Religion and the State

Religion and the State

A Comparative Sociology

Edited by
Jack Barbalet, Adam Possamai
and Bryan S. Turner

ANTHEM PRESS
LONDON · NEW YORK · DELHI

Anthem Press
An imprint of Wimbledon Publishing Company
www.anthempress.com

This edition first published in UK and USA 2013
by ANTHEM PRESS
75–76 Blackfriars Road, London SE1 8HA, UK
or PO Box 9779, London SW19 7ZG, UK
and
244 Madison Ave. #116, New York, NY 10016, USA

First published in hardback by Anthem Press in 2011

British Library Cataloguing-in-Publication Data
A catalogue record for this book is available from the British Library.

Library of Congress Cataloging-in-Publication Data
The Library of Congress has cataloged the hardcover edition as follows:
Religion and the state : a comparative sociology / edited by Jack Barbalet, Adam
Possamai, Bryan S. Turner.
p. cm.
Proceedings of a workshop held July 17–18, 2009 at the University of Western Sydney,
Parramatta Campus.
Includes bibliographical references and index.
ISBN 978-0-85728-798-4 (hardback : alk. paper)
1. Religion and state–Congresses. I. Barbalet, J. M., 1946– II. Possamai, Adam.
III. Turner, Bryan S.
BL65.S8R4455 2011
322'.1–dc23
2011039325

ISBN-13: 978 1 78308 066 3 (Pbk)
ISBN-10: 1 78308 066 3 (Pbk)

This title is also available as an ebook.

TABLE OF CONTENTS

Part II: From Pietism to Consumerism

Part III: Concluding Comments

ACKNOWLEDGEMENTS

On 17–18 July 2009, the Academy of Social Sciences in Australia and the College of Arts from the University of Western Sydney cosponsored a workshop, which was held at the University of Western Sydney (Parramatta Campus). The workshop addressed various relationships between religion and the state through comparative investigations of historical cases and contemporary developments, and this edited book is an outcome of that meeting. This volume includes a number of chapters that were first presented at that workshop as well as invited contributions.

The editors would like to thank Alan Nixon and Elena Knox for the help they provided with this workshop and book.

NOTES ON CONTRIBUTORS

Jack Barbalet is a professor of sociology and head of the Department of Sociology at Hong Kong Baptist University. He is also an adjunct professor in the Institute for Culture and Society at the University of Western Sydney, where he was previously a professorial fellow at the Centre for Citizenship and Public Policy and a foundation professor of sociology. He has also been a professor of sociology and head of department at the University of Leicester. Jack's most recent book is *Weber, Passion and Profits: "The Protestant Ethic and the Spirit of Capitalism" in Context* (Cambridge University Press, 2008). His recent papers have appeared in *Kölner Zeitschrift für Soziologie und Sozialpsychologie*, the *European Journal of Social Theory*, *Theory and Society*, the *Cambridge Journal of Economics*, *Max Weber Studies*, the *Journal for the Theory of Social Behaviour*, and the *British Journal of Sociology*.

James A. Beckford, Fellow of the British Academy, is a professor emeritus of sociology at the University of Warwick and was president of the Society for the Scientific Study of Religion 2010–11. His recent books include: *Social Theory and Religion* (Cambridge University Press, 2003), *Muslims in Prison: Challenge and Change in Britain and France* (with D. Joly and F. Khosrokhavar, Palgrave Macmillan, 2005); *Theorising Religion: Classical and Contemporary Debates* (edited with J. Walliss, Ashgate, 2006); and *The SAGE Handbook of the Sociology of Religion* (edited with N. J. Demerath, SAGE, 2007). His current research interests include religion and the state, prison chaplaincy and Muslims in Europe.

Stephen Chavura teaches in the Department of Politics and International Relations at Macquarie University, Sydney. His interests include religion and politics, church-state relations in Australia, and the history of political thought. He is the author of *Tudor Protestant Political Thought 1547–1603* (Brill, 2011).

Reza Hasmath (PhD, Cambridge) is a senior research lecturer in social sciences. His research examines the labor market experiences of urban ethnic minorities, and state and society interactions in China. He is the author of

The Ethnic Penalty: Immigration, Education and the Labour Market (Ashgate, 2011) and *A Comparative Study of Minority Development in China and Canada* (Palgrave Macmillan, 2010), and has edited the collections *The Chinese Corporatist State: Adaptation, Survival and Resistance* (with J. Hsu, forthcoming) *China in an Era of Transition: Understanding Contemporary State and Society Actors* (with J. Hsu, Palgrave Macmillan, 2009) and *Managing Ethnic Diversity: Meanings and Practices from an International Perspective* (Ashgate, 2011).

Gal Levy (PhD, LSE) is a senior teaching faculty at the Open University, Israel, and the director of New York University in Tel Aviv. His current interest in religion and the state stems from his long-lasting study of the Israeli ethnicized society. Following his dissertation, which explored the interrelationship between ethnic politics and educational policy, Gal became engaged in various research projects that aim to examine the triad relationship of education, ethnicity and citizenship. His most recent projects include a study on education and citizenship among children of labor-migrants and a large scale research project (coauthored with Dr M. Massalha and supported by an Israel Science Foundation grant) on alternative Arab education. His current book manuscript, which is under review at Cambridge University Press, is a political account of the history of education in Israel and its implications for the construction of contemporary ethnic identities and conceptions of citizenship. Gal has published locally and internationally on these topics, as well as on class and ethnic voting in the Israeli general elections.

Patrick Michel is a senior research fellow at the Centre National de la Recherche Scientifique, is president of the Political Science and Sociology of Organizations section of the Comité National de la Recherche Scientifique of France, and is full professor at the École des Hautes Études en Sciences Sociales (Paris). He is also the Director of the Centre Maurice Halbwachs in Paris. In addition to his primary interest in Central Europe, his research focuses on the theoretical aspects of the relation between politics and religion. His published works include *Religion(s) et identité(s) en Europe: L'épreuve du pluriel*, coedited with Antonela Capelle-Pogacean and Enzo Pace (Les Presses de Sciences Po, 2008), and *Politique et religion – La grande mutation* (Albin Michel, 1994).

Douglas Porpora is a professor of sociology in the Department of Culture and Communication at Drexel University in Philadelphia. Although he has written more widely on social theory in books such as *How Holocausts Happen: The US in Central America* (Temple University Press, 1990) and *Landscapes of the Soul: The Loss of Moral Meaning in American Life* (Oxford University Press, 2001), he has here focused on how Americans deal with macro-moral issues. He is currently writing a book on how Americans debated the 2003 attack on Iraq.

Adam Possamai is an associate professor in sociology at the University of Western Sydney (UWS). He is the author of *Sociology: A Down-to-Earth Approach* (with James Henslin and Alphia Possamai-Inesedy, Pearson, 2010), *Sociology of Religion for Generations X and Y* (Equinox, 2009), *Religion and Popular Culture: A Hyper-Real Testament* (Peter Lang, 2007) and *In Search of New Age Spiritualities* (Ashgate, 2005). He is the 2010–14 president of the executive board of ISA RC22 (Sociology of Religion), a former president of the Australian Association for the Study of Religions, and was the 2002–07 coeditor of the *Australian Religion Studies Review*. He was the program co-coordinator for the sociology of religion section of the recent World Congress of Sociology in 2010 in Sweden. He was also one of the associate heads of school at the School of Social Sciences at UWS (specializing in research), and he is currently the acting director of the Centre for the Study of Contemporary Muslim Societies. His work has been published in English, French, Spanish, Romanian and Slovakian.

Arathi Sriprakash is a lecturer in the sociology of education at the University of Western Sydney. With an interest in education and international development, she has conducted ethnographic research on the local translations of global development policies in the Indian context. Her forthcoming book *Pedagogies for Development* examines the politics and practices of child-centered education in poor communities in rural India.

Bryan Turner is the director of the Centre for the Study of Contemporary Muslim Societies at the University of Western Sydney and Presidential Professor of Sociology at the City University of New York. He has held professorships at Cambridge University and the National University of Singapore. He is the founding editor of the journals *Body & Society* (with Mike Featherstone), *Citizenship Studies* and *Journal of Classical Sociology* (with John O'Neill) and an editorial member of numerous journals, including the *British Journal of Sociology*, *Contemporary Islam* and the *Sociological Review*. He edited the *New Blackwell Companion to the Sociology of Religion* (Wiley-Blackwell, 2010).

Meyda Yeğenoğlu is a professor of cultural studies at Bilgi University, Istanbul. She has held visiting appointments at Columbia University, Oberlin College, Rutgers University, New York University, the University of Vienna and the University of Oxford. She is the author of *Colonial Fantasies: Towards a Feminist Reading of Orientalism* (Cambridge University Press, 1998). She has had numerous essays published in various journals and edited volumes, including:

Feminist Postcolonial Theory; *Postcolonialism, Feminism and Religious Discourse*; *Nineteenth Century Literature Criticism*; *Postmodern Culture*; *Race and Ethnic Relations*; *Culture and Religion*; *Inscriptions*; *Religion and Gender*; *Handbook of Contemporary Social and Political Theory*; *State, Religion and Secularization*; *Feminism and Hospitality*; *Toplum ve Bilim*; *Defter*; and *Doğu-Batı*. Her book entitled *Islam, Migrancy and Hospitality in Europe* (Palgrave-Macmillan) is forthcoming in March 2012.

Siniša Zrinščak is a professor of social policy at the University of Zagreb. His main scientific interests include comparative and European social policy, church-state relations, religious and social policy changes in post-communist societies and civil society development. He is president of the International Study of Religion in Central and Eastern Europe Association (ISORECEA), council member of the International Society for the Sociology of Religion (ISSR), and vice president of the International Sociological Association's Research Committee for the Sociology of Religion (ISA RC22). He has also served as president and vice president of the Croatian Sociological Association, head of the Department for Social Work at the University of Zagreb, and as editor in chief of the *Croatian Journal of Social Policy*.

LIST OF TABLES AND FIGURES

TABLES

FIGURES

INTRODUCTION:
STATES, CONSUMPTION
AND MANAGING RELIGIONS

Bryan S. Turner, Adam Possamai and Jack Barbalet

When sociologists refer to the contemporary crisis of multiculturalism, they are typically talking about how modern states, especially liberal democratic states, respond to the rise of "public religions." These religious conflicts and uncertainties about appropriate state responses to them have produced a general retreat from multiculturalism – at least in Europe (Joppke, 2004). More specifically, the contemporary problem of politics and religion has been increasingly orchestrated around the global revival of Islam and the emergence of a global Muslim community. However, the particular issues surrounding Muslim minorities in non-Muslim secular societies can be seen as simply one instance of the more general issue of state and religion relationships in modern complex societies. There is growing awareness about the limitations of the Westphalian solution to religious conflicts and hence political theory is undertaking a serious reconsideration of liberalism as the philosophical basis of political strategies to manage conflicting cultural, religious and ethnic interests. In the modern global world where state boundaries have been contested, there is a need to rethink how the competing claims of secular and religious citizens can be articulated and respected within public discourse (Habermas, 2008).

This question – how to manage the public expression of religion in multicultural and therefore multifaith societies – is not simply an issue for conventional liberal societies, because religious revivalism and community conflict raise political issues across a wide spectrum of modern societies. Throughout much of Asia (as subsequent chapters demonstrate), religious evangelism and the prospect of widespread conversions to expanding faiths cause difficulties for states that seek to balance the composition of civil society (Turner, 2009a).

Stales of very different political orientations and ideologies intervene to manage religions in the interests of public order. One example is Singapore, which has a strategy of "upgrading" Islam primarily through the agency of the Singapore Council for Muslims (MUIS) (Kamaludeen, Pereira and Turner, 2009). Singapore might be appropriately considered a "well-ordered hierarchical society" (Rawls, 2001) in which the various religions are not only managed but upgraded through various educational strategies. While Singapore is a small country in Southeast Asia, it presents an interesting social case study from which we can derive a number of sociological lessons.

While liberal democracies such as Australia, Canada, Britain and the United States also have similar strategies to manage religions, their religious policies will probably remain primarily implicit and minimal. One example is the difficulty in Britain where governments refused to include Muslims but included Jews and Sikhs under the Race Relations Act; hence Muslims felt they were discriminated against as a minority (Fetzer and Soper, 2005). This case study illustrates the problem which will be examined later as to whether religious groups in secular constitutions should be treated by the law as either voluntary associations or ethnic minorities. This question about the voluntary character of religious organizations was an important aspect of Brian Barry's criticisms of the immunities and privileges which religious groups such as the Amish enjoyed in liberal societies such as the United States (Barry, 2001).

Liberal post-secular consumer societies may be prevented from adopting explicit policies of intervention in religious management and are more likely to continue to treat – or attempt to treat – religion as a private matter, that is to treat religious groups as voluntary associations. Given the liberal commitment to freedom of religion, they will in all likelihood attempt to resist what José Casanova (1994) has called the "deprivatization" of religion by simply ignoring it. However, even liberal societies may be forced, albeit reluctantly, to take an interest in the goods and services that are delivered by religious groups. States have typically taken an interest in the exposure of minors to religious messages, fearing the possibility that they may be exposed to "brainwashing," and have frequently intervened to monitor, regulate or eliminate so-called "cults." A case in point is that of Scientology in contemporary France (Possamai and Lee, 2004). Attempts to manage religions in a more general sense may become more common in post-secular societies, especially if religion increasingly dominates the definition of ethnic identity.

This opening reflection on the management of religions in the contemporary world lends some support to the somewhat paradoxical claim that "religious liberty is a matter of government regulation" (Gill, 2008: 47). Pressure on the state to support religious tolerance will vary considerably in terms of majority-minority religious relations. Whereas dominant religious groups will seek state regulation of minority religions, religious liberty will be more vigorously pursued by marginalized minority religious movements and groups. It is in the interests of hegemonic religions such as an established church to prefer state regulation rather than religious competition in an open market, because their erstwhile monopolistic advantages may be eroded by such open religious competition. Effective governance is clearly more problematic in pluralistic environments, where there is plenty of scope for religious competition and conflict and where trust in governments may be eroded by policies that are seen to favor one religion over another. This problem of the perception of partiality on the part of secular states may explain the relative failure of British governments in their attempts to accommodate a growing and more assertive Muslim community in the late twentieth century (Joppke, 2009). Because virtually all modern societies are multicultural and multiracial, the "management of religion" is an inevitable component of modern government, despite the liberal preference for treating religion as a matter of private conscience and therefore of little overt concern to secular states. In other words, there is a paradox that, precisely because religion is important in modern life as the vehicle of personal identity, it has to be controlled, overtly or covertly, by the state to minimize the costs of government in reducing friction between competing groups and in avoiding more open examples of social conflict. Ultimately, the policies of securitization on the part of states in a global environment of uncertainty and conflict will require parallel policies to manage and regulate religion.

These issues constitute the substantive dilemmas that sit behind the philosophical debates of, among others, John Rawls and Jürgen Habermas. We can read Rawls' debate about "the original position" as a commentary on Hobbes' fiction of the state of nature. Rawls (1971) in *A Theory of Justice* adopts the idea of a "veil of ignorance" to say that we might imagine an ideal future society but not know what our position in such a thought experiment might be. In this hypothetical game, we would be unlikely to describe a slave society for fear that in the future we might be a slave. Reasonable and rational people would want to live in a decent and well-ordered society in which one's freedom would not impinge on somebody else and one's wealth would not seriously damage the life chances of another. Out of this thought experiment, Rawls (1993) created his famous model of liberalism in which he argued that a decent functional society was one in which there is tolerance of differences in belief but within the framework of a shared consensus about basic beliefs. However, it was his attempt to extend these arguments to international affairs in *The Laws of Peoples* (Rawls, 1999) that may be more relevant to our discussion here. In this later discussion, Rawls outlined a typology of societies within which liberal principles might operate. He argued that in a well-ordered but liberal society there would be an "overlapping consensus" of fundamental doctrines (1999: 171).

By contrast, authoritarian and hierarchical societies would rule by extralegal means. Rawls regarded his arguments as utopian but nevertheless realistic, because he assumed that reasonable and rational people would, given the veil of ignorance, want a society that was well ordered but also in his terms decent. A well-ordered society would depend less on the coercive force of law and more on the consensus of citizens in whose interest it is to protect institutions that satisfy their collective needs.

Barry's criticism of multiculturalism is probably compatible with Rawlsian liberalism in the sense that an overlapping consensus of beliefs might be difficult to sustain in a society that is too divided by incommensurable doctrines. Jürgen Habermas has also followed John Rawls' defense of liberal principles in his attempt to extend his original theory of communicative rationality to deal with societies in which religious fundamentalism has been growing. In *Between Facts and Norms*, Habermas (1996: 61) recognized that Rawls had "certainly shown that a normative theory of justice of the sort he proposes can gain entry to a culture in which the basic liberal convictions are already rooted through tradition and political socialization in everyday practices and in the institutions of individual citizens." In this respect, Rawls' political theory was both a normative view of justice and a defense of American democracy as a clear example of a society in which there is a "reasonable pluralism." In the traditional liberal position, different religions could be accommodated within the civil sphere on the condition that they remained merely private beliefs. Casanova's commentary on public religions sparked off an important debate about how and whether radical religious doctrines could be accommodated within a Rawlsian "reasonable pluralism."

In recent years, Habermas (2006, 2008; Habermas and Mendieta, 2002) has recognized that the conventional liberal view is in need of repair. He also recognized that the legality of the state was no automatic guarantee of the legitimacy of the public arena, because a well-ordered hierarchical society is not necessarily a wholly legitimate society. The contemporary situation has forced critical theorists like Habermas and pragmatists like Richard Rorty to start taking religion seriously. This is what they mean by the idea of a post-secular society. It does not mean suddenly that social life is pervaded by religion or that the conventional theory of secularization is dead. It simply means that organized religion cannot be ignored or dismissed precisely because it has erupted into the public domain. He has proposed that in a post-secular society it is necessary for both secular and religious citizens to engage in a public defense of their beliefs (Habermas and Mendieta, 2002; Habermas and

Ratzinger, 2006). It is not sufficient to say that humanism and secularism are self-evidently true or that religious conviction needs no justification because it is based on revelation. Communicative openness is a requirement of democratic norms in a public space and hence customs and beliefs have to be rationally justified and defended. This rule applies, for example, to secular humanists and to fundamentalists alike.

There are many aspects of this argument that are problematic. For one thing, holding to a religious belief, for example, in the sinfulness of mankind may be very different from believing that parliamentary institutions can offer a better defense of common interests. Religious beliefs tend to be affective and habitual, not neutral and deliberative. Furthermore, if I am already convinced that my beliefs are true by divine authority, what need have I to defend these in public? In short fundamentalist beliefs (in any religious tradition) may be as a matter of fact incommensurable with liberalism. These conflicts over "fundamental doctrines" become divisive in the public sphere when issues about conversion and apostasy come into play. The public order can become disrupted by radical conversionist movements, as happened frequently in the modern histories of India, Malaysia and Indonesia (Veer, 1996). It is precisely here – over the management of conversion, dress codes, religious education and interfaith marriages – that the state becomes involved in the management of religions. Of course, this discussion of religion and politics has so far tended to assume that we are talking about active citizens in a participatory democracy and active communities of the pious in the religious field. But is the citizen in a decent well-ordered democracy necessarily an active participant?

In this introduction, we claim that in modern liberal democracies the active citizen is becoming increasingly a passive consumer in which the traditional bases of effective civic participation through work, public service and reproduction are no longer the fundamental conditions of citizenship entitlement (Turner, 2008). This erosion of citizenship was dramatically illustrated by the credit crunch of 2008–10, in which citizens in Britain, Australia and the United States were admonished by their respective governments to shop in order to save both the economy and the society. The new duty of the responsible citizen is to consume in order to promote economic activity and paradoxically at the same time to save, because personal savings in Western societies are at an all time low. In post-industrial capitalism, there is a permanent tension between asceticism as the legacy of the Protestant ethic and acquisitiveness as the legacy of the consumer boom of the postwar economic strategy of the West. States have also adopted the same sales techniques that were originally developed by the advertising industries to promote consumerism. Political parties increasingly treat citizens as an audience that must be cultivated by sales techniques (focus groups, opinion polls, marketing strategies and national identity as branding) and the quality of political leadership is tested by ratings in the opinion polls. Policies are increasingly developed on the basis of focus-group data rather than long-term national needs. Of course, this development of political salesmanship is not especially compatible with the vision of communicative rationality in Habermas's theory or with Rawls' view of a liberal well-ordered society.

One colorful illustration of these developments might be taken from Italy under Silvio Berlusconi. Over the last two decades, the Italian economy grew by a mere 1.5 percent against the Organisation for Economic Co-operation and Development (OECD) average of 2.6 percent. In Italy only 12.9 percent of the population has a university degree compared to 26 percent in the other OECD countries. Italy was ranked 84 out of 128 countries in the World Economic Forum 2007 index of gender equality. Nevertheless, after years of public scandal and incompetent government, Berlusconi's popularity remained high and he appeared to be largely immune from criticism, because he controlled a large section of the Italian television and print media. In late 2010 and early 2011 of course, Berlusconi was faced by such a wave of new scandals, including alleged shady dealings with the Libyan leader Colonel Muammar Gaddafi, that it seemed even he could not service such a litany of public scandals. From different ends of the political spectrum, leaders like Berlusconi and Putin have achieved notoriety and celebrity status. Alongside the financialization of the state and "casino capitalism" (Strange, 1986), the passive consumer citizen is an appropriate figure in a world of political entertainment or "videocracy" (Stille, 2010).

At the same time, the rise of religious markets, megachurches, religious advertisements and the use of growth consultants to boost church membership also suggest that religion has become deeply embedded in the market (Turner, 2011). The commercialization of religion is true of both fundamentalist movements that promote the growth of congregational religion and the spirituality of New Age tendencies that are post-institutional, unorthodox and hybrid. The result is an important fusion between passive secular citizenship and the spiritual marketplace. With this critical erosion of active citizenship, the state has a political interest in the surveillance – and periodically in the supervision – of both the secular and religious markets. Our argument is that there is an important cultural and political development taking place with the growth of casino capitalism, celebrity politics and the growth of passive citizenship and consumer religion. This cultural mixture may throw a more critical light on the idea of a post-secular society.

The disciplinary management of religions in well-ordered hierarchical regimes such as Singapore and South Korea may obviously remain unavailable to liberal democratic regimes such as Australia, Britain and Canada, which may seek to contain religion within the private domain. Only when such conventional approaches fail are they likely to feel compelled to take up more interventionist strategies. Spirituality as a lifestyle is in any case unlikely to pose a significant public threat precisely because it is individualistic and inward in personal orientation. Only when religion becomes "deprivatized" and takes up a political agenda may the states be unable to maintain such laissez-faire attitudes. Faith becomes a political issue when religious and ethnic identities merge and religious minorities feel excluded from the common weal.

There is obviously a dystopian aspect to our argument. Insofar as liberal societies may slide inevitably towards authoritarian systems with the global development of securitization in response to real or imagined terrorist threats, then all governments will embrace more open policies regarding the management of religions. In such circumstances, religion may be banned or suppressed, and draconian measures may be put in place to eradicate religious leaders and their institutions. These strategies were of course common in centralized socialist states such as the Soviet Union, Vietnam and China during the cold war. Various chapters in this collection (5, 7 and 8) explore the problems of religion and centralized party politics in various communist and post-communist societies. However, repression has never been entirely successful (Yang, 2010) and authoritarian states may seek to cultivate passive religiosity during periods of liberalization under the guise of leisure and tourism. There is some indication that in contemporary China, religion can be revived because it is attractive to overseas Chinese who may wish to invest in post-communist China. While Falon Gong is seen as a threat to the monopoly of the Party, Buddhist monasteries may be rebuilt to stimulate religious tourism. While it is normally assumed that such minorities are suppressed (in Vietnam and China) because they are seen as a threat to the authority of the Party, we suggest that an alternative strategy for managing religions would be to commercialize them. There is some evidence from China that Buddhism and Daoism, for example, are being allowed to enjoy some partial revival but only as a form of cultural tourism (Luke, 1987; Yang, 2004). Shrines can grow and flourish only if they can be contained within religious theme parks – perhaps the counterparts of the science parks that are so popular in modern universities. Religion and science would therefore no longer need to compete with each other as both would contribute to the growth of the economy. Religious institutions can become valuable aspects of entertainment and leisure industries; they can be promoted in religious parks just as governments stimulate interest in science through science museums and exhibition sites. Religious commodification is a powerful force in Asia, but equally so in the West. The global interest in the death and funeral of Michael Jackson was a powerful example of the notion that citizens have become spectators to be entertained by spectacular events – the death of Lady Diana, the Olympic Games, the World Cup, American Idol and so forth. These events are as it were the Disneyland equivalent of the idea of civil religion (Bellah, 1967). They involve celebrity, orchestrated emotions and powerful rituals. They have a quasi-religious aura.

The Sociology of Secularization

While secularization and post-secular society are clearly issues in Western Europe, religion in its various and complex manifestations is obviously thriving in many parts of Asia, Africa and Latin America. The growth of Pentecostalism and the eruption of charismatic movements in Africa and Latin America are well-known developments outside the Western world that bring into question the narrow focus of much philosophical and sociological debate (Adogame, 2010). There is now a reverse missionary movement in which a revitalized Christianity is being brought back to the West by African missionaries working with diasporic communities of migrants. Islamic revivalism is important in Southeast Asia, but equally significant among migrant communities in the West. Approximately one-third of Muslims now live as minority communities outside the Middle East.

While it is widely held that the conventional secularization thesis of sociologists in the 1960s was limited and often therefore misguided and misleading, to abandon the secularization thesis in its entirety would be equally mistaken. There is an alternative thesis to the simple notion of secularization as membership decline and growing social irrelevance, namely that religion has been democratized through commercialization in which secularization is manifest through the growth of megachurches, drive-in confessionals, buy-a-prayer, religious films, commercial pilgrimages, a global spiritual literature and the sale of amulets and other religious paraphernalia. Religion has been modernized through religious markets that sell spiritual goods and services and as a result religion has at the same time become increasingly democratized. The relationship between the sacred and profane is no longer vertical in terms of a hierarchy of authority but horizontal as power is more equally shared with the laity.

One aspect of democratization is that the mysterious and unspeakable character of the sacred domain is arcane in societies that have at least in principle embraced values relating to equality and participation. Thus in Judaism, Christianity and Islam, the sacred realm was characterized by the ineffable character of the holy (Turner, 2009b). The sacred was located in a hierarchical world – a great chain of being – and this sacred reality was manifest in human affairs through the communication of intermediaries – prophets, angels, mythical creatures, mystical birds or spirits – but the communication from the sacred to the profane world was paradoxically unspeakable (Nancy, 2005). The other forms of exchange between the sacred and profane plane involved various sacrificial activities.

These intermediary systems are disappearing in modern societies where media are omnipresent, democratically devolved and spatially dispersed. We inhabit an information-saturated social environment in which communication comes from everywhere and invades the everyday world. In place of the ineffable character of the sacred realm, religion becomes fully available to the literate masses, because its message is made plain and simple through commercialized media and popular culture. In the West, the laity is just as likely to consume its religiosity through the fictional works of Dan Brown, the big screen productions of Mel Gibson or the sacrilegious music of Madonna as it is to attend a conventional church, synagogue or mosque. Perhaps the most compelling illustration of the democratization of the sacred is that the Lord has become our friend with whom we can communicate freely (Zabala, 2005: 17).

We can think of the secularization thesis as simply a subtheme of the more general notion of modernization and that modernity involved the differentiation of the various subsystems of society in which the religious becomes a specialized set of services alongside welfare and education. In a theory that followed Max Weber's notions about the rationalization and differentiation of society, Casanova identified three aspects of secularization: the differentiation of the various spheres of the social system; secularization in terms of the decline of religious belief and practice; and finally the marginalization of religion to the private sphere. Through a number of discrete comparative studies, Casanova argued that secularization as differentiation is indeed the key component of modern secularization. The sociology of religion has to evaluate these components separately, carefully and independently, because the decline of religious belief and practice is not necessarily the dominant and universal feature of religion in the modern world. Much of the variation in secularization is illustrated in this volume by chapters on Australia (Chavura), India (Sriprakash and Possamai), Israel (Levy) and Britain (Beckford).

Sociologists of religion have been forced to review their assumptions about secularization with the eruption of various public religions such as the Iranian Revolution, the rise of Solidarity, the involvement of Roman Catholicism in the Sandinista Revolution and the growth of the Christian Right in America. There is nevertheless much confusion surrounding the ideas of secularization and resacralization. We propose that the debate about secularization could be rendered conceptually more precise if we draw a simple distinction between "political secularization" which we might call the conventional differentiation thesis and "social secularization" which we might conveniently define as the anthropological thesis of commodification. The former refers specifically to the issues surrounding the historical separation of church and state, and to the contemporary differentiation of the spheres of the social system, namely the specialization of the subsystems of society around politics, culture, the economy, religion and so forth. The latter refers to religion in everyday life, namely the secularization of belief and practice through democratization and commercialization.

Political secularization is in fact the cornerstone of the liberal approach to tolerance in which we are free to hold our private beliefs provided these do not interfere negatively with public life. This liberal solution has its historical roots in the Anglican settlement of Richard Hooker's *Ecclesiastical Polity* of 1593 and its political manifestation in John Locke's *A Letter Concerning Tolerance* in 1689. It was reaffirmed in the colony of Virginia when the rejection of an established church paved the way to the constitutional recognition of secularization. In Europe, the legal division between church and state was originally a political solution to settle the conflicts between Catholics and Protestants. It is alleged that this settlement has broken down, because modern societies are typically multicultural, multiethnic and multifaith. Because religion often defines identity, it is difficult to sustain any simple division between the public and the private. Furthermore, these ethnoreligious identities are typically transnational and hence cannot be conveniently confined within the national boundaries of the modern state. The eruption of religions into the public domain means that the state, often reluctantly, clumsily and ineptly, enters into civil sphere with the management of religions, especially where multicultural and multifaith communities threaten social harmony and liberal tolerance. When the diversity of religions in society begins to disrupt civil harmony, states intervene either implicitly or explicitly in the regulation of religious affairs, for example by banning religious symbols in state schools. Having recognized these challenges, it would be fundamentally mistaken to assume that secularization as the division between state and religion (or more precisely the neutrality of the state towards religion) is no longer relevant. Indeed, it can be plausibly argued that in religiously diverse societies religions are best served by secularization that is the neutrality of the state (An-Na'im, 2008).

If political secularization refers to a macro-separation between church and state, then social secularization refers to the transformation of conventional forms of religious vitality – church membership, belief in God, religious experiences and acts of devotion such as prayer, religious festivals, days of abstinence and church attendance – by commercial values, institutions and practices. Sociologists of religion who are now critical of the secularization thesis have pointed to the fact that there is little evidence of religious decline outside of northern Europe. On the contrary, religion in the social sphere appears to be a lively and vital aspect of ordinary life. However, while there has indeed been evidence of religious revivalism, there has also been a commercialization and democratization of religion in the social sphere that renders religion increasingly compatible with and an important part of the world of secular consumerism. Religion as consumption is a secular practice and hence the tension between religion and "the world" that was the basis of Christian radicalism has largely disappeared – or at least that tension has been eroded.

This aspect of modern religious life provides a conceptually fruitful contrast to the role of religion in the public domain of politics – essentially the role of Catholicism in Poland and in various South American contexts, radical Islam in global politics, the Jewish ultraorthodox movements in Israel, and the Moral Majority in America – and the social domain of everyday life. In the social sphere, the market influences religion rather than vice versa. Religion, state and market may have become differentiated spheres, but they are also highly interconnected and furthermore it is the market which is increasingly shaping religion rather than religion shaping the market. In this respect, it is possible to defend a modified version of the secularization thesis by pointing to the various ways in which religion is influenced by secular consumerism.

While Casanova's seminal work on public religions was about differentiation and deprivatization, this analysis of commodification is more specifically focused on the transformations of the religious sphere by the values, practices and institutions of the market. With differentiation and the transformation of churches into denominations, religions have to compete with each other for influence and for customers, but they also have to compete with other lifestyle choices. Following the insights of the so-called economic interpretation of religion in the religious marketplace created by the separation of church and state, religions are forced to sell their services in a competitive environment and hence they have adopted many of the practices of the secular market to win new customers and to maintain brand loyalty of existing members (Warner, 2004). Although these marketing strategies are most obvious in the North American context with the growth of the megachurch, similar developments can be seen in Asia among a diverse range of religious traditions (Kitiarsa, 2008). Although Bryan Wilson has been consistently criticized by those sociologists who favor the idea of "resacralization," his analysis of commercial influences on religion, especially in the United States, can be sustained once we focus on the idea of the religious consumer.

The notion that modernization involves secularization was closely connected in classical sociology with Max Weber's sociology of religion. In *The Protestant Ethic and the Spirit of Capitalism* Weber explored the unique relationship between the ascetic ethic of the Protestant sects and modernity

(Weber, 2002). By contrast, the sociological tradition that we associate with Émile Durkheim and Marcel Mauss was an attempt not to study religions but an inquiry into the generic nature of religion. Durkheim depended on missionary and administrative reports emerging from late nineteenth-century colonialism to formulate a notion of the "elementary forms" of religion. The classical foundations of the sociology of religion in this interpretation were created by an inquiry into the cultural uniqueness of the Protestant Reformation (Max Weber and Ernst Troeltsch) and by an inquiry into the generic nature of religion as a system of elementary or "primitive" classification (Émile Durkheim, Marcel Mauss and Robert Hertz). In the first tradition, the scientific question was posed by the historical consequences of Protestantism on the rationalization of society. In the second tradition, the issue was to understand how religion in some generic sense contributed to social classification and hence to social life as such.

These two dimensions of religion were to some extent reflected in the very meaning of "religion" (*religio*), which has two somewhat distinct roots. First, *relegere* from *legere* means to pull together, to harvest or to gather (in), and secondly, *religare* from *ligare* means to tie or to bind together. The first meaning described the religious foundations of any social group that is gathered together and the second pointed to the disciplines or moral principles that are necessary for controlling human beings and creating a disciplined soul. These two etymological roots of the notion of religion further elucidate the separation in Kant's philosophical analysis between religion and morality. In Kant's essay on religion – *Religion within the Limits of Pure Reason* – there is a distinction between religion as cult (*des blossen Cultus*) in which the believer asks for favors from God through sacrifice to bring healing and wealth and religion as moral action (*die Religion des guten Lebenswandels*) that commands human beings through the discipline of self development rather than sacrifice to change behavior in order to lead better lives (Kant, 1960). Kant further elaborated on this point through an examination of "reflecting faith" that compels humans to strive for salvation through faith rather than through the possession of religious knowledge or through exacting religious rituals. The implication of Kant's distinction was that Protestant Christianity was the only genuine "reflecting faith" and therefore the model for an authentic religious life. Kant's distinction was fundamentally about those religious injunctions that call human beings to moral action, demanding that humans assert their autonomy and responsibility. This philosophical distinction can be translated into the anthropological distinction between health and wealth cults, on the one hand, and austere, ascetic systems of higher order religions on the other. To have autonomy, human beings need to act independently of God and without the support of ecclesiastical rituals and institutions.

In a paradoxical fashion, by calling upon people to embrace intellectual freedom and personal responsibility, Christianity implies the "death of God" and hence the Christian faith is ultimately self-defeating. If Christianity as a religion is successful, its adherents will no longer need it. Certainly the Kantian legacy had no need of a personal God or a loving relationship with Jesus or any notion of transcendence. A religion of salvation had been replaced by the categorical imperative of Kantian ethics.

These Kantian principles were eventually developed in *The Sociology of Religion*, where Weber distinguished between the religion of the masses and the religion of the virtuosi (Weber, 1996). While masses seek earthly comforts from religion, especially healing, the virtuosi fulfill the ethical demands of religion in search of spiritual salvation or enlightenment. The religion of the masses requires charismatic figures to satisfy their mundane needs, and hence charisma is inevitably corrupted by the very demand for miracles and magical spectacles. Weber's analysis of the religious quest for salvation produced a theory of the norms which govern the practical conduct of life (*Lebensführung*). In his inquiry into religious conduct, Weber distinguished between a theodicy of good fortune (*Glück*) and a theodicy of suffering (*Leid*). In coming to terms with fortune and suffering, human beings project their conceptions of their personal experiences beyond the everyday material world. It is these experiences of fortune and suffering which undermine the rational or purposive categories of pragmatic orientation to reality. There is no satisfactory rational explanation of suffering in this world where chance rather than virtue dominates. However, it was primarily within the monotheistic and ascetic religions that the rationalization of theodicy reached its ultimate fruition. The development of the concept of a universal God as the framework of history and salvation produced a rational theodicy of reality as such. In short, the legacy of the Judeo-Christian world, based upon the notions of ethical prophecy and monotheism, was crucial to the development of a radical solution to theodicy in terms of highly intellectual and systematic soteriologies. For example, the intellectual rationalism of the Protestant sects was critical in pushing European civilization towards a pattern of religious individualism involving strict norms of personal discipline and conduct. However, the everyday needs for health and wealth which characterize the religious needs and orientation of the disprivileged and the downtrodden were very different from the motivations that drove the elite virtuosi.

The Consumerization of Religion

Weber's sociology of religion provides an adequate description of a society in which the sacred world is still primarily vertical and in which the virtuosi remain culturally and politically hegemonic. We will attempt here to provide a summary of some of the major changes that one can observe in religion in modern societies by taking a comparative perspective. Firstly, whereas the religious system of communication in an age of revelation was hierarchical, unitary and authoritative, the system of communicative acts in a new media environment are horizontal, diverse and fragmented rather than unitary, the sources of authority are devolved rather than centralized and the authority of any message is negotiable and negotiated. The growth of these diverse centers of interpretation in a global communication system has produced a crisis of authority in the formal system of religious belief and practice. In Islam, for example, there has been an inflation of sources of authority since through some local and specific consensus almost any local teacher or *mullah* can issue a *fatwa* to guide a local community (Monshipouri, 2009; Volpi and Turner, 2007).

Secondly, the modern media contribute to a growing subjectivity and individualism that are very different from the rugged ascetic individualism of early Protestantism. The religious subjectivity of the modern world is a facet of the "expressive revolution" that had its roots in the student revolts and culture wars of the 1960s (Parsons, 1967). In the new individualism, people invent their own religious ideas, giving rise to what we might call a "do-it-yourself" religiosity. The result has been a social revolution flowing from both consumerism and individualism. As a result, "Capitalism's success eroded class rivalries and replaced the activist and utopian mass politics of the inter-war era with a more bloodless politics of consumption and management. Goods not gods were what people wanted" (Mazower, 1999: 306). Religious lifestyles get modeled on consumer lifestyles in which people can try out religions rather like they try out a new fashion in consumer goods. In a consumer society, people want goods not gods, and to a large extent their desires have been satisfied by cheap money, easy mortgages and consumer credit. A new industry has emerged concerned with spiritual advice about how to cope with the modern world while remaining pious and pure. As a result, pious lifestyles are marketed by religious entrepreneurs who need to brand their products in the spiritual marketplace.

The consequence of these developments is a growing division between "religion" and "spirituality" (Hunt, 2005). Globalization thus involves the spread of personal spirituality and these spiritualities typically provide both practical guidance in the everyday world and subjective, personalized avenues to meaning. Some aspects of the media and popular religion are explored by Adam Possamai in his chapter on "Jediism." Such religious phenomena are often combined with therapeutic or healing services, or the promise of personal enhancement through meditation. While Protestant fundamentalism with its norms of personal discipline appeals mostly to social groups that are upwardly socially mobile, such as the lower middle-class and newly educated couples, spirituality is more closely associated with middle-class singles that have been thoroughly influenced by Western consumer values. Pentecostalism can also been seen as a global religious movement that offers "technologies of the self" and personal expressivity that are highly compatible with the spirit of late capitalism (Martin, 2002). Whereas the traditionally religious find meaning in existing mainstream denominational Christianity, spiritual people can construct their own religious lifestyles in a spiritual marketplace, and self-consciously avoid any commitment to organized religious institutions and can experiment with diverse and unorthodox philosophies and theologies (Bender, 2003). The new religions are also closely associated with themes of therapy, peace and self-help. Of course the idea that religion, especially in the West, had become privatized was a common notion in sociology in the 1960s (Luckmann, 1967). However, these new forms of subjectivity and privatism are no longer confined to Protestantism or the American middle classes; they now have global implications.

Historians might complain that these forms of commercial religion could also be found in medieval Christian practice in which indulgences were sold to the faithful. These examples are telling, but in the Middle Ages the authority of the elite was not challenged either by commodification or by the unorthodox beliefs of the illiterate laity. In the modern world, universal literacy, the media and globalization have changed religious life. These commercial religious developments are no longer simply local cults, but burgeoning global popular religions carried by the internet, movies, rock music, popular television shows and "pulp fiction." In these pick 'n' mix religions, adherents borrow carelessly from a great range of religious beliefs and practices. This development is one aspect of "a new techno-mysticism most spectacularly presented to us in the use of special effects in blockbuster films" such as *Crouching Tiger, Hidden Dragon* and *House of Flying Daggers* (Ward, 2006: 18). These phenomena have been regarded as aspects of "new religious movements" that are, as we have seen, manifestations of the spiritual marketplace (Beckford, 2003). These forms of spirituality tend to be highly individualistic, unorthodox in the sense that they follow no official creed, characterized by their syncretism and have little or no connection with formal institutions such as churches, mosques or temples. They are post-institutional and in this sense they can be legitimately called "postmodern religions."

We live increasingly in a communication environment where images and symbols rather than the written word probably play an important role in interaction. This visual world is therefore iconic rather than literate and it requires new skills to interpret coded messages. These new skills emerge alongside new occupational structures and hierarchies that no longer duplicate the traditional hierarchies of the written word. It is also a new experimental context in which the iconic is frequently the iconoclastic as Madonna in her Catholic period switched to Rachel and for a while explored the Kabbalah (Hulsether, 2000). The new media world has emerged in parallel to a radical transformation of Western capitalism from an industrial system with a dominant capitalist class of industrialists to a financial and communication capitalism with new financial elites that are global (Epstein, 2005). We can interpret the globalization of religion – especially in the globalization of religious sites on the internet and the globalization of the religious publishing world (Stolow, 2010) – as the mirror image of this financialization of capitalism as the next stage of economic globalization.

Finally, we have described this combination of self-help systems, subjectivity, devolved authority structures, iconic discourses and do-it-yourself theology an example of "low intensity religion" (Turner, 2009b). It is a mobile spirituality that can be transported globally by mobile people to new sites where they can mix and match their religious or self-help needs without too much institutional constraint from hierarchical authorities. It is a religiosity that can travel without the encumbrance of too much cultural and ritualized baggage. It is a low-emotion religion because modern conversions tend to be more like a change in consumer brands rather than a searching of the soul. If the new religious lifestyles give rise to emotions, these are packaged in ways that can be easily consumed. Perhaps the harbinger of the new emotional packing of mobile spirituality was the chat show of Oprah Winfrey who brought a confessional culture on to the television screens not only in America but worldwide (Illouz, 2003).

Conclusion: The Structure of this Volume

In summary, the general framework of this book is organized around the issue of how the state relates to religion(s) through various orientations that include active management strategies or liberal indifference or direct control. Secondly, we are concerned to understand how religion develops at the social level through the processes of pietization and revival, and how those changes are influenced by consumerism and other secular forces. In other words, we are exploring two paradoxes. As religion (re)enters the public domain by so-called deprivatization, the state moves in to manage religions in the interests of securitization. Secondly, as religious lifestyles become more pious, they can also become more dominated by consumerism.

The first part of this book explores various ways in which religion appears to leave the private sphere of individual conscience and to enter the public domain, and how sometimes governments also work towards securitizing the presence of religion in the public sphere. The case studies below are connected to the wider process of global securitization.

Bryan S. Turner's "Religion in Authoritarian States" explores the top-down approach of this securitization process through a study of governmentality that aims to control religious tensions as they appear in the public sphere. As minority religious groups join the mainstream, Turner observes a process of domestication that reduces these groups' cultural distinctiveness. Focusing on various case studies, but most centrally on the Singaporean model, this chapter illustrates two important paradoxes. The first is that economic forces create multinational societies, but political forces must create national communities. The second is that while secular societies like Singapore strive to separate religion (as a private matter of the individual) from the public domain (of politics and economics), government must attempt to manage religion.

Moving to a more liberal case study, Jim Beckford observes with his "Religion in Prisons and in Partnership with the State" how the British state, even if constitutionally interlinked with two Christian churches, is also associated with other religious organizations in, for example, social welfare, education, healthcare, prisons and the armed forces. Compared to the United States and French cases, the approach of the British state to religious diversity is more one of a pragmatic adaptation, first by continuing the long-term relationship with the Church of England, other mainstream Christian churches and the Board of Deputies of British Jews, and secondly by widening its relationship with more recent religious groups. The basis of cooperation between religious groups and the state is officially seen as a type of partnership, but it needs to be underlined that this partnership is defined by the government. As researched by Beckford on faith communities, there is a new type of state corporatism that is quite state centered. Religious organizations have difficulties in working with state agencies, even to the point of being faced with tensions and conflict, and appear to be valued exclusively for instrumental reasons (e.g. utilizing the help provided to the community and dismissing the faith work central to these religious organizations).

In the Australian case study, Stephen Chavura's "The Secularisation Thesis and the Secular State: Reflections with Special Attention to Debates in Australia" reflects on, among other things, the different meanings of what a secular state is from country to country, but also from time to time. Although he agrees that in some ways, secularism is enforced through coercion, the case study in Australia is more refined than simply this. He traces the first use of the conception of the secular by the Fathers of Australian Federation (1901) who took secular to mean not nonreligious, but rather nonsectarian. According to him, while the Church of England was never established as the state church, there was always space for religious input in matters of social policy, education, welfare and national ceremony. Australia has neither an established church nor a constitution that is strong on separating the church and the state, and thus Australia cannot be seen as a model of exclusive secularism where the government and its institutions are void of any religious presence.

Hasmath's "Managing China's Muslim Minorities: Migration, Labor and the Rise of Ethnoreligious Consciousness among Uyghurs in Urban Xinjiang" underlines the fact that China is not as ethnically homogenous as one would think. Hasmath explores in this chapter the ethnic tension between the Muslim Uyghurs and the Hans (the national majority) and explores various periods of "soft" and "hard" policies from the state to manage this Muslim minority. To understand the state approach to a religious minority, Hasmath studies the migratory and urbanization patterns in urban Xinjiang to confirm this oppression of a minority group by a state, but also how intense competition for resources, educational and labor market is also a strong factor in this ethnic conflict.

Levy's "Secularism, Religion and the Status Quo" brings us to Israel, which appears to be an exception to the secularization thesis, as this nation-state refused to let religion die in the heyday of secularization, by establishing Judaism as its major foundation. This specificity is framed within the political principle of the status quo emerging from a pact between the Zionist and the Jewish political elites which prevents the disentangling between state and religion and leads to a type of semitheocratic state.

Porpora's "The Tension between State and Religion in American Foreign Policy" crosses the Pacific to analyze 500 opinion pieces published in newspapers and magazines between August and October 2002. He discovers that it was mainly the religious sphere that was critical of the war in Iraq on moral grounds, whereas the more mainstream and secular press focused more on pragmatics (e.g. would this war be another Vietnam and/or exacerbate terrorism?). Although the state aims at securitizing religion, Porpora found that traditional and organized religion continues to pack a counterhegemonic punch.

Zrinščak's "Church, State, and Society in Post-communist Europe" argues that although there is not one single European model of church-state relations, there is nevertheless evidence of a distinctive European dimension. He discovers that even in a post-communist environment pre-communist history is not the only salient element in the current church-state relationship; pre-communist national founding myths and the perceived identity shared by the various populations are also present. This would explain the different church-state arrangements between European post-communist countries.

The second part of this book observes how religions move from various forms of piety towards a more consumerist approach, and this in relation with the state.

Barbalet's "Chinese Religion, Market Society and the State" gives another approach to the case study of China by studying the growth of certain religions such as the Buddhist and Daoist revivalist movements which attract overseas Chinese contributors to the capitalist economy of the mainland. We discover in this chapter how the program of temple rebuilding has been encouraged through donations made by overseas Chinese individuals and families. While this type of family capitalism is not the only factor in the development of the post-1978 Chinese market, it is surely an important one.

Sriprakash and Possamai's "Hindu Normalization, Nationalism, and Consumer Mobilization" explores how Hindutva (loosely "Hindu-ness"), an ideology advocated by Hindu nationalist movements, exerts significant influence in parliamentary politics and, arguably more insidiously, in social life in contemporary India. This religious and social movement is able to develop its relationship with the state though consuming practices. To understand this new type of synergy between religion, state and consumerism, this chapter revises classical theories on consumption, especially the work of Bourdieu and the Frankfurt School, to understand the specific relation between this field in not only India, but also within its diaspora.

Yegenoglu's "Clash of Secularity and Religiosity: The Staging of Secularism and Islam through the Icons of Atatürk and the Veil in Turkey" studies how different groups are trying to assert themselves in the public spheres of a consumerist culture. Whereas Muslim groups make their religion more visible, through the use of the headscarf for example, secularist groups are doing the same to make their politics visible as well, through the display of Atatürk icons (e.g. posters, statues and even tattoos). Through these two different consuming paths, there is a complex interplay between the imaginary of the past and the desire for a specific future that rests behind the discourse that registers Islam as a threat or danger.

Possamai's "Gramsci, Jediism, the Standardization of Popular Religion and the State" adapts Gramsci's work on hegemony and popular religion to current fluid religions. It also reworks the classical understanding of the state to a transnational one that continues to operate its hegemony across nations. Gramsci thought that there were revolutionary elements in certain popular religions of his time. Using Jediism as a case study, Possamai claims that this new form of popular religion thriving on the internet, a space with no limitations or boundaries, does not have this revolutionary element. It is a paradox to discover that Jediism, this hyperreal religion inspired by the *Star Wars* franchise, is not attuned to fighting against any corrupted "empire," but focuses only on the work of the spiritual self.

In the "Concluding Comments," Michel's "Concerning the Current Recompositions of Religion and of Politics" addresses these tensions between believers and the range of public institutions that have been discussed in this book. He even wonders if religion is still disappearing or endlessly reemerging. Taking into account the end of the political utopia of 1989–92, it can be argued that the disenchantment of the world today affects the political arena as well and as Certeau claims, when politics gives ground, the religious comes back. Michel underlines the strong fluidity between religion, economy and politics and discovers a triple crisis that emerges from a political deficit, explosion/inadequacy of the supply of meaning and the strong decrease/withdrawal of credibility. These case studies illustrate a variety of common patterns in different societies and in terms of various religious traditions, while also paying attention to variations in relations between state and religion that are the product of local circumstances. One conclusion is however unavoidable – the overriding importance of religion in any understanding of modern politics.

References

Adogame, Afe. 2010. "Pentecostal and Charismatic Movements in a Global Perspective." In Bryan S. Turner (ed.), *The New Blackwell Companion to the Sociology of Religion*, 498–518. Oxford: Wiley-Blackwell.

An-Na'im, Abdullahi Ahmed. 2008. *Islam and the Secular State: Negotiating the Future of Shari'a*. Cambridge, MA: Harvard University Press.

Barry, Brian. 2001. *Culture & Equality: An Egalitarian Critique of Multiculturalism*. Cambridge, MA: Harvard University Press.

Beckford, James A. 2003. *Social Theory and Religion*. Cambridge: Cambridge University Press.

Bellah, Robert N. 1967. "Civil Religion in America." *Daedalus* 96: 1–27.

Bender, Cortney. 2003. *Heaven's Kitchen: Living Religion at God's Love We Deliver*. Chicago and London: University of Chicago Press.

Casanova, José. 1994. *Public Religions in the Modern World*. Chicago: University of Chicago Press.

Epstein, G. A. (ed.) 2005. *Financialization and the World Economy*. London: Routledge.

Fetzer, Joel S. and J. Christopher Soper. 2005. *Muslims and the State in Britain, France and Germany*. Cambridge: Cambridge University Press.

Gill, Anthony. 2008. *The Political Origins of Religious Liberty*. Cambridge: Cambridge University Press.

Habermas, Jürgen. 1996. *Between Facts and Norms: Contributions to a Discourse Theory of Law and Democracy* (trans. William Rehg). Cambridge, MA: MIT Press.

_____. 2006. "Religion in the Public Sphere." *European Journal of Philosophy* 14.1: 1–25.

_____. 2008. *Between Naturalism and Religion*. Cambridge: Polity Press.

Habermas, Jürgen and Eduardo Mendieta. 2002. *Religion and Rationality: Essays on Reason, God, and Modernity*. Cambridge, MA: MIT Press.

Habermas, Jürgen and Joseph Ratzinger. 2006. *The Dialectics of Secularization: On Reason and Religion*. San Francisco: Ignatius.

Hooker, Richard. 1982. *On the Laws of Ecclesiastical Polity*. Cambridge, MA: Belknap Press of Harvard University Press.

Hulsether, Mark D. 2000. "Like a Sermon: Popular religion in Madonna videos." In Bruce David Forbes and Jeffrey H. Mahan (eds), *Religion and Popular Culture*, 77–100. Berkeley, CA: University of California Press.

Hunt, Stephen. 2005. *Religion and Everyday Life*. London: Routledge.

Illouz, Eva. 2003. *Oprah Winfrey and the Glamour of Misery: An Essay on Popular Culture*. New York: Columbia University Press.

Joppke, Christian. 2004. "The Retreat of Multiculturalism in the Liberal State: Theory and Policy." *British Journal of Sociology* 55.2: 237–57.

———. 2009. *Veil: Mirror of Identity*. Cambridge: Polity.

Kamaludeen, Nasir Mohamed, Alexius Pereira and Bryan S. Turner. 2009. *Muslims in Singapore*. London: Routledge.

Kant, Immanuel. 1960. *Religion within the Limits of Pure Reason*. New York: Harper & Row.

Kitiarsa, Pattana (ed.) 2008. *Religious Commodifications in Asia: Marketing Gods*. London and New York: Routledge.

Locke, John. 1991. *A Letter Concerning Toleration*. London: Routledge.

Luckmann, Thomas. 1967. *The Invisible Religion: The Problem of Religion in Modern Society*. New York: Macmillan.

Luke, Timothy W. 1987. "Civil Religion and Secularization: Ideological Revitalization in Post-Revolutionary Communist Systems." *Sociological Forum* 2.1: 108–34.

Martin, David. 2002. *Pentecostalism: The World Their Parish*. Oxford: Blackwell.

Mazower, Mark. 1998. *Dark Continent. Europe's Twentieth Century*. London: Penguin.

Monshipouri, Mahmood. 2009. *Muslims in Global Politics. Identities, Interests and Human Rights*. Philadelphia: University of Pennsylvania Press.

Manby, Bronwen. 2009. *Struggles for Citizenship in Africa*. London: Verso.

Nancy, Jean-Luc. 2005. *The Ground of the Image*. New York: Fordham University Press.

Parsons, Talcott. 1963. "Christianity and modern industrial society." In Edward A. Tiryakian (ed.), *Sociological Theory, Values and Sociocultural Change: Essays in Honor of Pitrim A. Sorokin*, 33–70. New York: Free Press.

———. 1999. "Belief, Unbelief and Disbelief." In Bryan S. Turner (ed.), *The Talcott Parsons Reader*. Oxford: Blackwell.

Possamai, Adam and Murray Lee. 2004. "New Religious Movements and the Fear of Crime." *Journal of Contemporary Religion* 19.3: 337–52.

Rawls, John. 1993. *Political Liberalism*. New York: Columbia University Press.

———. 1999. *The Law of Peoples*. Cambridge, MA: Harvard University Press.

Stille, Alexander. 2010. "The Corrupt Reign of Emperor Silvio." *New York Review of Books* 57.6: 18–22.

Stolow, Jeremy. 2010. *Orthodox by Design*. Berkeley, CA: University of California Press.

Strange, Susan. 1986. *Casino Capitalism*. Oxford: Basil Blackwell.

Turner, Bryan S. 2007. "The Enclave Society: Towards a Sociology of Immobility." *European Journal of Social Theory* 10.2: 287–303.

———. 2008. "New spiritualities, the media and global religion: *Da Vinci Code* and *The Passion of Christ*." In Pattana Kitiarsa (ed.), *Religious Commodifications in Asia: Marketing Gods*, 31–45. London and New York: Routledge.

———. "Evangelism, state and subjectivity." In Julius Bautista and Francis Khek Gee Lim (eds), *Christianity and the State in Asia: Complicity and Conflict*, 18–35. London: Routledge.

———. "Religious Speech. The Ineffable Nature of Religious Communication in the Information Age." *Theory Culture & Society* 25.7–8: 219–35.

Veer, Peter van der (ed.) 1996. *Conversion to Modernities: The Globalization of Christianity*. New York and London: Routledge.

Volpi, Frederic and Bryan S. Turner. 2007. "Making Islamic Authority Matter." *Theory Culture & Society* 24.2: 1–19.

Ward, Graham. 2006. "The Future of Religion." *Journal of the American Academy of Religion* 74.1: 179–86.

Warner, R. Stephen. 2004. "Enlisting Smelser's Theory of Ambivalence to Maintaining Progress in Sociology of Religion's New Paradigm." In Jeffrey C. Alexander, Gary T. Marx and Christine L. Williams (eds), *Self, Social Structure and Beliefs: Explorations in Sociology*, 103–21. Berkeley, CA: University of California Press.

_____. 1952. *Ancient Judaism*. Glencoe, IL: Free Press.

_____. 1966. *Sociology of Religion*. London: Methuen.

_____. 2002. *The Protestant Ethic and the Spirit of Capitalism*. London: Penguin.

Yang, Fenggang. 2004. "Between Secularist Ideology and Desecularizing Reality: The Birth and Growth of Religious Research in Communist China." *The Sociology of Religion, A Quarterly Review* 65.2: 101–19.

_____. 2010. "Religious Awakening in China under Communist Rule: A political economy approach." In Bryan S. Turner (ed.), *The New Blackwell Companion to the Sociology of Religion*, 431–55. Oxford: Wiley-Blackwell.

Zabala, Santiago (ed.) 2004. *The Future of Religion*. New York: Columbia University Press.

Part I

FROM DEPRIVITIZATION
TO SECURITIZATION

Chapter 1

RELIGION IN LIBERAL AND AUTHORITARIAN STATES[1]

Bryan S. Turner

The City University of New York and University of Western Sydney

Introduction: The Paradox of the Politics and Economics of Migration

Two aspects of the modern liberal state can be considered basic conditions that influence the place of religion in modern society. The first is the problem of national identity in the face of cultural diversity. Most modern states are culturally, ethnically and religiously diverse. For most states, this diversity is a consequence of massive migration, either historically or more recently. With the globalization of the labor market, host societies have become more complex and diverse, and in addition they have become more difficult to govern. Singapore is an important Asian case where migration, before and after its independence, created a multicultural society; however, today it must deal with even more diversity. Like many other Asian societies, Singapore has a declining fertility rate despite all government attempts to correct that downward trend. As a result, the state must constantly seek to import labor, especially talented labor. With its current population at just over four million and with little opportunity to recover more usable land, the state has decided to increase its population to just over six million. Unless there are very direct controls on the ethnic composition of migrants, economic openness inevitably results in greater ethnic diversity. At the same time, the state has an interest in protecting its own territorial sovereignty and in order to assert its sovereignty

---

1 A version of this chapter was originally published in Kamaludeen Mohamed Nasir, Alexius A. Pereira and Bryan S. Turner, *Muslims in Singapore* (London: Routledge, 2009).

over society, it must create the political myth of a morally coherent and integrated society (Kamaludeen, Pereira and Turner, 2009).

Benedict Anderson (1983) has famously written about how nation-states create "imagined communities" through the spread of print media, and this mythical creation essentially involves the construction of a nationalist ideology. Like other states, Singapore must find ways of projecting a common purpose around the state and the image of a unified national community. In particular, it must foster a vivid and meaningful sense of what it is to be a "Singaporean," rather than, for example, a Chinese person living on the island of Singapore whose familial memories are more likely to be connected with mainland China. It must achieve a delicate balancing act between nationalism, internal harmony and openness to foreign talent by avoiding any impression that it favors one community over another. Therefore, the first paradox is that economic forces create multinational societies, but political forces must create national communities. Sociologists occasionally refer to this nation-building activity of the state in terms of building the cultural fabric – the great arch – of the society as the real foundation of political power (Corrigan and Sayer, 1985). This paradox holds true for small countries such as Singapore, but it is also central to the recent migration and population dilemmas of relatively large European societies such as Italy and the United Kingdom. In both societies, there is a rightwing opposition to migration, whereas with a declining and aging population these societies need to accept migrants to avoid a shrinking workforce.

The second paradox is that while secular societies like Singapore strive to separate religion (as a private matter of the individual) from the public domain (of politics and economics), governments must attempt to manage religions. Owing to the first paradox, the government cannot ignore the fact that religious diversity without management will in all probability result in communal tensions, if not in open social conflict. Other things being equal, the practice of religious piety will create a certain social distance between social groups and eventually these social divisions can harden into separate enclaves. These issues have dominated much of American history and are probably more salient now than in the past. Following the work of Robert Putnam (2000), we can argue that religious communities tend to build social bonding rather than social bridging. Other things being equal, piety movements will tend to reinforce exclusive tendencies and reinforce separate identities. The role of the state is to manage such social processes in the interest of creating social unity. Where possible, it should seek to convince its citizens that such social harmony is not simply artificial. In their recent *American Grace*, Robert Putnam and David Campbell (2010) take an excessively optimistic view of the capacity of American society to absorb religious diversity and proclaim its national coherence. By contrast, resentment rather than grace appears to dominate religion and politics in the United States, especially after 9/11 and more recently after the credit crunch. The aggravated public debate about the proposal to build a Muslim cultural center in the vicinity of the site of the Twin Towers at Ground Zero is simply one recent manifestation of the problems of Muslim integration. William E. Connolly (1995) has grasped this general sense of resentment in his account of the creation of a fundamentalist ideology, the rise of the Republican Right, the crisis of a number of foreign adventures from the Vietnam War to modern day Iraq, Afghanistan and Libya against the backdrop of the transformation of manufacturing industry and the financialization of American capitalism. For example, he argues that the Southern Baptist Church was originally consolidated through a shared sense of betrayal and resentment. This combination of military defeat, deep resentment against the outside world and aggressive moralization to overturn those evils forms the persistent basis of American religious fundamentalism (Connolly, 2008). The political fundamentalism of the South was part of a constituency that felt under siege from middle-class feminism, the welfare program of the Great Society, and more recently the election of President Obama. This resentment has gathered momentum against migration, especially illegal migration across the Mexican border and specifically against the growth of the Muslim population and what is seen to be the creeping threat of the Shari'a.

These alienated sectors of the blue-collar labor force, who have already been victims of the rust belt and the internet bubble, have now been subjected to the housing market crisis, the liquidity crisis, the slide in the value of the dollar, the banking meltdown, the economic recession and the legal scandals around mortgages and foreclosure. Tea Party politics might be suitably regarded as a contemporary example of status politics and political conservatism, and as such it has a long tradition in American political culture such as the People's Party of the 1890s in its opposition to big government, east-coast intellectuals, and Washington politicians. The message of the Tea Party is consistent with the basic elements of conservative thought: promote lower personal taxation, smaller government, ownership of guns, limited migration and more individual liberty. The title of the "Tea Party Manifesto" by Dick Amery and Matt Kibbe is "Give us Liberty" (2010). The politics of the Tea Party are a manifestation of the paradox that I am describing in terms of a tension between the politics of the nation-state and the labor requirements of economic growth.

Of course, not all liberal democratic societies have the same public issues regarding religion, diversity and migration. The ways in which states manage religions will clearly differ according to their histories and social structures. Canada and the United States, while they share the same land mass, do not share the same history with respect to slavery, migration and multiculturalism. America's border with Mexico has produced a set of somewhat specific conditions. The steady flow of illegal Mexican migrants is fueling anti-migrant xenophobia in states like Arizona and Nevada, whereas Canada has retained an openness to migration, taking 281,000 legal immigrants in 2010, the majority of whom came from the Philippines, India and China. Canada has of course had highly public contests with its Muslim culture following the failed experiment to develop Shari'a arbitration courts in Ontario in the late 1990s (Turner and Arslan, 2011). With a booming domestic economy and expanding energy industries, Canada has not been faced with a critical problem of illegal immigration and has retained a much more positive view of multiculturalism, which was in any case a policy invented by Pierre Trudeau.

With its history of slavery and racial conflict, the United States has been the site of communal tension and violence for the last two centuries. Clearly the scale of racial conflict in Singapore is vastly different, but the contradictory structure of nationhood and open borders remains the same. Singapore has experienced racial and religious tensions in the past. There were riots in 1951 over the religious identity of Maria Hertog, a European girl who had been raised by a Malay family (Aljunied, 2009). The government has responded to this religious diversity by preventing religious labels from playing any overt public role. The Maintenance of Religious Harmony Act of 1990 prevents the use of religion for political ends. The state has also been willing to respond forcefully to eliminate any signs of religious opposition to the government, exemplified by its response to what it saw as a Marxist conspiracy among Catholic intellectuals in 1987. Twenty-two members of Catholic Church organizations who had promoted awareness of the plight of foreign workers were arrested on the grounds that they were plotting a Marxist revolt against the state. These arrests were carried out under the Internal Security Act, but this blunt instrument was inappropriate in such a case. The Maintenance of Religious Harmony Act was designed to separate faith from social activism. However, the paradox is that in order to keep religion and politics apart, the state must actively intervene in civil society to guarantee that religious services – preaching, teaching, healing, praying and so forth – are compatible with public security, social stability and nationalist goals.

In the Singapore case, this "management of religion" has two dimensions, each of which is characterized by further ambiguities. The first dimension is the unintended consequence of creating religious enclaves. This outcome arises because the Singapore state categorically divides the population primarily into four distinct ethnic communities: Chinese, Malay, Indian and other. The consequence is that these ethnic identities inevitably play an important role in public life. Furthermore, since these ethnic categories are also in practice religious categories, it means that religion is significant in defining public identities. To illustrate this point, Malays are typically Muslim, Indians are typically Hindu and the Chinese are typically Buddhist, although there are a sizable number of Chinese who are Christian. Thus, there is an official ethnic definition of groups despite the government's attempts to break down the cultural division between various communities to foster the national identity of being "Singaporean."

The second dimension is the specific management of Islam in Singapore. This policy is seen as necessary because of the long-standing "Malay problem," namely the social and economic backwardness of the Malay Singaporeans. Singapore's government prides itself on its technological rationality, ranging from economic and urban planning to its family and cultural policies. Thus, the state has a range of strategies that are designed to "upgrade" its own population. These upgrading strategies include everything from health (mosquito control and encouraging weight control to prevent obesity) to automobile restrictions to education (including policies on "Religious Knowledge"). The Singaporean authorities have regarded individualism and "shapeless multiculturalism" as aspects of Western decadence, contrasted with the moral superiority of Confucian Asia (Harvey, 2006). The upgrading therefore manifests itself through the self-assumed responsibility of the state to intervene directly in the arenas of religion, morals, reproduction and family life. Singapore's strategies towards its Muslim population are encapsulated in Majlis Ugama Islam Singapura (MUIS, or the Islamic Religious Council of Singapore) and its related policies of improving Muslim education, modernizing the Shari'a and its courts, and seeking to regulate and improve Muslim family life.

Although Singapore is a small island city-state in Southeast Asia surrounded by societies that have much larger populations and resources, it is a society that is highly instructive from a sociological point of view. Singapore illustrates in clear terms the paradoxes of free-market capitalism. While the dominant form of global capitalism has been neoliberal, few Asian societies have simultaneously embraced deregulation in economics and liberalism in social life. The idea of a harmonious society based on a strong state and Confucian values has continued to be more attractive than Western liberalism – in other words, the rule of virtue rather than the rule of law. Asian societies have generally sought to regulate family and religion in the interest of social stability. The Singaporean experience shows that any society that wants to separate religion and politics (in order to guarantee freedom of religious belief and practice) must interfere systematically in society to manage religions. The success or failure of these policies will have profound implications for the wealth and well-being of its citizens and the regions that surround the island.

Although Singapore has not as yet been the target of a successful terrorist attack, there is considerable anxiety in the city-state that such an attack would have devastating social and economic consequences. It is also obvious that as a secular capitalist state, Singapore must be a potential target of some significance. Economically advanced societies can no longer rely on the conventional division between politics and religion and have entered into a new phase that will have to involve the direct management of religions. In the current context of global anxieties over security, liberal states have evolved from policies of benign neglect towards religious belief and racial identity to active management of religious institutions. In practice, these new strategies are in fact concerned with "managing Muslims" under the umbrella of social pluralism and multiculturalism. These developments can be understood in terms of Michel Foucault's concept of "governmentality," since managing religions is a recent adjunct of the more general functions of the administrative state (Foucault, 2000). Managing religions is important if the state is to reassert its authority over civil society – especially over those religious institutions that seek to articulate an alternative vision of power and truth – and if it is to command the loyalty of its citizens over and above other claims of membership.

Managing Religions

I have argued that the modern state has a contradictory relationship with multiculturalism and migration on the one hand and to security and sovereignty on the other. Security would be relatively effective and inexpensive in a society where virtually all of the citizens spoke the same language, practiced the same religion, adhered to the same dress code and supported the same cricket teams. The modern world is generally not like this. In a capitalist society in particular, the state seeks to encourage labor migration, porous political boundaries and minimal constraints on the flexibility of the labor market. At the same time, the state is under considerable pressure from economic elites to reduce the resistance of labor to the destructive logic of enterprise and capital accumulation. One solution to the resistance of organized labor to structural change in the economy is to regulate trade unions, make strikes illegal and import foreign labor to reduce the unit costs of production. Singapore has been remarkably successful in achieving these economic goals. Under Mrs Thatcher's Conservative governments, similar inroads were made into the effectiveness of trade unions in influencing wage levels and conditions of employment. However, the state also has an interest in sustaining its own sovereignty, and hence wants to create and impose a cultural and moral unity on society. The modern state is an administrative order that seeks to maximize the social potential of its population (hence it has an interest in supporting migration), but it also has an interest in the enforcement of a particular type of governmentality.

This contradiction means that we can expect state policies towards citizenship and migration to vacillate between treating migration and multiculturalism as aspects of economic policy and constructing multiculturalism within a framework of asserting national sovereignty. While some sociologists have noted that "we are all multicultural now" (Glazer, 1997; Kymlicka, 1995), much of the recent evidence from Western societies is that multiculturalism is in retreat because there is now a growing emphasis on security and careful regulation of migration. More importantly, critics argue that multicultural policies often appear to have divided rather than united societies (Barry, 2001; Joppke, 2004; Levy, 2000). Recent political crises in the liberal democracies – Britain, France, Germany, Italy, the Netherlands, Denmark and Australia – have only served to reinforce this critical standpoint. European societies have all faced this postwar cultural and ethnic fragmentation, but in Britain – given its imperial history – these social changes have been both rapid and profound. The history of Singapore is somewhat different. As an international port, it has always been a migrant society and its Chinese majority, although the political elite, are also a migrant community. Singapore has been largely successful in embracing multiculturalism – or multiracialism to use on its own terms – without jeopardizing the social supremacy of the Chinese.

Theories of multiculturalism have attempted to make a distinction between its social and cultural dimensions, thereby constructing four types, namely cosmopolitanism, fragmented pluralism, interactive pluralism and assimilation (Hartmann and Gerteis, 2005). This theory suggests that multiculturalism can involve a variety of combinations, including a situation where social groups retain their internal solidarity, but the society as a whole is fragmented. This situation is often described in terms of a system of parallel communities. In this typology, social groups can be both in conflict and in competitive relationships with each other. Assimilation is probably not strictly speaking a multicultural strategy, since it is based on the assumption that difference is harmful or at least undesirable and should be suppressed or suspended in the process of assimilating foreigners into a host society. Finally, interactive multiculturalism celebrates differences, recognizes group rights and accepts principles of recognition and reciprocity. Cosmopolitanism involves a distinctively normative vision of this cultural diversity in which individual civil liberties are preserved (Appiah, 2006).

Typologies of state responses to religion should be regarded as merely heuristic devices that are only more or less useful. The following typology attempts to categorize government policies as either inclusive or exclusive. Obviously, any one government may have several policy strategies in place simultaneously, and these policies may not be necessarily compatible or coherent. Governments may try out several strategies over time depending on local circumstances and the changing nature of state politics. The more extreme state policies might involve a form of social quarantine resulting in the formation of ghettos or parallel communities. These extreme forms of separation and exclusion would also include repatriation and expulsion on the one hand and extermination and ethnic cleansing on the other.

Repatriation, denaturalization and the forceful expulsion of minorities have unfortunately made up a common pattern of political conflict in Africa (Manby, 2009). Similarly, the laws that were enacted in Germany in the 1930s to declare that Jews were not citizens were in some sense extraordinary laws (Agamben, 1998). However, repatriation, expulsion or genocide constitute extreme strategies and are unlikely practices in democratic governments. In short, draconian policies of repatriation, expulsion and genocide are incompatible with human rights legislation and would be difficult to implement because their very enactment would be likely to contradict the rules of procedural justice in a functioning democracy. For similar reasons, the use of "extraordinary rendition" by United States security agencies appears to contradict the principles of the rule of law upon which American democracy is based.

Inclusive policies, although in some circumstances benign, can nevertheless be criticized as patronizing. Through an inclusive policy of "adaptive upgrading," I adopt a term from Talcott Parsons's sociological theory of social systems (Parsons, 1999: 76) to suggest that some governments may adopt strategies to improve the education and social status of migrants. They adopt these strategies with the view that such policies may help to bring them into the middle class and that the training of their leadership will make them more moderate in political terms. Parsons defined "adaptive upgrading" as "the reevaluation of the older, previously downgraded components to constitute assets from the point of view of the broader system" (1999: 76). The opposite strategy would be to downgrade or even to degrade a population by transforming it into a minority whose main function in society would be to provide manual labor and to undertake stigmatized services that the host population might reject. Degrading prevents a group from achieving even the minimum standards of dignity and civility. Degrading creates an underclass and such policies would transform a minority into a "pariah group" in the long run (Weber, 1952: 3).

Integration and assimilation are well-known multicultural strategies that aim to bring a subordinate or minority group into the mainstream, but with assimilation there is the implication that over time such minorities would abandon their cultural distinctiveness. These strategies are in effect strategies of domestication. The opposite strategy – the creation of an "enclave society" (Turner, 2007) – is to force minorities into segregated areas using physical impediments such as walls to stop the flow of people. Perhaps the most encouraging strategy would be to embrace some form of cosmopolitanism that would integrate minorities without robbing them of their cultural distinctiveness. However, cosmopolitanism is ambiguous. It has been criticized by some as an elitist strategy that recognizes differences from a position of privilege. Although recognition appears to be an essential step in the development of cosmopolitanism as a moral attitude and as a strategy necessary for social harmony in complex multicultural societies, there are by that very fact ample opportunities for misrecognition and resentment. These various strategies can be summarized in this typology:

Table 1.1. Typology of state management

Positive state policies	Negative state policies
Inclusive policies	Exclusive policies
Upgrading	Downgrading or degrading
Integration/assimilation	Enclavement
Cosmopolitanism	Cultural indifference
Politics of recognition	Politics of misrecognition

When we consider the relationship between the state and religion in any typology of management strategies, we have also to keep in mind that "religion" may take many forms along a continuum from individualistic spirituality to collective expressions of identity. One aspect of my argument is that the modern eruption of spirituality is unlikely to pose problems for the state, because it is by definition post-institutional and private. Religion may cause the state to intervene when it takes on a fundamentalist orientation involving a movement to increase conversions or when religion becomes largely equivalent to an ethnic identity. In short, it is mainly when religions become "public religions" that states are forced to respond with much more than mere indifference (Casanova, 1994).

Legal Regulation and the Quality of Religious Services

My argument is that all states, with significant variation of course, are now involved in some form of management of religions. In this chapter, I shall simplify the picture by looking at the sharp contrast between liberal democratic states and post-communist authoritarian ones. In the majority of liberal democracies before 9/11, there was an inclusive laissez-faire policy in which the state guaranteed freedom of conscience on the principle that religion is a private affair. The main exception has been the treatment of so-called cults; states in liberal democracies have been forced to intervene in what they have seen to be problematic implications of cultic groups for society. States tend to intervene when there is a perceived threat to minors, namely when children or the vulnerable are seen to be at risk from the evangelical activities of cults. Such behavior – for example, conversion techniques – tends to be regarded as merely brainwashing and hence a basis for legal intervention. The classical example in the West would be the Moonies. With the development of consumerism in both market and religion more recently, states more regularly intervene to ensure the quality of the product, such as in the case of Scientology in France. Liberal states nevertheless are slow to intervene and only reluctantly become active in religious management.

The management of religion under communism comes in this typology under the category of downgrading or degrading. Religion in general was regarded simply as a superstition from the feudal past and as a threat to the monopolistic role of the Party. In the period of the Cultural Revolution in China, Mao attempted to liquidate Confucianism as a feudal system and directly attacked the traditional customs of filial piety. However, it is said that both Stalin and Mao came implicitly to support some aspects of religion insofar as it could be useful in supporting or legitimating the Party. In Vietnam, Roman Catholicism was seen by the Party as a remnant of French colonialism, and under American influence the Diem regime came to support Catholicism as a state religion against Buddhism. Despite these conflicts, it is possible to argue that Confucianism remained an official ideology and its commitment to an orderly society often served Party objectives.

The traditional legal arrangements of imperial China were based on Confucian values and can be described as a system of moral "familialism." This system involved unconditional filial piety, the welfare of the dominant status group over the individual and a reverence for seniority. The "Confucianization of the law" meant that both judge and ruler drew directly from morality, especially where strictly juridical guidelines were absent or ambiguous. This traditional Confucian system promoted the idea of rules of law and virtue. The criminal law was the cornerstone of this system, because it was the basis of social control. This legal system broke down during the Cultural Revolution and one can interpret the post–Cultural Revolution period of institution building and law reform as an attempt to prevent another relapse into the excesses of class struggle and generational conflict. The 1999 National Plan for Managing Public Order sought to contain the growth of criminal gangs, the production of fake agricultural goods, the proliferation of cults, the emergence of juvenile delinquency and to manage China's floating, dislocated populations With these reforms, there has been a political emphasis on the need to combine rule of law with the rule of virtue. As an antidote to "blind Westernization," Chinese citizens are called upon to embrace Confucian virtue in the form of the "four beautiful virtues" (*si mei*) of beautiful thought, language, behavior and environment and the "four haves" (*si you*) of consciousness, morality, culture and discipline.

China's legal reforms and modernization are in many respects a reassertion of traditional Confucian norms of respect, duty and stability. This feature of traditional rule and the failures of China's criminal law institutions is perhaps nowhere better illustrated than in the Party's response to the "Falun Gong problem." Between 1949 and 1997, cults were regarded as secret societies and hence constructed by the political elite as counterrevolutionary movements. The current treatment of Falun Gong continues a tradition of such criticism and displays the worst aspects of legal flexibility in which policy needs replace legal procedure. The ethos of "state instrumentalism" and the use of the notion of "social harm" give rise to considerable human rights abuses. The worst features of state instrumentalism include detention without trial, extralegal detention and custody for investigation. These procedures are enforced on the basis of the extrajudicial authority of public agencies.

Falun Gong ("Wheel of Law"), which combines Buddhist-Daoist beliefs and traditional exercises, claimed the right to assemble to practice healing exercises in public spaces. Its founder Li Hongzhi was born in 1952 and embraced the teachings of *qigong* at an early age. He established his own school of traditional healing in 1992 and initially gained political approval for these practices. Falun Gong appealed to the powerless and the dispossessed, but when it was banned by the Ministry of Civil Affairs in 1999, Falun Gong members often responded with acts of civil disobedience. The authorities have responded with a mixture of extrajudicial measures that amount to administrative discipline: hard labor for reeducation, "custody for repatriation," detention for "further investigation," loss of jobs and so forth. The Chinese Communist Party has defined religious heresy as a crime and employed state institutions to reinforce "socialist spiritual civilization" against "feudal superstition" such as the beliefs and practices of Falun Gong. On 12 July 2006 it was reported in the Canadian foreign policy newsletter *Embassy* that the Canadian government had announced its intention to investigate allegations that Falun Gong prisoners in Chinese jails were being murdered and their organs sold to transplant patients. One piece of evidence is that prior to 1999 – when Falun Gong was banned – the state was harvesting organs from 1,600 prisoners executed each year. After 1999, there has been a rapid increase in organ transplants and it is estimated that some 41,500 organ donors in that period are unaccounted for. If these allegations prove to be true, the removal of prisoner's organs without consent will give "extrajudicial procedures" a new and sinister meaning.

Both Muslims and Buddhists in China have recently come to the attention of the international media because their suppression has become more obvious and blatant. Some aspects of this repression were evident during the Olympic Games and more recently, conflicts with Huigra in the Xinjiang province and with Buddhists in Tibet have raised issues about the failures of citizenship and the erosion of religious freedom. At present, the prospects for human rights in China are not promising. Merle Goldman's analysis of the erosion of the achievements of the new liberalism of 1997 to 1998 in *From Comrade to Citizen* (2005) is depressing reading. In reviewing China's achievements, it is useful to make a comparison with the recent history of Russia.

Like China, Russia is faced with serious problems resulting from the alienation of its Muslim population. With the collapse of the Soviet empire in 1992, there was of course considerable optimism about the prospects of human rights improvements. However, in November 1994 President Yeltsin decided to attack the Chechen capital Grozny to crush the separatist movement of Jokhar Dudayev. Human rights critics of the war such as Sergei Kovalev, having been denounced as enemies of Russia, predicted that the war would result in intolerance, revenge and civil violence (Gilligan, 2005). These criticisms became horribly true at the school massacre in Beslan in September 2004. While Kovalev was highly critical of the Chechen leadership, he argued that the second war in Chechnya allowed Vladimir Putin to consolidate his power. Putin, who has done much to curtail human rights, undermine foreign NGOs, silence opposition and restore centralized power, has enforced the ideology of Russia as the Great Power and the doctrine of *derzhavnost*, the view that the state is a superior mystical being that every citizen must serve without question. The good citizen is a *derzhavnik* who is indifferent to the fate of other citizens and accepts state crimes as necessary and justified. It has proved difficult to contain the conflict in North Caucasus, where the violence has erupted in many provinces – Dagestan, Ingushetia and Karbardino-Balkaria. Radical Islam has become increasingly important in these conflicts as the region has been opened up to Middle Eastern trade, pilgrimage and the internet (King and Menon, 2010). However, while Islam has become important in the contemporary conflict, the region is an ancient location of opposition to the Russian state.

An equally appropriate example of the differences between political and social secularization can be taken from the modern history of the Russian Orthodox Church in relation to society and state. Although the church was severely repressed in the early years of the Russian Revolution, the close relationship between Orthodoxy and nationalism meant that Orthodox Christianity could also play a useful role in secular Russian politics. Since the fall of the Soviet system, the Orthodox Church has made an important comeback under the skilful political direction of Patriarch Alexy II, who has forged a powerful alliance with both Vladimir Putin and Dmitry Medvedev (Garrad and Garrad, 2009). In 1983, the patriarch was successful in securing the return of the Don Monastery in central Moscow to ecclesiastical use. In 1991, he managed to restore the veneration of St Seraphim of Sarov who, dying in 1833, was revered as a patriot by Tsar Nicholas II. The saint's relics were restored to the Cathedral of Sarov. In 1997, a law on the freedom of religious conscience gave a privileged status to Orthodoxy, while Roman Catholicism has been politically marginalized. For obvious reasons, Islam and evangelical Protestantism have been the target of much state intervention and have been suppressed when necessary. Under Medvedev, Orthodoxy has continued to prosper as an official religion offering some degree of spiritual and national legitimacy to the Party and the state. There is also a close relationship between the military and the Orthodox Church in that religious icons are used to bless warships and the patriarch offered a thanksgiving service on the anniversary of the creation of the Soviet nuclear arsenal.

Although the public role of Orthodoxy has been largely restored, the church's influence is largely based on cultural nationalism rather than on its spiritual authority. Thus while some 80 percent of Russians describe themselves as "Orthodox," just over 40 percent call themselves "believers." This relationship between the political and the social allows us to say that, while Orthodoxy is a powerful public religion and public space has been partially resacralized, Russian society remains secular. The same is true of modern China. While there is considerable evidence of religious revival in both folk religion and the world religions, social surveys show that the Chinese population is predominantly secular (Yang, 2010). The legacy of atheism and secularism from the past still has a hold over the everyday social world even when religion now plays a considerable part in a nationalist revival. Therefore, in any assessment of the notion of "a post-secular society" in both liberal and authoritarian states, we need to be careful about whether secularization refers to formal institutions at the political level or whether it refers to lived religion at the social level. It is my contention that the philosophical analysis of the role of religion by Habermas in public culture is very important, but it may tell us relatively little about how religion is embodied in the social world.

Many of these issues are illustrated by the modern history of Tibet. Tibetans have unusually high urban illiteracy rates and it is the Han migrants who benefit most from Chinese economic investment. Tibetans have become an urban underclass, while those remaining in rural areas have suffered from

limited economic opportunities and rural poverty (Fischer, 2005). While there
has been a significant decline in the number of Buddhist monks, some 1,550
out of 1,886 monasteries have been rebuilt in eastern Tibetan areas (Kolas and
Thowsen, 2005). However, Chinese promotion of Buddhist sites in China may
also be generally connected with the expansion of what we might legitimately
call "religious tourism." This commercial development of religious sites
is common in China and more generally in Asia. This commodification of
religion is also consistent with greater state intervention in the management
of religion in China since the 1990s, and those groups that cannot achieve
recognition from the state as a religion may attempt to flourish as cultural or
tourist sites under the regulation of local state agencies (Ashiwa and Wank,
2006). In short, both Russia and China can be said to be engaging in a modest
level of "cultural upgrading" of Buddhism and Orthodoxy in the interests
of their foreign relations. At the same time, they are engaged in degrading
and exclusionary policies towards their Muslim minorities which are generally
labeled as terrorist movements.

Conclusion

These authoritarian state examples probably confirm the Western view that
despite liberalization, state authorities often harass religious minorities because
they are seen to be a challenge from within civil society to the authority of the
state. A similar story could be told about modern Vietnam where, despite
the so-called Renovation Period, ethnic minorities in border areas are seen
to be both backward and disruptive. The growth of Protestant evangelism
in these border areas of Vietnam has been of particular concern to the state.
Although authoritarian states tend to suppress cults by forceful and violent
means if necessary, the commercial development of religions in both China
and Vietnam could offer an alternative strategy. One solution to the Tibet
problem and to the Muslim threat for the Chinese authorities would be to
commodify these religions, thereby developing Tibet into a tourist site – a
religious Disneyland under the control of the state.

   Although Western liberal critics are quick to demonstrate the shortcomings
of such authoritarian states, there is a reasonable concern that modern
states could in general slide towards the "Singapore model" in which there
is relatively tight and illiberal regulation of religion in a period of global
securitization. However, the Singapore model does present a challenge to
Western liberal views, especially to those positions that are inspired by the
work of John Rawls or Jürgen Habermas's interpretation of it. Western
liberals argue that democracy and secularization (in the basic meaning of the
separation of religion and politics) provide the best conditions within which

religious and sectarian conflict can be avoided. One recent illustration of this argument appears in Irfan Ahmad's *Islamism and Democracy in India* (2009), where he shows how the original and radical version of Jamaat-e-Islami Hind, which was founded in 1941 by Syed Abul Ala Maududi, has gradually evolved towards overt acceptance of secular political values and institutions. His explanation is that, because the Indian Constitution guaranteed secularism and democracy, Jamaat leaders came to accept secular political institutions as their best defense against the violence being promoted by the anti-Muslim Hindutva. Even Indira Ghandi's decision in 1975 to ban all opposition parties did not turn the Jamaat back to the position advocated by Maududi that Muslims should reject democracy as *haram*. A similar argument is presented in Mohammed Hafez's *Why Muslims Rebel* (2003), in which he argues, comparing Egypt and Algeria, that representing repressive and authoritarian attempts to suppress radical religious groups is counterproductive, as they drive the moderates into the arms of the radicals.

These arguments provide comforting ammunition to secular liberals who want to protect the basic institutions and values of liberal democracy as the best foundation for individual rights and tolerance. Against such examples, the "Singapore model" presents an important alternative. Singapore clearly has a history that is very different from either Russia or China, but it is equally and clearly different from Britain and America in its strategy. If through careful and technical management of religions, Singapore can successfully build a harmonious and successful modern society, then it provides an obvious contrast to laissez-faire traditions of the liberal West. The paradox is, of course, that Singapore represents a form of "soft authoritarianism" that is grounded in the legality of the state, but it is not the tolerance that liberals have admired and cherished.

References

Agamben, Giorgio. 1998. *Homo Sacer: Sovereign Power and Bare Life*. Stanford, CA: Stanford University Press.

Ahmad, Irfan. 2009. *Islamism and Democracy in India: The Transformation of Jamaat-e-Islami*. Princeton, NJ: Princeton University Press.

Aljunied, Syed Muhd Khairudin. 2009. *Colonialism, Violence and Muslims in Southeast Asia: The Maria Hertogh Controversy and Its Aftermath*. London: Routledge.

Amery, Dick and Matt Kibbe. 2010. *Give Us Liberty: A Tea Party Manifesto*. New York: HarperCollins.

Anderson, Benedict. 1991. *Imagined Communities: Reflections on the Origin and Spread of Nationalism*. London: Verso Books.

Appiah, Kwame A. 2006. *Cosmopolitanism: Ethics in a World of Strangers*. New York: W. W. Norton.

Ashiwa, Yoshiko and David L. Wank. 2006. "The Politics of a Reviving Buddhist Temple: State, association and religion in Southeast China." *The Journal of Asian Studies* 65.2: 337–59.

Barry, Brian M. 2001. *Culture and Equality: An Egalitarian Critique of Multiculturalism.* Cambridge, MA: Harvard University Press.

Casanova, José. 1994. *Public Religions in the Modern World.* Chicago: University of Chicago Press.

Connolly, William E. 1995. *The Ethos of Pluralisation.* Minneapolis: University of Minnesota Press.

————. 2008. *Capitalism and Christianity, American Style.* Durham, NC and London: Duke University Press.

Corrigan, Philip and Derek Sayer. 1985. *The Great Arch: English State Formation as Cultural Revolution.* Oxford: Blackwell.

Fischer, Andrew Martin. 2005. *State Growth and Social Exclusion in Tibet: Challenges of Recent Economic Growth.* Copenhagen: IAS Press.

Foucault. Michel. 2000. *"Governmentality" in Power: The Essential Works of Michel Foucault, Vol. 3.* London: Allen Lane.

Garrad, John and Carol Garrad. 2009. *Russian Orthodoxy Resurgent: Faith and Power in the New Russia.* Princeton, NJ: Princeton University Press.

Gilligan, Emma. 2005. *Defending Human Rights in Russia: Sergei Kovalyov, Dissident and Human Rights Commissioner 1969–2003.* London: Routledge Curzon.

Glazer, Nathan. 1997. *We Are All Multiculturalists Now.* Cambridge, MA: Harvard University Press.

Hafez, Mohammed. 2003. *Why Muslims Rebel.* Boulder, CO: Lynne Reinner.

Hartmann, Douglas and Joseph Gerteis. 2005. "Dealing with Diversity: Mapping multiculturalism in sociological terms." *Sociological Theory* 232.2: 218–40.

Harvey, David. 2006. *Spaces of Global Development.* London: Verso.

Joppke, Christian. 2004. "The Retreat of Multiculturalism in the Liberal State: Theory and policy." *British Journal of Sociology* 55.2: 237–57.

Kamaludeen, Nasir Mohamed, Alexius A. Pereira and Bryan. S. Turner. 2009. *Muslims in Singapore.* London: Routledge.

King, Charles and Rajan Menon. 2010. "Prisoners of the Caucasus: Russia's invisible civil war." *Foreign Affairs* 89.4: 20–34.

Kolas, Ashild and Monika P. Thowsen. 2005. *On the Margins of Tibet: Cultural Survival on the Sino-Tibetan Frontier.* Seattle: University of Washington Press.

Kymlicka, Will. 1995. *Multicultural Citizenship: A Liberal Theory of Minority Rights.* Oxford: Oxford University Press.

Levy, Jacob. 2000. *The Multiculturalism of Fear.* Oxford: Oxford University Press.

Manby, Bronwen. 2009. *Struggles for Citizenship in Africa.* London: Verso.

Parsons, Talcott. 1999. "Belief, Unbelief and Disbelief." In Bryan S. Turner (ed.), *The Talcott Parsons Reader,* 51–79. Oxford: Blackwell.

Putnam, Robert. 2000. *Bowling Alone: The Collapse and Revival of American Community.* New York: Simon & Schuster.

Putnam, Robert and David Campbell. 2010. *American Grace: How Religion Divides and Unites Us.* London: Simon & Schuster.

Turner, Bryan S. 2007. "The Enclave Society: Towards a sociology of immobility." *European Journal of Social Theory* 10.2: 287–303.

Turner, Bryan S. and Berna Zengin Arslan. 2011. "*Shari'a* and legal pluralism in the West." *European Journal of Social Theory* 14.2: 139–59.

Weber, Max. 1952. *Ancient Judaism.* Glencoe, IL: Free Press.

Yang, Fenggang. 2010. "Religious Awakening in China under Communist Rule: A political economy approach." In Bryan S. Turner (ed.), *The New Blackwell Companion to the Sociology of Religion*, 431–55. Oxford: Wiley-Blackwell.

Chapter 2

RELIGION IN PRISONS AND IN PARTNERSHIP WITH THE STATE

James A. Beckford

University of Warwick

Introduction

"Religion" and "state" are contested concepts. A particularly heated debate has been raging about these concepts for a decade or more among practitioners of religious studies. On the one hand, the majority view is that the terms "religion" and "state" are difficult to define but that they are in principle good enough for analytical purposes. On the other hand is the view of a group of self-styled critical theorists that both terms are illegitimate abstractions that mask ideological positions (Fitzgerald, 2000, 2007; McCutcheon, 2003).

I find this debate intriguing, although it has very few implications for this chapter. This is because I choose to take a social constructionist approach to the sociological understanding of religion (Beckford, 2003). This means that, instead of using generic notions of religion and the state that purport to be valid for all times and places, I prefer to focus on the social processes whereby the meanings of these terms are generated, attributed, deployed and contested in particular social and cultural contexts. This allows me to work with rough and ready definitions that merely identify the outer limits of common usage. For my purposes, then, *religion* has to do with beliefs, values, motivations, feelings, activities, normative codes, institutions and organizations that relate to claims about the ultimate significance or perceived wholeness of life. Loosely following Max Weber's example, I understand *states* as formal political collectivities that successfully claim legitimacy over the exclusive exercise of authority, backed by force if necessary, in relation to all human activity in their territories.

Relations between religions and states, understood in these terms, have historically run the full gamut of positions between total inseparability and mutual exclusion. The Islamic Republic of Iran represents an extreme position of virtual identity between a religion and a state. The former communist regime of Albania represents the opposite extreme, approximating to mutual exclusion between a state and all religions. Despite problems of definition, all the states in the world can in principle be situated on this continuum between polar extremes.

The sociological importance of relations between religions and states is reflected in the fact that at least three specialist journals (*The Journal of Church and State*; *Religion, State and Society*; and *Religion-Staat-Gesellschaft*) now deal with the topic. In addition, other journals and books continue to publish extensive analyses of the religion-state nexus, beginning in the 1980s with *Religion and the State* (Wood, 1985) and *Church-State Relations. Tensions and Transitions* (Robbins and Robertson, 1987). One of the most recent is Jonathan Fox's *A World Survey of Religion and the State* (2008). At the same time, studies of the legal frameworks and regulatory mechanisms governing relations between religions and states, especially in the United States, add further complexity to the picture (Grim and Finke, 2006). Winnifred Sullivan's *The Impossibility of Religious Freedom* (2005) and Marci Hamilton's *God vs. the Gavel* (2005) show just how contentious the picture can be. Meanwhile, there is extensive overlap with the much more voluminous literature on religion and politics.

One of the most productive developments in this field was the deployment of a neoinstitutionalist approach (Powell and DiMaggio, 1991; Koenig, 2007). This refers to a loose set of assumptions and questions about the capacity of institutions to give cognitive and normative shape to social life. From this point of view, a critical aspect of relations between religions and states is how, over time, they have been molded into distinctive forms that are largely taken for granted and resilient. The focus of this approach is on the ideas, routines, values, rules and laws that help to make particular relations between religions and states appear to be natural or normal. I shall refer to these phenomena as "institutional frameworks." They simultaneously make certain things possible and other things virtually unthinkable. The advantage of this perspective is that it facilitates comparisons of the institutional frameworks that structure relations between religions and states in different countries.

This chapter has three main sections. The first will outline a neoinstitutionalist perspective on questions about relations between states and religions in France, the United States and the United Kingdom. As Minkenberg (2002, 2003), Koenig (2007) and Bader (2007) have shown, the pattern of religion-state relations remains impressively diverse even among the member states of the European Union. Using evidence about the different patterns of spiritual and religious care that France, the United States and the United Kingdom provide for prisoners, I shall show that religion-state relations have a major impact on the official recognition and resourcing of religions in prison establishments. The chapter's second section will develop this argument further with specific reference to the interest that recent British governments have shown in pursuing partnerships with faith communities and faith-based organizations at a time of growing religious diversity. Since 1997 in particular, a wide range of public policies have favored investment in not only consultation with faith communities but also investment in their capacity to act as partners with the state in the design and delivery of services in relation to education, health, community cohesion and welfare. However, the final section of the chapter will challenge the idea that partnerships between the state and the "faith sector" of British society have been unproblematic. It will also argue that claims about a resurgence of religion in the public sphere tend to overlook the effect of government strategies for managing ethnic and religious diversity on the increased salience accorded to religion in public life.

The thread that runs through all three sections of the chapter is the argument that relations between states and religions are much more complex than mere outworkings of political and theological ideas. Religion-state relations are subtle and provisional outcomes of the shifting interplay between many different interests and forces. The growth of religious and ethnic diversity in liberal democracies since the mid-twentieth century has elicited policy responses which vary loosely with each country's evolving framework of religion-state relations. However, these frameworks do not determine the outcomes in a mechanical fashion (Bowen, 2007). Discussion of religion in prisons and of the British government's strategies for entering into partnerships with religions for the sake of achieving policy objectives will show how varied and paradoxical the nexus of relations between states and religions can be.

Religious Diversity in the Context of State-Religion Relations

(a) France

In constitutional terms, France is a secular republic, which in principle has had no formal links with any religion for more than one hundred years. The principle of *laïcité*, or republican secularism, governs the public sphere in France and is particularly powerful in keeping religious influences out of state institutions, especially state schools (Caron, 2007). Indeed, Jonathan Fox's *World Survey of Religion and the State* claims that "the French government tends to take a slightly negative view of religion" (2008: 135) and that its position is best categorized as "hostile" to religion. This is certainly the case with its heavy-handed "vigilance" against "cultic aberrations" (Beckford, 2004; Altglas, 2008). Nevertheless, the republic is constitutionally bound to respect its citizens' freedom of conscience and religion; Catholic culture remains active in the private lives of large segments of the population; and the state pays for the upkeep of churches that existed before 1905. The presence of about half a million Jews and 5 million Muslims also helps to ensure that religious organizations and activities continue to thrive in the communal and voluntary sectors of French society. At the same time, central bureaucracies of the French state are responsible for registering organizations that choose to be categorized as religious in order to benefit from fiscal advantages. And even more surprisingly, there is no separation of religion and the state in the Alsace-Moselle region of eastern France on the border with Germany or in some of France's overseas territories. In short, the picture is mixed and even contradictory in some respects (Altglas, 2010), but no other state in Western Europe does more than France to distance itself from religion (Bowen, 2007).

The French Republic's response to religious diversity is distinctive and clear. Starting from the constitutional principle that the republic is unitary and secular (*laïque*), questions about religious diversity are virtually unthinkable in the state's institutions. The state in France is more than neutral or evenhanded in matters of religion: its laws and policies come close to excluding religion from most of the public sphere. This means that the state is indifferent to the number or variety of religions that operate in its territory, provided that the citizens who participate in these religions do not allow their religious commitments to interfere with their supposedly primary identification with and loyalty to the republic. In other words, religions are largely confined to the spheres of private life and voluntary associations. Citizens are free to give expression to religions in their private lives but not in areas of public life that are the preserve of the state.

The boundary between religious activities and the republic is monitored and policed by two official organizations. On the one hand, the Bureau des Cultes is responsible for administering the registration of religious groups that choose to be incorporated under a law of 1901 and for overseeing the concordat with various religious communities that are still operative in the Alsace-Moselle region and in some overseas territories. On the other hand, the Interministerial Mission of Vigilance and Struggle Against Cultic Aberrations (Mission interministérielle de vigilance et de lutte contre les dérives sectaires, or MIVILUDES) answers directly to the prime minister for coordinating the republic's campaign to prevent sectarian or cultic groups from taking unfair advantage of weak and vulnerable members or potential recruits. MIVILUDES's attention has been focused in recent years on allegations of abuse allegedly perpetrated by unscrupulous groups – under the cover of religion – in relation to the home schooling of children, alternative therapies and vocational training (Altglas, 2010).[1] Political support in France is extremely strong for the work of MIVILUDES, which is often portrayed as a bulwark against irrationality or transnational conspiracies in the name of bogus religions to subvert the republic or simply to make immoral profits.

Against this background, agencies of the French Republic have taken a variety of positions but rarely recognize the existence of religious or ethnic minorities. Questions concerning justice and equality in relation to minorities simply do not arise because public policies must be aimed at all citizens, who supposedly enjoy equal rights. Very few policies or programs deliberately or explicitly target minorities as such, although the growing body of laws against discrimination – mostly in response to directives from the European Union – is beginning to change the picture. At the same time, the republic took the leading role in establishing regional and national structures that seek to coordinate and represent Muslims living in France. But this has much more to do with co-opting and integrating Muslims than with acknowledging that they might form intermediary bodies with political functions independent of the state. Fears that religious "communalism" will corrode the republic's integrity lie behind the unwillingness to regard the diversity of religions in France as having implications for public policy. Instead, policy is framed in terms of concepts such as "young people from troubled neighbourhoods,"[2] which attempt to naturalize controversial or constitutionally illicit social categories by referring to them by geographical location.

When it comes to the treatment of religious minorities in French prisons, the prison service – l'Administration pénitentiaire – follows the pattern of the republic's other institutions by seeking to avoid giving the impression that it officially favors any religion. The Criminal Law recognizes the right of France's 62,252[3] inmates to practice their religions, but the prison service provides only meager resources or opportunities to facilitate this. Very few prison chaplains are employed by the state; most are volunteers. The space and time for collective worship are hard to find. Chaplains and chaplaincy volunteers are

---

1 See the annual reports of MIVILUDES and of its predecessor MILS online at: http://www.miviludes.gouv.fr/-Rapports-?iddiv=3 (accessed 17 June 2011).

2 "Les jeunes des quartiers en difficulté," in the words of the "Charte de la laïcité dans les services publics et autres avis," Haut Conseil à l'Intégration, 31 January 2007. Online at: http://lesrapports.ladocumentationfrancaise.fr/BRP/074000341/0000.pdf (accessed 6 September 2009).

3 L'Administration pénitentiaire, "Les chiffres clés de l'administration pénitentiaire au 1er janvier 2009." Online at: http://www.justice.gouv.fr/index.php?rubrique=10036&ssrubrique=10041&article=17322 (accessed 10 January 2010).

not well integrated into the structures of management or support services. Responsibility for the recruitment, training, coordination and professional development of chaplains is left mainly to religious organizations. And, despite the fact that Muslims are heavily overrepresented in the French prison population, provisions for their spiritual and religious care are rudimentary (Beckford, Joly and Khosrokhavar, 2005). For example, requests for *halal* diet often meet with the response that Muslim inmates should either choose vegetarian options or buy their own food in the prison shop. In part, this is because prison administrators tend to interpret the principle of *laïcité* in the most restrictive fashion to mean that the republic should not accommodate for religious obligations or differences.

(b) USA

The celebrated First Amendment to the United States Constitution prevents the federal state from showing favor towards any particular religion whilst at the same time protecting the right of its citizens to express their religion (Greenawalt, 2006, 2008). The so-called wall of separation between the state and religion is perhaps not as impassable as the figure of speech implies, but continuous processes of litigation have at least averted any significant breaches or collapses. Nevertheless, while the level of state "entanglement" in religion is unusually low in comparison with most other countries, Americans display exceptionally high levels of commitment to religious beliefs, activities and organizations. In the United States, religious activity looms large in civil society; political activity gives ready expression to religious values; and the delivery of social welfare is entrusted in large part to religious organizations (Farnsley, 2007). Not surprisingly, generations of immigrants have successfully navigated their way into American society by participating in religious groups.

The constitution of the United States may appear to resemble that of France insofar as the federal state is required to show neutrality towards all religions and must not prevent its citizens from expressing their religious views. But in practice, the two systems of "separation" produce quite different outcomes. The main purpose of the separation of religions from the state in France is to protect the state against the risk of religious interference. By contrast, the separation in the United States serves primarily to protect religions against the risk that the state might try to co-opt or control them. These differences stem mainly from the two countries' contrasting histories in the eighteenth and nineteenth centuries.

Against the background of a powerful form of civil religion and of the prominent display of religious symbols on banknotes and in prayers in Congress – to say nothing of the carefully staged public demonstrations of the personal piety of leading United States politicians – extensive legal and campaigning activities prevent individual states and the federal state from either backing or blocking any religions in particular. Admittedly, the boundary between "entanglement" and "separation" is permanently disputed territory in courts of law, academic forums and the public square, but the First Amendment doctrines are rarely called into question. As a result, diversity in religion is widely acknowledged as a sign that United States citizens really are free to express their religions in private *and* public without fear of interference from the state. Indeed, advocates of theoretical positions allied to rational choice theory or subjective rationality attribute the vitality and diversity of American religion to the lack of state interference in religion (Finke, 1990; Stark and Finke, 2000). The only significant constraints applied by the state to religious freedom arise from concerns phrased in terms of public and national security. It is on these grounds that federal, state and local agencies have occasionally tried to stem the activities of minority movements such as Mormons, Jehovah's Witnesses, Scientologists and the Nation of Islam.

The United States Bureau of Prisons (BOP), which is responsible for 115 federal prisons and other correctional institutions but not for each state's own prison system, is also bound to operate in accordance with a constitution that separates religions from the state. But the "free exercise" clause of the First Amendment is also honored in such a way that a wide array of statutory and voluntary provisions are made for the spiritual and religious care of inmates. Roughly 250 chaplains are currently working in the BOP's Religious Services Branch on full-time contracts, serving approximately 204,000 inmates.[4] Many other chaplains and volunteers are provided by "religious contractors" and local religious groups. The principal justification for this apparent entanglement of the state with religions is that, since inmates – like other "institutionalized persons" – are not able to exercise their right to practice religion by attending local places of study or worship, the state must make suitable provisions on their behalf (Dolan, 2008). But, in order to minimize the risk that the state could be accused of unconstitutional entanglement with religions in prison, the provision of facilities for religion is subject to stringent limits. For example, it must be strictly evenhanded between different religions; it must not breach security regulations; and "institutional chaplains" must make themselves

---

4 See http://www.bop.gov/about/index.jsp (accessed 11 June 2009). Only 12.5 percent of the 1.6 million inmates held in the United States in 2007 were in the jurisdiction of federal authorities. See also United States Department of Justice, Office of Justice Programs, Bureau of Justice Statistics Bulletin: "Prison inmates at mid-year 2007." Online at: http://www.ojp.usdoj.gov/bjs/pub/pdf/pim07.pdf accessed (11 June 2009).

available to *all* prisoners. On the other hand, courts of law have also imposed limits on the power of prison authorities to deny the claims that prisoners make for the free exercise of their religions (US Commission on Civil Rights, 2008). All these issues are subject to more or less continuous processes of litigation that extend up to the United States Supreme Court on occasion (Hammond, Machacek and Mazur, 2004; Hamilton, 2005; Sullivan, 2009).[5]

(c) UK

The Anglican Church remains "established in law" in England, and the Presbyterian Church enjoys a similar legal status in Scotland. Although they are both "national churches" rather than "state churches," their entanglement with the apparatus of monarchy, parliament and state is close and complex. Publicly funded chaplaincies are central to the operation of prisons, hospitals and military institutions in all four countries of the United Kingdom: England, Scotland, Wales and Northern Ireland. In addition, the British state has long maintained a "dual system" of school-level education in which close to one quarter of students are taught in schools owned and/or managed by religious – mostly Christian – organizations. Moreover, all state schools are required by law to teach religious education and to conduct a daily act of collective worship. The state also authorizes the clergy of certain religious communities to solemnize marriages without the need for separate civil ceremonies. And broadcasting authorities are required by law not only to provide a certain amount of religious programming but also to regulate the form and content of advertising sponsored by religious organizations. Nevertheless, the level of active participation in public or private religious activities in the United Kingdom is among the lowest in Western Europe, albeit with wide variations between different faith communities, ethnic groups, social classes, regions and generations.

In contrast to France and the United States, the British state is not only constitutionally intertwined with two Christian churches but is also associated at local, regional and national levels with many other religious organizations in fields such as social welfare (Beckford et al., 2006; Prochaska, 2006), education, healthcare, prisons and the armed forces. In the absence of a constitutional separation of state and religions, British governments

---

5 The framework of federal law includes the Civil Rights of Institutionalized Persons Act (1980), the Religious Freedom Restoration Act (1993, revoked in 1996), and the Religious Land Use and Institutionalized Persons Act (2000). Leading cases include *Employment Div. v. Smith* US 872 (1990); *City of Boerne v. Flores*, 521 US 507, 532 (1997); and *Cutter v. Wilkinson*, 544 US 709 (2005).

have discriminated against some religions and actively cooperated with others (Barker, 1987; Beckford, 1993). This uneven pattern is characteristic of other European countries such as Andorra and Liechtenstein that fall into Fox's (2008) category of "historical or cultural state religion." Some religious organizations can derive tax benefits from registration with the Charity Commission, while this privilege is denied to others. In addition, a category of "religiously aggravated" offenses has been framed in criminal law and discrimination on the grounds of religion in many spheres of life now breaches civil law.

Two developments that have occurred since the first New Labour government took office in 1997 indicate a new phase in relations between the British state and selected religions. The first is the ideological commitment of successive governments to the promotion of the value of *diversity* in ethnicity and religion. But, following the violence of 11 September 2001 and 7 July 2005, the emphasis of government policies has shifted away from diversity for its own sake towards the need to ensure that diversity does not undermine social cohesion and "British identity" by engendering "parallel lives." The ideological thrust is now towards making diversity in religion and other bases of identity serve the overarching goal of strengthening "Britishness."

The second recent development is the policy of fostering *partnerships* between the state and selected actors in civil society – so-called faith communities in particular (Beckford, 2010). In an extension of Margaret Thatcher's neoliberal policy of "rolling back the state" and privatizing wide swaths of the public service, New Labour governments have sought to "outsource" many public functions to private or civil society organizations – but without necessarily relaxing the state's oversight of how these functions are carried out.[6] It is particularly in the field of "urban governance" (Chapman, 2009) that the state has sought partners among religious organizations.

The British state's current response to religious diversity is best characterized as a pragmatic adaptation of the long-standing pattern of cooperating with the Church of England, other mainstream Christian churches and the Board of Deputies of British Jews in the provision of educational and welfare services. The selection of religions and services has been widened in recent decades and the basis of cooperation is now partnership, as defined by government (Beckford, 2010).

This pattern of partnership between state and religions is particularly evident in the prisons of England and Wales (Beckford and Gilliat, 1998).[7]

---

6 Hundreds of quangos (quasi-autonomous nongovernmental organizations) have been created to monitor and regulate the performance of its partners or service providers on behalf of government. Their official designation is "nondepartmental public body."

7 Scotland and Northern Ireland operate their own prison services.

Christian chaplains have been an integral part of these prisons for about two hundred years. Indeed, Christian theological ideas lie at the root of the theory and the practice of regimes such as solitary confinement. All prisons in England and Wales are still required by law to have a Church of England chaplain and such others as are necessary to meet the spiritual and religious needs of inmates. There were about 200 Christian chaplains and 50 Muslim chaplains working full-time among the 84,000 inmates in 2010. Part-time and voluntary workers in prison chaplaincy numbered about 8,000. Chaplains were involved in a wide range of activities including sentence planning, the preparation of parole reports and participation in prison committees.

The chaplain general of the Prison Service Chaplaincy is a senior Anglican priest. He is assisted by several assistant chaplains general and a Muslim adviser to the prison service. In addition, a chaplaincy council and a group of faith advisers representing the major faith traditions in England and Wales act as further consultants and advisers. Under pressure from the representatives of minority faiths, prison chaplaincies have responded to the growth of religious diversity in the prison population since the 1980s by adopting aspects of a multifaith ethos and by accommodating many of the demands for the official recognition of religiously based diets, forms of clothing and festivals.

In short, France, the United States and the United Kingdom clearly display markedly different frameworks of relations between the state and religions. Each of these frameworks, in turn, gives rise to a distinctive way of framing and responding to religious diversity. Nowhere is the distinctiveness of these processes of framing religious diversity clearer than in the context of prisons. This is where the state really shows its hand when it comes to relations with religions.

The second section of this chapter will now develop these points further by examining in detail the highly distinctive configuration of religion-state relations which has evolved over the long haul in England and Wales. It centers on cooperative partnerships between the state and what it identifies as "the faith sector."

Partnership between the British State and Faith Communities

Whereas the French and United States administrations are constitutionally obliged to avoid close relations with religions, no such legal provisions have ever deterred agencies of the British state from "close encounters of the religious kind." Neither the French preoccupation with the evolution of *laïcité* in the face of religious diversity nor the American preoccupation with determining how reasonable the state should be in its "reasonable accommodation" of religious differences finds any echo in the United Kingdom. Instead, the United Kingdom seems to be heading in a completely different direction – towards ever closer forms of partnership with faith communities in its cautious embrace of diversity.

The United Kingdom's membership of the European Union and the compatibility of its laws with the provisions of European treaties have strengthened notions of citizenship, rights and equality. Nevertheless, the policies of British governments of all political complexions in the past few decades have continued to frame key issues in terms of certain *collective* identities alongside notions of individual rights. Categories of gender, disability "race" and ethnicity have more recently been joined by religion as points of reference in the framing of public policies designed to promote equality and justice (Woodhead with Catto, 2009).[8] Tony Blair's vision for Britain in the late 1990s was as a "community of communities." Diversity of communities was celebrated as a vital force in British society. But following the terrorist attacks on the United States, Britain and Spain – as well as the violent disturbances that took place in some British cities in 2001 – the emphasis has shifted away from the celebration of diversity for its own sake towards a more instrumental strategy of harnessing diversity as a search for social cohesion (Home Office, 2001). This does not amount to a wholesale abandonment of multiculturalism (pace Joppke, 2004, 2009) but is rather a pragmatic response to the real and perceived threats from terrorism and "communal" tensions in areas of deprivation.

Instead of encouraging unlimited diversity for its own sake, the current objective of government policy is to ensure that "ethnic, religious or cultural differences do not define people's life chances and that people with different backgrounds work together to build a shared future" (Home Office, 2004: 4). This statement implicitly acknowledges that diversity can be problematic. Indeed, a Home Office (2004: 7) consultation document captured the new orientation as follows:

> Respecting and valuing diversity is an essential part of building a successful, integrated society. But respect for diversity must take place within a framework of rights and responsibilities that are recognised by and apply to all – to abide by the law, to reject extremism and intolerance and make a positive contribution to UK society. One of the results of this re-orientation of policy is that applicants for British nationality now have to demonstrate their competence in the English language and their understanding of "life in the UK."

---

8 For a critical assessment, see Baumann and Sunier (1995) and Baumann (1999).

In terms of government machinery, the Race, Cohesion and Faith Unit of the Department for Communities and Local Government takes the lead on questions concerning religious diversity. The title of a research project sponsored by this unit indicates just how far the concepts of ethnicity and religion are now conflated: "Understanding Muslim ethnic communities."[9] Each of the reports on these communities emphasizes the need for policy to respond to the communities' internal diversity.

Further attention is focused on ethnic and religious communities by the government's strategy of fostering partnerships with voluntary and communal associations that claim to represent these communities. Three examples include:

- The 2005 formation of the Faith and Voluntary Sector Alliance for the purpose of making better use of faith-based organizations in the delivery of local government services
- The plan to integrate faith-based organizations into the strategies of the National Offender Management Service for reducing rates of reoffending among youths and adults (NOMS, 2007)
- The launch of the Department for Communities and Local Government's detailed "framework for partnership in our multi-faith society" (DCLG, 2008)

The term "partnership" recurs in official documents about these, and other, schemes for harnessing the resources of faith-based organizations to the achievement of government policy objectives.[10] I am tempted to categorize these schemes as evidence of a new kind of *state corporatism*. This is doubly ironic. First, the schemes involve the use of voluntary resources in pursuit of the state's objectives. Secondly, they display a high degree of *dirigisme* or state-centeredness, which is more characteristic of the secular French Republic than of the supposedly more devolved and pluralistic British regime. Indeed, the religious diversity of the United Kingdom is conveniently packaged and smoothed over for government consumption by the United Kingdom

---

9 For reports on 13 "Muslim ethnic diaspora communities in England," see http:// webarchive.nationalarchives.gov.uk/20100513032259/http://communities.gov.uk/ publications/communities/summarymuslimcommunity (accessed 24 August 2011).

10 For example, a report on faith schools published in 2007 by the Department for Children, Schools and Families highlighted "the very positive contribution which schools with a religious character make as valuable, engaged partners in the school system and in their local communities and beyond" (1). The report also drew attention to "the new duty on all maintained schools to promote community cohesion" (15) that was introduced by the Education and Inspections Act in 2006.

Inter-Faith Network's practice of stipulating that there are five major faiths and four minor faiths in the country. This reinforces the impression that a distinctive "faith sector" exists in the United Kingdom and that it consists exclusively of the participants in the interfaith network. Indeed, government relies heavily on the United Kingdom Inter-Faith Network to be the gatekeeper of suitable partners for the state.[11] New or controversial religious movements are not among its member organizations.

Partnerships between the British state and religious organizations have a long history, especially in the fields of education and prisons. But my argument is that relations between religions and the state have changed significantly since the 1950s for two main reasons. One is the substantial growth of religious diversity. The other is the slow crystallization of laws and administrative procedures designed to promote equality of opportunity and to penalize unjust discrimination on the grounds of religion. The result of this combination of factors is that the privileges and priorities previously accorded only to mainstream Christian churches have largely given way to a marketized set of relationships between the state as a purchaser and religious organizations as suppliers of various religious goods and services. The ground for this development had been prepared in the early 1980s, when the Conservative governments of Mrs Thatcher implemented neoliberal policies designed to contract out responsibility for the provision of many state services – especially in the welfare sector – to private, profit-seeking companies and to community and voluntary organizations. For a wide variety of reasons, faith-based organizations took the opportunity to enter the market as contractors to the state in an increasingly mixed economy of statutory and nonstatutory service providers. When the first New Labour government came to power in 1997, faith-based organizations were particularly well placed to compete for contracts to deliver services that were then expected to be tailored to the personal needs and circumstances of service users.

Unlike the United States, however, the British market for religious contractors is less than fully open; it is restricted to those suppliers who are able to meet the government's contractual conditions. The state enters into contractual relations with religious organizations within a framework of equalities legislation. To complicate matters further, the inducements for faith-based organizations to enter this market have increased at a time when many of them are struggling to find enough members at the level of local groups to carry out their own internal tasks (Cameron, 2003). As a result, the relationship between the state and faith-based organizations is not one of equal

---

11 "At the point at which it recognizes the need to engage with religions, therefore, the state can find interfaith mediating bodies very attractive." (Weller, 2009: 76)

power. The partnership is heavily one-sided in terms of the power to specify tasks, conditions and rewards.[12] But it also offers financial rewards, a degree of prestige and a heightened probability of being appointed or co-opted to official bodies such as Regional Assemblies, Regional Development Agencies and Local Strategic Partnerships (Church Urban Fund, 2006; Finneron, 2007). Specific schemes involving faith-based organizations in partnership with the British state include the National Strategy for Neighbourhood Renewal, the New Deal for Communities, regional Faith Forums, and the Faith Communities Capacity Building Fund.

In addition, special bodies have been formed for the purpose of facilitating relations between faith-based organizations and the state. For example, the Muslim Contact Unit and the Muslim Safety Forum bring together representatives of the Metropolitan Police Service and Muslims (Spalek, El Awa and McDonald, 2009). The Faith and Voluntary and Community Sector Alliance, hosted by the Ministry of Justice, seeks to bring together a wide range of groups working towards the reduction of crime and recidivism.[13] The Charity Commission recently set up its own Faith and Social Cohesion Unit whose "aim is to enhance and advance high standards of governance and accountability among faith-based groups, promote the benefits of registering as a charity, and promote the valuable contribution these charities make to society."[14] In common with a growing number of public bodies, the Charity Commission also has plans for a Faith Advisory Group. Meanwhile, the Faith Communities Consultative Council, chaired by a Minister at the Department for Communities and Local Government, has been acting since 2006 as an umbrella body for facilitating and monitoring consultation at all levels between government and faith communities.

In short, the closing decades of the twentieth century and the opening decade of the twenty-first century marked a period of progressively closer relations between the British state and the faith communities that comprise "the faith sector." Contrary to the claims that successive British governments have tried to exclude religions – especially Christianity – from public life (Trigg, 2007), faith communities have accepted invitations and inducements to enter into partnerships with the state in areas such as education, welfare services,

---

12 This is not unique to faith-based organizations but is true for many community and voluntary organizations. See Deakin (2001).

13 See http://noms.justice.gov.uk/about-us/working-with-partners/alliances/faith-community-volun-alliance/ (accessed 6 May 2009).

14 "Faith in Focus: The Newsletter of the Faith and Social Cohesion Unit" (London: The Charity Commission). Online at: http://www.charitycommission.gov.uk/Charity_requirements_guidance/Specialist_guidance/Faith/faithnews2.aspx (accessed 24 August 2011).

community cohesion and the prevention of terrorism. As I shall argue in the next section, these developments have strengthened the questionable claim that the United Kingdom has experienced a resurgence of public religion.

Resurgence of Public Religion?

The fact that recent governments in the United Kingdom have strengthened the policy of entering into partnerships with faith-based organizations has led some commentators to employ celebratory – if not triumphalist – expressions such as "the revival of public religion" or "the return of religion to the public sphere." Indeed, some have gone so far as to speculate that secularism and secularity have been ousted by post-secularism and post-secularity (Beckford, 2010). A variant interpretation in France is that advanced democracies have entered a phase of "ultra modernity" in which secularism has itself been secularized, thereby creating more space for religion in the public sphere (Willaime, 2006). The question for me is whether the evidence supports these contentions about the resurgence of public religion in the United Kingdom.[15] On the one hand, there is no doubt that the British state has implemented many policies intended to foster partnerships with faith-based organizations. But, on the other, there are three reasons for doubting whether these partnerships necessarily reflect a resurgence of religion in the public sphere.

First, some religious organizations have readily acknowledged that working in partnership with agencies of the state can be difficult. A particularly perceptive report by the Church of England's Commission on Urban Life and Faith (2006: 72) on "Faithful cities" concluded, for example, that government policy had not "provided a secure and consistent relationship between faith communities and government at all levels. There needs to be greater clarity over expectations in partnerships." Even stronger criticisms of the very notion of partnership emerged from a three-year study of the results of more than twenty years of attempts to regenerate inner-city neighborhoods in Manchester and to deal effectively with their problems of poverty (William Temple Foundation, 2003). It highlighted the feelings of "disempowerment" expressed most clearly by those with direct responsibility for implementing central government policies for regeneration. "The focal point for this sense of disempowerment was the concept of partnership, but more especially the concept of consultation. Ironically, these are the two cornerstones of New Labour's regeneration policy designed to create empowerment and

15 I make no comment here about the claims made for the upsurge of religious organizations and activities in many other regions of the world outside Western Europe. See, for example, Jenkins (2002), Juergensmeyer (2006) and Benthall (2008).

participation" (William Temple Foundation, 2003: 57–8). Moreover, "there is growing evidence...that the *faith sector is not necessarily willing or able to fulfil the role expected of it by government rhetoric*" (emphasis in original). Indeed, a report two years later confirmed that, against the background of the "very high levels of contribution made by faith-groups to wider society" (Baker and Skinner, 2005: 82), "the hope that there might be a distinctive language that churches could bring to the regeneration debate has proved...to be elusive." Consequently, "gaps of understanding and knowledge between faith and non-faith-based sectors are wide and levels of real communication poor" (Baker and Skinner, 2005: 86). Strong opposition to the government's policies on partnership with faith-based organizations has also come from the British Humanist Association and the National Secular Society.

Second, while the opportunity for religious groups to enter into partnerships with the British state has undoubtedly helped to "normalize" relations with some relatively excluded communities, it has also aggravated tensions and conflicts in other cases. For example, a report by the Conservative think-tank Policy Exchange (2007: 26) claims that competition for the resources that accompany partnerships has "created a fierce competition" among contenders for official recognition. It adds that "the shift at local level from secular to religious partners" has inspired some of the new contenders for recognition to "challenge the dominance of older, secular traditions," thereby further fragmenting the already divided Muslim communities. Research by the National Council for Voluntary Organisations (2007) also showed that faith-based groups in rural areas felt marginalized by the government's focus on social cohesion in urban areas. They also voiced the concern that groups belonging to the Christian majority faith might feel sidelined by the focus on minorities. A broader concern is that the state may be unwittingly fermenting divisions between faith-based organizations by framing policies in terms of generic partnerships with them, without taking full account of their differences at the local level (Farnell and Ramsay, 2007: 15). Fear that the current policy of promoting "faith schools" within the state system of education will reinforce already high levels of segregation between faith communities in some localities also feeds into concerns about divisiveness.

Third, research on small faith-based organizations, especially in rural areas, has uncovered skepticism about the government's "instrumentalist approach to the involvement of faith-based organisations" because it allegedly failed to take account of the "faith dimension of their work" (NCVO, 2007: 20). There are echoes of this view in other studies that have identified a high risk of "mission drift" among faith-based organizations that work in partnership with agencies of the state. Allegations of the government's instrumentalism are widespread; and there are even suggestions that government is actually suspicious of faith itself (Jochum, Pratten and Wilding, 2007: 21). The grounds for this suspicion rest on the dual accusations that in many settings faith-based organizations have been "highly pernicious in their influence, siding with elites against the interests of the poor and marginalised, stirring ethnic and religious divisions, and maintaining patriarchal social structures which oppress women and homosexuals" and that their own structures and cultures are rarely democratic (Jochum, Pratten and Wilding, 2007: 26). Indeed, some faith-based organizations struggle to conform to the legal requirement that services delivered to the public, with state funding, do not unfairly discriminate against people on the grounds of ethnicity, religion, sexual orientation, gender or disability.

It is certainly not difficult to understand the British government's reasons for using faith-based organizations as partners or deliverers of services in fields as diverse as welfare, health and education. The reasons are particularly cogent in the case of services aimed at ethnic minorities and categories of such vulnerable people as refugees and asylum seekers, "rough sleepers" and released prisoners. Faith-based organizations with their own premises offer additional advantages as partners with the state. Their financial and human resources as well as their educational and managerial structures and social networks are also part of what many well-established faith-based organizations can bring to the partnership. Discourse about symbolic, human and social capital is common in this area. However, evidence that the British government's hopes and expectations for partnership have been fulfilled is not plentiful – and certainly not convincing enough to outweigh all the difficulties that faith-based organizations and government departments have experienced in trying to work in partnership.

The British state now has substantial machinery for consulting with faith communities and for engaging them in a wide range of schemes to promote social cohesion and to reduce inequalities. Is this evidence of a "resurgence" of faith in the public sphere? In my view, it signifies the *continuing* contribution of religious organizations and faith communities to civil society in the United Kingdom, not an upsurge or a resurgence. More importantly, the evidence also points to the growth of an instrumental attitude (Farnell, 2009: 185) among policymakers to the capacity of religious organizations to help government to achieve its policy objectives in the fields of social cohesion, local governance, education and social welfare. In this context, religious organizations and faith communities are mainly valued for instrumental reasons – and not unreasonably, in view of the contributions that they make towards day-to-day living in many localities.

The pressure and the inducements to involve religious groups in partnerships with the British state have come from its agencies at national and local levels.[16] In part, this is because recent governments have followed ideological principles of neoliberal communitarianism, which favor the strengthening of the community and voluntary sectors of civil society – and this includes religious groups. In other respects, the post-2001 focus on national security, the "war on terror" and the ethnoreligious tensions in certain British cities have also given a strong impetus to policies promoting social cohesion and partnerships between "communities" and state. Again, faith communities and religious organizations have been targeted as potential allies of government. In short, *expediency* lies behind many of the official strategies and schemes for consulting and "using" faith or religion as a vehicle for the delivery of government policies. The result is undoubtedly a higher public profile for faith and religion – particularly in the sphere of state-controlled institutions. In this sense, the salience of public religion has increased. But I see no warrant for talking of an independent resurgence or return of religion elsewhere in British public life. Nor is there evidence that religious organizations have succeeded in exercising significant influence over the shape or direction of government policies. This is not to forget the limited success that religious lobbyists have achieved in obtaining exemption from legislation against discrimination in recent years (Sandberg and Doe, 2007).

Conclusions

This chapter's arguments fall into three main parts. The first is that France, the United States and the United Kingdom display differences not only between their constitutional frameworks for managing relations with religions but also between their respective responses to the growth of religious diversity. These three states all subscribe to many of the same international codes of human rights and religious freedom, but their practical implementation of the codes displays wide variations. This is clear in relation to their respective responses to the growing diversity of religions and in terms of the kind of provisions that their prison systems make for inmates to practice religions. Admittedly, this is an unusual angle from which to approach questions about these relations, but it throws into sharp relief the limits that states impose on the recognition and accommodation of religious diversity.

---

16 "Thus, in contrast with the 1970s and much of the 1980s, when many religious organisations and groups often felt frozen out from participation in local authority-driven development, a situation has developed in which religious groups are being positively 'wooed' to join in partnership as part of a new approach to the development of local governance." (Weller, 2009: 71)

The second part of my argument is not only that the British state's response to the growth of religious diversity differs sharply from that of France and the United States, but also that recent British government policies have fostered increasingly close partnerships between the state and faith communities. In pursuit of policy goals related to equality, social cohesion and national security, agencies of the state routinely engage with selected religious partners. This helps to reinforce the differences between the United Kingdom and countries such as France and the United States, which maintain at least a constitutional separation between religion and the state.

The British state's expedient use of partnerships with faith communities may have boosted the impression that a resurgence of religion was taking place in the public sphere and that the country was somehow becoming "post-secular." But the third part of my argument is that such an impression would be misleading. In fact, the heightened salience of religion in the public sphere owes at least as much to government policies and strategies aimed at drawing faith communities into partnerships with the British state as to any significant upsurge in religious convictions, consciousness or action. This suggests that the distinctive configuration of religion-state relations in Britain is not merely the backdrop to religious activity: it actually helps to shape the activity and its salience in public life.

References

Altglas, Veronique. 2008. "French cult controversy at the turn of the new millennium: Escalation, dissensions and new forms of mobilisations across the battlefield." In Eileen V. Barker (ed), *The Centrality of Religion in Social Life: Essays in Honour of James A. Beckford*, 55–68. Aldershot: Ashgate.

———. 2010. "Laïcité is what laïcité does: Rethinking the French cult controversy." *Current Sociology* 58.3: 489–510.

Bader, Veit. 2007. *Secularism or Democracy? Associational Governance of Religious Diversity*. Amsterdam: University of Amsterdam Press.

Baker, Chris and Hannah Skinner. 2005. *Year Two. Telling the stories: How churches are contributing to social capital*. Manchester: William Temple Foundation.

Barker, Eileen V. 1987. "The British right to discriminate." In Thomas Robbins and Roland Robertson (eds), *Church-State Relations*, 269–80. New Brunswick, NJ: Transaction Books.

Baumann, Gerd. 1999. *The Multicultural Riddle: Rethinking National, Ethnic, and Religious Identities*. London: Routledge.

Baumann, Gerd and Thijl Sunier (eds). 1995. *Post-Migration Ethnicity: De-Essentializing Cohesion, Commitments and Comparison*. The Hague: Martinus Nijhoff.

Beckford, James A. 1993. "States, governments and the management of controversial new religious movements." In Eileen V. Barker, James A. Beckford and Karel Dobbelaere (eds), *Secularization, Rationalism and Sectarianism*, 125–43. Oxford: Clarendon Press.

———. 2003. *Social Theory and Religion*. Cambridge: Cambridge University Press.

———. 2004. "'Laïcité,' 'Dystopia,' and the Reaction to New Religious Movements in France." In James T. Richardson (ed.), *Regulating Religion: Cases Studies from around the Globe*, 27–40. Dordrecht: Kluwer Academic/Plenum Publishers.

_____. 2010. "The uses of religion in public institutions: the case of prisons." In Arie Molendijk, Justin Beaumont and Christoph Jedan (eds), *Exploring the Postsecular: The Religious, the Political and the Urban*, 381–401. Leiden: Brill.

Beckford, James A. and Sophie Gilliat. 1998. *Religion in Prison: Equal Rites in a Multi-Faith Society*. Cambridge: Cambridge University Press.

Beckford, James A., Richard Gale, David Owen, Ceri Peach and Paul Weller. 2006. *Review of the Evidence Base on Faith Communities*. London: Office of the Deputy Prime Minister. Online at: http://www.communities.gov.uk/publications/communities/review (accessed 5 October 2011).

Beckford, James A., Danièle Joly and Farhad Khosrokhavar. 2005. *Muslims in Prison: Challenge and Change in Britain and France*. Basingstoke: Palgrave.

Benthall, Jonathan. 2008. *Returning to Religion: Why a Secular Age is Haunted by Faith*. London: I.B. Tauris.

Berger, Peter L., Grace Davie and Effie Fokas. 2008. *Religious America, Secular Europe?* Aldershot: Ashgate.

Bowen, John. 2007. "A view from France on the internal complexity of national models." *Journal of Ethnic and Migration Studies* 33.6: 1003–16.

Cameron, Helen. 2003. "The decline of the Church in England as a local membership organization: Predicting the nature of civil society in 2050." In Grace Davie, Paul Heelas and Linda Woodhead (eds), *Predicting Religion: Christian, Secular and Alternative Futures*, 109–19. Aldershot: Ashgate.

Caron, Nathalie. 2007. "*Laïcité* and secular attitudes in France." In Barry A. Kosmin and Ariela Keysar (eds), *Secularism and Secularity*, 113–24. Hartford, CT: Institute for the Study of Secularism in Society and Culture.

Chapman, Rachael. 2009. "Faith and the voluntary sector in urban governance." In Adam Dinham, Robert Furbey and Vivien Lowndes (eds), *Faith in the Public Realm*, 203–22. Bristol: Policy Press.

Church Urban Fund. 2006. *Faithful Representation: Faith Representatives on Local Public Partnerships*. London: Church Urban Fund.

Commission on Urban Life and Culture. 2006. *Faithful Cities: A Call for Celebration, Vision and Justice*. London: Church House Publishing and Methodist Publishing House.

Deakin, Nicolas. 2001. *In Search of Civil Society*. Basingstoke: Palgrave.

Department for Children, Schools and Families. 2007. *Faith in the System: The Role of Schools with a Religious Character in English Education and Society*. London: Department for Children, Schools and Families.

Department of Communities and Local Government. 2008. *Face to Face and Side by Side: A Framework for Partnership in Our Multi Faith Society*. London: Department of Communities and Local Government.

Dolan, Mary J. 2008. "Government-sponsored chaplains and crisis: Walking the fine line in disaster response and daily life." *Hastings Constitutional Law Quarterly* 35 (Spring): 505–46.

Farnell, Richard. 2009. "Faiths, government and regeneration: a contested discourse." In Adam Dinham, Robert Furbey and Vivien Lowndes (eds), *Faith in the Public Realm*, 183–202. Bristol: Policy Press.

Farnell, Richard and Sally Ramsay. 2007. *Faith in Lewisham*. Coventry: Coventry University.

Farnsley, Arthur E. II. 2007. "Faith-based initiatives." In James A. Beckford and N. J. Demerath (eds), *The SAGE Handbook of the Sociology of Religion*, 345–56 London: SAGE.

Finke, Roger. 1990. "Religious deregulation: Origins and consequences." *Journal of Church and State* 32.3: 609–26.

Finneron, Doreen. 2007. "Local governance, representation and faith-based organisations." In Véronique Jochum, Belinda Pratten and Karl Wilding (eds), *Faith and Voluntary Action*, 39–42. London: National Council for Voluntary Organizations.

Fitzgerald, Timothy. 2000. *The Ideology of Religious Studies*. New York: Oxford University Press.

———. 2007. *Discourse on Civility and Barbarity: A Critical History of Religion and Related Categories*. Oxford: Oxford University Press.

Fox, Jonathan. 2008. *A World Survey of Religion and the State*. Cambridge: Cambridge University Press.

Greenawalt, Kent. 2006. *Religion and the Constitution, Vol. 1: Free Exercise and Fairness*. Princeton, NJ: Princeton University Press.

———. 2008. *Religion and the Constitution, Vol. 2: Establishment and Fairness*. Princeton, NJ: Princeton University Press.

Grim, Brian J. and Roger Finke. 2006. "International Religion Indexes: Government regulation, government favoritism, and social regulation of religion." *Interdisciplinary Journal of Research on Religion* 2: 1–40.

Hammond, Phillip E., David W. Machacek and Eric M. Mazur. 2004. *Religion on Trial: How Supreme Court Trends Threaten Freedom of Conscience in America*. Walnut Creek, CA: Altamira.

Hamilton, Marci. A. 2005. *God vs. the Gavel: Religion and the Rule of Law*. New York: Cambridge University Press.

Home Office. 2001. *Community Cohesion: A Report of the Independent Review Team*. Under the chairmanship of Ted Cantle. London: Home Office.

———. 2004. *Strength in Diversity: Towards a Community Cohesion and Race Equality Strategy*. Home Office Consultation Paper. London: Home Office Communications Directorate.

Jenkins, Phillip. 2002. *The Next Christendom: The Coming of Global Christianity*. New York: Oxford University Press.

Jochum, Véronique, Belinda Pratten and Karl Wilding. 2007. *Faith and Voluntary Action: An Overview of Current Evidence and Debates*. London: National Council for Voluntary Organizations.

Joppke, Christian. 2004. "The retreat of multiculturalism in the liberal state: Theory and policy." *British Journal of Sociology* 55.2: 237–57.

———. 2009. "Limits of integration policy: Britain and her Muslims." *Journal of Ethnic and Migration Studies* 35.3: 453–72.

Juergensmeyer, Mark (ed.) 2006. *Religion in Global Civil Society*. New York: Oxford University Press.

Koenig, Matthias. 2007. "Europeanising the governance of religious diversity: An institutionalist account of Muslim struggles for public recognition." *Journal of Ethnic and Migration Studies* 33.6: 911–32.

McCutcheon, Russell T. 2003. *The Discipline of Religion: Structure, Meaning, Rhetoric*. London: Routledge.

Minkenberg, Michael. 2002. "Religion and public policy. Institutional, cultural, and political impact on the shaping of abortion policies in Western democracies." *Comparative Political Studies* 35.2: 221–47.

———. 2003. "The policy impact of church-state relations: Family policy and abortion in Britain, France, and Germany." *West European Politics* 26.1: 195–217.

National Council for Voluntary Organizations. 2007. *Faith and Voluntary Action*. London: NCVO.

National Offender Management System. 2007. *Believing We Can. Promoting the Contribution Faith-Based Organisations Can Make to Reducing Adult and Youth Re-offending*. London: National Offender Management Service. 1–33.

Palmer, Susan J. 2008. "France's 'War on Sects': A Post-9/11 Update." *Nova Religio* 11.3: 104–20.

Policy Exchange. 2007. *Living Apart Together*. London: Policy Exchange. 1–99.

Powell, Walter W. and Paul J. DiMaggio. 1991. *The New Institutionalism in Organizational Analysis*. Chicago: University of Chicago Press.

Prochaska, Frank. 2006. *Christianity and Social Service in Modern Britain: The Disinherited Spirit*. Oxford: Oxford University Press.

Robbins, Thomas and Roland Robertson (eds). 1987. *Church-State Relations: Tensions and Transitions*. New Brunswick, NJ: Transaction Books.

Sandberg, Russell and Norman Doe. 2007. "Religious exemption in discrimination law." *Cambridge Law Journal* 66.2: 302–12.

Spalek, Basia, Salwa El Awa and Laura Z. McDonald. 2009. *Police-Muslim Engagement and Partnerships for the Purpose of Counter-terrorism: An Examination*. Birmingham: University of Birmingham.

Stark, Rodney and Roger Finke. 2000. *Acts of Faith: Explaining the Human Side of Religion*. Berkeley, CA: University of California Press.

Sullivan, Winnifred Fallers. 2005. *The Impossibility of Religious Freedom*. Princeton, NJ: Princeton University Press.

_____. 2009. *Prison Religion: Faith-Based Reform and the Constitution*. Princeton, NJ: Princeton University Press.

Trigg, Roger. 2007. *Religion in Public Life: Must Faith be Privatized?* Oxford: Oxford University Press.

US Commission on Civil Rights. 2008. *Enforcing Religious Freedom in Prison*. Washington DC: United States Commission on Civil Rights.

Weller, Paul. 2009. "How participation changes things: 'Inter-faith,' 'multi-faith' and a new public imaginary." In Adam Dinham, Robert Furbey and Vivien Lowndes (eds), *Faith in the Public Realm*, 63–81. Bristol: Policy Press.

Willaime, Jean-Paul. 2006. "Religion in ultramodernity." In James A. Beckford and John Walliss (eds), *Theorising Religion. Classical and Contemporary Debates*, 77–89. Aldershot: Ashgate.

William Temple Foundation. 2003. *Regenerating Communities: A Theological and Strategic Critique*. Manchester: William Temple Foundation.

Wood, James E. (ed.) 1985. *Religion and the State: Essays in Honour of Leo Pfeffer*. Waco, TX: Baylor University Press.

Woodhead, Linda with Rebecca Catto. 2009. *"Religion or belief": Identifying issues and priorities*. Research Report 48. London, Equality and Human Rights Commission. Online at: http://www. equalityhumanrights.com/uploaded_files/research/research_report_48__religion_ or_belief.pdf (accessed 1 June 2010).

Chapter 3

THE SECULARIZATION THESIS AND THE SECULAR STATE: REFLECTIONS WITH SPECIAL ATTENTION TO DEBATES IN AUSTRALIA[1]

Stephen Chavura

Macquarie University, Sydney

Introduction

Contrary to the modernist expectation that religion would recede from the public sphere, José Casanova has identified a recent social and cultural shift that he calls the "deprivatization of religion" or the rise of "public religion." In short, Casanova (1994: 65–6) describes "a process whereby religion abandons its assigned place in the private sphere and enters the undifferentiated public sphere of civil society to take part in the ongoing process of contestation, discursive legitimation, and redrawing the boundaries."[2] Reflecting on similar phenomena, Jürgen Habermas (2008: 116) has recently observed that "Viewed in terms of world history, Max Weber's 'Occidental Rationalism' now appears to be the actual deviation." Indeed "religious traditions appear to be sweeping away with undiminished strength the thresholds hitherto upheld between 'traditional' and 'modern societies...'" While it would seem queer to say that there has been no secularization at all, religion has proven far more resilient

---

1 I wish to thank Eric Jones and Dr Ian Tregenza for reading various manuscripts of this chapter and offering valuable advice. The comments of the anonymous reviewers were also challenging and constructive. I also acknowledge valuable conversations with Dr Bruce Kaye, Dr John Tate, Dr Greg Melleuish, Dr Steve Mutch, and Emeritus Professor Graham Maddox. The argument here does not necessarily represent anyone's views but my own.

2 See also Hanson (2006), Norris and Inglehart (2004) and Berger (1999).

and adaptive than classical sociologists imagined. This chapter considers how political theorists can apply the lessons of the secularization debate to the problem of defining the secular state. Advocates of political secularism have tended to assume a single model of the secular state as the state and its institutions *emptied or exclusive of* religion. I show this by offering a case study on the debate on religion and politics that has been taking place in Australia since the mid-1990s. This view of the secular as *exclusive of* religion has provoked critiques of the secular state from both religious conservatives and social pluralists, the latter calling for a shift from the secular state to the pluralist state. Yet the argument of this chapter is that this exclusive understanding of secularism is only one, and by no means the dominant, historical conception of secularity to be found in European political traditions. Furthermore, I argue that the recovery of the alternative conception of the secular as a realm merely *distinct from* but not necessarily hostile to or suspicious of religion is preferable to contemporary fundamentalist and pluralist movements to abandon the secular paradigm altogether.[3] Notions of the secular state, like the democratic state, should be clear enough to protect basic political goods yet open enough to allow the unique religious heritage and national character of each state and citizen to express itself in the public sphere.

The Secularization Debate

Briefly, the secularization thesis is the idea that with the progress of modernity, loosely understood to be the rise of the sovereign state, the progress of capitalism, and the advance of the empirical sciences, religion would lose its relevance and eventually disappear in modernized countries. Yet its early advocates assumed the theory as a matter of Enlightenment triumphalism, if not mere prejudice, and the theory started to come under attack as soon as defenders started seriously to attempt to vindicate it empirically, exposing its weaknesses along with its strengths. Some attack the thesis, saying that there was never a golden age of faith, thus the idea of desacralization is inherently problematic (Stark, 1999; cf. Casanova, 1994: 16–17). Others say that secularization has occurred, but the nature of actual secularization

---

3 The conception of the secular as a realm exclusive of religion is best captured by the rhetoric of *laïcité* from the French Revolution to the present as well as the United States Supreme Court reading of the "Establishment Clause," post–World War II. This is very different from the idea of the secular that was around Europe before the French Revolution and has remained in most European countries and Britain since the Revolution, which referred to a realm merely distinct from the religious, in that its aims were not identical to the aims of the church, but saw value in the contribution religion could make to citizenship and was not opposed to partnership.

is equivalent to the deinstitutionalization of religion (Bouma, 2006: 5). Recently, Charles Taylor has argued that the nature of secularization is simply that religion has shifted from the center or from the epistemically and socially given to the periphery. Put another way, religious adherence is merely one option among many, not even the default option, in modern societies (Taylor, 2007: 14).[4] There is also the view that secularization has not occurred, but rather that the very opposite has occurred: religion has not only survived in most modernized countries but has undergone a revival in developing countries.[5]

This debate has largely been confined to sociologists, with occasional contributions by historians. Political scientists and theorists, on the other hand, have been more concerned with the nature of the secular state. The two debates are very different. Sociologists must try to measure the religiosity of a people, which is no easy task, if it is even possible. Political scientists, on the other hand, try to examine how the state actually relates to religion as well as how it ought to. Although the sociological and political interests in the secular are different, they are not wholly unrelated and political science has certainly benefitted from sociology. For example, we know from analysis of constitutions and social behavior that a vigorous and healthy democracy is not incompatible with a religious populace or with a state that establishes a religion (Monsma and Soper, 1996; Fox, 2008). Very religious societies, such as the United States, can maintain their democracy over a long period of time and states with established religions such as England still have healthy multicultural democracies. Thus, the idea that religion and democracy are incompatible faces serious challenges from sociological analysis, or at the very least, sociology forces the claim to clarify itself in the face of obvious counterexamples. Another way that recent sociological analysis helps clarify the idea of the secular state is in its potential in discouraging categorical assertions on exactly what the secular state is, as though the secular state is any less flexible and ambiguous in its nature than the democratic state. One of the great contributions of recent analysis of the manner in which states relate to religion is our awareness that individual states – especially liberal democratic states – have their own unique way of relating to religion (Monsma and Soper, 1996; Fox, 2008: 136–9). Thus, any model of *the* secular state is not likely perfectly to fit all secular states. This should lead to modesty among political theorists so as not dogmatically to set out the

---

4 For an overview of secularization theory from the nineteenth century to the present see McLeod (2000: 1–12).

5 Casanova (1994), Huntington (1996), Berger (1999), Jenkins (2002, 2006, 2007), Hanson (2006), Fox (2008).

minutiae of the secular state without considering the plurality of secular models now existing.

"*Saeculum*" in European History

Notwithstanding the numerous uses of "secular" throughout European history, Casanova is right to say that the very existence of a secular realm involved dualistic conceptions of reality. In fact, there was a double dualism: dualism "between" and dualism "within." There was a dualism *between* this world (*saeculum*) and the other world, and a dualism *within* this world between secular institutions and religious institutions (Casanova, 1994: 15). J. G. A. Pocock has pointed out that *saeculum*, meaning, "age" or, in Christian terms, *this age*, as opposed to the *nunc-stans*, or God's standpoint from eternity, carried implications of temporality and finitude; thus the *saeculum* was in some respects "nonsacred because noneternal" (Pocock, 2003: 8). In the Bible there are several polarities that roughly equate to the sacred and secular distinction: the Israelites as God's children as opposed to the nations; kingdoms of exile as opposed to the Promised Land; those who walk in the light and those who walk in the darkness; this world and its things which are perishing and the eternal world to come. St Augustine divided people into citizens of the *civitas terrena* and the *civitas Dei*. Those of the former fix their eyes on the things of this world to satiate their earthly desires as ends in themselves, whereas those in the latter fix their hope on God, considering all carnal things as merely a means to being able eternally to enjoy him.[6] The dichotomy between two realms carried into the medieval tradition yet became hierarchical in subordinating secular politics and institutions to the church *within* this *saeculum*. Thus Pope Gelasius I in 494 AD drew a distinction between the *auctoritas* of the priesthood and the *potestas* of political government. Because of the sacred nature of *autoritas*, Gelasius could admonish Emperor Anastasius to "piously bow the neck to those who have charge of divine affairs..." (Tierney, 1964: 13). In the thirteenth century, Aquinas (1988: 69) wrote that "The secular power is subject to the spiritual power as the body is subject to the soul." The *saeculum* was distinct from the transcendent, but the two interacted, albeit on hierarchical terms. With the Protestant Reformation of the sixteenth century, the distinction between the two realms was kept but different varieties of Protestantism offered different models of subordination. Because the clear subordination of the state to the church was removed, most Protestant models involved a fragile balance between the two institutions. Luther spoke of the "Two Swords"

---

6 See, for example his *City of God against the Pagans*, written from 417–426/7AD: I.1, I.25, X.3, XI.25, XIV.28, XIX.17.

needed in this age: the spiritual sword of the gospel to provide a means for salvation and the carnal sword of the state and its legitimate use of violence to preserve justice and peace (Luther, 1991). The state was no longer subordinate to the church but remained subordinate to the word of God, obliging the magistrate to receive counsel from able preachers and theologians. With the Anabaptist radicals the *saeculum* was considered evil and its institutions of little concern to the holy. The *Schleitheim Articles* of 1527 sought a total withdrawal from the *saeculum*, limiting its legitimate authority to the unregenerate children of darkness. For the Anabaptists, there was to be no relationship or interaction at all between the sacred and the secular (Baylor, 1991: 175–8). The second generation of reformers based in Switzerland would offer separate models still. John Calvin presided over a system in Geneva where the church had full autonomy from the state whereas the Zurich theology of Heinrich Bullinger and Peter Martyr Vermingli would encourage rulers to take charge of the church and see that it was properly reformed. The Zurich theologians were deeply involved with the progress of religious reform in England during the reign of Edward VI (1547–53) and the early reign of Elizabeth I (1558–1603), teaching both monarchs that part of their office was the *cura religionis*, or care for religion (Kirby, 2007). The English model that emerged from Henry VIII's dispute with Rome, except for a brief hiatus during the Catholic reign of Mary I (1553–58), was of the Royal Supremacy over both temporal and spiritual realms. The distinction between the secular and the sacred remained, but authority over institutions representing both realms was with the prince. This model had different results in different countries. In England, it led to an intense interest in the Church of England, resulting in royally prescribed sermons, liturgies, dress and legitimate topics of theological discussion. The distinction between secular and religious institutions found its expression in all important European thinkers. Even a materialist theorist like Thomas Hobbes, who denied any transcendent interpretation of an age to come, interpreting the Kingdom of God as "a Civil Common-wealth… wherein he [God] reigneth by his Vicar, or Lieutenant…" distinguished between the "secular" and "ecclesiastical." For Hobbes, the distinction was between laws and institutions aiming at civil peace and those aimed at salvation.[7]

In this tradition, things pertaining to the secular are not things pertaining to the sacred, yet the former did not exclude the latter from its sphere. For, despite the fact that politics was considered a sphere very distinct from the sacred, both Catholic and Protestant theology pressed the public religious duties of the ruler for the *cura religionis*. Indeed, rulers obliged, seeing religion as essential to the general good and their own legitimacy. Although the sacred

---

7 For the quote see Hobbes (1991: 311); for Hobbes' use of "secular" see page 388 of the same volume.

and secular were distinguished, they were not divorced, though their marriage was not always smooth. Just as the epistemological categories of faith and reason met and often overlapped in scholastic learning, so did state and church, the former still remaining secular.

It was only with the French Revolution and the thought of the *philosophes* that the secular took an antireligious meaning. France did not go through a Protestant Reformation and thus the French experience of religion was still of an ancient, hierarchical, intolerant Catholic Church against which the *philosophes* and the Revolution defined themselves. The church tended to be seen as a rival to the new regime, either to be extinguished or functionalized into an apparatus of the state. The program of European secularization as conceived by theorists and administrators of the Revolution was never permanently realized, yet its rhetoric of "the absolute secularization of the political" has remained with the modern French tradition of *laïcité* as defended by French intellectuals and politicians (Fehér, 1990: 193–4; Bowen, 2007: 6–21). It was with the Revolution that the European tradition of the secular as merely *distinct from* the religious seems to have been confronted with the very different notion of the secular as *exclusive of* the religious. Although France's secular tradition has never been a consistent nor a coherent one in practice, its narrators often describe it as a coherent tradition progressing over 200 years towards "the removal of religion from the public sphere" (Bowen, 2007: 6). French secularism was very different to the secularization of institutions in Germany and England during the second half of the nineteenth century, which was more a case of removing privileges, disadvantages and inequalities rather than religion per se in public institutions and schools. Indeed, many public institutions in both Germany and England, though no longer committed to the social domination of their national churches, remained strongly religious and yet secular in that they were not constitutionally bound to protect the exclusive hegemony of the national religion in educational and political institutions (McLeod, 2000: 52–80).

The French tradition of secularism seems to resonate in the post–World War II United States Supreme Court tradition of interpreting the First Amendment "Establishment Clause." In *Everson v. Board of Education* (1947) the Establishment Clause was first interpreted along the lines of separation of church and state, which itself was interpreted as disallowing the state from offering any support or endorsement of religion.[8] This interpretation led to the banning of school prayers with *Engel v. Vitale* (1962), the banning of devotional readings of the Bible in class with *Abington v. Schempp* (1963), as well

---

8 On church-state issues in American jurisprudence see Eastland (1995), Patrick and Long (1999), Greenawalt (2006) and Davis (2010).

as the banning of religious displays in schools with *Stone v. Graham* (1980). The 1971 "Lemon Test,"[9] which was supposed to function as the guideline for all legal decisions regarding the state and religion, had three criteria:

1. The government's action must have a secular legislative purpose.
2. The government's action must not have the primary effect of either advancing or inhibiting religion.
3. The government's action must not result in "an excessive government entanglement" with religion.

The second criterion in the Lemon Test resulted in Judeo-Christian displays in public institutions being withdrawn owing to the commitment to religious neutrality.[10] Despite the fact that the Lemon Test has in recent years been much relaxed in United States jurisprudence,[11] its wider effect seems to be an impression in the minds of secularists that secularism is a process of dereligionization. This understanding of state secularism was later defended in the political philosophy of John Rawls (1993) with emphasis in his later career on Public Reason as a monological discourse stripped of appeal to comprehensive doctrines, including religion. If the public realm is a realm filled only with Public Reason, then the public has no room for religion. Thus the secular has become redefined as a realm where religion can have no presence. This conception of the secular as a realm *exclusive of* religion is strikingly different from the older European tradition, surviving in some states like England and Australia, of the secular as a realm merely *distinct from* yet at the same time *open to* religion. The former cannot allow religion any influence

---

9 *Lemon v. Kurtzman* (1971).
10 In *Torcaso v. Watkins* (1961) Secular Humanism was recognized as a religion by the Supreme Court.
11 I thank an anonymous reviewer for pointing out the relaxation of the "Lemon Test" in United States constitutional law. Notwithstanding this, even though over the last 20 years the funding received by religious institutions from the state has increased in range and amount, the Supreme Court has not deviated in principle from the first rule of the Lemon Test, that funding cannot have a religious purpose, interpreted as funding not going directly to a religious cause. Thus, state funding has found its way into the hands of religious schools, but indirectly via grants for blind people to spend on higher education (in this case, theological) (*Witters v. Washington Department of Services for the Blind* (1986)), confessional school students entitled to state-funded disability services (*Zobrest v. Catalina Foothills School District* (1993)) and underprivileged children to spend on the private education of their choice *Zelman v. Simmons-Harris* (2002). Most recently the Supreme Court has allowed school vouchers to be used at religious schools. See *Arizona Christian School Tuition Organization v. Winn* and *Arizona Department of Revenue v. Winn* (2011).

or presence within its realm, whereas the latter is open to the presence of religion so long as the ends of the realm itself remain secular and free from religious domination.

The Secular State

One of the great contributions of recent studies in religion and the state is to have shown the pluralist nature of global state secularism, that is, religion and government have different relationships from state to state, even in so-called secular liberal democracies (Fox, 2008; Monsma and Soper, 1996). Despite this scholarship, much of the contemporary debate on the secular state in politics still tends to be guided by the misconception that there is some single, clear and properly liberal democratic model of the secular state that all too often is being subverted in the present political sphere. This form of secularism tends to be of the exclusive kind of a realm emptied of or devoid of religion. Thus secular lobbyists in Europe, the United States and Australia tend to lobby for the abolition of policy and practices such as state aid to religious schools, religious education in state schools, exemptions from discrimination laws for religious institutions, tax exemptions for religious organizations, state-funded religious welfare services, the presence of religious rites and symbols in state institutions, religious voices in public debate and clerics holding state offices as though such policy flows perforce from the mere notion of the secular.

The controversy over the secular state springs from the very nature of the state itself. The normative nature of much political analysis is rooted in the very nature of the state as an institution which refers beyond itself to another realm (the nation) upon which it seeks to impose some order according to certain ideals that define the particular state. Let us take the classic definition of the state found in Max Weber's famous 1919 address, "The Profession and Vocation of Politics," which defines the state as "that human community which (successfully) lays claim to the *monopoly of legitimate physical violence* within a certain territory…" (Weber, 1994: 310–11). Now, Weber admits that the monopoly of legitimate violence is not the only way the state realizes its aims. Yet in every type of state, whether it is democratic, socialist, liberal or, as is most common, a cluster of these ideologies, the ideals that characterize the state are closely related to the coercive activity of the state; that is, the rights and duties that give form to the welfare state, democratic state or the liberal state are maintained to a significant extent by coercion. There are penalties for those who do not pay tax in any state, and the welfare state depends on this. Also, there are penalties for those who seek to undermine the democratic process through deliberately misinforming the public, misleading parliament, or, in Australia, not voting. The same goes for the liberal state, whose individual rights are partially maintained through punishing those who fail their duties towards the rights-holders.

It is important to keep the nature of the state in mind when contemplating the secular state for, given the coercive nature of the state, in some way secularism will be enforced. Somehow, under a secular state, individuals (whether in the sphere of government or citizens in general) are forced with the threat of deprivation of liberty to be secular. How does secularism relate to the state in this instance? Who is it enforced upon? Of course the answers to these questions vary from state to state. Take three examples of states which are either explicitly secular (Turkey), or at least generally considered to be so (United States and Australia). In Turkey, for example, there is a feeling among the cogoverning military elite that the secularization process begun by Atatürk after World War I is in perennial jeopardy owing to popular Islam, hence every measure to manage and control religion by enforcing the secular ideals of Kemalism both on the political party system and on the citizens is pursued when possible. Thus, Article 24 of the Turkish constitution bans the basing of "the fundamental, social, economic, political, and legal order of the state on religious tenets," while Article 136 establishes the Department of Religious Affairs, which operates according to "the principles of secularism." Mosques outside of state-designated areas are illegal, many clerics are chosen and appointed by the state, traditional Muslim female headcoverings are banned in the civil service and in universities and there has recently been significant tension between the secularist military and the Erdoğan government, commonly perceived by military elites as overly sympathetic towards Islam (Fox, 2008: 246–7; Fuller, 2008: 51–6, 70). In Turkey, the secularism of the state regulates political parties, politicians and state institutions as much as it does the religious lives of the citizens.

In the United States, however, the situation is quite different, with secularism mainly restricted to civil institutions like the courts and schools. The Supreme Court defines separation of church and state as the state neither helping nor hindering the program of religion, that is, total indifference. At the same time, politicians are not discouraged from openly voting according to religious views and religious garb may be freely displayed. Yet religious symbols are often banned from schools and courthouses and although private prayer is allowed in schools, teachers are not allowed to organize or encourage it. Ironically, the United States has a strong rhetoric of exclusive secularism and separation of church and state but also an equally strong tradition of civil religion with religious oaths, iconography and rhetoric infusing all levels of politics. Thus, United States state secularism is imposed mainly on juristic and educational institutions, but hardly at all at the governmental and popular level.

In Australia, the situation is different still. Section 116 of the constitution guarantees that there will be no established religion, that people can worship freely and that there will be no religious tests to enter the public service. The state finances religious schools and pays chaplains to enter schools to provide religious counsel. Prayers are recited at federal and state parliaments daily, the preamble to the constitution reads "humbly relying on the blessing of Almighty God," and the Christian Democratic Party currently has two MPs in the New South Wales Legislative Council (Frame, 2006; Monsma and Soper, 1997: 87–119). There are no laws against religious displays or prayers in public schools, though these are not common except in holiday seasons, and religious chaplains are funded by the state. Australian secularism guarantees that the federal government will not coerce citizens to adhere to a particular religion, while at the same time funding all sorts of religious enterprises at the federal, state and local levels of government. Thus, we see that there are varieties of state secularism that range from hostile management and control to liberal indifference and support. Indeed, the meaning of the secular state varies from country to country and is more determined by national character and history than by abstract notions of the secular (cf. Randell-Moon, 2009: 327). However, as will be shown, the exclusive secularism of *laïcité* as well as the United States Supreme Court tradition of secularism and its philosophical defense by John Rawls has started to inform national debates on the relation between religion and the state outside those countries that practice it.[12] This secularism is an abstract notion of a realm devoid of the religious which overrides any traditional place religion may have in society and the state. Although United States and French secularist rhetoric is being used in both Western and Islamic contexts, I will focus on the Western case, simply because the issues involved in bringing secularism to Islamic nations are so different from those of the secular state in the West that they require a whole study in themselves. To mention a single example, to many postcolonial Muslim theocrats anything short of a Shari'a state is a secular (godless) state. Thus, the state, no matter how accommodating to Islam in its policy and ceremony, remains thoroughly secular if it is not a Shari'a state. This narrow definition of the secular state as the non-Shari'a state is very different from Western definitions, making a discussion of the secular state in both Western and Islamic contexts too large for this particular essay. Australia may be a helpful case study to evaluate the transplantation of French and United States secularist rhetoric because it is typical both in its liberal democratic institutions and in its mildly religious population. It closely resembles European states in its political

---

12 Indeed, Rawls himself saw the Supreme Court as the "exemplar of public reason" (1993: 231–40).

institutions and broadly in its religious demographic. It also closely resembles the culture of predominantly Anglophone liberal democracies like England, the United States, Canada and New Zealand, the latter three all sharing a British heritage as well as being multicultural societies with a bias towards Christianity of the Catholic and Protestant varieties.[13]

The Australian Debate on the Secular State

Australia is commonly identified by political scientists as possessing a secular state. But increasingly, this notion of the secular state is being interpreted along the lines of exclusive secularism espoused by the rhetoric of *laïcité* and the United States Supreme Court. For example, in a recent symposium over the meaning and validity of the concept of the "Australian Settlement" Geoffrey Stokes recommended the addition of "state secularism" to the terms and conditions of the Australian Federation (Stokes, 2004). Stokes (11) defines "state secularism" as "a rejection of religion or religious considerations in public affairs" and refers to "the constitutional reference to secularism" in s.116:

> The Commonwealth shall not make any law for establishing any religion, or for imposing any religious observance, or for prohibiting the free exercise of any religion, and no religious test shall be required as a qualification for any office or public trust under the Commonwealth.

The problem with Stokes' interpretation of s.116 is that the section does not support his notion of exclusive state secularism; it says nothing about "a rejection of religion or religious considerations in public affairs." The most that can be said is that it prohibits consideration of a citizen's religious convictions as a qualification for holding public office. But this hardly entails a secularism prohibiting public policy informed by religious ideas or, to use the terminology of John Rawls, "comprehensive doctrine" that is often read into the constitution (Rawls, 1993). Yet the Rawlsian position that the public sphere must be emptied of all discourse other than Public Reason (by its very nature nonreligious) has become almost an assumed truth by many commentators of religion and the state in Australia. Most recently, Anna Crabb documents the incline of Christian discourse in no less than 2,422 speeches delivered by federal politicians from 2000–06. Her research shows that after 2001, the invocation of Christian concepts and vocabulary spiked and reached a level

---

13 Political sociologists often place Australia within the broad category of liberal democracies such as states in Europe and the United States. See Huntington (1996) and Fox (2008).

not seen since the sectarian debates of the 1950s in Labor Party politics (Crabb, 2009). Crabb goes on to say that such discourse "weakened adherence to Rawls' liberal consensus (exclusion of religious beliefs from the public forum) and normalized the use of Christian terminology and ideas in Australian political discourse" (2009: 261). One could be forgiven for concluding after reading much of the literature on religion and politics in Australia that part of the Australian political settlement of the early twentieth century involved adherence to late twentieth-century Rawlsian liberalism!

In her recent study Marion Maddox (2005) preserves much of the debate during the Howard years on the nature of the state's relationship with religion. Her aim is to document "Howard's assault on *assumed* separations…" (315, my italics). She lists some of the following (311):

1. Promoting the discrediting of indigenous religion
2. Restricting the church's ability to critique
3. Funding church agencies (faith-based social services)
4. Promoting conservative Christian schools

It is hard to deduce a single meaning for separationism from these examples of its "assumed" violations. Elsewhere throughout the book, Marion Maddox cites other examples of church-state boundary blurring. For example, Western Australia governor-general Michael Jeffrey's frequent proclamations of Jesus as "the greatest example of leadership who ever lived" (M. Maddox, 2005: 311) and parliamentary members' private religious beliefs informing their policy are both cited as bringing church and state closer together (314). Marion Maddox's analysis rightly judges any government attempt to silence religious critique as domination, but why is secularism or separationism violated with the funding of conservative Christian schools or public servants espousing or following their religious beliefs in office? Historically in Australia it has not been unusual for politicians to be informed by their religious convictions. Furthermore, the High Court has decided that there is no violation of s.116 of the Australian constitution in publicly funded religious schools.[14]

An awareness of the nonexclusive possibilities of the secular is not lost on all commentators in the Australian debate, but it is often abandoned for an exclusivist agenda when the discussion turns towards policy critique and

---

14 The notion that state funding of religious schools is a violation of s.116 of the Australian constitution, which promises that there will be no law regarding the establishing of any religion, was legally put to rest in the High Court of Australia with the 1981 Defence of Government Schools (DOGS) case, where "establishment" was taken to mean setting up a state religion rather than merely supporting religion (Frame, 2006: 54–7).

construction. Amanda Lohrey (2006: 42–3) states that "To be secular is not to be anti-religion, but to be anti-theocracy. Secular doesn't mean without; it doesn't mean empty. On the contrary, in the context of liberal democracy it means multiple and diverse or, to pursue the special metaphor, 'full.'" Then, following a discussion of s.116, Lohrey offers a definition of separationism in Australia: "…freedom of religious observance and nondiscrimination on the basis of religious faith" (42). This looks pretty faithful to the constitution. Yet when Lohrey goes on to identify several examples of alleged "blurring" of the boundaries between church and state, none of them seem clearly to flow from her nonexclusivist discussion of secularism or her definition of separationism as religious freedom. Examples of blurring the boundaries are:

- Clerical calls to consider Christianity as a worthy candidate to fill the cultural void created by secular, liberal democracy (36, 40)
- Commending the life and teachings of Jesus in the national values debate (37)
- The Christian Right's attempt to court and cultivate a Christian constituency amongst voters (39)
- State funding of religious schools (63)

It is not clear how any of these are violations of Lohrey's principle of Australian secularism and hence "blurrings" of the separation of church and state. What they reflect, however, is an exclusive secularism very reminiscent of French laicist and United States secularist rhetoric that endeavors to remove religion from the public by ensuring that it does not inform public values via schools, influence the outcome of democratic culture or receive public funding.

What seems to be happening in much of the debate is that United States-style Supreme Court secularism and the rhetoric of *laïcité* is being seen as an exemplar against which Australia compares poorly. For example, former Australian Democrat senator Lyn Allison on numerous occasions accused the former Howard government of breaching the separation of church and state. Ultimately she defines closely along Rawlsian lines: "…self-identified Christians should not make religiously motivated decisions for those who do not share their beliefs."[15] This is not an uncommon view amongst Australian politicians (M. Maddox, 2005: 62). For secularists like Allison, the whole political realm and its institutions must become completely emptied and divorced from

---

15 See Lyn Allison, "The Role of Religion in Australian Politics – Senator Allison Speaks to the Peaceful Pill Conference for Exist International" (5 November 2005). Online at: http://www.democrats.org.au/speeches/index.htm?speech_id=1731 (accessed 20 June 2008).

religion to be properly secular. In a senate speech on the separation of church and state Allison listed three perceived violations:

- Religious references in oaths and pledges
- Prayer before parliamentary sessions
- Advantages and exceptions for religious institutions[16]

Actually, none of these need necessarily be religiously motivated. One could imagine approving of, say, prayers in parliament or religious oaths on the grounds that such ceremony accords with tradition or with the religious sentiments of the majority of Australians. In fact, there are documented examples of such approval by atheists.[17] Certainly advantages and exceptions to religious institutions require no religious justification at all. Other instances of Allison identifying church-state "entanglement" are the presence of Catholics in the coalition, parliamentary prayer networks, the Lyons Forum, faith-based social services and individual politicians making policy informed by their religious convictions.[18] The most profound problem with the debate on church and state in Australia is the obliviousness shown by many commentators to the plural, ambiguous and contested nature of state secularism exercised by Western liberal democracies, which sustains the common but mistaken belief that *the* secular state is the state that resembles France or the United States – the two most famous "showcase" secular states. This has led to two unhelpful tendencies in the Australian debate:

1. Terms like "religion" and "establishment" are understood in light of French laicist rhetoric or the post–World War II United States secularist tradition rather than according to a distinct Australian tradition which borrows both

---

16 See Lyn Allison, "Separation of Church and State: Speech Delivered to Parliament House, Canberra on 1 March 2006." Online at: http://www.democrats.org.au/motions/?id=11 (accessed 20 June 2008).

17 For example, at the 1998 Constitutional Convention, Pat O'Shane, who described herself as "probably the most committed atheist in the chamber" was happy to have the reference to Almighty God retained in the preamble because, she said, "I happen to respect the spiritual and religious beliefs of my fellow Australians" (M. Maddox 2001a: 55). My point here is not to suggest that prayer for most people does not have a religious motivation but to show the limits of religious motivation as a test for keeping religion out of politics. Someone could be politically or practically motivated to have prayers in parliament. Alternatively, someone could be religiously motivated to keep religion out of parliament. Motivation is itself difficult to discern and it cannot be predicted that secular politics will flow from a secular motive or that a religious motive will result in distinctively religious politics.

18 See Lyn Allison, "Separating Church and State Conference 2006: Does God have a place in government?" Online at: http://www.democrats.org.au/speeches/index.htm?speech_id=1861(accessed 20 June 2008).

an appreciation for supporting religion as a social good from its British heritage and also a hostility to religious domination from the United States. Consequently, aspects of Australian political culture that seem to run afoul of the rhetoric and policy of French laicism or many Supreme Court rulings are interpreted as violating secularism or the separation of church and state.

2. Analysts see that French and United States secularist rhetoric and policy is absent in Australia's judicial and political history, concluding that there is no separationism in Australia or that Australia does not have a secular state.

On this second point, there are those who conclude that Australia has no separation of church and state, at least nothing clearly defined and enshrined in the Commonwealth Constitution. Lyn Allison speaks of the "absence of formal separation of church and state" in Australia.[19] An Australian Democrats Discussion Paper released in October 2006 made the claim that "there is in fact no clearly articulated separation of church and state in our Constitution."[20] Professor Graham Maddox writes similarly, "Australia has neither an established church nor a strongly entrenched constitutional separation of church and state" (G. Maddox, 2007: 511). To return to Marion Maddox's work, at no point does she say that certain events *actually* violate a legal separation of church and state in Australia. Her more subtle claim is merely that certain "*assumed* separations" have been assaulted.[21]

The conception of secular as a place from which religion is excluded seems to inform contemporary activists of secular politics. Steve Mutch (2010: 12–13) sums up the program of political secularist organizations such as the Australia New Zealand Secular Association, the Republican Party of Australia and the Secular Party of Australia:

There are many…areas of state regulation and funding that are central to any discussion of a normative version of separation. These include: official recognition of religious rituals, such as marriage celebration; religious inclusion on state occasions, such as parliamentary prayers or

19 Allison, "The Role of Religion in Australian Politics."
20 See *Separation of Church and State: Politics, Religion, Policy and Law in Australia*, Australian Democrats Discussion Paper, October 2006. Online at: http://www.democrats.org.au/docs/2006/DiscussionPaper_SeparationChurchState_Oct2006.pdf (accessed 17 June 2011).
21 For an excellent and recent discussion on whether Australia has a separation of church and state see M. Maddox (2009: 349–54).

official commemorations involving clergy; religious classes or displays of religious allegiance in state schools; religious displays in state buildings; the provision of state services by religious organizations; religious vilification laws; religious exemptions from employment, antidiscrimination, charitable collection or conscription laws; payments and access provided to clergy in official capacities as prison or military or school chaplains; rating exemptions; and tax-deductible donations for church building funds, *inter alia*.

Mutch then lists other issues of interest for "strict secularists" including banning ordained clergy in state offices and banning religious political parties. Mutch notes that these latter two regulations are the norm in Turkey, though precisely why Australia should be striving to imitate Turkish national politics is a question strict political secularists still need to address. Indeed, if my analysis is correct and the idea of the secular has various historical meanings and its political manifestation is different from state to state, than "the task of achieving a generally accepted model" (Mutch, 2010: 17) is probably impossible and without clear justification.

Marion Maddox (2001b, 8; cf. Warhurst, 2008: 36–7) captures the essence of much recent analysis of religion and politics in Australia:

The expectation underlying much public commentary is that, while Members and Senators may have religious beliefs, they should not exercise them politically; and the absence of religious convictions from parliament is one safeguard of the political process.

When faced with the concept of the secular as a realm exclusive of religion, religion becomes something to be rooted out from the public sphere. This has been the characteristic trait of recent advocates of a secular state in Australia.[22] It has gotten to the stage where the *Freedom of Religion and Belief in the 21st Century. Discussion Paper* put out by the Human Rights and Equal Opportunity Commission in 2008 feels the need to discuss whether there is "a role for religious voices, alongside others in the policy debates of the nation"

---

22 A typical example is the Secular Party of Australia, which seeks completely to remove religion from public institutions. Its website advocates the banning of religious dress from public schools, reversing state funding of religious schools, removing religious organizations from tax exemptions, removing religious references in the constitution and in public oaths – in the latter case unless specifically requested, and that public policy not be informed ("misled") by "religiously inspired…prohibitions." See http://www.secular.org.au/mnu-policy-details (accessed 17 June 2011).

(2008: 9). An amazing question, given that religious voices have always had a public presence in Australian policy debates! Arguably, exclusivist secularism was never the intention of the Fathers of Federation, who for the most part took secular at its most common nineteenth-century meaning as nonsectarian rather than nonreligious.[23] The secular state was the state not constitutionally bound to defend the ecclesiastical hegemony of any particular Christian religion or denomination. Although the framers of s.116 lifted the language from the First Amendment, at that time the United States legislature did not interpret the First Amendment along the strict separationist lines that later came to characterize the Supreme Court from 1947 onwards (see Dreisbach, 2010: 216). Thus, while the Church of England was never established in Federated Australia, there was always space for religious input in matters of social policy, education, welfare and national ceremony. Australian secularism, like British secularism, has always been open; yet like America and unlike Britain, it has rejected ecclesiastical establishment.

The Australian debate on the place of religion in the state highlights how contemporary critics of religion and state interaction tend to draw upon a particular discourse of the secular as a realm that excludes religion to give substance to their critiques. Objections to this conception of the secular state as the state exclusive of religion have led some activists and theorists in Australia and elsewhere to critique state secularism or to call for a paradigm shift from state secularism to state pluralism. It is these movements against the secular state that we will now consider.

Farewell to the Secular State? Conservatives and Pluralists

The meaning of "secular" shifted in revolutionary France and then in the United States from being merely *distinct from* the religious to *exclusive of* the religious. Thus, schools formerly could contain prayers and scripture classes and still be called secular in that their aim was not to secure salvation but to produce good citizens. Now with the exclusive meaning of "secular," scripture, prayers or even evidence of a possible transcendent reality (intelligent design) are deemed intrusive. This has led to reaction against the secular state from several angles, most sensationally the Religious Right, but also the religious pluralists. The Religious Right is an umbrella term for organized groups in the United States and Australia who see the secular state as a threat to national religious heritage, religious freedom and morality. This would typify the Moral Majority movement of the 1980s in the United States and the strong evangelical and conservative Catholic presence in Australian federal

---

23 See Hughes (2003: 133), Frame (2006: 56–7) and Ely (1976: 88).

politics, especially during the Howard period (1996–2007) (M. Maddox, 2005; Martin, 1997; Lambert, 2008: 184–217). The Religious Right in the United States has not gone away; indeed, organizations like Focus on the Family and the Witherspoon Institute lobby for and defend a traditional Christian understanding of the family, sexuality and the sanctity of human life as well as religious freedom (against secularism and multiculturalism) and a reinvigorated grassroots democracy. Typically groups belonging to the Religious Right see their calling as restorative; that is, they seek to restore a traditional sense of Christian nationhood, morality and the family. This manifests in campaigns to bring back prayer in schools, teach intelligent design in science classes, regulate or ban abortion, keep Christian iconography in public spaces and state institutions and outlaw same-sex marriage, to identify but a few of their concerns. The Religious Right sees itself as a counterforce to the perceived secular exclusion of religion from public and civic life.

The pluralist movement, on the other hand, calls for a paradigm shift away from the secular state model altogether and towards a pluralist model more reflective of the fact of religious pluralism (not secularism) that has emerged at the national level in modernized countries over the last generation. Pluralists begin by exposing several myths:

1. The myth of modernity as a force of social secularization
2. The myth that liberal states are, in fact, neutral towards religion
3. The myth that state recognition and even establishment of religions is incompatible with democracy and liberalism

Pluralism raises objections against the model of the secular state that implements a policy of negative equality. In an effort to promote religious equality, it banishes or negates religion from the public sphere, ensuring everyone is equally without representation. Yet pluralists like Veit Bader (2003a: 6) argue that "To treat people fairly does not mean that we have to abstract from all their cultural and religious particularities but to take them into account in an evenhanded manner." The pluralist model rejects both monistic establishmentarianism and exclusive state secularism. In their place, it suggests that a plurality of national religions, probably the major ones and the major-minority ones, are recognized and institutionalized within the political system in the sense that their voice has a special and constitutional right to be heard (Bader, 2003b: 56). In the end, the polity is about preserving democracy, not suppressing religion (Bader, 1999: 602). In short, pluralists believe that the problem with exclusive secularism is that it militates against religion simply because it is not secular, rather than because it is especially and uniquely harmful to politics. If the state and its institutions are to reflect the identities of its citizens, then the pluralist state rather than the secular state is the most appropriate and legitimate type, given the fact of social pluralism.

Both the Religious Right and pluralists critique the secular state, the latter declaring its illegitimacy and explicitly calling for a paradigm shift away from state secularism. Yet the secularism that these critics are responding to is an exclusive secularist rhetoric that seeks to shut out religion from civic life, leaving the alternative model of open secularism that has typified religion/state relations in the United Kingdom, much of Europe, Australia, and, to some extent, the United States, unscathed.

Rawlsian Secularism

Indeed, the idea of a state emptied of religion, a nation where religion is wholly confined to the private sphere with the exception of occasional token ceremonial appearance is remarkably novel in most countries and its necessity is not obvious. Yet there are well-known arguments for the total exclusion of religion from the public sphere. Take the most celebrated defense of the exclusive secular state, John Rawls' *Political Liberalism* (1993). The social fact giving occasion to Rawls' theory is the "fact of reasonable pluralism." For Rawls, modern democratic societies contain numerous incompatible yet "reasonable" worldviews and religions, what Rawls calls "comprehensive doctrines." Furthermore, this social pluralism is not a passing trend, "it is a permanent feature of the public culture of democracy" (36). In fact, any state that does not contain a plurality of opposing ideas of the good is probably undemocratic and illiberal, for homogeneity "can be maintained only by the oppressive use of state power" (37). Now, what is the implication of the fact of reasonable pluralism for political philosophy? Rawls says that it is Public Reason. Essentially, Public Reason is a method of dialogue that is based on "appeal only to presently accepted general beliefs and forms of reasoning found in common sense, and the methods and conclusions of science when these are not controversial" (224). Yet this common reason turns out to be rather narrow upon closer analysis. In this way, public servants and citizens are prohibited from appealing to their comprehensive doctrines when formulating or interpreting policy and law. Utilitarianism, Marxism and natural law theories are excluded owing to their dependence on broad metaphysical conceptions of human nature, agency and the good, not to mention various strands of liberalism which count on contested theories such as value pluralism and varieties of perfectionism. Indeed, even private citizens must be able to give a public answer if they are called to vote on "fundamental political questions" (219).

The Rawlsian state is one where religion is almost wholly confined to the private sphere, where the state and its institutions are devoid of religious discourse and input. Rawls' followers have taken the logic even further, ruling out not only nonpublic reasons for actions with political consequences but also nonpublic motives. Robert Audi (2000: 96) recommends a "*principle of secular motivation*" whereby one has an "obligation to abstain from advocacy or support of a law or public policy that restricts human conduct, unless in advocating or supporting it one is sufficiently motivated by (normatively) adequate secular reason." Indeed, as shown above in the discussion of recent Australian debates on the nature of state secularism, Rawls' philosophy has become the de facto norm against which various constitutions and institutions are measured. But must the secular state be the exclusive Rawlsian state? Must the secular state be emptied of religion, as opposed to its aims being merely nonreligious yet open to the presence and contribution of organized religion? Perhaps the answer is contained in the overall question Rawls' political liberalism seeks to address: "How is it possible that there may exist over time a stable and just society of free and equal citizens profoundly divided by reasonable though incompatible religious, philosophical, and moral doctrines?" (xviii). For Rawls, if comprehensive doctrines, even reasonable ones, get a foothold in public institutions, then sectarian strife at the political and social level will ensue (38, 129). Now this may be the case in countries with vital religious animosities and hostilities, where participation in government is simply seen as an opportunity to suppress all religious opposition, or states where the presence of any religious group in the institutions of state is perceived by others as a threat justifying sectarian violence. But how reasonable is this justification in the context of modernized liberal democracies which tend not to be characterized by deep religious division and animosity and which allow citizens to participate in the process of government and not to be helplessly dominated by religious interests?

Liberalism has never been a single coherent tradition and certainly cannot be reduced to a single principle of avoiding controversial comprehensive doctrines as justifications for restraint, as Audi wishes to do (2000: 67). It will frequently be the case in a liberal democracy that citizens will find themselves forced to suffer decisions whose justifications they do not accept and, furthermore, think only the irrational or indoctrinated could possibly accept: welfare, free-markets, unilateral divorce, abortion, indigenous land rights, affirmative action, privatization or socialization of industries and utilities, national responses to climate change, to name but a few. Our most important political concepts, including freedom, equality, justice and democracy are complex, normative and in W. G. Gallie's

(1955–56) words, "essentially contestable." Once one starts inquiring into the meaning of the essential concepts of liberal democracy, one sees the futility in demanding a polity based only upon noncontroversial concepts. Historically, liberal democracy has not sought to liberate people from being subject to arguments they find misguided or alienating by exorcising such arguments from the public and political sphere; it liberates people by giving them the opportunity to speak out and become active in promoting their alternative conception. In other words, there is a danger in much debate on the place of religion in the public square that democracy as a preservative against alienation is being marginalized. If it is impossible to legislate and govern in a single discourse with which all citizens can identify, the best remedy against resentment may well be the democratic right of all citizens to voice their comprehensive doctrines in the public square. Possibly, as Habermas (2008: 131) says, "Secular citizens or those of other religious persuasions can also learn something from religious contributions…" One may object and say that such a model could only beget conflict. First, as pointed out earlier, this has not been borne out by the history of modern liberal democracy. Second, surely the absence of conflict or tension in the political realm is as much indicative of illiberal and undemocratic coercion as the absence of reasonable pluralism in the civil sphere. Given the fact of social pluralism – indeed, the fact that there are numerous worldviews that cannot be reduced to a single principle, which are very often incompatible with one another, and, as Habermas (2008: 135) points out, whose lack of universal adherence "cannot be resolved at the cognitive level" – how could a monological public discourse possibly reflect and represent citizens so divided? The impulse of much recent liberalism to impose a single logic to public dialogue seeks to overcome irresolvable difference by disallowing all but one voice. Admittedly, the rest may participate, but only if they are able to mimic the voice of Public Reason.[24] The business of the liberal state is not to overcome or transcend dialogical conflict but to try to manage it and ensure that it does not undermine the essentials of the liberal democratic order. We deal with pluralism not by removing all reasons except Public Reason, but by allowing all voices to be heard and potentially become effective, *in dialogue with* the fundamental principles of liberalism: democracy perfects liberalism, and vice versa.[25]

---

24 See Nicholas Wolterstorff's discussion (Audi and Wolterstorff, 1997: 105) of how Rawls' Public Reason violates the conscience of the deeply religious and forces an "impious" divorce between the believer's religious worldview and his public voice.

25 On the notion of religious freedom within the context of broadly accepted social norms – "managed pluralism" – see Nikolas K. Gvosdev (2010).

Restoring the Secular State

The exclusive secular state cannot be justified in modernized societies by appealing to a perpetual threat of conflict or minority alienation.[26] In this sense, a public sphere emptied of religion is simply unnecessary and – given the fact that in most, if not all, stable modernized societies the public sphere is not emptied of religion – any call for exclusive secularism of the public needs justification.[27]

There is good political reason to reject the legitimacy of exclusive secularism, and this has to do with citizenship. As Wayne Hudson has pointed out, citizenship is multilevel, heterogeneous and differential. That is, there can be levels of citizenship from national, transnational and global, as well as dual citizenship between states, representing a plurality of attributes such as race and gender (2003: 425–6). The complex nature of citizenship has implications for the religion-state debate (426):

> Once citizenship is approached in this broad way, and not reduced to matters of immigration and passports…it makes sense to refer to religious citizenship as one of the citizenships persons might attract.

Furthermore, as Raymond Plant has said, "If religious beliefs are identity-creating in much the same way as gender and race, these beliefs and their content will be likely to dominate over all other considerations…" (2001: 302). Hudson believes that the secular conception of society and state commonly used when describing liberal democracies simply does not reflect the pluralistic nature of citizens, hence a shift from "secular" to "pluralist" needs to take place when nations consider their identity (429). Yet, if my distinction between exclusive and open secularism holds, there is no necessary contradiction between a nation seeing itself as pluralist, or, more realistically (for example, European states, Australia and New Zealand, the United Kingdom, the United States and Canada), pluralist with an overwhelming Christian majority and at the same time having a secular state. So long as the religious identity

---

26 The research of Tariq Modood in the 1990s showed that secularism rather than religious establishmentarianism was seen as threatening to British Muslims. Thus, for secularists to justify their stance by appealing to a disaffected religious minority is seriously flawed; indeed, religious minorities, by their very nature, are skeptical about the legitimacy of a religionless public space. See Modood (1994) cited in Monsma and Soper (1997: 133), Modood (1997) and Ahdar (1998–9: 467).

27 Fox (2008) in his survey of 175 constitutions and governments concludes that only the United States has full separation of religion and state. However, as pointed out above, the United States has a strong civil religion which shows no sign of decline.

of the citizens as individuals and the nation as a whole is not *excluded* from the public sphere simply because it is religious, there is no contradiction. This is, of course, Hudson and Bader's problem with the current exclusivist secular discourse, for within this discourse "many writers on politics assume that religion has no legitimate political role" (Hudson, 2003: 425). In this way, religious monists and exclusive secularists fall into the same trap, that is, imposing a rigid model of religion-state interaction (or noninteraction) that does not reflect actual practice, national identity, and recognition of the unique contribution of long-standing historical religions. Both religious monism and contemporary exclusive secularism fail the test of representation. Making a single religion an element or condition of citizenship fails religious minorities and nonadherents in their quest for representation qua religious minorities or nonadherents. Equally though, completely emptying religion from the rights of citizenship – political activity, education, office holding in politics – makes the citizen completely unrecognizable to the religious self; that is, the individual, biographical, situated self has little in common with the citizen he or she is urged to be. Consequently, in both models, when the individual is confronted with the citizen, he or she is confronted with a stranger.

Contrary to the pluralist response to secularism, the solution to the increasingly alienating nature of contemporary secularism need not be to shift the paradigm away from secularism but to restore the historical concept of the secular as a realm *distinct from* rather than *exclusive of* religion. The traditional conception of inclusive secularism is arguably more amenable to liberal democracy than exclusive secularism. At the very least, it has been shown that not only is religion, even established religion, not necessarily harmful to liberal democracy, it can actually facilitate it through programs of social welfare, not to mention the democratic nature of many churches providing a good training ground for civic participation.[28] The secular state need not be the state devoid of religion, but it must be the state which refuses to coerce with regard to religion. If the essence of the state is to coerce, then the state separated from religion is the state which does not coerce religious adherence or nonadherence. This means that any state which has religious freedom ought to be considered at least minimally secular, for its coercive activity does not adopt a religious agenda of salvation or adherence to dogma or religious practice. Indeed, when examining states whose constitutions explicitly endorse secularism, we see that its meaning is not stable but almost always involves religious freedom, though in some instances restricting religious involvement in politics and state funding of

---

28 See Smidt (2003), Bellah et al. (1996), Campbell (2004), and *Faith and International Affairs* (2009).

religious institutions.[29] Most states could probably be considered secular by the most minimum standard of allowing religious freedom. Thus we can sensibly speak of secular Christian, secular Muslim and secular Jewish states, that is, states that may favor a particular religion, officially or not, based on national history and demographic, yet allow lawful freedom of dissent. Although the idea of a Christian or Islamic secular state may be questioned by some advocates of religious equality (Randell-Moon, 2009), it may well be possible to give all religions some sort of representation without denying the special status of distinctive religious heritages which all countries possess. Any call for "exclusive" secularism in terms of removing religious iconography from institutions, outlawing religious political parties, removing public expressions of religion, may in fact be justified, but not by appealing to the ideal of "the secular state." Other considerations such as the potential of national conflict as well as the nature of the political parties themselves may well justify state regulation of religion within the public sphere. This would obviously apply to countries with deep and violent sectarian animosities or with militant religious movements seeking control.

Conclusion

The global persistence of religion at the social and political level has led sociologists to scrutinize the secularization thesis and to refine it to reflect the complex nature of religion and society in the modern world. The sociological debate has not gone unnoticed by political scientists, who have mapped the relationship between religion and the state both nationally and globally. The two lessons to be learned from this literature are that, first, secularization at the level of individual religiosity, though doubtlessly occurring, has been exaggerated, and that second, there is no universal model of state interaction with religion that can be called *the* secular state model. This lesson still needs to be learned, for as shown with the Australian case study, many commentators see the secular state as a simple model of exclusive secularism where the

---

29 See, for example, the following constitutions explicitly referring to their states as "secular states/republics": Angola (Art. 8); Benin (Title I, Arts 2, 10, 14); Burkina Faso (Art. 31) (see Fox, 2008: 273); Cameroon (Preamble); Cape Verde (Art. 48); Chad (Arts 1, 14); Ethiopia (Art. 11); Gabonese Republic (Art. 2); Second Republic of Gambia (see the theological Preamble as well as Art. 1); Second Republic of Guinea (Preamble, Art. 1); Liberia (see theological Preamble as well as Art. 14); Mali (Preamble, Arts 4, 18, 25); Namibia (Preamble, Arts 10, 20, 21); Cuba (Art. 8); India (Preamble); Japan (Art. 20); South Korea (Arts 19, 20); Kyrgyz Republic (Arts 1, 15, 16); Tajikistan (Arts 1, 8, 26) (see Fox, 2008: 174–5); Turkmenistan (Arts 1, 11); Albania (Art. 7); Azerbaijan (Arts 7, 18).

government and its institutions are emptied of any religious presence. This model of the secular state as the state devoid of religion is unnecessary in most liberal democracies. The result has been attacks against the secular state from various parties dissatisfied with its hostility towards or suspicion of religion. Conceptual and practical problems with state secularism can be solved within the secular paradigm, though through restoring a notion of the secular as a realm open to religion but not open to the state becoming a function by which a particular religion may dominate citizens. The secularity of the state – its exclusiveness or inclusiveness – is something to be determined by numerous factors including national character, political stability, and abstract political ideas. Because national character and politics vary from country to country, the extent of religious involvement in the state and vice versa will vary from country to country. The lesson is that just because one state does not practice the United States model of state indifference or the French model of *laïcité* does not mean that it is not a secular state. If we acknowledge a historic and still-practiced tradition of "secular" as merely a realm *distinct from* the religious, whose aims are not religious but not necessarily opposed to or incompatible with religion, then the thinnest meaning of the secular state is simply a state that does not coerce religious adherence, a state that is not merely a function of organized religion. Whether the state goes beyond this is to be determined by time and place.

References

Ahdar, Rex J. 1998–99. "A Christian State?" *Journal of Law and Religion* 13.2: 453–82.

Aquinas, Thomas. 1988. *St Thomas Aquinas on Politics and Ethics* (trans. and ed. Paul E. Sigmund). New York: Norton.

Audi, Robert. 2000. *Religious Commitment and Secular Reason*. Cambridge: Cambridge University Press.

Audi, Robert and Nicholas Wolterstorff. 1997. *Religion in the Public Square*. Lanham, MD: Rowman & Littlefield.

Augustine. 1995. *City of God* (trans. Marcus Dods). Peabody, MA: Hendrickson.

Bader, Veit. 1999. "Religious Pluralism: Secularism or Priority for Democracy?" *Political Theory* 27.5: 597–633.

_____. 2003a. "Taking Religious Pluralism Seriously. Arguing for an Institutional Turn." *Ethical Theory and Practice* 6.1: 3–22.

_____. 2003b. "Religions and States. A New Typology and a Plea for Non-Constitutional Pluralism." *Ethical Theory and Moral Practice* 16.1: 55–91.

_____. 2003c. "Religious Diversity and Democratic Institutional Pluralism." *Political Theory* 31.2: 265–94.

Bellah, Robert, Richard Madsen, William M. Sullivan, Ann Swidler and Steven M. Tipton. 1996. *Habits of the Heart: Individualism and Commitment in American Life*. Berkeley, CA: University of California Press.

Berger, Peter. L. (ed.) 1999. *The Desecularization of the World: Resurgent Religion and World Politics*. Ethics and Public Policy Center, Washington DC. Grand Rapids, MI: Eerdmans.

Baylor, Michael G. (ed.) 1991. *The Radical Reformation*. Cambridge: Cambridge University Press.

Bowen, John R. 2007. *Why the French Don't Like Headscarves: Islam, the State, and Public Space*. Princeton, NJ and Oxford: Princeton University Press.

Bouma, Gary. 2006. *Australian Soul: Religion and Spirituality in the Twenty-first Century*. Cambridge: Cambridge University Press.

Campbell, David E. 2004. "Acts of Faith: Churches and Political Engagement." *Political Behavior* 26.2: 155–80.

Casanova, José. 1994. *Public Religions in the Modern World*. Chicago and London: University of Chicago Press.

Crabb, Anna. 2009. "Invoking Religion in Australian Politics." *Australian Journal of Political Science* 44.2: 259–79.

Davis, Derek H. (ed.) 2010. *The Oxford Handbook of Church and State in the United States*. Oxford: Oxford University Press.

Dreisbach, Daniel. 2010. "The Meaning of the Separation of Church and State." In Derek H. Davis (ed.), *The Oxford Handbook of Church and State in the United States*, 207–25. Oxford: Oxford University Press.

Eastland, Terry (ed.) 2005. *Religious Liberty in the Supreme Court: The Cases that Define the Debate over Church and State*. Grand Rapids, MI: Eerdmans.

Ely, Richard. 1976. *Unto God and Caesar: Religious Issues in the Emerging Commonwealth 1891–1906*. Melbourne: Melbourne University Press.

Fehér, Ferenc (ed.) 1990. *The French Revolution and the Birth of Modernity*. Berkeley, CA: University of California Press.

Fox, Jonathan. 2008. *A World Survey of Religion and the State*. Cambridge: Cambridge University Press.

Frame, Tom. 2006. *Church and State: Australia's Imaginary Wall*. Sydney: University of New South Wales Press.

Freedom of Religion and Belief in the 21st Century: Discussion Paper. 2008. Human Rights and Equal Opportunity Commission.

Fuller, Graham E. 2008. *The New Turkish Republic: Turkey as a Pivotal State in the Muslim World*. Washington DC: United States Institute of Peace Press.

Gallie, Walter Bryce. 1955–56. "Essentially Contested Concepts." *Proceedings of the Aristotelian Society* 56: 167–98.

Greenawalt, Kent. 2006. *Religion and the Constitution*. 2 vols. Princeton, NJ and Oxford: Princeton University Press.

Gvosdev, Nikolas K. 2010. "Managed Pluralism: The Emerging Church-State Model in the United States." In Derek H. Davis (ed.), *The Oxford Handbook of Church and State in the United States*, 226–48. Oxford: Oxford University Press.

Habermas, Jürgen. 2008. *Between Naturalism and Religion*. Cambridge: Polity.

Hanson, Eric O. 2006. *Religion and Politics in the International System Today*. Cambridge: Cambridge University Press.

Hobbes, Thomas. 1996. *Leviathan* (ed. Richard Tuck). Cambridge: Cambridge University Press.

Hudson, Wayne. 2003. "Religious Citizenship." *Australian Journal of Politics and History* 49.3: 425–9.

Hughes, Philip. 2003. "Social Capital and Religion in Contemporary Australia." In Brian Howe and Philip Hughes (eds), *Spirit of Australia II: Religion in Citizenship and National Life*, 131–44. AFT: Adelaide.

Huntington, Samuel P. 1996. *The Clash of Civilizations and the Remaking of World Order*. New York: Simon & Schuster.

Jenkins, Phillip. 2002. *The New Christendom: The Coming of Global Christianity*. Oxford: Oxford University Press.

_____. 2006. *The New Faces of Christianity: Believing the Bible in the Global South*. Oxford: Oxford University Press.

_____. 2007. *God's Continent: Christianity, Islam, and Europe's Religious Crisis*. Oxford: Oxford University Press.

Kirby, W. J. Torrance. 2007. *The Zurich Connection and Tudor Political Theology*. Leiden: Brill.

Lambert, Frank. 2008. *Religion in American Politics: A Short History*. Princeton, NJ and Oxford: Princeton University Press.

Lohrey, Amanda. 2006. "Voting for Jesus: Christianity and Politics in Australia." *Quarterly Essay* 22: 1–79.

Luther, Martin. 1991. *Luther and Calvin on Secular Authority* (trans. and ed. H. Höpfl) Cambridge: Cambridge University Press.

McLeod, Hugh. 2000. *Secularisation in Western Europe, 1848–1914*. London: Macmillan.

Maddox, Graham. 2007. "Religion and Politics." In Brian Galligan and Winsome Roberts (eds), *The Oxford Companion to Australian Politics*, 131–44. South Melbourne: Oxford University Press.

Maddox, Marion. 2001a. *For God and Country: Religious Dynamics in Australian Federal Politics*. Canberra: Department of the Parliamentary Library, Information and Research Services.

_____. 2001b. "So Help Me God: The Sacred and the State in Australia." *St Mark's Review* 185.2: 3–10.

_____. 2005. *God under Howard: The Rise of the Religious Right in Australian Politics*. Crows Nest, NSW: Allen & Unwin.

_____. 2009. "An Argument for More, Not Less, Religion in Australian Politics." *Australian Religion Studies Review* 22.3: 345–67.

Martin, William. 1996. *With God on Our Side: The Rise of the Religious Right in America*. New York: Broadway Books.

Modood, Tariq. (ed.) 1997. *Church, State and Religious Minorities*. London: Policy Studies Unit.

Monsma, Stephen and Christopher Soper. 1996. *The Challenge of Pluralism: Church and State in Five Democracies*. Oxford: Rowman & Littlefield.

Mutch, Stephen. 2010. "Political Secularism in Australia." *Australian Quarterly* 82.1: 12–17.

Norris, Pippa and Ronald Inglehart. 2004. *Sacred and Secular: Religion and Politics Worldwide*. Cambridge: Cambridge University Press.

Patrick, John J. and Gerald P. Long (eds). 1999. *Constitutional Debates on Freedom of Religion: A Documentary History*. Westport, CT: Greenwood Press.

Plant, Raymond. 2001. *Politics, Theology, and History*. Cambridge: Cambridge University Press.

Pocock, John. G. A. [1975] 2003. *The Machiavellian Moment: Florentine Political Thought and the Atlantic Republican Tradition*. Princeton, NJ: Princeton University Press.

Randell-Moon, Holly. 2009. "Tolerating Religious 'Others': Some Thoughts on Secular Neutrality and Religious Tolerance in Australia." *Australian Religion Studies Review* 22.3: 324–44.

Rawls, John. 1993. *Political Liberalism*. New York: Columbia University Press.

Smidt, Corwin. 2003. *Religion as Social Capital: Producing the Common Good*. Waco, TX: Baylor University Press.

Stark, Rodney. 1999. "Secularization, R.I.P." *Sociology of Religion* 60.3: 249–73.

Stokes, Geoffrey. 2004. "The 'Australian Settlement' and Australian Political Thought." *Australian Journal of Political Science* 39.1: 5–22.

Taylor, Charles. 2007. *A Secular Age.* Cambridge, MA: Belknap Press of Harvard University Press.

Tierney, Brian (ed.) 1964. *The Crisis of Church and State 1050–1300.* Englewood Cliffs, NJ: Prentice-Hall.

Warhurst, John. 2008. "Lessons from the 2007 Federal Election about Religion and Politics." *St Mark's Review* 204.1: 35–43.

Weber, Max. 1994. *Political Writings* (ed. Peter Lassman and Ronald Speirs). Cambridge: Cambridge University Press.

Chapter 4

SECULARISM, RELIGION AND THE STATUS QUO[1]

Gal Levy

The Open University of Israel and New York University Tel Aviv

> The secularity of a Zionist ought to be different than that of a simple non-Zionist, in as much as the religiosity of a Zionist is different than that of a non-Zionist.
>
> —David Ben-Gurion[2]

Introduction

Israel, it is commonly thought, is an emblematic case of conflation of state and religion seen, and now even designated by law, as a *Jewish and democratic state*. It might therefore be totally inadequate to question the state-religion relationship in Israel within the framework of the secularization thesis. Yet, although Israel is not a typical Western democracy built upon the separation of church and state, its modernistic features as well as its democratic procedures are required by the state to adhere to the principle of separation, even if at the end the state renounces its relevance to the Israeli context. An apt example to this duality is the relation of the state to religions other than Judaism. As amply shown by Karayanni (2006), the very definition of the state as Jewish entails relegating all religious affairs of non-Jewish communities to the private realm, presumably a de facto separation of state and church. Still, defining this situation in terms of separation is rather misleading. Not only

---

1 I would like to thank Shlomo Fischer, Hanna Herzog and Dana Kaplan for their insightful reading of this text.
2 David Ben-Gurion, cited in Elam (2001: 74).

is the conception of state-church relations embedded in a Christian world history (Asad, 1993; Haynes, 2009: 1051), it is also the case that in Israel the idea of an established rabbinate as the institution analogous to church has come to existence based on the ideas of nationhood and statehood. Suffice to say that while in European-Christian history the modern state rose against a politicized church, Zionist nationalism gave birth to a politicized, institutionalized Jewish religion. This entanglement of nationality, religiosity and citizenship in a *Jewish and democratic state* has definitely determined the Israeli road to secularization, an idea that recently surfaced in the Israeli political debate.

In this chapter, I ask what happened to state secularism in light of recent interest in secularization in Israel. Whereas the state-religion relationship is mostly viewed in isolation, I seek to place it within the dual context of citizenship and ethnicity and to examine it in relation to the elusive boundary between state and society (Mitchell, 1991). By focusing on the ethnicized relationship between state and society in Israel and on the social boundaries that cut across the Israeli citizenship, I propose to elucidate why secularization in Israel has been forestalled and why, despite the prominence of religious politics, secularization remains a marginal political issue. I find the recent turn to secularization a significant contribution to and turning point in the discussion of state and religion in Israel. Yet I suggest that the ensuing debate is still missing a significant aspect, namely explanation of the persistence of the *status quo* as the conceptual framework that organizes and normalizes the relationship between state and religion. I therefore revisit the concept of the status quo, thus reexamining its power in rendering the question of secularization apolitical. I propose this in order to better account for why secularism fails to attract political agency and who beyond "the religious" enjoys the persistence of the status quo.

In Israel, the state-religion relationship has been a matter of continuous debate (Smooha, 1978; Cohen and Susser, 2000; Shafir and Peled, 2002), and Israelis frequently experience disputes on this subject, often culminating in physical violence. So the question of why secularization has rarely posed a political problem for most Israelis still calls for an answer (Elam, 2000; Shenhav, 2007: 23). In the 1950s and 1960s, secularization was a marginal political issue and similarly of a minor academic concern. This contradicted the fact that at that time, the heyday of the modernization paradigm, (structuralist-functionalist) sociologists and anthropologists recorded religious diversification at the societal level and the centrality of religious politics at the state level (e.g. Shokeid, 2001: 22). Secularization was generally seen as an ideological or cultural problem rather than as a theoretical or normative issue for social scientists to address. Moreover, it was assumed that Zionist ideology was capable of absorbing this (dysfunctional) tension between the secular and the religious by molding a relatively cohesive Jewish-Zionist national society (Elam, 2000: 74).[3]

Interestingly, secularization has also remained low on the agenda of the school of critical sociology that has emerged since the 1980s (Ram, 1995). Religion and secularization were seen as surrogates to other, more germane political concerns, especially the Arab-Israeli conflict and intra-Israeli ethnicity (Smooha, 1978). Concurrently, a new generation of political scientists, mostly sympathetic to the Zionist-religious outlook, sought to understand and restore the allegedly failed consociational order as the framework for managing the state-religion relationship (Cohen and Susser, 2000; Cohen and Rynhold, 2005). Only recently has the question of secularization resurfaced and become a matter for political and scholarly debate (e.g. Elam, 2000; Levy, 2007; Shenhav, 2007; Ram, 2008). Two political developments may be considered responsible for this: the expansion of Jewish settlement in the occupied territories led by ultranationalist religious Zionists (Eisenstadt, 2008: 212–3) and the political ascendance of Jewish ultraorthodox ethnic political parties (Peled, 1998). Still, the ensuing debate was limited in scope and failed to transcend what seemed to be the Zionist imperative, namely accommodating the relationship between state and religion within the confines of the status quo. In other words, secularization has still remained a nonissue in both political and academic debates.

To explain why secularization was a nonissue and how recent concerns may or may not be reflected the political sphere, I aim to unpack the concept of the status quo and reframe it in the context of citizenship and ethnicity. I intend to transcend the debate over the status quo as a particular mechanism that characterizes the (exclusively Jewish) consociational model (Cohen and Susser, 2000), and present it as a discursive articulation of the conundrum of a *Jewish and democratic* state. Thus I refrain from seeing the status quo arrangement as obsolete, as occasionally argued. Rather, it is the debate over secularization

---

3 In retrospect, the anthropologist Shokeid (2001: 21) writes: "Sociologists, and later the anthropologists, who entered immigrant settlements, often encountered 'traditional' systems of belief that conflicted with the structure of the social institutions and the norms of behaviour to which the immigrants were expected to conform... Unlike the sociologists, the anthropologists, for example, were well aware of the centrality of religion in the life of immigrants from Middle Eastern countries. They did not assume it was a passing phenomenon destined to disappear with the adoption of modernity. The anthropologists' research methods brought them into close contact with the religious domain in the immigrants' life. They spent long hours in their company, in the villages and development towns. Staying there during the Sabbath and the holidays, they could not ignore the impact of synagogue life."

as a sociopolitical phenomenon that was rendered obsolete, leaving religion as a powerful mechanism of social differentiation that undermines the concept of a secularized Israeli citizenship.

The Return of Religion? A Theoretical Prelude

The status quo – a shorthand term to describe the sociopolitical arrangement of state-religion relations in Israel – has never stopped occupying the minds of Israelis. In recent years, debates were seen and occasionally framed within the context of the global phenomenon of the "return of religion." One famous thesis is José Casanova's "deprivatization" thesis, emphasizing the (renewed) role of religion in the public domain. Other theses have focused on religious revival in the social sphere and still others have focused on how religion has been influenced by consumerism and how this led to the commodification of religious practices (see this volume's introduction). While these phenomena are evident to various degrees in Israel, some even leaving an imprint on the public sphere (see Goodman and Yonah, 2004; Ben-Porat and Feniger, 2009), religion in Israel is mostly seen through its value to Zionist ideology and its impact on politics. Indeed, politicized religion engendered anticlerical sentiments amongst the Jewish middle class. This heated political debate won a spectacular 15 out of 120 parliamentary seats for Shinui, a previously minor anticlerical party, at its peak in the 2003 elections. Interestingly, by the following elections in 2006 this party had evaporated. In 2009, the slump by the remaining liberal party, Meretz, to a meager three seats left the political arena to the religious parties. Against this backdrop and in light of the constant centrality of politicized religion in the debate over the future of the occupied territories, two answers were proposed to the question of whether Israel ought, or could be, secularized.

Not long after modernization theory came under attack, secularization as both a theoretical matter and a social judgment was revisited from two related perspectives. The post-Zionist school repudiated modernization theory for its ideological assumptions regarding the inevitability of secularization (Kimmerling, 1999; Ram, 2008). In this view, premised on criticism of modernist linear perception of social progress, anticipation of the demise of religion was not merely theoretically flawed. Rather, it overlooked the interests that had kept religion alive. As Ram (2008: 71) concludes: "the separation of state and synagogue in Israel is stalled not because of the power of the 'old' synagogue but, on the contrary, because of the 'new state and its dominant [Jewish] ethnicity." The postcolonial critique followed suit in rejecting idealizations of the state as a fair agent of modernization. Adopting a post-secular outlook, it also asked to be rid of the invariably hierarchical presuppositions of the post-Zionist stance (Goodman and Yonah, 2004; Shenhav, 2008). Driven by a multiculturalist agenda, it called to abandon binary conceptions of social identities that unjustifiably sever the secular discourse from the religious one. Instead, postcolonialists seek to treat more sensibly the value of religion in the eyes of modern men and women and to refrain from presupposing the need to remove religion in order to make room for a more equitable society (Goodman and Yonah, 2004: 23; Shenhav, 2007, 2008). For them, the need for a post-secular perspective is ontological as well as epistemological (Shenhav, 2007: 25).

Both critiques agree that the rise of religion in Israeli politics since the early 1970s can be attributed to the political demise of the Labor Party (Eisenstadt, 2008: 210) that reinforced the interconnection between nationalism and religiosity. Subsequently, Mizrahi (Oriental) Jews, religious Zionists and non-Zionists, and the Arab-Palestinian citizens have risen to center stage. These new political forces perhaps did not change the foundational (im)balance of power in Israeli society. But this shift did accentuate the historic pivotal role of religion in creating and maintaining social hierarchies (Levy, 2002; Shenhav, 2006). Equally, it uncovered the democratizing effect of religion, which has become a vehicle for nonhegemonic groups to bring to the fore their own conceptions of the secular and the sacred (Levy and Emmerich, 2001; Goodman and Yonah, 2004: 23; Eisenstadt, 2008: 210; Jamal, 2009: 1144). In both critiques, it was agreed that secularization is not bound to happen, whether because it is ontologically impossible (Shenhav, 2008), politically undesirable (Ram, 2008) or simply infeasible (Kimmerling, 1999). What was missing from the theory, though, was a satisfactory response to the need to create and maintain a secularized space where a civic conception of citizenship would emerge (Turner, 2001: 132).

Whether one considers positively the deprivatization of religion (Goodman and Yonah, 2004; Shenhav, 2008) as marking the voice of the *unaffiliated* (Rose, 1996: 343) or if one's concern is privatizing religion to make a much-needed secular space for the middle class (Ram, 2008), the concept of secularization needs to be unpacked. If, as Turner posits, religion "is assumed to contain the seeds of social life as such" (2009: 194), my endeavor is to explore how the uneven spread of modernity and hence secularization yielded a conception of a *Jewish and democratic* state in which secularism is absent from the public debate. I therefore see the "problem of secularization" in Israel as a flawed process of differentiation (Casanova, 1994), impaired by the entanglement of ethnicity and citizenship. In this respect, the status quo may be seen as an exceptional way to bypass the imperative to differentiate the religious from the secular. Yet, rejecting understandings as a unitary concept or social institution, the status quo is not merely the incarnation of a successful (or failed) consociational democratic order (Cohen and Susser, 2000; Cohen and Rynhold, 2005). Nor is it an ideological vehicle for politicians, secular or religious, to gain political power (Elam, 2000). I follow and expand Boas (2002: 107) in understanding the status quo as a mechanism of "quasi-mythic presence in the interrelationship between religious and secular," and a determinant of social categorizations. Alluding to three historical moments – reflecting the citizenship stories of Mizrahim, Arabs and immigrants from the Former Soviet Union – I propose to show the status quo "at work" and so to point out how the status quo functions as it becomes a "taken-for-granted" descriptor of social reality; it becomes this descriptor first in the categorization processes of the marginalized and second in inscribing in the minds of Israelis the inevitability of the status quo as the only solution to the tension between state and religion. I will thus demonstrate how the status quo and hence religion differentiates between citizens and how it precludes the discourse of secularization from public debate. Israel is an exemplar of a state which is at once religiously ethnocentric and democratic. Therefore, it may also serve as a case in point for exploring the interrelationship between secularization and desecularization as a determinant of the extent of social and political freedoms in contemporary states where the boundary between the sacred and secular is blurred and the extant social structure is changing (McLennan, 2007: 864).

The Status Quo and the History of the State-Religion Relationship

The origins of the status quo, it is commonly argued, lie in a letter from David Ben-Gurion, then chair of the Zionist executive committee in Palestine, to the anti-Zionist ultraorthodox Jewish leadership that set the terms of agreement on how to maintain Jewish life in the Jewish state's public sphere in exchange for the latter's political support in the partition plan that would resolve the Zionist quest for a state. It is of little significance whether this was the true intent of the letter or that its principles have no legal bearing. Eventually, this "compromise" had been reinforced by a pact within the Zionist and Jewish political elite that was seen as a manifestation of a consociational democratic order (Friedman, 1990: 47–8; Cohen and Susser, 2000: 18; Elam, 2001: 83–4; Boas, 2002: 107; Corinaldi, 2003: 290). In contemporary Israel, the status quo letter is considered an inspiration to legislation on the scope and limits of the freedom of religion and consciousness (Corinaldi, 2003; Ram, 2008). Thus, consecutive coalition agreements reiterated these principles comprising the status quo, which include keeping public kitchens kosher and the Sabbath as the official rest day, but more importantly securing the autonomy of religious education and forming a religious monopoly in personal status law (Radai, 2005: 80; Ram, 2008; Jamal, 2009: 1158).[4] Over the years, the status quo has become a cardinal political issue, a target for political and legal dispute from the liberal inclining political parties and even more from feminist activists, who remain its most vociferous contesters (Elam, 2001: 103–4; Boas, 2002: 109). To date, despite significant shifts in the makeup and content of the public sphere, the status quo is still seen as a pillar of a Jewish consensus (Fogiel-Bijaoui, 2003; Corinaldi, 2003; Karayanni, 2006; Jamal, 2009). This chapter seeks to answer the question of why this is so.

While many deliberations on ethnic relations acknowledge the affiliation between ethnicity and religiosity, rarely has this relation been observed from the perspective of the sociology of religion. My second question, then, is how the state-religion relationship conflict is implicated in the ethnic one. This question is especially called for in the context of contemporary scholarship that sees the prevalence of ethnicity in the lives of Israelis. My analysis of educational history has led me to see Israeli society as an *ethnicized society*, where issues of conflict and control are readily explained in terms of "ethnic differences" (Levy, 2005: 280; Herzog, 1985). Shafir and Peled (2002) also contend that Israeli citizenship is ethnicized, or predominately ethnorepublican. Indeed, Israelis consider their citizenship as being predominantly ethnic, identifying themselves primarily as Arabs or Jews, before they indicate a common Israeli identity (Levy, 2005: 273; Ram, 2008: 67). Still, issues pertaining to religiosity have remained confined to an ethnic-free zone. For example, an early critical analysis of social conflicts in Israel pertinently differentiated the religious-secular divide from the intra-Jewish ethnic schism, designating to each a varied degree of resolvability. The Arab-Jewish divide was considered as yet another conflict (Smooha, 1978). This theoretical segregation has changed, especially after the rise in 1984 of Shas, a Mizrahi ethnic and religiously ultraorthodox political party that conflated religious and ethnic agendas (Peled, 1998). Since then, these social schisms have evolved into an explicitly overlapping conflict over culture and power that in recent elections have played a significant role in determining the voting pattern of the non-Arab constituency (Peled, 1998; Shalev and Kis, 1999; Shalev and Levy, 2004). With a parallel rise of Islamism amongst the Arab electorate (Ali, 2004), no longer were the politics of religion seen as divorced from ethnic and ethnonational politics.

---

4 Paradoxically or not, the latter principle is not as controversial as it looks. Secular leaders such as Ben-Gurion and Golda Meir reiterated a Zionist interest in the governance of religious law in marriage and divorce as a means to maintain a unified Jewish people (Elam, 2001: 71, 127–8).

Yet it is not my intent to focus on recent moments of conflation of ethnicity and religiosity. Such a focus may lead to an erroneous impression that this overlap bears upon mainly, if not merely, Arab-Jewish dynamics (Kimmerling, 1999; Ram, 2008; Jamal, 2009: 1158) or that it is nothing but a manifestation of sheer political manipulation, as is occasionally portrayed in public debates. Instead of clinging to the anecdotal, as do contemporary critics, we need to see the dynamics of religiosity and secularity as particular manifestations of acts of categorization (Boas, 2002; Goodman and Yonah, 2004; Goodman and Fisher, 2004; Shenhav, 2007, 2008). So what calls for an explanation is how the status quo shapes the contours of citizenship and ethnicity, within and without Jewish society.

In asking why the status quo prevails and how it shapes citizenship, I thus refrain from seeing it as a political compromise to ameliorate the tension either between a Jewish and democratic state (e.g. Gavison, 1998: 217; but see Elam, 2001: 65–81) or between secularism and religiousness (Cohen and Rynhold, 2005: 728). Instead, I seek to understand the endurance of the status quo in relation to processes of ethnicization. Following Mitchell (1991), I claim the status quo is another mechanism of the elusive boundary between state and society and it delineates ethnicized boundaries that are at once drawing the limits of secularization. Thus, beyond delimiting secular freedoms in the public sphere (e.g. by imposing the kosher diet or limiting public transportation), it legitimizes an ethnic-Jewish conception of Israeli citizenship and naturalizes its supremacy over territorially bounded conceptions of citizenship (e.g. Weiss, 2002). In this sense, the status quo and ethnicization work hand in hand to impact the contours of citizenship beyond any institutional (state-religion separation) or political (consociational democracy) arrangements. Paradoxically, this elusiveness also allows a relatively high maneuverability for secularism at the societal level without impinging its endurance at the state level. Each of the following three citizenship tales bears evidence of these processes. Combined, they are meant to show the status quo's foundational role in drawing social boundaries and rendering the concept of a *Jewish and democratic state* irrevocable in the minds of Israelis, both Jews and Arabs.

Secularization and Beyond?

When José Casanova challenged the "old" secularization thesis, he did not consider the secularization theory redundant. He argued for three distinct meanings of secularization as a concept: "differentiation of the secular spheres from religious institutions and norms...a decline of religious beliefs and practices, and...marginalization of religion to a privatized sphere"

(Casanova, 1994: 211). By seeing and theoretically identifying deprivatization as an acute social phenomenon, Casanova in fact reapproved the usefulness of a theory of secularization, rendering it readily applicable to the study of particular processes of secularization and desecularization. In this way, he sought to "rethink systematically the relationship of religion and modernity, and the possible roles religions may play in the public sphere of modern societies" (ibid.).

Currently, it is hardly questioned that religion plays various roles in the political, social and economic spheres of contemporary societies (Haynes, 2009: 1042). However, this is not necessarily due to a "return to the sacred," nor a testimony to the withering away of religion in earlier phases of modernization (Demerath, 2007: 57; see also this chapter's introduction). In fact, as modernization spread unevenly throughout societies, religion became only partly privatized, making space for new forms of both public and private religiosity. Likewise, secularization was neither universal nor total (Fox, 2005: 297) and is better understood in its relation to sacralization (Demerath, 2007), or further as pertaining to culture at large (see Bruce 2006). Thus, the dialectics of secularization and sacralization have yielded several paradoxes (Demerath, 2007: 67–9) and new forms of religiosity. In recent years, these processes have also become implicated in globalization, where globalization seems to replace modernization as their determinant (Beyer, 2007: 99). Globalization, though not necessarily the reason for the changing relations of secularism and religion, contributes to the deprivatization of religion, to its diversification and primarily to the prominence of consumerism and securitization in redefining the relationship between states, religions and societies (Beckford and Demerath, 2007: 7–8).

Contemporary studies show that Israelis become more religious (Levy et al., 2004), and that religiosity plays a significant role in public life, primarily in the context of the relationship between religion and nationalism (Goodman and Yonah, 2004; Jamal, 2009; Sorek and Ceobanu, 2009), in light of reconfigurations in the politics of religion (Peled, 1998; Cohen and Susser, 2000; Ali, 2004) or by generating new forms of consumerism (Ben-Porat and Feniger, 2009). Similarly, the class-biased privatization of religion has bearings on the politicization of religion and on the particular role of the middle class in challenging the monopolistic power of religious orthodoxy (Levy, 2007). These aspects of (de)secularization notwithstanding, my interest is in secularization as differentiation. I particularly refrain from asking whether or not there is, or was, a decline in religious beliefs in Israeli society, or to what extent religion has been privatized. This aspect of differentiation is what Casanova refers to as the historical process, whereby the (medievalist) dualistic structure of "this world" and the "other world" is replaced by "only one single 'this world,' the secular one, within which religion will have to find its own place" (Casanova, 1994: 15). In "this world," a new conception of citizenship was bound to emerge.

In today's "this world" religion has found a place, though it is a different place than that which modernists like Talcott Parsons assigned to it (Turner, 2001: 133). Instead of being completely privatized, it reappeared on center stage (McLennan, 2007). To some extent, post-secularism is a timely corrective, required after the "significance of religion used for political ends has...grown the world over" (Habermas, 2006: 2) and inasmuch as religion played a greater political role in the state and the public sphere (ibid.: 3). Habermas's conception of civil society has shifted, acknowledging a need to make a space for the religious person to partake in the public debate (McLennan, 2007: 866; also Habermas, 2010). This does not obviate his secularism (Habermas, 2006: 19), but many of the post-secular moves are "much easier said than done" (McLennan, 2007: 859). Finally, religion and secularity changed indeed, but, to cite Bruce (2006), occasionally they are simply formed differently.

Finally, if the *myth* of secularization is rightly to be dismissed, this does not necessarily mean that the secularization project is or ought to be done away with (Bruce, 2006: 45). Indeed, as the dialectics of secularization and sacralization manifest themselves in contemporary social, economic and political dynamics, differentiation (Casanova, 1994) is an even greater challenge, particularly with relation to determining the scope and depth of citizenship. In Israel, a narrow conception of secularization as differentiation resulted in a differential structure of sovereignty based on the concept of *mamlakhtiyut* (see below). It was therefore not surprising that the Israeli notion of a consociational democracy (Cohen and Susser, 2000) was not a comprehensive order and was in fact an exclusive "Jewish consociation" (Jamal, 2009: 1162). Driven also by intra-Jewish ethnic stratification, this order reinforced a hierarchical order of citizenship, sandwiching Mizrahi Jews between the Ashkenazi hegemonic elite and the excluded Arab citizenry (Shafir and Peled, 2002). It is to these dynamics that my discussion now turns.

1. Mizrahim and the Zionist-modernist order

Like many of his contemporaries, Shmuel N. Eisenstadt was a true believer in the powers of the modern state. Long before he developed the concept of "multiple modernities" to overcome the drawbacks of the modernization thesis, he became a prominent speaker of Jewish nation-building qua modernization.[5] In his view, founded on the structuralist-functionalist school, failed secularization was regarded as a social problem that would hinder modernization (see also Goodman and Fisher, 2004: 353). In a monograph published in 1947 focused on what would become Israel's major challenge in the years to come, the absorption of immigration, Eisenstadt foresaw the failure of Israel's modernization. His analysis was premised empirically on examining the problems of Oriental Jews in British mandate Palestine as epitomizing the future failed adjustment of non-European Jews to modernity (Levy, 2002). Theoretically, his foresight relied on the determinative presuppositions of the modernization approach, particularly its tendency to depoliticize social problems. Especially, this approach relinquished political and class determinants to social marginality, offering instead cultural explanatory factors that held the new immigrants themselves responsible for their maladjustment to society (Ram, 1995). Conceptually, Eisenstadt's analysis adhered to a common distinction at the time between an "immigrant" and "Oleh," the latter term replacing the Hebrew word for immigrant with a concept that bears theological and ideological meanings (Levy, 2002). Interestingly, this distinction made use of a religious discourse in distinguishing the "Oleh," a self-motivated modern pioneer, from the "immigrant," a passive adherent to messianic fatalism. In other words, while the Ashkenazi (European Jews) were "making Alyia," as active agents, Mizrahi immigrants were passively (and reluctantly) drawn to confront modernity.

Until the late 1970s it had been the mainstay of Israeli public and academic discourses, in explaining away the failed integration of Mizrahim, to label them "traditionalists" or in other words, religious (Ram, 2008: 68). Even when a new generation of scholars rose to defy the culturalistic view, proposing materialistic reasons instead and reproblematizing the social categories of "pre-modern" or "primitive," the question of religiosity had remained unasked (Smooha, 1978; Swirski, 1981). While recognizing power relations as an explanatory factor in forestalling the modernization of the Mizrahim, hardly anyone asked why they were all "religious." Of course, not "all" were religious. This is exactly the point: this discourse had left little room for presenting or representing the Mizrahim otherwise. As early as the 1940s, religiosity was attached to ethnicity (Levy, 2002; Shenhav, 2006). Following the eruption of conflicts over the education of Yemenite children in the transitory camps in the early 1950s – what came to be known as "the struggle over education" – a Judicial Commission of Inquiry was set up to inquire into allegations of religious and antireligious coercion in

---

5 Any attempt to encompass Eisenstadt's work will do him injustice. His idea of "multiple modernities" (Eisenstadt, 2000) became useful in explicating uneven and indeterminate processes of secularization. I restrict myself to what I believe is his earliest work (Eisenstadt, 1947) which was only a precursor to his voluminous work on nation-building.

the camps (Zameret, 2002). In its conclusions, the commission adopted a "compromise" between the political parties over the backs of the Yemenite immigrant children, who were sent en masse to religious schools. This not only paved the way for the deepening of an ethnic division of education, but further entrenched ethnicity and religion. When a new state education system was founded in 1953, this compromise normalized the separation between religious and nonreligious schools (Levy, 2002), consigning the idea of a secular state to an uncertain future (Swirski, 1999). It also determined the view that to be Mizrahi was to be religious. Mizrahi Jews did not simply fail to modernize. They were confined to the quarters of religion, not meant to secularize (Levy, 2002; also cf. Shenhav, 2006: 77; Shenhav, 2007: 3). Some three and half decades later in 1984, Mizrahi Jews reclaimed their citizenship by vehemently supporting an ultraorthodox religious ethnic party, Shas, that defied the monopoly held by Ashkenazi Jews on who is designated a Zionist, an Israeli, a Jew. For many Mizrahim at this point adhering to the status quo proved to be unavoidable, because beyond ensuring the political power of religion, it supported their becoming Israelis merely by being Jews (Peled, 1998; Levy and Emmerich, 2001).

2. Israeli-Arabs and the military administration

The second story is more easily argued, even though its relation to the status quo is less obvious. It is not difficult to view the Palestinians who remained within the borders of the newly self-declared Israeli state as ethnonationals. The distinction between them and Jewish-Israelis was made all the more marked after the state imposed military administration upon the Arab-populated areas (1950–66), which implied a curtailed type of citizenship (Lustick, 1980; Levy, 2005). Thus, against an ideal of a territorially bounded state, a particular designated Arab space had been created within which a new Arab-Palestinian society had emerged. The limits on movement, employment and political mobilization restricted the processes of proletarianization and urbanization and hence delimited the modernization of the Arab society. Its members were therefore destined to be the drawers of water and hewers of wood for the rising Jewish middle class (Rosenfeld and Carmi, 1976). The opportunity to modernize came only in 1966, when the struggle against the military administration resulted in its disbandment. The Palestinians gained more than formal political rights, as the new freedoms materialized in the organization of new political leadership and the time became ripe for claiming their citizenship rights (Peled, 1992). These changes were reflected in a new reform in Arab education that eventually delineated the limits of Arabs' inclusion in the Israeli state and society.

In 1972, state officials became concerned with the increasing alienation of Arab pupils from the state and sought new ways to tackle this issue (Peres and Yuval-Davis, 1969; Al-Haj, 1995: 139). A short report on "Basic trends in Arab education" summed up the work of the Ministry of Education on this matter and drew new guidelines for an educational policy that emphasized the need to strengthen the Arab pupils' identification with the state. Its importance, according to sociologist of Arab education Majid Al-Haj (1995: 140), "lies in the very fact that for the first time wide public attention was given to the uniqueness of Arab education and the need to formulate particular aims for the Arab pupils." Still, the report was rejected and severely criticized by Arab leaders for creating a "'unique Israeli Arab' divorced from his [sic] genuine national and cultural roots" (Al-Haj, 1995: 140; Mar'i, 1978: 53; Levy, 2005: 282). Yet this is also where its greater significance lay. The need to define "who is an Arab (Israeli)?" was crucial. The new educational goals reflected this ambiguous new social category of "Israeli-Arabs" which was, on the one hand, meant to include the Arabs within the Israeli citizenry and distinguish them from the Palestinians in the recently occupied Palestinian territories and on the other hand meant to distinguish them from the Jewish citizens by culturally designating them as Arabs and Muslims (Levy, 2005: 283).

"Israeli-Arab" citizens could neither become fully integrated as citizens nor be recognized as national-Palestinians (Jamal, 2009: 1162), yet the political demand was that they should become Israelis in their own right (Karayani, 2007: 49). But inasmuch as their ethnicization as "Arabs" was carved deep into the conception of Israeli citizenship which in turn was imbued with Jewish meaning (Peled, 1992; Ram, 2008; Jamal, 2009: 1158), the state could not play a neutral liberal hand (Karaynai, 2007: 50). Indeed, state institutions became proactive in favoring certain Arab groups over others. Ironically or not, occasionally this implied cooperating with Islamists against the rise of a more nationalistically oriented, yet secular and democratic leadership. This was the case in Yaffa, where the municipality sought to undermine the establishment of an Arab democratic school at the cost of supporting the Islamist movement (Levy and Massalha, 2010). In the end, Arab citizens, as with veiled Muslim women in liberal contexts, felt safer in their religious identity and have forsaken their secular one in order to maintain their place within the Israeli democracy. Paradoxically, as Karayanni (2007) demonstrated (and as is often evidenced in public debates), the Palestinian citizens may benefit from supporting the continuation of the status quo that justifies redrawing the boundaries that separate and distinguish them from the Jewish society.

3. Non-Jewish Russians in a Zionist state

In Israeli public and academic discourses, both the stories of the Mizrahim and the Palestinians are conveniently framed within the tale of "belated modernization." The case of the "Russians" may be considered within an almost opposite framework. Comprising over one million immigrants from all republics of the Former Soviet Union, the Russian immigration, now distinguished according to the immigrants' European or Asian origins, was commonly hailed for its highly educated and modern characteristics and hence for its qualitative contribution to society. Indeed, this immigration had a major impact on all spheres of life and has also induced contest. One criticism immediately following the opening of the Former Soviet Union for immigration (and waning soon after) was typically voiced by Mizrahi activists. These activists feared that the "Russians" would tip the balance against the Mizrahim just as they were making inroads into the echelons of power, as had happened in the 1970s. A second line of disapproval reflected concerns about the growing numbers (up to one-third) of "non-Jewish" immigrants, who were still eligible returnees by the Law of Return. This latter criticism coincided with discontent regarding the inclination of the new immigrants to refute the Zionist diktat to assimilate in the Hebrew culture by holding on to their own language and culture (cf. Yonah, 2005: 130). Concerns about the lack of Jewish biological and cultural roots, which the state seemingly seeks to bypass in order to allow the integration of these immigrants into society, become implicated in societal approaches that defy the attempt to separate ethnicity from religion.

Since its legislation (before there was even an effective citizenship law), the Law of Return (1950) was a matter of political debate (Elam, 2001) that brought the government (not for the first time) to the verge of a crisis in 1970. Following a High Court of Justice ruling in favor of an Israeli navy officer who demanded to register his children as Jewish nationals despite their being born to a non-Jewish mother (on the Shalit affair, see Hofnung, 1996), the Law of Return was amended in two seemingly opposing ways. On the one hand, the law included the Jewish principle of maternal lineage in determining "who is (an eligible) Jew?," thus solidifying the role of religion in determining who is an eligible "returnee." On the other, the law extended the right of return to third generation siblings of Jews, despite their failing the religious criteria. It is no secret that the legislators had their eyes on the Soviet Union, where hundreds of thousands of Jews disconnected from their Jewish ancestry due to mixed marriages (Weiss, 2002: 94) made a reservoir of potential returnees. In due time, about a third of the "Russian" immigrants were "non-Jews." Yet as one commentator observed, these immigrants were also non-Arab, which counts far more in Zionist eyes (Lustick, 1999). Indeed, not being a "kosher" Jew was a minor imperfection vis-à-vis being Arab, but a drawback within Jewish society (Yelenevskaya and Fialkova, 2004).

When the 1989 immigration began, "ethnicity" rather than "religion" seemed to dictate its course in the Israeli society. For many Israelis, it was reminiscent of the early 1970s, when Israel welcomed hundreds of thousands of Jewish immigrants from the Soviet Union and offered them considerable economic benefits. This generosity was one trigger in the rise of the Israeli Black Panthers, who organized to fight the struggle of the Mizrahi lower class and for whom these benefits epitomized the state's continuous indifference to the fate of the Mizrahim when they were making headway to center stage (Bernstein, 1984: 132). Almost two decades later in the late 1980s as Shas was rising to prominence, a new wave of "Russians" was welcomed as filling the dwindling ranks of the old elite, that is, (re)shifting the ethnic balance from Mizrahi to Ashkenazi Jews.[6] Against this shift, the terminology of modernization was evoked once more as the Russians' education was contrasted with the "primitivism" and lack of modernity of the Mizrahim (Shumsky, 2002; Yelenevskaya and Fialkova, 2004). This immigration was extolled for its scientific promise and economic contribution, but no less importantly for its potentiality to reshape Israeli culture (Kalekin-Fishman, 2004: 255; Smooha, 2008).

Ultimately, the Russians did not easily assimilate into the Ashkenazi society (Shumsky, 2002). Nor did they align with the Mizrahim, whose neighbors they became and with whom they competed in the secondary labor market. Two cultural markers played a significant role in their relative seclusion within their new society. First, by rejecting the Zionist cultural homogeneity they retained their mother tongue and culture and also created their own educational enclaves, mainly in major cities (Kalekin-Fishman, 2004: 260). Secondly, by holding on to their nonreligious and especially nonkosher dietary, they broke with the tacit agreement to maintain the public sphere ostensibly Jewish (Ben-Porat and Feniger, 2009). In the context of the 1990s, this enhanced a newly emerging image of a multicultural society and a new secularized conception of the public sphere (Yonah and Shenhav, 2005; Ram, 2008), which was amplified by Tel Aviv becoming globally renowned for its young, "club culture." "Russian" thus was a "tainted" category, not only in terms of not being properly "Jewish." Its "problem" for Israeli society was its conspicuous atheism that further accentuated the possibility for a secularized public sphere against the ambiguous secularism of Zionism.

---

6 Kalekin-Fishman (2004: 249) mentions, matter-of-factly, that a "veiled motivation was the desire to repair the balance between the Sephardi [read: Mizrahi] population and the population that claimed Ashkenazi ancestry."

The "Russians" placed the state in a political strait, between its commitment to the status quo and the need to address the immigrants' concerns. Paradoxically, this extended the state's intervention in religion. While the question of burial was resolved by allowing for noncongregational cemeteries, the issue of marriage remained moot in the absence of civil marriages in Israel. The state set up special rabbinical courts, which were deeply involved in a process of mass religious conversion (Goodman, 2008: 381). Their practice exposed the duality of the concept of "absorption of immigration," namely the will to preserve a model of citizenship based on modernity, secularity and Western-ness coupled with the need to mobilize Judaism as the core component of the national and civic identity. Put differently, lacking other means to distinguish the "Russian non-Jews" from other non-Jews, the state conveniently resorted to the rabbinical courts to do this classification work for it. However, this came at a price: deepening the division between Arabs and Jews, but also cutting through the "Jewish society," which was becoming even more ethnicized. The contrast in the experiences of Ethiopian and Russian immigrants in these courts is telling. As Goodman (2008) shows, immigrants from Ethiopia who arrived parallel to the great immigration from the FSU, being considered dubious Jews, were being forced to convert, whereas Russian non-Jews could convert by free will at their own convenience – mainly when seeking marriage (Gitelman, 2004: 97–8). The naturalization of new immigrants also proved to be subdued by "religion" and by reinforcing ethnic boundaries within society.

Back to Now

Can these stories of Mizrahi Jews, Arabs and Russians be woven into one history of state and religion? What do they teach us about what the status quo means contemporarily? How do they inform us about the failure to open up a secularized space and allow a conception of inclusive citizenship to emerge? And above all, can these citizenship stories explicate why secularization has remained apolitical for most Israelis? In my final analysis, I propose to read them as relating to contemporary manifestations of the politics of religion. Specifically, I explore the "old consociational order," which dominated through the hegemony of the Labor Party (1930s–70s) and reexamine the dynamics of the status quo in light of its demise. Under this hegemonic order, acts of naming and practices of categorization created "ethnicities" while determining also "who is a Jew?" Still, these acts delineate the limits of Israeli citizenship and reveal the elusive ways in which the state constitutes itself as distinct from society (Mitchell, 1991: 78). The status quo is, then, one effect of the relation between state and society which, I argue, is responsible for "produc[ing] *abstract* citizens for a state which is, as idea, everywhere yet nowhere" (Lloyd and Thomas, 1998: 125). To put this slightly differently, the production of abstract citizens has been represented and maintained by an exclusively Jewish consociational democratic order (Cohen and Susser, 2004) that at once symbolized a compromise between state and religion and their seeming separation and the predominance of the Ashkenazi middle class over the Mizrahi lower class (Levy, 2002). In this sense, the mythical notion of the status quo (Boas, 2002: 113) has been more than a consensual political mechanism. As our stories show, the status quo became implicated in an ethnicized discourse of citizenship. This, I argue, undermines the claims of the *Jewish and democratic* state to be at once particularistic and universalistic and still be seen as a legitimate representative of society as a whole (compare Lloyd and Thomas, 1998: 5). I conclude, then, by discussing the ethnic aspects of the old consociational order and pointing out its limitations in becoming a democratic order.

The debate over the status quo has usually been ethnically blind (as it was gender blind (Boas, 2002)). However, ethnicity and class impacted significantly on rendering the status quo a constitutive factor of Israel's state-religion order. Yigal Elam, in his meticulous history of the status quo, understood it as *the perimeter*, the bounded outer surface within which the struggle over state and religion takes place, but of which no one really wants to dispose (Elam, 2000: 96). Contrary to typical advocates of the status quo (Cohen and Susser, 2000; Cohen and Rynhold, 2005: 728; and of course Gavison and Medan, n.d.), what Elam proposed was to see the status quo not simply as the best (or least worse) compromise the Israeli society could or should achieve. Rather, he claimed, the status quo is the most that the political elites of either side *were willing* to have (see also Kimmerling, 1999; Ram, 2008; Shenhav, 2007). Anything more would be unbearable for either the seculars or the religious. Or, put in the context of the secularization thesis, the failure to differentiate "the other worldly" from "this worldly" was neither a political mishap, nor an expression of lack of political power or legitimacy to act upon this issue. For both political elites, transcending *the perimeter* would undermine their representative status in the eyes of each respective constituency and in society at large.[7] Thus (and here the citizenship stories I have outlined take Elam's observation a

---

7 Elam offers several examples of this, including, on one side, Ben-Gurion's refusal to abandon religious personal law, and on the other, the religious parties' failure to propose a religiously acceptable Sabbath law for a Jewish state. Interestingly, Rabbi Wasserman (2002: 297) similarly demonstrates how the status quo serves the religious leadership by allowing the rabbinical elite to dissociate itself from the religious political one, thus enlarging their room for maneuver in the political arena.

step further), instead of seeing the "seculars" and the "religious" as adversaries in a struggle over state and religion, we should ask how the status quo became a common ground for these political sides to gain control over the state, for whom, and at whose expense. The citizenship (hi)stories of the marginalized show the status quo as a determinant of social boundaries and as preempting a social secular consciousness of the citizens to be.

The status quo is all but static. Over the years the secular and the religious have pulled and pushed it, tallying victories and losses both big and small. It became a source of power, primarily for the religious parties but also for its rivals (for one, see in Levy, 2007). Yet in recent decades, its power seemed to wither away and its political pillar, the National Religious Party (NRP), gradually dissipated, receiving its final blow during the term of the 18th Knesset when it ceased to exist even by name. Ever since the political "upheaval" of 1977, when the Likud toppled Labor using the support of the Mizrahi working class, the NRP has been losing its pivotal role as a mediator of a dual tension: between the religious (the ultraorthodox segment to their right) and the secular (Labor and its socialist allies to the left) and between the Ashkenazi middle class and the Mizrahi working class. The dual role of religious Zionism had been built steadily since the early days of Zionism and revealed itself in the field of education (Swirski, 1999; Levy, 2002). In the 1920s, the Zionist religious movement had taken over religious education in an attempt to contain the more religiously extreme anti-Zionist ultraorthodoxy. Later, in the 1950s, the dominant labor party (*Mapai*) again co-opted the Zionist religious parties (that merged in 1956 to create the NRP), this time to contain the Mizrahim, who immigrated en masse, threatening to tip the demographic balance against the Ashkenazim.

This partnership, known as the "historical alliance" between Labor and religious-Zionism, forged the status quo. Both parties, whose political flag and ideology was *mamlakhtiyut*[8], surfaced as the moderate, rational factors capable of appeasing the tension between state and religion. This was made evident in the "struggle over education," which brought the *yishuv*'s partisan educational order to an end but left intact the religious factions' control over education. This revealed two underpinnings of the new state order and of the evolving conception of Israeli citizenship. First, that the "historical alliance" was based on a partnership that was not solely ideological (Zionist) or political but also class motivated. This alliance was led by the rising state-made Jewish middle class, both religious and nonreligious (see Rosenfeld and Carmi, 1976), vis-à-vis the emerging (Jewish) proletariat that was

---

8 This term, which translates to kingdomship, was imbued with a strong ideology of *étatisme* and social unity at all cost.

typically Mizrahi. More importantly, it evolved against what had been seen and sociologically defined as an emotional, irrational and messianic type of Zionism, represented by Mizrahi Jews (Eisenstadt, 1947; Shenhav, 2006). Secondly, the replacement of the *yishuv*'s school system with a bifurcated religious/nonreligious one confirmed that the religious schism was not the major source of fear for the political elites. Rather, the division of power and of spheres of influence between Labor and the NRP reinforced a consensus between these parties that Jewishness would remain constitutive in the Zionist conception of Israeli citizenship. Alas, this conception was imbued with Ashkenazi symbols of pioneering that had left the Mizrahi immigrants secluded from the Zionist, modernist ethos (Shafir and Peled, 2002). In the 1970s the Mizrahim turned away from the hegemonic conceptions of nationalism and Zionism, thus marking the decline of the old Ashkenazi-religious alliance and setting the stage for a new state-religion alliance to appear. From the 1980s, Shas led this new ethnoreligious partnership that further reinforced the place of the status quo.[9]

The changes in the interrelationship between the Mizrahim and the state were not strictly political or educational. They were taking place as the rise of the Israeli Black Panthers (1970–71) threatened to destabilize the social order and the Israeli economy was in transition to a market-based economy (Shalev, 1999). In this historical context of the aftermath of the 1967 war, the social boundaries between Jews and Arabs were redefined and the conception of Israeli citizenship remolded once more. Then, when the military administration within Israel had been removed only to be restored in the newly occupied territories, a new social marker was drawn along the Green Line (the pre-1967 armistice border). Put differently, while the political successors and offspring of the Zionist religious movement were exerting all effort to blur the Green Line – "for the Land and the Lord" (Lustick, 1988) – the Green Line was integral to the Palestinians' very identity. The Palestinian workers from the occupied territories were entering the Israeli labor market but remained "the enemy," while those who resided within the Green Line were required to see themselves as Israelis. Citizenship became meaningful for the Palestinians in Israel, and a way to become active members in society. But this upgrade in their citizenship status could not be unrestricted. This again rendered the continuation of the status quo pertinent, not only for

---

9 Interestingly, this centrality of Shas and of the ultraorthodox Jewish parties in this new alliance brought about an attempt to create a counteralliance. In 2001 Shinui, the most vocal anticlerical Ashkenazi middle-class party, collaborated with the NRP, the Jewish Orthodox religious party, to propose a new basic law that would determine Israel's character as a Zionist, Jewish and democratic state. Maybe its most salient uniqueness was that this alliance was ostensibly non-Mizrahi (see Levy, 2007).

the sake of maintaining the boundary between Jews and Arabs (as *who was a Jew* was still more important than *who was an Israeli*). The fate of the Black Panthers was telling; any attempt to turn it into a class-based struggle for both Palestinian and Jewish workers had been curtailed and delegitimized as opposing the national imperative and unity (Bernstein, 1984). Moreover, as the Mizrahim were stepping towards center stage, their Jewishness became an indispensible asset and their political move to the right and to the religious parties therefore became inevitable. Religion had again become the common denominator for politicians, now mostly from the right and from the ethno-religious political parties. These politicians sought to reiterate the centrality, indeed the supremacy of the status quo in maintaining the social order. As argued before, Shas was the centerpiece of this new order.

Soon after Shas bloomed in the political arena as the new pivotal party determining the fates of ruling coalitions, the influx of immigrants from the Former Soviet Union threatened to undermine, if not overthrow, the enduring status quo. The "Russian" immigration was ostensibly nonreligious (as well as partly non-Jewish) (Goldstein and Gitelman, 2005: 251). Had it collaborated with the anticlerical forces, it would minimize the political clout of "the religious." However, the political trajectory of this new electorate was different, and not only did it not eventually topple the "religious" parties, it practically reinforced the importance of religion as a marker of citizenship. In the political arena, this was made evident by the eventual demise of the "Russian ethnic parties" that, at one point, seemed to form a counterethnic, counterreligious political force.

The "problem" of the "Russian immigration" was of a dual nature. One question was whether this immigration would integrate into society and into the existing political and social order. Since many of the immigrants were pushed out of Russia rather than pulled by their Zionist zeal, it was feared that their preference for holding on to their own language and culture would also imply their preclusion from the main quarters of society. Apparently, this fear was allayed as the new immigrants proved to be secular but ideologically right wing (Shalev and Levy, 2005: 181; Goldstein and Gitelman, 2005: 249). The second question concerned non-Jewish immigrants. Conversion was not a mass solution, but rather a personal one limited to those who were willing to undergo conversion. Consequently, the "Russian immigration" has retained a considerable non-Jewish component, contributing to the reluctance of its majority to conform in keeping the public sphere seemingly Jewish. One major example is the flourishing of nonkosher butcheries and supermarkets that previously were kept from the public eye (Ben-Porat and Feinger, 2008). This occasionally conflicted with the religious feelings of peripheral Mizrahim, contributing to the accentuation of "religion" as the dividing line. In this sense, the emerging animosity between "Russians" and Mizrahim, especially where the latter were drawn to Shas and "back to religion," was not simply an extension of xenophobic inclinations from the "old" homeland (Shumsky, 2002; Caneti-Nisim et al., 2006). It was "Israeli-made" racism that fueled the ethnicization of citizenship. The following story testifies to how far this went.

The entrenchment of religiosity, ethnicity and nationalism had taken a somewhat surprising turn in the West Bank Jewish settlement of Nokdim. Recently, the members of this mixed religious-secular community of mostly immigrants from the Russian republics decided to bar non-Jewish Russian-Israelis from owning houses in the settlement for, to cite Nokdim's secretary:

> If you accept 10 families in which the mother isn't Jewish, then soon there will be 30 children, and tomorrow your son could fall in love with the good-looking girl next door. It's a real problem. (Levinson, 2010)

Accentuating a general hardline right-wing position amongst this constituency, another speaker did not hesitate in comparing these Israeli citizens to terrorists, adding that,

> We have to separate ourselves from the gentiles in commerce and everything else – particularly when it comes to living with them. It could lead to assimilation or idol worship; it opens the door to all kinds of trouble. They might lead us into committing offenses that Jews normally don't do, like idolatry and incest and all kinds of other perversions. (Levinson, 2010)

Conclusion

The relationship between state and religion in Israel is embedded in every aspect of social life and as such, religion matters beyond its institutional arrangements and the political agreements that it entails. There is no disputing the impact of religion on, say, the fate of the Israeli-Palestinian conflict, the future of labor-migrants or even the content of heritage studies at elementary school. Yet it is its presence in the mundane and quotidian aspects of Israeli lives (Karrayani, 2007) that renders the debate over whether and how the interrelationship between state, nationalism and religion should be understood as complex and conflictive. Indeed, as shown here, the very questions of who the Israelis are – Mizrahim, Arabs or Russians – and hence of what Israeli society is, are determined by the interplay of modernization, secularization/desecularization and ethnicization. It is in this sense that the status quo becomes not merely a political mechanism delimiting the extent of state-religion relationship or determining the particular makeup of the political alliance that supports it (Cohen and Susser, 2000: 18). What makes the status quo germane and practically indispensable is that it defines for many Israelis their social order, or the *perimeter* beyond the scope of which religion should not be questioned (Elam, 2000). In closing I intend to revisit this observation by relating it to the interplay between ethnicity, citizenship and religion.

Maybe the most perplexing aspect of the status quo is the discrepancy between its formal characteristics – mainly the absence of civil marriages and, in general, the precedence of "personal law" over a statist conception of "territorial law" in all related matters – and the façade of a Westernized, secularized public sphere. In light of the prominence of "religious politics" manifested in the salience of religious political parties and in the visibility of "religious issues," it is striking that no major force seeks to politicize the concept of secularization. Regarding the marginalized groups of Arabs, Mizrahim and Russians, I argue that the entrenchment of the status quo in processes and practices of ethnic categorization in the sense of implicating nationalism, ethnicity and religion in these groups' conceptions of citizenship gave them a vested interest in its continuation. These processes, elevating the existence of the status quo to a point of indisputability, eventually caused the nonreligious elites and their constituencies to lose interest in changing the status quo. In other words, it is commonly suggested that "religion" is intrinsic to the identity of ethnic and lower-class categories, whether as a result of their being "traditionalists" as more conservative sociologists tend to argue or being marked as "religious" through practices of "religionization" as critical observers claim (Levy and Emmerich, 2001; Shenhav, 2006). However, what is neglected is that a similar interest in the continuation of the status quo that pertains to the ethnic (Ashkenazi) and national (Jewish) identity of the middle class prevents them from being the vanguard of secularization.

Secularizing the state is not equivalent to secularizing the public sphere, which occurs as part of everyday consumerism and in line with the rise of new cosmopolitan lifestyles (Ben-Porat and Feniger, 2009; Kaplan, 2011). In final analysis, what the "seculars" fear is the loss of Israel's Jewish identity, were they to follow the logic of secularization and require from the state and from themselves to be rid of the ethnic elements – both Jewish and Ashkenazi – of Israeli citizenship. If the state were to disengage from its Jewish component, "secular" Jews would fear being submerged in an Orient that still haunts them. Had Israel given the Palestinian citizens "full and equal rights," as recently contended by Shlomo Avineri (2010), a left-leaning political theorist, there would be no escape from Israel's eventually becoming "Falastin." This fear echoes and reinforces an "internal fear" that resonated in the roar of the crowd in 1999: "Anything but Shas" (Shalev and

Levy, 2005: 181). At that time, when the option of a political partnership between the purportedly all-encompassing "One Israel" political alliance and Shas was within reach, the Ashkenazi middle-class supporters of "One Israel" seemed to prefer revitalizing the "old" consociational order with the (by then) ultranationalistic right-wing National Religious Party. Shas was declined as a legitimate partner, despite its supporting a peaceful resolution of the Israeli-Palestinian conflict. In other words, neither the possibility of peace nor the opportunity to redefine the relationship between state and religion were worth the price of unraveling the elusiveness of the status quo and ridding the Israeli citizenship of its ethnic array.

References

Al-Haj, Majid. 1995. *Education, Empowerment, and Control: The Case of the Arabs in Israel*. Albany, NY: SUNY Press.

Ali, Nohad. 2004. "The Islamic Movement in Israel: Between Religion, Nationalism and Modernity." In Yossi Yonah and Yehuda Goodman (eds), *Maelstrom of Identities: A Critical Look at Religion and Secularity in Israel*, 132–64. Tel Aviv: Van Leer Institute and Hakibbutz Hameuchad Publishing House.

Asad, Talal. 1993. *Genealogies of Religion: Discipline and Reasons of Power in Christianity and Islam*. Baltimore, MD: Johns Hopkins University Press.

Avineri, Shlomo. 2010. "Biladi, Biladi – what's in a name?" Haaretz.com, 8 September 2010. Online at: http://www.haaretz.com/print-edition/opinion/biladi-biladi-what-s-in-a-name-1.312848 (accessed 23 September 2010).

Beckford James A. and N. J. Demerath. 2007. "Introduction." In James A. Beckford and N. J. Demerath (eds), *The SAGE Handbook of the Sociology of Religion*, 1–16. London: SAGE.

Ben-Porat, Guy and Yariv Feniger. 2009. "Live and Let Buy? Consumerism, Secularization, and Liberalism." *Comparative Politics* 41.3: 293–313.

Bernstein, Deborah. 1984. "Conflict and Protest in Israeli Society: The Case of the Black Panthers of Israel." *Youth & Society* 16.2: 129–52.

Bernstein, Deborah and Shlomo Swirski. 1982. "The Rapid Economic Development of Israel and the Emergence of the Ethnic Division of Labor." *The British Journal of Sociology* 33.1: 64–85.

Beyer, Peter. "Globalization and Glocalization." In James A. Beckford and N. J. Demerath (eds), *The SAGE Handbook of the Sociology of Religion*, 98–117. London: SAGE.

Boas, Hagai. 2002. "The Affair of the Struggle for the Suffrage of Women in the *Yishuv*: The Status Quo and the formation of Social Categories." *Theory and Criticism* 21: 107–31. In Hebrew.

Bruce, Steve. 2006. "Secularization and the Impotence of Individualized Religion." *Hedgehog Review* 8.1–2: 35–45

Casanova, José. 1994. *Public Religion in the Modern World*. Chicago: University of Chicago Press.

_____. 2006. "Rethinking secularization: A global comparative perspective." *Hedgehog Review*. 8.1–2: 7–22.

Cohen, Asher. 2005. "Religious Zionism and the National Religious Party in the 2003 Elections: An Attempt to Respond to the Challenges of Religious, Ethnic and Political

Schism." In Asher Arian and Michal Shamir (eds), *The Elections in Israel, 2003*, 187–214. New Brunswick, NJ and London: Transaction Publishers.

Cohen, Asher and Bernard Susser. 2000. *Israel and the Politics of Jewish Identity: The Secular-Religious Impasse*. Baltimore, MD: Johns Hopkins University Press.

Cohen, Asher and Jonathan Rynhold. 2005. "Social Covenants: The Solution to the Crisis of Religion and State in Israel?" *Journal of Church and State* 47.4: 725–45.

Corinaldi, Michael. 2003. "Freedom of religion in Israel: Changes in the '*status quo*.'" *Sha'arei Mishpat* (Special Issue: Religion and State) 3.2: 287–339. In Hebrew.

Demerath, N. J. "Secularization and Sacralization Deconstructed and Reconstructed." In James A. Beckford and N. J. Demerath (eds), *The SAGE Handbook of the Sociology of Religion*, 27–80. London: SAGE.

Eisenstadt, Shmuel N. 1947. *Introduction to the Study of the Sociological Structure of the Oriental Communities*. Jerusalem: The Szold Institute.

_____. 2000. "Multiple Modernities." *Daedalus* 129.1: 1–29.

_____. 2008. "Collective identities, public spheres, civil society and citizenship in the contemporary era – with some observations on the Israeli scene." *Citizenship Studies* 12.3: 203–13.

Elam, Yigal. 2000. *End of Judaism: The Religion-Nation and the Kingdom*. Tel Aviv: Yediot Achronot. In Hebrew.

_____. 2001. *Judaism as a Status Quo: The Who is a Jew Controversy in 1958 and Some Remarks on Secular-Religious Relations in Israel*. Tel Aviv: Am Oved Publishers. In Hebrew.

Fogiel-Bijaui, Silvie. 2003. "Why Won't There Be Civil Marriage Any Time Soon in Israel? Or: Personal Law – The Silenced Issue of the Israeli-Palestinian Conflict." *Nashim: A Journal of Jewish Women's Studies & Gender Issues* 6: 28–34.

Fox, Judith. 2005. "Secularization." In John R. Hinnells (ed.), *The Routledge Companion to the Study of Religion*, 291–305. London and New York: Routledge.

Friedman, Menachem. 1990. "And this is the history of the Status Quo." In Varda Pilovsky (ed.), *The Transition from Yishuv to Statehood 1947–1949: Continuity and Changes*, 47–79. Haifa: Herzl Institute. In Hebrew.

Gavison, Ruth. 1998. "A Jewish and Democratic State: Challenges and Risks." In Menachem Mautner, Avi. Sagi and Ronen Shamir (eds), *Multiculturalism in a Democratic and Jewish State*, 213–78. Tel Aviv: Ramot – Tel Aviv University. In Hebrew.

Gavison, Ruth and Yaaov Medan. n.d. *The Gavison-Medan Covenant*. Online at: http://www.gavison-medan.org.il/english/ (accessed 17 June 2011).

Ghanem, Asad and Ilan Saban. 2010. "There are more than two options." Haaretz.com, 17 September 2010. Online at: http://www.haaretz.com/print-edition/opinion/there-are-more-than-two-options-1.314314 (accessed 23 September 2010).

Gitelman, Zvi. 2004. "The 'Russian Revolution' in Israel." In Alan Dowty (ed.), *Critical Issues in Israeli Society*, 95–108. Westport, CT: Greenwood Publishing Group.

Goldstein, Ken and Zvi Gitelman. 2005. "From 'Russians' to Israelis?" In Asher Arian and Michal Shamir (eds), *The Elections in Israel, 2003*, 245–60. New Brunswick, NJ and London: Transaction Publishers.

Goodman, Yehuda. 2008. "Citizenship, Modernity and Faith in the Nation-State: Racialization and de-recialization in the conversion of Russian and Ethiopian in Israel." In Yehouda Shenhav and Y. Yohan (eds), *Racism in Israel*, 381–415. Tel Aviv: Van Leer Institute and Hakibbutz Hameuchad Publishing House.

Goodman, Yehuda and Shlomo Fisher. 2004. "Towards an Understanding of Secularism and Religiosity in Israel: The Secularization Thesis and Possible Alternatives." In

Yossi Yonah and Yehuda Goodman (eds), *Maelstrom of Identities: A Critical Look at Religion and Secularity in Israel*, 346–90. Tel Aviv: Van Leer Institute and Hakibbutz Hameuchad Publishing House.

Goodman, Yehuda and Yossi Yonah. 2004. "Introduction: Religiousness and Secularity in Israel – Alternative Perspectives." In Yossi Yonah and Yehuda Goodman (eds), *Maelstrom of Identities: A Critical Look at Religion and Secularity in Israel*, 9–45. Tel Aviv: Van Leer Institute and Hakibbutz Hameuchad Publishing House.

Gordon, Andrew and Trevor Stack. 2007. "Citizenship Beyond the State: Thinking with Early Modern Citizenship in the Contemporary World." *Citizenship Studies* 11.2: 117.

Habermas, Jürgen. 2006. "Religion in the Public Sphere." *European Journal of Philosophy* 14.1: 1–25.

_____. 2010. *An Awareness of What is Missing: Faith and Reason in a Post-secular Age.* Cambridge: Polity Press.

Haynes, Jeffrey. 2009. "Religion and democratizations: an introduction." *Democratization* 16.6: 1041.

Herzog, Hanna 1985. "Ethnicity as a Negotiated Issue in the Israeli Political Order: The 'Ethnic Lists' to the Delegates' Assembly and the Knesset (1920–1977)." In Alex Weingrod (ed.), *Studies in Israeli Ethnicity: After the Ingathering* 159–78. New York: Gordon & Breach Science Publishers.

Hofnung, Menachem. 1996. "The Unintended Consequences of Unplanned Constitutional Reform: Constitutional Politics in Israel." *American Journal of Comparative Law* 44: 585–604

Jamal, Amal. 2009. "Democratizing state-religion relations: A comparative study of Turkey, Egypt and Israel." *Democratization* 16.6: 1143–71

Kalekin-Fishman, Devorah. 2004. *Ideology, Policy, and Practice: Education for Immigrants and Minorities in Israel Today.* New York: Kluwer Academic.

Kaplan, Dana. 2011. "Sexual Liberation and the creative class in Israel." In Steven Seidman, Nancy Fisher and Chet Meeks (eds), *Introducing the New Sexuality Studies*, 357–63. London: Routledge.

Karayanni, Michael M. 2006. "Separate Nature of the Religious Accommodations for the Palestinian-Arab Minority in Israel." *The Northwestern University Journal of International Human Rights* 5.1: 41–71.

_____. 2007. "Multiculture Me No More! On Multicultural Qualifications and the Palestinian-Arab Minority of Israel." *Diogenes* 54.3: 39–58.

Kimmerling, Baruch. 1999. "Religion, Nationalism and Democracy in Israel." *Constellations: An International Journal of Critical & Democratic Theory* 6.3: 339–63.

Lehmann, David and Batia Siebzehner. 2008. "Self-exclusion as a strategy of inclusion: The case of Shas." *Citizenship Studies* 12.3: 233–47.

Levinson, Chaim. 2010. "Lieberman's settlement bars Russian-Israeli families from buying homes." Haaretz.com, 11 July. Online at: http://www.haaretz.com/print-edition/news/lieberman-s-settlement-bars-russian-israeli-families-from-buying-homes-1.301170 (accessed 31 August 2010).

Levy, Daniel and Yfaat Weiss (eds). 2002. *Challenging Ethnic Citizenship: German and Israeli Perspectives on Immigration.* New York and Oxford: Berghahn Books.

Levy, Gal. 2002. "Ethnicity and Education: Nation-Building, State-Formation and the Construction of the Israeli Education System." PhD dissertation, London School of Economics.

_____. 2005. "From Subjects to Citizens: On Educational Reforms and the Demarcation of the Israeli-Arabs." *Citizenship Studies* 9.3: 271–91.

_____. 2007. "On Change and Continuity: Shinui and the Lost Secular Revolution." *The Public Sphere: Tel Aviv Journal of Political Science* 1: 135–47. In Hebrew.

Levy, Gal and Mohammad Massalha. 2010. "Yaffa: A school of their choice?" *British Journal of Sociology of Education* 31.2: 171.

Levy, Gal and Zeev Emmerich. 2001. "Shas and the 'Ethnic Phantom.'" In Yoav Peled (ed.), *Shas: The Challenge of Israeliness*, 126–58. Tel Aviv: Yediot Ahronot Books and Chemed Books. In Hebrew.

Levy, Shlomit, Hanna Levinshon and Elihu Katz. 2004. "The Many Faces of Jewishness in Israel." In Uzi Rebhun and Chaim I. Waxman (eds), *Jews in Israel: Contemporary Social and Cultural Patterns*, 265–84. Lebanon, NH: Brandeis University Press.

Lloyd, David and Paul Thomas. 1998. *Culture and the State*. New York and London: Routledge.

Lustick, Ian. 1980. *Arabs in the Jewish State*. Austin, TX: University of Texas Press.

_____. 1988. *For the Land and the Lord: Jewish Fundamentalism in Israel*. New York: Council on Foreign Relations Press.

_____. 1999. "Israel as a Non-Arab State: The Political Implications of Mass Immigration of Non-Jews." *Middle East Journal* 53.3: 417–33.

Mar'i, Sami Khalil. 1978. *Arab Education in Israel*. Syracuse, NY: Syracuse University Press.

McLennan, Gregor. 2007. "Towards Postsecular Sociology?" *Sociology* 41.5: 857–70.

Mitchell, Timothy. 1991. "The Limits of the State: Beyond Statist Approaches and Their Critics." *American Political Science Review* 85.1: 77–96.

Peled, Yoav. 1992. "Ethnic Democracy and the Legal Construction of Citizenship: Arab Citizens of the Jewish State." *American Political Science Review* 86.2: 432–43.

_____. 1998. "Towards a redefinition of Jewish nationalism in Israel? The enigma of Shas." *Ethnic and Racial Studies* 21.4: 703–27.

Raday, Frances. 2005. "Women's Human Rights: Dichotomy between Religion and Secularism in Israel." *Israel Affairs* 11.1: 78–94.

Ram, Uri. 1995. *The Changing Agenda of Israeli Sociology: Theory, Ideology, and Identity*. Albany, NY: SUNY Press.

_____. 2008. "Why Secularism Fails? Secular Nationalism and Religious Revivalism in Israel." *International Journal of Politics, Culture, and Society* 21.1: 57–73.

Reder, Michael and Josef Schmidt. 2010. "Habermas and Religion." In Jürgen Habermas, *An Awareness of What is Missing: Faith and Reason in a Post-secular Age*, 1–14. Cambridge: Polity Press.

Rose, Nikolas. 1996. "The death of the social? Re-figuring the territory of government." *Economy and Society* 25.3: 327–56.

Rosenfeld, Henry and Shulamit Carmi. 1976. "The Privatization of Public Means, the State-Made Middle Class, and the Realization of Family Value in Israel." In John G. Peristiany (ed.), *Kinship and Modernization in Mediterranean Society*, 131–59. Rome: Center for Mediterranean Studies, American Universities Field Staff.

Shafir, Gershon and Yoav Peled. 2002. *Being Israeli: The Dynamics of Multiple Citizenship*. Cambridge: Cambridge University Press.

Shalev, Michael and Sigal Kis. 2002. "Social Cleavages among Non-Arab Voters: A New Analysis." In Asher Arian and Michal Shamir (eds), *The Elections in Israel, 1999*, 67–96. Albany, NY: SUNY Press.

Shalev, Michael and Gal Levy. 2005. "The Winners and Losers of 2003: Ideology, Social Structure and Political Change." In Asher Arian and Michal Shamir (eds), *The Elections in Israel, 2003*, 167–86. New Brunswick, NJ and London: Transaction Publishers.

Shenhav, Yehouda. 2006. *The Arab Jews: A Postcolonial Reading of Nationalism, Religion, and Ethnicity*. Stanford, CA: Stanford University Press.

_____. 2007. "Modernity and the hybridization of nationalism and religion: Zionism and the Jews of the Middle East as a heuristic case." *Theory and Society* 36.1: 1–30.

_____. 2008. "Invitation to a Post-secular outline for the study of the society in Israel." *Israeli Sociology (Sociologia Israelit)* 10.1: 161–88.

Shokeid, Moshe. 2001. "On the Sin We Did Not Commit in the Research of Oriental Jews." *Israel Studies* 6.1: 15–33.

Shumsky, Dimitry. 2002. "Ethnicity and Citizenship in the Perception of Russian Israelis." In Daniel Levy and Yfaat Weiss (eds), *Challenging Ethnic Citizenship: German and Israeli Perspectives on Immigration*, 154–80. New York and Oxford: Berghahn Books.

Smooha, Sammy. 1978. *Israel: Pluralism and Conflict*. Berkeley and Los Angeles: University of California Press.

_____. 2008. "The mass immigrations to Israel: A comparison of the failure of the Mizrahi immigrants of the 1950s with the success of the Russian immigrants of the 1990s." *Journal of Israeli History: Politics, Society, Culture* 27.1: 1–27.

Sorek, Tamir and Alin M. Ceobanu. 2009. "Religiosity, National Identity and Legitimacy: Israel as an Extreme Case." *Sociology* 43.3: 477–96.

Swirski, Shlomo. 1989. *Israel: The Oriental Majority*. London: Zed Books.

_____. 1999. *Politics and Education in Israel: Comparisons with the United States*. London: Falmer Press.

Sznaider, Natan. 2000. "Consumerism as a Civilizing Process: Israel and Judaism in the Second Age of Modernity." *International Journal of Politics, Culture, and Society* 14.2: 297–314.

Turner, Bryan S. 2001. "Cosmopolitan Virtue: On Religion in a Global Age." *European Journal of Social Theory* 4.2: 131–52.

Wasserman, Abraham. 2002. "Status Quo." In Nathan Langenthal and S. Friedman (eds), *The Conflict: Religion and State in Israel*, 287–301. Tel Aviv: Yediot Achronot. In Hebrew.

Yelenevskaya, Maria N. and Larisa Fialkova. 2004. "My poor cousin, my feared enemy: The image of Arabs in personal narratives of former Soviets in Israel." *Folklore* 115.1: 77.

Yonah, Yossi. 2005. *In Virtue of Difference: The Multicultural Project in Israel*. Tel Aviv: Van Leer Institute and Hakibbutz Hameuchad Publishing House.

Zameret, Zvi. 2002. *The Melting Pot in Israel: The Commission of Inquiry Concerning the Education of Immigrant Children During the Early Years of the State*. Albany, NY: SUNY Press.

Zelniker, Shimshon and Michael Kahan. 1976. "Religion and Nascent Cleavages: The Case of Israel's National Religious Party." *Comparative Politics* 9.1: 21–48.

Chapter 5

MANAGING CHINA'S MUSLIM MINORITIES: MIGRATION, LABOR AND THE RISE OF ETHNORELIGIOUS CONSCIOUSNESS AMONG UYGHURS IN URBAN XINJIANG

Reza Hasmath

University of Western Sydney

Introduction

Although China is commonly perceived as being ethnically homogenous, nearly 9 percent of the total population consists of ethnic minorities whose importance for China's long-term development is disproportionate to their numbers. Among the estimated 106.4 million ethnic minorities, the majority have traditionally concentrated in the resource-rich western areas of the nation (NBS/EAC, 2003). Foremost among these areas is the Xinjiang Uyghur Autonomous Region (XUAR) in China's northwest – occupying one-sixth of the country's total land mass and holding one of the nation's largest and most strategically important natural gas and oil reserves[1] – where nearly 8.4 million Uyghurs,[2] a Turkic, mostly Sunni-Muslim ethnic minority,[3] reside in the majority.[4]

---

1 The issue of energy is not negligible in discussions about ethnoreligious relations in Xinjiang. Given the region's rich energy resources and geographical positioning, Xinjiang has become indispensable as a distributor of oil and natural gas to energy-guzzling Central Asia and the surrounding Chinese provinces.

2 Islamic identity among Uyghurs is older than the concept of Uyghurs as an ethnic minority group. As a result, it has historically been a common habit among Uyghurs (and non-Uyghurs alike) to conflate "Uyghur" with "Muslim," and to ascertain that all "Muslim Uyghurs" are united as Muslims. This is not entirely accurate. Although

Tensions between Muslim Uyghurs and Han Chinese (the national majority) have dominated discussions in the region as a result of historical and contemporary incidents between both groups. For instance, during the Gulja Incident during the Muslim holy month of Ramadan in February 1997, a series of riots and demonstrations occurred due to crackdowns by Chinese authorities on traditional Uyghur culture, including most notably the banning of traditional social gatherings (*meshrep*). More recently in July 2009, violent riots in the region's capital, Urumqi, resulted in 197 Uyghur and Han deaths and 1,721 injured (Hao et al., 2009). In general, contributing factors behind Muslim Uyghur-Han Chinese tensions revolve around policies that limit religious practice or aim to phase out Uyghur language instruction in schools. For example, public sector employees are not allowed to wear Islamic head scarves or coverings (including the *doppa* cap for males), nor fast during Ramadan.[5] Individuals under the age of 18 are not allowed to enter religious places such as mosques or pray in schools.[6] The study of the Koran is only allowed in designated government schools, and Imams cannot teach the Koran in private. There are documented accounts by Muslim Uyghurs who report that government informers regularly attend their prayer services in local mosques, especially the Friday sermon (see Fuller and Lipman, 2004).

Islam is a common marker of Uyghur identity, a common cultural heritage, diet and language are other salient markers as well. Moreover, there are competing Sufi and non-Sufi factions, and linguistic discrepancies among this minority nationality. Notwithstanding, the increasing arrival and presence of Hans in Xinjiang have only intensified closer linkages between Islam and Uyghur identity to the point they are often seen as synonymous on the ground.

3 While there is a lively scholarly debate on the utility of using the terms "ethnic minorities," "ethnic groups" (*zuqun*) and "minority nationalities" (*shaoshu minzu*) in P. R. China (see Ma, 2001), until academic consensus is reached, and for the purposes of this chapter, the three terms will be used with a similar intentionality.

4 Islam in Xinjiang has been influenced by the region's proximity to Central Asia. Islam entered Xinjiang from central Asia in the tenth century. By the mid-fifteenth century the Turkic speakers of the Tarim basin oases had almost universally converted to Islam (Fuller and Lipman, 2004).

5 All Communist Party members and employees on the state payroll, Uyghurs inclusive, cannot attend prayers of religious practices.

6 This can potentially lead to a process of deculturalization by depriving youths grounding in Muslim Uyghur traditional community values. Put another way, the distance from Islam at a young age may encourage more Uyghurs to adopt the secular ideology of the Chinese state rather than to practice Islam from the age of 18 onwards. The effects on this policy, coupled with the growing numerical presence of non-Muslim Han Chinese, has lead many older Muslim Uyghurs to worry that their offspring will be drawn away from their ancestral faith by the attraction of Han materialism (see Fuller and Lipman, 2004).

Furthermore, Chinese authorities have slowly phased out the use of the Uyghur language in the majority of schools and universities, leaving Mandarin Chinese as the main mode of instruction.[7] As one Uyghur woman commented in the aftermath of the July 2009 riots, Hans "don't respect our lifestyle... we want our dignity" (Wong, 2009).

The state's response to potential outbursts of Muslim Uyghur dissent has consisted of periods of "soft" and "hard" policies. Clarke (2010) characterizes the "soft" approach to acquiesce the Muslim Uyghur population as relative tolerance of institutionalized Islam, viz. state funding of the Chinese Islamic Association, and the building and upkeep of mosques. There are over twenty thousand mosques in Xinjiang reported by the Information Office of the State Council (2000), which makes this endeavor relatively significant. The "hard" approach is illustrated by "re-educating" and "reforming" religious leaders[8] and clamping down on "illegal" mosque construction when the state perceives them to be a threat to security.

Coiled within this unnerving interaction between Muslim Uyghurs and Hans, commentators have noted there is a growing rise of ethnoreligious consciousness among Muslim Uyghurs which often revolves around highlighting differences to Hans.[9] As Gladney (1996) argues, Muslim Uyghurs are subscribing to certain identities under highly contextualized moments of social relations. That is, the close link between Islam and Uyghur identity has meant that any shifts by state authorities in regulating religious practice via varying "soft" or "hard" policies has been a source of contention for Muslim Uyghurs who believe it is a attack on their personal identity. From the state's perspective, a heightened religious consciousness among Muslim Uyghurs, if not adequately managed, can lead to dissent in this strategically

---

7 State authorities generally respond that the shift to a near-universal use of Mandarin Chinese in schools and universities is to ensure that Uyghurs can compete on equal footing with Hans in the labor market, and relatedly to maximize their educational potential.

8 The goal of "reeducation" is to ensure that religious leaders do not advocate Islamic "fundamentalism" or "radicalism" as defined by the state or forge connections between Muslims in China and elsewhere.

9 For example, many Uyghurs attend mosque on Friday as a means of reinforcing the distinctiveness of the Uyghur community (see Fuller and Lipman, 2004). In addition, since Islamic diet requires meat to be prepared in accordance to religious practice, and it strictly prohibits the consumption of pork – a staple among Hans – there is the potential for reduced social interactions between Muslim Uyghurs and Hans. Perhaps the most culpable barrier for Muslim Uyghur interactions with Hans is the institutionalization of ethnic groups by the CPC itself. The official system of categorization constantly reminds Uyghurs that they are members of a fixed and specific ethnic group differing from the dominant majority Hans.

important area of China. Finley (2007: 628) goes a step further than Gladney, specifically outlining three ways Uyghur ethnoreligious consciousness manifests on the ground: (1) daily repetition of negative stereotypes of Han Chinese; (2) symbolic, spatial and social segregation from Han Chinese; and (3) dissemination of alternative representations of Han/Uyghur as colonizer/colonized through the medium of popular Uyghur song. By utilizing these strategies, Muslim Uyghurs seemingly create a discourse that rejects national unity and reemphasizes Uyghur cultural and social differences from Hans. Of course, those "same differences apparently did not prevent Uyghurs from interacting with the Han in the past... nor do those differences stop Uyghurs from interacting with Han Chinese in the present context when it suits them to do so" (Smith, 2002: 156).

While the studies cited thus far correctly attribute cultural repression as the main culprit behind the rise of ethnoreligious consciousness among Uyghurs, the State Ethnic Minorities Commissioner suggests an alternative explanation, arguing that the increased minority migration to urban areas is the main reason behind the "disrupted social harmony" between Muslim Uyghurs and Hans (see Mittenhal, 2002). While increased numbers of Uyghur and Han migrants are heading into Xinjiang's cities, pushed by demographic pressures and pulled by economic structural transformations, the commissioner's comments are worth exploring. Are the burgeoning numbers of Uyghur migrants entering Xinjiang's urban entities potentially creating new social mosaics to such an extent that they are the main source of increased levels of ethnoreligious consciousness? Put another way, what contributory roles do socioeconomic factors such as labor shares and sectoral distribution in major occupational categories and the likewise growing Han migration have on ethnoreligious consciousness among Uyghurs?

The aim of this chapter is thus to examine the potential role of increasing migration on the management of Muslim Uyghur and Han Chinese interactions in urban Xinjiang. The first section will provide a brief contextualization of Uyghur and Han presence in Xinjiang, followed by a discussion of the spatial inequalities indicative of urbanization patterns that favor Han internal migrants. The chapter will proceed to describe Xinjiang's division of labor and subsequently the potential linkages social stratification has for the rise of contemporary ethnoreligious consciousness among the Uyghur population.

Migratory and Urbanization Patterns

Before Xinjiang was annexed in 1760 by the Qing Dynasty, the region never constituted a single polity but rather was crisscrossed by fluid borders and contested by innumerable warlords and imperial powers including the

Mongol, Russian and British empires.[10] In 1884, a weakened Qing empire converted Xinjiang to provincial status, shifting the capital from Ili to Urumqi. After the Qing Dynasty was replaced by the Republic of China in 1912, two short-lived Eastern Turkestan republics were established until September 1949, where the Communist Party of China (CPC) proclaimed it "liberated" the region. By October 1955 it established the Xinjiang Uyghur Autonomous Region.[11]

After "liberation" the CPC instituted a program of resettlement of Hans to "rusticate" urban youths and integrate the non-Han population into China proper. As a result, Xinjiang's Han population has increased steadily, save for a rapid leap between 1958 and 1960 – the period of the Great Leap Forward and ensuing calamitous Great Leap famine that killed roughly 30 million. The sudden escalation of Han residents during this period has two primary causes. First, unsustainable expansion of industry and accompanying urbanization and second, Xinjiang did not suffer severe food shortages during this time and therefore received an influx of internal migrants from other parts of China in search of food (Pannell and Ma, 1997). In aggregate terms, between 1953 and 2000 the Han Chinese population increased their share of the region's total population from 6.1 percent to 40.6 percent.

The Chinese have historically controlled Xinjiang through the construction of garrisons and urban settlements (Gaubatz, 1996; Van Wie Davis, 2008). In this tradition, the CPC have continued to use these methods of control in tandem with agricultural settlements in the form of the still very active Xinjiang Production and Construction Corps (XPCC) established in 1954 and originally created to employ demobilized troops. The XPCC is one of Xinjiang's three main administrative organs which operates as an autonomous society with its own public security and judicial organs. In 1996 it was elevated to the same political status as the Xinjiang government (see Seymour, 2000 for further details). One of the practical consequences of consolidating power through this administrative setup is that it places Muslim Uyghurs in structural competition with other minority groups, retaining executive power in the hands of predominantly Han upper-level officials (see Millward and Tursun, 2004). For example, the XPCC currently reserves approximately 800 of 840 civil servant job openings for Han Chinese.

---

10 Uyghurs and Hans generally disagree on which group has a legitimate historical claim to the region. Uyghurs assert that they are indigenous to the area, whereas Chinese authorities consider Xinjiang to have belonged to China since the Han Dynasty (202 BC–220 AD).

11 This was a renunciation of the earlier CPC 1934 Basic Law, which stipulated the right of all national minorities to separate from China and to create their own autonomous state.

Xinjiang's Hans have a tendency to settle in wealthier urban areas, while Uyghurs tend to constitute the majority in rural areas or the poorer urban areas of southern Xinjiang (see Cao, 2010). Officially, 80.8 percent of Uyghurs reside in rural areas, in comparison to 46.4 percent for Hans; 9 percent and 10.1 percent of Uyghurs live in the town and city, with a corresponding figure of 13.0 percent and 40.6 percent for the Han population (calculated using NBS/EAC, 2003).[12] The strong Han presence in cities encourages claims that a form of internal Han colonization through encirclement or population swamping is taking place in the region – a matter that will be explored in further depth in a later section. Fueling this claim are statistics that indicate that between 1991 and 2000, Han presence in Xinjiang's urban areas increased at a positive rate of about 2 percent, almost the inverse of the corresponding rate for Uyghurs, −1.9 percent. Moreover, as Table 5.1 suggests, between 1991 and 2000 Uyghurs' share of the urban population declined significantly in nearly all major cities, except for Kashgar and Hotan, both of which are located in the penurious south and whose economies are highly dependent upon agriculture.

The urban percentage changes for Han and Uyghur form mirror images. Han markedly increased in proportion in major cities, by over 5 percent in Korla, Aksu, Hami, Turpan, Bortala and Yi'ning. Korla, whose economy is buttressed by the oil and gas industries, is one of the three main centers of production in Xinjiang (the other two being Urumqi and Karamay). Aksu, Xinjiang's third biggest city, witnessed the most dramatic change to ethnic population distribution. In this city Han increased their population by 127,824 between 1991 and 2000. The corresponding figure for Uyghurs was only 31,012 (NBS/EAC, 2003). Aksu, despite being in the poorer Tarim basin, generates far more industrial activity than Kashgar or Khotan. Furthermore, it has a large, mainly Han XPCC presence, and is a destination for many interprovincial migrants. The only exception to mounting sinification of the cities is Altay in the far north. Altay is in a county with a relatively low per capita GDP (approximately 4,000 RMB, or ~590 USD) so it may not attract many interprovincial Hans.

---

12 The legacy of the *hukou* (household registration) system, instituted since 1958, must be factored in to the creation of this demographic urban-rural discrepancy among Uyghurs. According to the *hukou* system, all individuals must be registered in the locale where they commonly reside – categorized further as either "nonagricultural" (urban) or "agricultural" (rural) – whereby entitlements such as housing, education and employment rights are administered accordingly. As a consequence, the *hukou* system has to a great extent controlled the mobility of rural to urban migration (see Wu and Treiman, 2004 for further details).

Table 5.1. Uyghur and Han population shares in Xinjiang's major cities, 1991–2000

	Uyghurs			Hans		
	1991 (%)	2000 (%)	Change (%)	1991 (%)	2000 (%)	Change (%)
Urumqi	12.43	12.79	0.37	72.88	75.30	2.42
Karamay	15.27	13.78	−1.49	75.97	78.07	2.10
Shihezi	1.04	1.20	0.15	95.50	94.53	−0.98
Kuitun	0.28	0.47	0.19	95.43	94.62	−0.81
Yi'ning	51.29	45.54	−5.75	32.11	38.77	6.66
Tacheng	3.64	3.19	−0.44	64.02	63.73	−0.29
Altay	2.63	2.80	0.17	59.60	54.55	−5.06
Bortala	19.17	15.44	−3.74	61.01	67.97	6.95
Changji	3.13	2.87	−0.26	75.85	77.46	1.61
Turpan	72.67	70.38	−2.30	19.48	21.95	2.47
Hami	26.17	21.19	−4.98	65.94	71.73	5.79
Korla	32.29	26.36	−5.92	64.52	69.84	5.33
Aksu	46.01	38.07	−7.93	52.73	60.06	7.33
Artush	81.76	79.75	−2.01	6.22	8.10	1.88
Kashgar	74.89	77.36	2.47	24.02	21.78	−2.24
Hotan	81.06	82.40	1.34	18.60	17.01	−1.60

Source: Calculated using NBS/EAC (2003).

From another standpoint, the birth rate among Hans (1.5 percent) in Xinjiang is quite low in comparison to Uyghurs (4.3 percent) (*Xinjiang Statistical Yearbook*, 2001). Therefore, it is reasonable to assume that the increase in the Han urban population principally results from increased Han internal migration. The Han bias in urbanization is a key demographic and development issue within Xinjiang. As Hasmath and Hsu (2007) argue in the case of the Tibet Autonomous Region, the urgent development issue for minorities is not population dominance but access to the privileged trappings of urban development – the locus of economic and political power. In the context of Xinjiang, regional and ethnic inequality is worsening as demonstrated in the next section despite its GDP per capita ranking twelfth among China's 31 provinces and regions in 2000. The Han population is disproportionately concentrated in locations where average income is highest. There is a clear and significant correlation between GDP per capita and the proportion of Han residents as Tables 5.2 and 5.3 attest. In fact, every percentage point increase in the non-Han share of the population is associated with an expected

Table 5.2. Labor shares and GDP/labor share ratios (in parentheses), 2000

	Primary	Secondary	Tertiary
XUAR	55.90	13.60	30.50
	(0.34)	(3.10)	(1.27)
China	50.00	21.40	28.60
	(0.31)	(2.39)	(1.17)

Source: Calculated using *Xinjiang Population Census 2000* (2002).

Table 5.3. Sectoral distribution by ethnicity, 2000

	Uyghurs	Hans	Other
Primary	59.87	25.13	15.00
Secondary	18.16	75.61	6.24
Tertiary	25.56	62.62	11.81

Source: Calculated using *Xinjiang Population Census 2000* (2002).

decrease in GDP per capita of 44 RMB (~6.50 USD) (see Wiemer, 2004 for calculations).

Economic Situation

The division of labor in Xinjiang is greatly shaped by migration and urbanization patterns. In particular the oasis settlements where the majority of Muslim Uyghurs reside, land is scarce and the small plots cultivated are insufficient to satisfy subsistence needs and provide work to all the available labor force in the household (Beller-Hann, 1997). As elsewhere in China following the advent of the rural responsibility system, the agriculture sector was unable to absorb surplus labor. In addition, due to a lack of markets, infrastructure and the high dispersion of the population, rural industrial and transport activities are very limited. Whereas 26 percent of China's township and village enterprises (TVEs) involve industry or transport, the corresponding figure for Xinjiang TVEs is 8.6 percent (Sautman, 2000).

The economic structural forces underlying urbanization can be illustrated by comparing GDP to labor share ratios. These indicate the relative productivity of labor within different industries in terms of its value-added contribution to GDP. Table 5.2 illustrates the labor shares (percentage of employed persons) and GDP to labor share ratios in the primary, secondary and tertiary industries.

What is observed is that the GDP/labor share ratio is highest in the secondary industry, which – it should be noted – generally has higher capital inputs. Thus, the relative GDP contribution of one worker in this industry is higher than in the primary and tertiary industries. The value added contribution includes wages and profits. In short, the high secondary and tertiary ratios reflect the relatively high salary levels in these industries (approximately 14,000 RMB (2,070 USD) per annum). These are more than double the primary industry (approximately 6,500 RMB (960 USD) per annum), which has particularly low remuneration (Sautman, 2000). In Xinjiang, the secondary and tertiary industries are more productive than in China as a whole – a gauge of the relative structural dominance of these industries in Xinjiang's economic development.

The critical issue here is that while Uyghurs have a saturated concentration in primary industries, Hans dominate the secondary and tertiary industries (see Table 5.3). Put another way, key strategic resources of the region such as electricity, gas and water are managed and concentrated by Han Chinese (odds ratio: 0.06).[13] The types and quality of jobs Uyghurs receive are crucial to understanding this stratification. Hans have moved into the private sector – where minorities are not faring well – as the formal urban state and collective sector diminishes in economic importance. Note that total employment in work units has slumped drastically in a background where the total number of Xinjiang inhabitants of working age has grown. In 2000, 2,762,260 were "formal employees" and 4,175,900 were "urban individuals" or "rural laborers" (*Xinjiang Statistical Yearbook*, 2001). The minority share of employment in local state-owned units (40.7 percent in 1991; 43.2 percent in 1996) greatly outweighs their share of employment in central state-owned units (9.4 percent in 1991; 10.5 percent in 1996) (*Xinjiang Statistical Yearbook*, 1992, 1997). Official statistics in later years do not differentiate minority share by these divisions. However, such figures, ignored in debates on internal Han colonialism in Xinjiang, are a strong sign of unequal distribution of political power. Note also that in the secondary sector – industry – there has been a decrease of 1 percent of minority participation and a negligible increase (0.3 percent) in construction. Most noteworthy is the labor force shift to the tertiary sector, especially wholesale and retail trade and the decrease in importance of the secondary sector.

Many of the Han Chinese interprovincial migrants are spontaneous, not part of state-directed population transfers. Their presence within urban areas and within high-status, high-paying occupations (defined in this instance as above the average annual wage of 10,278 RMB (1,517 USD)) contributes

---

13 Unlike measures of difference, odd ratios are not influenced by ceiling and floor effects.

to the perception of urban Xinjiang being an internal Han colony. As Table 5.4 illustrates, Hans are overrepresented in high-status and high-paying occupations where over 25 percent of the Han working population reside, in comparison to 9 percent for Uyghurs. On the other hand, Uyghurs are overrepresented in agriculture where over 80 percent of the group's working population is presently (odds ratio: 4.66).

The transformation from a state-planned to market-based economy during the 1980s and early 1990s slowly created an ownership structure in Xinjiang that shifted towards the private sector (see Dreyer 2000 for further details).

Table 5.4. Occupation sector concentration and odds ratios by Uyghur and Han population in Xinjiang, 2000

	Occupational sector	Uyghur %	Han %	Odds ratios (Uyghur/Han)*
High-status, high-paying occupations	Banking, security and insurance	0.06	0.52	0.43
	Scientific research and technical services	3.33	3.80	0.77
	Electricity, gas and water	0.43	1.76	0.06
	Public management and social organization	2.54	4.84	0.28
	Health, social securities and social welfare	0.04	0.46	0.01
	Education and culture, sports and entertainment	2.09	4.84	0.08
	Geologic prospecting and management of water conservance	0.51	6.92	0.01
	Restaurant and retail trade	4.04	12.83	0.10
Low-status, low-paying occupations	Other professions	0.39	1.13	0.12
	Real estate	0.26	1.48	0.03
	Transport, storage and post	1.26	5.51	0.05
	Manufacturing	3.79	12.80	0.09
	Mining	0.39	2.28	0.03
	Construction	0.27	0.97	0.08
	Farming, forestry and animal	80.60	37.32	4.66

Source: Calculated using NBS/EAC (2003).

*The odds ratios compare the odds of working in an occupational sector [p(outcome) / (1–p(outcome))] for Uyghurs (numerator) and Hans (denominator). An odds ratio value of 1 thus indicates group equity; an odds ratio value that is > 1 indicates that Uyghurs are more likely to work in that particular occupational sector; conversely, an odds ratio value that is < 1 indicates that Uyghurs are less likely to work in the respected occupational sector. Occupational Categories set by the National Bureau of Statistics.

While the private sector is relatively weak in Xinjiang compared to other western provinces, its importance has grown rapidly, accounting for about 20 percent of the region's total GDP in 2003. Between 1995 and 2002, the urban state sector in Xinjiang shed 884,000 jobs and its share in overall urban employment dropped from 80.6 percent to 59.0 percent. In contrast, Xinjiang's total number of *getihu* (private businesses with fewer than eight employees) and *siying qiye* (more than eight employees) has burgeoned. By December 2003, Xinjiang had 36,617 *siying qiye* employing 491,657 persons. This amounted to a rise of 31.1 percent and 27 percent respectively over the previous year. The number of *getihu* also increased over the same 12 months to 449,911 (4.2 percent increase), employing some 706,556 persons (7.7 percent increase).

Muslim Uyghurs are faring relatively poorly in the private sector and are far less inclined towards self-employment than Han. The private sector attracts many Han internal migrants, as does the XPCC. For this reason, some commentators have recommended that reducing the size of the XPCC would also reduce pressure on local employment by cutting down on the large population of itinerant Han migrant workers (see Vicziany and Zhang, 2004). While this recommendation could potentially be fruitful, deeper processes linked to the marketization of the economy and social networks that manufacture social exclusion must be fully factored in any recommendations for change as the following sections suggest.

Marketization and the Rise of Ethnoreligious Consciousness

The current migration, urbanization and economic patterns may lead one to reasonably conclude that there is a growing internal Han colony in Xinjiang's political economy (see Sautman, 2000). To attribute this reality entirely to state policy may not be entirely accurate. State policy does not wholeheartedly perpetuate a cultural division of labor, notwithstanding XPCC civil servant hiring practices. Indeed, there are numerous preferential policies in hiring and promotion, school admissions, the financing and taxation of businesses which, at least as to higher-status, high-paying occupations, ultimately benefit Muslim Uyghurs. Moreover, when both Uyghurs and Hans are abundant in low-status, low-paying occupations (91 and 75 percent respectively), the lack of a cultural division of labor diminishes ethnoreligious solidarity. Arguably, what is increasing ethnoreligious solidarity and consciousness among Uyghurs in particular are the effects of the marketization of an emerging capitalist economy in Xinjiang.[14]

---

14 The same operations can potentially be used to understand contemporary Buddhist and Daoist revivalism as discussed in Barbalet's chapter.

As Hasmath's (2011) research in Beijing illustrates, in spite of having higher educational attainment, minority nationalities generally have lower employment rates and wages than their Han counterparts. Hans seemingly tend to use their social connections to find occupational opportunities in the capital city in greater instances than minorities – two-thirds of all positions found by Hans were found in this fashion, whereas the corresponding figure for minority nationalities were one-twelfth of all positions found. Similar processes are at work in Xinjiang. Under a socialist mode of production, the state was compelled to integrate Uyghurs and was able to accomplish this task by providing "iron rice bowl" jobs (*tie fan wan*) in state-owned and collective-owned enterprises.[15] Essentially, in Xinjiang as well as the rest of China, there was an institutional system of "organized dependence" (Walder, 1986) whereby the individual was tied to his or her work unit for life in exchange for secure employment irrespective of ethnicity. However, by the late 1980s and early 1990s after nearly a decade of market reforms, the job assignment system was abandoned. Individuals were subsequently urged to create jobs for themselves and seek employment in an emerging private sector. In fact, as noted earlier, most new acts of hiring in Xinjiang now occur in the private sector, rendering government preferential policies too weak to control occupational stratification (see Iredale et al., 2001 for further discussion). A 2001 high-level investigation report of the Xinjiang CPC Committee candidly disclosed that

> the strategy of choosing from both sides [Han and Uyghurs] in hiring has been challenged following the establishment and perfecting of the market economic system…the power of intervention of the government has continuously decreased…and the difficulty of finding a job for minority labourers have become bigger…and implementing equal opportunities measures have become less practicable… (Quoted in Becquelin, 2004: 375)

Both Hans and Muslim Uyghurs rely on group networks, particularly strong ties (relatives, distant family or close friends), for information on job openings (see Ma and Xiang, 1998; Hasmath, 2011). Specifically, native-place or local-origin networks are in operation.[16] In effect, such networks embed labor

---

15 Although the state provided secure employment for one's working life, it was quite common for many to be severely underemployed both in SOEs and COEs. That is, there was an underutilization of labor on two fronts (1) an individual's high skills may not match their occupational tasks, which often occurred since the labor market did not clear using wage adjustments; and, (2) an overstaffing of employees at SOEs and COEs (see Hasmath, 2011).

16 That is, continuous social ties originally forged among Han or Muslim Uyghur members from their "home locality" carrying over to their "host locality."

market behavior to the degree that it ultimately produces sectoral group divisions. As demonstrated earlier in Table 5.4, Uyghurs have a tendency to skew towards low-status, low-paying positions particularly in the service sector while Hans occupy positions in high-wage-labor, capital-intensive industries. The internal group division may run deeper. For instance, many Uyghurs only conduct business with fellow Uyghurs and vice versa (see Gilley, 2001). Unfortunately, such behavior significantly reduces both sides' incomes, and unequally affects Uyghurs in a worst-off manner, given the tendency for the group to be in lower status and lower paying occupations. Suffice to say, the partitioning of the political economy as a result of loosened market forces and migration patterns creates spatial divisions. Uyghurs reside in relatively closed ethnic communities and on the whole only interact with Han in the economic sphere (see Cao, 2010 for further discussion). Their living conditions are also poorer than those of Han as a result of earning lower incomes and paying lower rents.

Two classic sociological theories may provide guidance in further analyzing this situation. Split labor market theory argues that ethnic antagonism emerges when two or more ethnoracially distinct groups of workers compete for the same jobs. Job competition thus leads to friction between, and hence the political crystallization of, a particular group (see Bonacich, 1972; Wilson, 1980). Conversely, labor segmentation theory can potentially illustrate capital's exploitation of ethnic group divisions for economic gain (see Reich et al., 1973). Contrary to neoclassical economic theories that suggest the existence of a unified market for labor whereby varying wages and occupational outcomes arise from individual differences in human capital, labor market segmentation theory points out that the labor market is not perfect. Institutions such as professional associations, unions or government agencies may interfere to produce varying results for workers with the same human capital.

An argument can be held using both theories that within China's transitional economy, social actors negotiate the antagonism between planned and market economy through the use of social capital to obtain employment. As urbanization continues apace in Xinjiang, market relations are precipitating an urban sectoral division of labor. Consequently, despite the counterclaims of an internal Han colonialism, affirmative action state policy is becoming ineffective in controlling occupational stratification – skewing high-status, high-wage positions for Han dominance. Since occupational stratification in the case of urban Xinjiang does involve competition between Hans and Muslim Uyghurs to the exclusion of one group from the rewards of material development, there is a strong potential for increased intergroup tension. In short, the current labor market processes – involving agency (social capital, labor movement) and structure (market and reforming socialist institutions) – are shaping a split and segmented labor market in Xinjiang, which in the case of Muslim Uyghurs mainly contributes to heightened ethnoreligious consciousness. Instances such as the Gulja Incident or the riots in July 2009 are a manifestation and expression of an acute ethnoreligious consciousness stemming from Muslim Uyghurs current economic reality.

Conclusion

The consequences of heightened ethnoreligious consciousness created by a split and segmented labor market can be understood in twofold. The first treats the Muslim Uyghur situation in Xinjiang as a struggle between the dominant state and the oppressed minority group. The second attributes group conflict to intense competition for resources, educational and labor market opportunities. As Schein (2000) notes, the Chinese state is often conceived of as much stronger than society. Under this guise, minority nationality issues are often treated as identity struggles in which the state is usually conflated with the Han majority and minorities with "civil society." The material dimensions of conflict, while recognized, are attributed to the colonizing intentions or inadequacies of the state (see Moneyhon, 2004). Everyday social processes such as discrimination, ethnic divisions of labor and migration are given short shrift. This chapter has sought to go beyond the common people versus the state model through which center-periphery relations in China are often conceived.

Instead, the chapter has contended that the political economy is the context within which to understand the new urban formations of post-reform China. Institutional changes have loosened peasants from their enforced tie to the land of their birth and given freer rein to private enterprises in spite the continuation of the *hukou* system. This has brought about migration to cities of burgeoning numbers of Han and Uyghurs. Amid such threatening developments, migrants rely upon their group or hometown connections to gain an entry on urban life. Social processes like invidious discrimination and exploitation of laborers have greater range of movement within such a structure. They therefore sharpen divisions of labor and capital, perpetuating sociocultural segregation in the urban milieu. As the chapter suggests, intergroup tension and a rise of ethnoreligious consciousness in the case of Muslim Uyghurs ensue as the group's job options are limited to low-status and low-paying positions.

One cannot escape the idea that tensions between Muslim Uyghurs and Han Chinese is not simply a reaction against the state. On the one hand, Muslim Uyghur resentment is directed at what is perceived to be a largely Han state – indeed Han cadres outnumber minority cadres in Xinjiang. On the other hand, underlying tensions are reproduced by unregulated labor markets and the ensuing inter- and intragroup competition and living conditions under which Xinjiang's Uyghur poor subsist. A Uyghur muezzin who had fought in the "Three District Army" in 1944 framed his resentment this decade as such:

> The "Open Door" policy and "Develop the West" policy mean less work for Uyghurs. They are just abolishing the Uyghurs now. Even buildings (like my house) are not in the Uyghur style. All the market now is doing is letting more Hans come from *neidi* (inner land) and they're taking all the jobs. (Quoted in Millward and Tursun, 2004: 82)

Paradoxically, the same segregated and segmented labor markets bind Muslim Uyghurs together and arguably form part and parcel of the recent surge in Uyghur ethnoreligious consciousness.

Ironically, economic incentives continue to be one of the main tools Chinese authorities use to manage the Muslim Uyghur population, in spite of their poor economic performance in the labor market compared to Hans. The underlying idea behind authorities' strong belief in this strategy is that Muslim Uyghurs primarily want a comfortable economic life for themselves and their offspring – a reasonable premise for any group. However, complications arise – in spite of improved labor market performances among Uyghurs since market reforms – as this reality has not come to pass when using Han experiences as a gauge for success, which the majority of Muslim Uyghurs seemingly use as a yardstick. Muslim Uyghurs continue to watch the better paying jobs go to Han Chinese while the more labor-intensive, poorer paying positions are given to Uyghurs. Until this situation has been corrected in the labor market, Uyghur ethnoreligious consciousness will be acute and Muslim Uyghur-Han Chinese conflict will continue to play a significant role in the history of Xinjiang.

References

Becquelin, Nicolas. 2004. "Staged Development in Xinjiang." *China Quarterly* 178: 358–78.

Beller-Hann, Ildiko. 1997. "The Peasant Condition in Xinjiang." *Journal of Peasant Studies* 24.4: 87–112.

Bonacich, Edna. 1972. "A Theory of Ethnic Antagonism: The Split Labor Market." *American Sociological Review* 37.5: 547–59.

Cao, Huhua. 2010. "Urban-Rural Income Disparity and Urbanization: What is the Role of Spatial Distribution of Ethnic Groups? A Case Study of Xinjiang Uygur Autonomous Region in Western China." *Regional Studies* 44.8: 965–82.

Chan, Kam Wing. 2009. "The Chinese Hukou System at 50." *Eurasian Geography and Economics* 50.2: 197–221.

Clarke, Michael. 2010. "Widening the Net: China's Anti-Terror Laws and Human Rights in the Xinjiang Autonomous Region." *International Journal of Human Rights* 14.4: 542–58.

Dreyer, June Tuefel. 2000. "Ethnicity and Economic Development in Xinjiang." *Inner Asia* 2.2: 137–54.

Finley, Joanne Smith. 2007. "Chinese Oppression in Xinjiang, Middle Eastern Conflicts and Global Islamic Solidarities Among the Uyghurs." *Journal of Contemporary China* 16.53: 627–54.

Fuller, Graham. E. and Jonathan N. Lipman. 2004. "Islam in Xinjiang." In S. Frederick Starr (ed.), *Xinjiang: China's Muslim Borderland*, 320–52. Armonk, NY: M. E. Sharpe.

Gaubatz, Piper Rae. 1996. *Beyond the Great Wall: Urban Form and Transformation on the Chinese Frontiers*. Palo Alto, CA: Stanford University Press.

Gilley, Bruce. 2001. "Uighurs Need Not Apply." *Far Eastern Economic Review*. 23 August.

Gladney, Dru. 1996. "Relational Alterity: Constructing Dungan (Hui), Uyghur, and Kazakh Identities Across Asia, Central Asia, and Turkey." *History and Anthropology* 9.4: 445–77.

Hasmath, Reza. 2011. "From Job Search to Hiring to Advancement: The Labor Market Experiences of Ethnic Minorities in Beijing." *International Labor Review* 150.1: 189–201.

Hasmath, Reza and Jennifer Hsu. 2007. "Social Development in the Tibet Autonomous Region: A Contemporary and Historical Analysis." *International Journal of Development Issues* 6.2: 125–41.

Hao, Yan, Geng Ruibin and Yuan Ye. 2009. "Xinjiang Riot Hits Regional Anti-Terror Nerve." Xinhua, 18 July. Online at: http://news.xinhuanet.com/english/2009-07/18/content_11727782.htm (accessed 22 June 2011).

Information Office of the State Council of the People's Republic of China. 2000. "Fifty Years of Progress in China's Human Rights." *Beijing Review* 43.9. Online at: http://www.china.org.cn/e-white/3/index.htm (accessed 25 August 2011).

Iredale, Robyn, Naran Bilik, Wang Su, Fei Guo and Caroline Hoy. 2001. *Contemporary Minority Migration, Education and Ethnicity in China*. Cheltenham and Northampton: Edward Elgar Publishing.

Ma, Laurence and Xiang Biao. 1998. "Native Place, Migration and the Emergence of Peasant Enclaves in Beijing." *China Quarterly* 155: 546–81.

Ma, Rong. 2001. *Ethnicity and Social Development*. Beijing: Minzu Press.

Mackerras, Colin. 2004. "Ethnicity in China: The Case of Xinjiang." *Harvard Asia Quarterly* 8: 1.

Millward, James. A. and Tursun Nabijan. 2004. "Political History and Strategies of Control, 1884–1978." In S. Frederick Starr (ed.), *Xinjiang: China's Muslim Borderland*, 63–98. Armonk, NY: M. E. Sharpe.

Mittenhal, L. 2002. "Inter-Ethnic Strife Prompts Review of Migration Policies." *China News Digest*, 19 January 2002. Online at: http://www.hartford-hwp.com/archives/55/343.html (accessed 22 June 2011).

Moneyhon, Mathew D. 2004. "Taming China's 'Wild West': Ethnic Conflict in Xinjiang." *Peace, Conflict, and Development: An Interdisciplinary Journal* 5.5: 2–23.

National Bureau of Statistics and Ethnic Affairs Commission (NBS/EAC). 2003. *Tabulation on Nationalities of 2000 Population Census of China, Vols 1 and 2*. Beijing: The Ethnic Publishing House.

Pannell, Clifton W. and Laurence J. C. Ma. 1997. "Urban Transition and Interstate Relations in a Dynamic Post-Soviet Borderland: The Xinjiang Uyghur Autonomous Region of China." *Post-Soviet Geography and Economics* 38.4: 206–29.

Reich, Michael, David Gordon and Richard Edwards. 1973. "A Theory of Labor Market Segmentation." *American Economic Review* 63: 359–65.

Sautman, Barry. 2000. "Is Xinjiang an Internal Colony?" *Inner Asia* 2.2: 239–71.

Schein, Louisa. 2000. *Minority Rules: The Miao and the Feminine in China's Cultural Politics*. Durham, NC: Duke University Press.

Seymour, James D. 2000. "Xinjiang's Production and Construction Corps, and the Sinification of Eastern Turkestan." *Inner Asia* 2.2: 171–93.

Smith, Joanne N. 2002. "'Making Culture Matter': Symbolic, Spatial and Social Boundaries Between Uyghurs and Han Chinese." *Asian Ethnicity* 3.2: 153–74.

Van Wie Davs, Elizabeth. 2008. "Uyghur Muslim Ethnic Separatism in Xinjiang, China." *Asian Affairs: An American Review* 35.1: 15–30.

Vicziany, Marika and Guibin Zhang. 2004. "The Rise of the Private Sector in Xinjiang: Han and Uyghur Entrepreneurship." In Robert Cribb (ed.), *Asia Examined: Proceedings of the 15th Biennial Conference of the ASAA*. Canberra: Asian Studies Association of Australia (ASAA). Online at: http://coombs.anu.edu.au/SpecialProj/ASAA/biennial-conference/2004/Vicziany+Zhang-ASAA2004.pdf (accessed 22 June 2011).

Walder, Andrew G. 1986. *Communist Neo-Traditionalism: Work and Authority in Chinese Industry*. Berkeley, CA: University of California Press.

Wiemer, Calla. 2004. "The Economy of Xinjiang." In S. Frederick Starr (ed.), *Xinjiang: China's Muslim Borderland*, 163–89. New York: M. E. Sharpe.

Wilson, William J. 1980. *The Declining Significance of Race*. Chicago: University of Chicago Press.

Wong, Edward. 2009. "Clashes in China Shed Light on Ethnic Divide." *New York Times*, 7 July 2009. Online at: http://www.nytimes.com/2009/07/08/world/asia/08china.html?partner=rss&emc=rss (accessed 22 June 2011).

Xinjiang Population Census 2000. 2002. Urumqi: People's Publisher.

Xinjiang Statistical Yearbook, 1991. 1992. Beijing: China Statistics Press.

Xinjiang Statistical Yearbook, 1996. 1997. Beijing: China Statistics Press.

Xinjiang Statistical Yearbook, 2001. 2001. Beijing: China Statistics Press.

Chapter 6

THE TENSION BETWEEN STATE AND RELIGION IN AMERICAN FOREIGN POLICY

Douglas Porpora

Drexel University, Philadelphia

This chapter calls attention to four post-9/11 episodes involving religion and United States foreign policy in an attempt to show the need for greater nuance in our understanding of the relation between religion and state. A number of observations will be drawn from these four cases. For example, it will be seen that at least in the United States, religion is neither entirely privatized nor entirely commodified and that traditional organized religion continues to pack a counterhegemonic punch. However, it will further be seen that this counterhegemonic face of religion finds only little voice in the American public sphere, which remains more open to conservative and – in the current case – imperial deployments of religion. It thus also becomes clear from the cases exhibited that how religion surfaces in the public sphere is not simply an inexorable effect of modernity but rather the result of contestation (see the contributions in Smith, 2003 for a similar line of argument based on other cases). Finally, in the cases under consideration here, there is a stark indication of what may be lost when we lose religion entirely from the public sphere: the loss also of a distinctly moral appraisal of state matters that properly should be appraised morally. Thus, for all the unhelpful moralism traditional religion brings to politics, it may also be that when the public square is entirely naked religiously (Neuhaus, 1986), it ends up morally naked as well.

The Privatization and Commodification of Religion

In all four of the cases to be considered, the backdrop is the privatization and commodification of religion. Although arguably the privatization and commodification of religion are two analytically separate phenomena, they are sometimes viewed together, with the commodification of religion regarded as a consequence of religion's privatization. Both together are sometimes presumed to be the fallout of a worldwide, historical trend toward secularization.

The secularization thesis is the idea going back at least to Weber (1946) that with modernity, the world is becoming increasingly "disenchanted," less oriented toward otherworldly explanations, forces and values. In this sense, secularization refers to the diminution of a religious mentality or what the French *Annales* School would call a *mentalité* (Swatos and Christiano, 1999).

It is not, however, just a religious mentality that is considered to be lost with secularization but also the sway or provenance of religion over society at large. It was Parsons (1977) who argued that with increasing modernity, society becomes increasingly differentiated so that many aspects of public life – like politics and the economy – become ever more detached from religion. Instead, religious governance retreats to private life (Berger, 1967; Luckmann, 1967, 1996, 1997). This retreat of religion to the private sphere is what is meant by the privatization of religion. Religion no longer governs communal matters in the public sphere but becomes a private matter, characterized, as Luckmann puts it, by syncretism, low levels of transcendence and a "commercialized, cultic milieu."

> The new, basically de-institutionalized privatized social form of religion seemed to be relying on an open market of diffuse, syncretistic packages of meaning, typically connected to low levels of transcendence and produced in a partly or fully commercialized cultic milieu. The new situation permitted, even encouraged individual bricolage. Relying for its essential legitimations upon the modern myth of the autonomous individual, it had a pronounced elective affinity for the sacralization of subjectivisms. (Luckmann, 1996: 73)

For Luckmann, then, the privatization of religion coincides with greater subjectivism on the religious front. People individually and syncretistically put together their own religions, much like Sheila in *Habits of the Heart* (Bellah et al., 1984). That subjectivism in turn seems to encourage cliental forms of religion organized around "minor charismatics, commercialized enterprises in astrology, the consciousness-expanding line and the like" (Luckmann, 1996: 73). Thus, along with the privatization of religion, we get a commodification of religion organized around an ethic of self-fulfillment. Like Zizek (2009) after him, Luckmann is particularly critical of the consumerist tendencies within the New Age movement.

The New Age movement lays stress on the spiritual development of each individual. Sometimes it revives elements of older religious traditions that were canonized and that it interprets in unorthodox (often far-fetched) ways. It collects abundant psychological, therapeutic, magic, marginally scientific and older esoteric materials, repackages them, and offers them for individual consumption and further private syncretism. . . This allows for the formation of commercially exploitable cultic milieu. (Luckmann, 1996: 75)

Missing, Luckmann argues, from religious forms organized around individual self-fulfillment is both a moral purview greater than the individual self and commonly accepted ways of addressing macro-social matters of a moral nature. In effect, morality, too, like religion becomes privatized.

The institutionalization of rules of conduct, enforceable by the apparatus of the public agents of an (increasingly secular) political system, legalized but potentially also de-moralized these rules ("norms"). The "upper reaches" of morals, those which legitimated the meaning of the rules of conduct by reference to a transcendent universe, remained in close attachment to the sacred universes and mundane institutions of religion. In the long process of functional differentiation of the political, legal and economic functions of social life, religious institutions too were increasingly defined as their special function, the individual soul in its relation to a sacred level of reality. The social reach and influence of religious institutions began to shrink, and so did the social reach and influence of the legitimatory level of morals. (Luckmann, 1996: 79)

As Luckmann describes this process, it all seems rather inexorable. That judgment, however, is too hasty. For all her privatized, syncretistic religion, even the eponymous Sheila of *Habits* lives by a code that is deeply moral (see McGuire's 2008 defence of Sheilaism). Similarly, here in this chapter, we will observe more complexity across the terrain of United States foreign policy debate. To be sure, we will see the contraction of religion's social reach and the *demoralization* it leaves behind. Contrariwise, however, we will see two counterphenomena. First, for better or worse, religion remains an important resource for American political integration that continues to rally Americans in such times as war. Second, the very demoralization of politics left in religion's wake is made more visible by the contrastingly strong moral critiques of hegemonic politics emanating from the still far from dead organized religions in America. Finally, in these and other ways we will see that the privatization of religion is not an inexorable product of social forces but contested by active agents.

Four Post-9/11 Cases of Religion and the American State in International Politics

The first episode begins immediately with 9/11. It is former president George W. Bush's explicit use of religious language to frame the war on terror and eventually the attack on Iraq.

Such use of religious language may come as no surprise. It exemplifies what many believe is the problem that results when religion intrudes into politics, and it seems to befit the image of America as the religiously exceptional place it is – at least in comparison with a more secularized Europe and Australia.

However, the conventional image of religious America misunderstands the place of religion in America and overstates it. And we must beware of drawing too totalizing a view of religion's role in politics from George Bush's use of it. Instead, in the second and third episodes to be recounted, we will observe religion in a counterhegemonic role.

The second episode is how the American public sphere went on to debate the post-9/11 attack on Iraq. In that discussion, we observe how moral considerations seem to be limited to religious sources, illustrating the privatization of morality that accompanies the privatization of religion but also the persistence in America of an organized religious sphere that escapes privatization and commercialization.

The third episode is the discussion in the American public sphere following the revelations about Abu Ghraib. In this extreme case, the secular American public sphere did voice more moral content, but it was still subdued in comparison with official religious reaction and very mixed with the logic of instrumental rationality.

Together, the second and third episodes suggest the problem at the macro-level when religion becomes privatized. With the privatization of morality that accompanies the privatization of religion, society seems to lose the ability to deliberate morally about matters that actually are moral in nature. Although at the micro-level one need not be religious in order to be moral, the evidence here suggests otherwise at the macro-level.

The final episode is the flap during the 2008 presidential election over candidate Barack Obama's pastor, Reverend Jeremiah Wright. It is a case in which what was again a largely secularized American public sphere confronted a form of religion it could not grasp, one not interpretable as a private lifestyle, namely, an African American liberationist form of religion that packed a highly critical, political edge. It exemplifies something to which Bryan Turner refers, namely the disciplining of religion into something politically safe and anemic, although carried out by the media rather than government. In Foucauldian language, it was an exercise in *governmentality* (see Burchell et al., 1991).

The Response of the Bush Administration to 9/11

We begin with President Bush's response to the 9/11 attacks. That response must be understood against the backdrop of political realism, which dominates elite opinion both in the academy and government, not just internationally but even in the United States (Hollis and Smith, 1990).

Realism is a kind of liberal, secular, enlightenment view, according to which it is virtually a moral principle to exclude moral principles from the conduct or analysis of foreign affairs. Instead, each nation is to pursue its own self-interest without couching those pursuits within a larger cosmic framework. Often, of course, when faced with the task of rallying their nations against external threats, political leaders do resort to grander language. Within the cosmopolitan West, however, including the United States, the strong tradition of political realism has generally held such rhetoric in check. Thus, realism in effect ideologically enforces the differentiation between politics on the one hand and religion and morality on the other.

Knowledge of this realist background is required to understand the audacity and offense of Bush's declaration to the West Point cadets in his June 2002 address to them: "And America will call evil by its name." This declaration repudiated – consciously and deliberately so – the entire Western, cosmopolitan, political culture of realism. It was the return of good and, especially, evil in Bush's language that was simultaneously a scandal to European and American liberals and an inspiration to the neoconservatives in America that Ronald Reagan had left behind.

From the beginning, Bush framed the 9/11 attacks and the American response to them in mythic terms. In the opening remarks of his 9/11 speech, Bush observed that "our way of life, our very freedom" had come under attack. Yet, just moments later, Bush explained that it was not only the *American* way of life and *American* freedom that had been attacked. Instead, according to Bush, "America was targeted for attack because we [Americans] are the brightest beacon for freedom and opportunity in the world." Attacked in other words was not just America and American freedom but what America stands for – freedom itself.

Bush's remark might be dismissed as the usual bombast of American exceptionalism, except that it is bombast Americans believe and that such bombast accordingly functioned – at least for the American listener – to elevate the 9/11 attacks and the American response to a mythic register.

In particular, Bush's remarks presume – and invite his American listeners to remember that they too presume – that unlike any other country, America is iconic. America stands for something. America, in the American mind, stands for freedom. It is as if America is itself the very incarnation of freedom in the world, a light shining into what otherwise would be darkness. It follows that any attack on America is necessarily lifted to a sacred plane. Thus, by the end of the 9/11 speech, the segue is complete and Bush is able to usher his listeners forward to defend not just America but "freedom and all that is good and just in our world."

As in his remarks to the cadets at West Point, Bush's post-9/11 speeches continued to invoke the language of good and evil. For example, the language again surfaced in Bush's 2002 State of the Union Address, where the world first learned of "an axis of evil." Evil now was no longer just shadowy. Evil, we now learned, also had a place – or places – where it materialized and took shape, where it could more easily be targeted for attack. And Iraq, of course, would subsequently become that target.

It was not always the binary opposition between good and evil that Bush invoked. At other times, the opposing forces represented on the one side "civilization," "order," "freedom" and "law," with "tyranny," "terror," "fear" and "chaos" on the other side. Always, however, the struggle was depicted as Manichean and apocalyptic.

It was not just religious *rhetoric* that was operative here. Behind it, within the neoconservative sector of the Bush administration, there was also a genuine *religious worldview* of an imperialistic nature. As John McCain put it in one of his debates with Barack Obama, "America is the greatest force for good in the world." That viewpoint was certainly held by the neoconservatives in Bush's cabinet, who let it be known early on that "this force for good" would no longer be stymied by the putative laws or norms of what Condoleezza Rice (2000) called an "illusory international community." Consequently, within the Bush administration there was not only a willingness but even an outright eagerness to wage war unilaterally without United Nations authorization. The attack on Iraq was actually to be the first step in which the world's only remaining superpower consolidated what was to be a "new American Century," that is, a new world order in which not the United Nations but America and American goodness would preside (see Kagan et al., 2000).

The rhetoric invoked by Bush arguably represents the kind of civil religion described by Bellah (1967). It is religion nonetheless, functioning as functionalists thought religion should function in the public sphere – to bind a society around common courses of action. The persistence of this form accordingly seems to indicate a continuing need – at least in America – for the kind of integration nonprivatized religion is ideally suited to supply.

The Debate about Iraq

The moral rhetoric expressed by the *Project for a New American Century* might have been anathema to political realist sensibility but the objective was not, at least once purged of religious sentiment. According to realism, nations should pursue their national interests, conceptualized especially in terms of power. Thus, if the world's only remaining superpower had the chance to establish its hegemony over the world, why should that superpower have forgone it? There might have been normative (i.e. legal or moral) reasons why not, but for realism, legal and moral considerations do not signify. Thus, it was perhaps no aberration that the attack on Iraq drew the support of arch-realist Henry Kissinger.

What should be the response when a nation, in this case the world's only superpower, proposes to attack another sovereign nation without provocation and in defiance of international law? At the time, the attack was condemned worldwide, but on what grounds? It was illegal, but if it could do otherwise, why should a superpower accede to legality? Why not just return the answer the Athenians gave the Melians during the Peloponnesian War: "The strong do what they can, and the weak suffer what they must" (Thucydides, 2009).

Ultimately, the only answer to Athenian realism is a moral one and it is important to know what remains today of moral discourse about such macro-moral matters. To find out how the American public sphere morally debated the proposed attack on Iraq is something my colleagues and I set out to determine. How did an exceptionally religious and moralistic nation debate as morally grave a matter as preemptive war?

To investigate the question, we looked at multiple sectors of the American public sphere, among them the internet and the opinion pages of newspapers and news magazines. We looked specifically at the period between 15 August and 15 October 2002. These two months were pivotal. Late August was when the Bush administration abandoned months of dark hints and finally admitted publicly that it sought to replace Saddam Hussein, by force if necessary. Mid-October was when the United States Congress formally authorized Bush to do so. The public debate in between was thus particularly consequential.

One part of our study (e.g. see Nikolaev and Porpora, 2007) examined all the 500 opinion pieces written during this period in 26 newspapers and news magazines that employed the words "Iraq" and "war." The 26 sources we examined spanned the political spectrum from left to right, including the six elite publications, the *New York Times*, the *Washington Post*, the *Christian Science Monitor*, the *Wall Street Journal*, *Time Magazine* and *Newsweek*.

We looked not just at secular publications but at religious ones as well. Only one of the conservative religious publications we examined, *Christianity Today*, commented on the war during this period. On the left, however, there were three: the Jewish *Tikkun*, the Protestant *Christian Century*, and the Catholic *Commonweal*.

Our unit of analysis was the individual opinion piece, and we coded each at both a macro- and micro-level, the macro-level referring to the piece as a whole and the micro-level to discrete argumentative points raised within (see Van Dijk, 1985 for the distinction). At the macro-level, we coded for the piece's orientation toward war (for, against or neutral) and whether or not its argument overall was moral in nature.

Aside from the argument type as a whole, we also coded the more specific, micro-level argumentative points that might be raised in the course of a piece. In all, we identified 56 such points. Over half of the pieces contained at least two. These included the widely cited points raised by the Bush administration: That Saddam had weapons of mass destruction, that Saddam was evil, etc. Counterpoints often raised were that the United States had other options besides war or that hostilities with Iraq would distract the United States from the war on terrorism. A common worry, quite prescient as it turned out, was that the Bush administration did not have adequate postwar plans.

Basically, coding was done by having a graduate student read through the pieces and mark an X next to a checklist of the 56 points if and when one appeared in a text. To prepare the student to do so, we went over the codes and then practiced on a sample. To insure interrater reliability, we examined consistency among a random sample of 50 pieces in the corpus, co-coded by two different readers.

At the macro-level, reliability was 86 percent for whether or not a piece was for or against the war and 98 percent for whether or not the overall argument was moral in nature. Reliability was also generally high in percentage terms at the micro-level, with only one of the 56 points falling below 80 percent. Besides percent agreement, we also calculated reliability controlling for chance using Krippendorf's α. Because of the way most of the variables were distributed – i.e. highly skewed with few occurrences of each – reliability controlling for chance often dropped. For the majority, however, α remained above 5.0, and we did not do any analysis with points having reliability below $\alpha = 4.0$, which for such data is considered at least fair (see Neuendorf, 2002).

A number of interesting patterns surfaced in our study. For example, the power of the presidency to set the agenda of debate is very evident. Thus, across the board almost half the pieces referenced the Bush administration's rationales for war: weapons of mass destruction, Saddam's ties to terrorism, the brutality of his regime and Saddam's general embodiment of evil. These concerns often had to be addressed even by pieces opposed to war (on agenda setting, see Lukes, 2004).

Of more direct relevance to this volume was the almost complete marginalization of specifically moral reasoning to the periphery – both left and right – and particularly to religious outlets. It was almost as if a religiously naked public square was required to be morally naked as well. At the elite center of debate, a privatization of morality did seem to follow the privatization of religion.

Overall, across the spectrum, fewer than 20 percent of pieces made arguments for or against war that were as a whole moral or legal in nature. In the elite press, these were most frequent in the right leaning opinion pages of the *Wall Street Journal* and least frequently in the *New York Times* (10 percent). A majority of these pieces were pro-war, with only about 6 percent offering principled moral or legal arguments against war.

Against war, micro-points of principle, that is, legal or moral points, were sparse in the elite press. The war's immorality, for example, was suggested by only 2 out of 239 pieces in the elite press and not at all by the secular left. In contrast, among the 12 pieces in the publications of the religious left, 4 – or one third – declared outright that the proposed attack would be immoral (a statistically significant result; in fact, despite the small number of religious cases, the effect sizes were all sufficiently large that all differences were statistically significant at the 0.05 level or, often, well below).

That without United Nations authorization the proposed attack would be internationally *illegal* was mentioned by Only 3 percent of the pieces in the elite press and only a little over 10 percent of the pieces in the mainstream press beyond the elite organs. The 24 pieces in the secular left totally ignored the point. In contrast, it was again predominantly in the religious press that the matter of international legality found a hearing, mentioned by a full third of the pieces.

Again, in four out of 12 opinion pieces in the religious press, it was pointed out that as an attack on Iraq would be unprovoked, it would be an aggressive action. The aggressiveness of the action was likewise pointed out by four pieces in the elite press. But in the elite press, that would be four out 239 pieces. Again, the effect size of this difference is highly significant statistically.

Forty-two percent of the religious pieces worried about the danger to Iraqi civilians. Here, the religious left was joined by the secular left, which also mentioned the danger in 22 percent of its 24 pieces. In contrast, concern for Iraqi civilians was cited by only 7 percent of the pieces in the elite press.

The most comprehensive framework for the moral evaluation of armed conflict is the Just War Theory (JWT). Although it goes back to Roman thought, it reached its fullest development in Roman Catholic theology, where a distinction was made between *Jus ad Bellum* – the just or moral reasons for going to war – and *Jus in Bellum*, which concerns the moral conduct of war. It was used by Francesca de Vittoria, for example, to condemn the Spanish conquest of America. According to the *Jus ad Bellum* criteria, a war is justly waged only if, among other things, it is a last resort; done for a just cause, most particularly self-defense from an external attack; and right intention, which is only for the sake of the just cause rather than ulterior motives such as material gain.

Today, because it brings together coherently so many of the moral factors that bear on the justice of warfare, JWT has become the main way to judge the ethics of warfare even among secular theorists (see, for example, Walzer, 2000). It is thus another measure of the privatization of morality how rarely JWT surfaced in the debate outside of religious sources. Consider for a moment the debate in online discussion groups. Between August and October 2002, the period of study, online discussion groups hosted some 57,000 threads on the prospective attack on Iraq. In that corpus, the phrase *just war* appeared just 200 times and JWT itself only 20 – mostly in religious forums.

Back on the opinion pages of the press, JWT was cited by 67 percent of the pieces in the religious publications, including the Jewish *Tikkun* and in the conservative *Christianity Today*. Almost all the pieces citing JWT considered the proposed attack unethical, 42 percent of the religious pieces overall.

Again, however, outside of the religious press, JWT was hardly mentioned – in the elite press by only 1 percent of the pieces. Again, it might be objected that JWT is an intrinsically religious approach unfamiliar to many. But what then is the alternative? Secular, *communitarian* arguments about traditional American values were hardly mentioned either (on communitarianism, see, for example, Etzioni, 2004). The point here is that whatever moral considerations one might imagine in connection with the attack on Iraq, they were marginalized in the American public sphere to the right and left but mostly to the religious sphere. It was mostly the religious sphere in other words that carried on national self-critique of a specifically moral nature. The mainstream and particularly elite press focused on pragmatics: Would this venture be another Vietnam, would it exacerbate terrorism?

Although there is little space to go into it, the marginalization of morality was not simply quantitative. It was qualitative as well. In the form of arguments made in the mainstream and particularly elite press, a definite *moral muting* could be observed (see Porpora and Nikolaev, 2008).

In fact, at the center of the secular American public sphere, moral arguments were frequently disguised as prudential arguments as if there were embarrassment or unease about straight-out moral argument. On close reading, for example, if American mainstream pundits commended morality and legality, they were careful to do so not as ends in themselves but more as instrumental means to maintain America's good image or moral authority. John Kerry was a master of this technique:

> For the American people to accept the legitimacy of this conflict and give their consent to it, the Bush administration must first present detailed evidence of the threat of Iraq's weapons of mass destruction and then prove that all other avenues of protecting our nation's security interests have been exhausted. Exhaustion of remedies is critical to winning the consent of a civilized people in the decision to go to war. And consent, as we have learned before, is essential to carrying out the mission... Legitimacy in the conduct of war, among our people, and our allies, is not a waste of time, but an essential foundation of success. (Kerry, 2002)

On one, perhaps the most natural reading, Kerry is offering moral counsel; he is detailing the moral criteria that would make for a legitimate war. He speaks in moralistic language of "legitimacy" and the demands of "civilization" and of "a civilized people." Even the notion of "consent" has moral weight.

Kerry's logic, however, is actually prudential, for he *instrumentalizes* the moral criteria he cites. What Kerry technically argues is that the administration should observe moral standards not for the sake of what is right or good but in order to gain the consent of the American people. It is significant perhaps that Kerry speaks twice of what has "legitimacy" as opposed to what is "legitimate," lexically suggesting almost that for the purposes of "winning... consent," appearance matters more than reality. Consent then itself also is *instrumentalized*. It too is not to be pursued as a moral end in itself but, rather, because it is the means to an end, mission success. Logically, mission success is the ultimate goal with legitimacy and consent demoted to instrumental goals. Although a strong aura of moral counsel remains, through *instrumentalization* morality has actually been subordinated to prudence.

Is it Kerry's belief that naked moral argument is unseemly in the American public sphere, or just less compelling than argument based on national self-interest? Either way, the prevalence of such form bespeaks a public sphere in which moral discourse has lost its standing.

In the secular mainstream, the moral muting took other forms as well, particularly the form linguists call *mitigation* or downgrading. In one such instance of mitigation, an obligatory moral requirement was downgraded by reframing it as an optional matter of mere prudence. Specifically, in opposition to the war, the American elite press clamored not for United Nations *approval* but rather for international *support*, approval being a legal requirement and support merely a contingency of prudence.

Commentary on the Abu Ghraib Scandal

The secular American public sphere seems not completely closed to moral consideration of macro-moral issues. However, it took the revelations of torture at Abu Ghraib to elicit specifically moral outrage, the *Washington Post* calling the interrogation techniques "shocking" and "reprehensible" and the *New York Times* describing them as "horrific," "inhumane" or at least "morally dubious."

However, in the case of Abu Ghraib as well the elite press tended to subordinate morality to self-interest. Thus, in several editorials, the *Times'* emphasis was on Abu Ghraib as "a gratuitous propaganda victory" for America's enemies. Similarly, David Ignatius in the *Post* worried that the war was "unraveling in ways that could harm America's interests for a generation." For example, consider more closely the following argument against torture offered by Eugene Robinson in the *Washington Post*:

> Look at the big picture: This is a wholesale trashing of our own ideals, an abandonment of the rule of law. It's already a huge scandal in the rest of the world, undoubtedly creating more enemies of the United States than it has taken out of circulation. And it was the White House that set this policy, not a bunch of poorly trained reservists at Abu Ghraib. (Robinson, 2005)

Robinson's piece seems morally hard hitting. In referring to our ideals, Robinson makes a moral *communitarian* argument. He then goes on to cite a legal argument. Yet what is striking about the argument and what it shares with many such arguments in the elite press is the way it fails to rest with a moral condemnation. Instead, Robinson ends the argument by appeal to prudential concerns – how the policy is a scandal creating rather than eliminating enemies for the United States. Coming at the end as it does, the prudential point assumes greater weight rhetorically than the moral points that preceded it. It is again as if Robinson does not fully trust a secularized American audience to respond to considerations that are purely moral, which again connotes a public sphere in which specifically moral discourse has lost its standing.

Contrast Robinson's mixed messages with the purely principled declarations of the religious opposition. "Torture is a moral issue," wrote the National Religious Campaign Against Torture (2006). "Nothing less is at stake in the torture abuse crisis than the soul of our nation." According to Rabbis for Human Rights (2006), "Jewish tradition teaches that human beings are created in God's image, and obliges us to protect human life and dignity." For their part, the United States Catholic Bishops (2007) specifically rejected "a morality based on the attitude that 'desperate times call for desperate measures' or 'the end justifies the means.'"

Again, it certainly ought not to be necessary to be religious in order to be moral, and the presence of some moral critique also in the secular left demonstrates as much. Further, many religious people in America, especially, it seems, Evangelicals and Catholics, are actually quite okay with torture (Gilgoff, 2009). At the macro-level, however, it was again from the religious sources that the strongest moral critiques consistently came.

The Flap Over Reverend Jeremiah Wright

As a number of pieces in this volume suggest, with the privatization of religion as far along as it is, religion largely functions as a private lifestyle choice. However, the privatization of religion is not entirely an inexorable result of modernization but the effect also of active agency. There are those who want to keep religion so safely contained in the private sphere (see Smith, 2003).

That agential containment of religion is what happened during the last United States presidential election in the case of Barack Obama's pastor, Reverend Jeremiah Wright. Briefly, while Obama was campaigning for the nomination of the Democratic Party, commentators on the conservative Fox News disclosed that the pastor of Obama's church was given to radical diatribes against America. On 16 September 2001, for example, the Sunday after 9/11, Jeremiah Wright told his congregation "We bombed Hiroshima, we bombed Nagasaki, and we nuked far more than the thousands in New York and the Pentagon, and we never batted an eye... The stuff we have done overseas is now brought right back to our own front yards. America's chickens are coming home to roost."

In another sermon, Wright objected to being asked to sing *God Bless America*. "No, no, no," he declaimed, "God damn America, that's in the Bible for killing innocent people. God damn America for treating our citizens as less than human. God damn America for as long as she acts like she is God and she is supreme."

Within the mainstream secular American public sphere, Wright's commentary was beyond the pale. For weeks, the media endlessly looped YouTube snippets featuring "God damn America" and "The chickens coming home to roost." Between 18 March and 15 June, the *Washington Post* published 29 articles featuring Jeremiah Wright – 22 news stories and 7 opinion pieces. From 19 March to 5 June, the *New York Times* published 24 news stories and 9 opinion pieces in which Wright is prominently mentioned (a total of 32 articles). In this corpus, these are the words used (in descending order of frequency) by journalists to describe Reverend Dr Jeremiah A. Wright, Jr, who holds master's degrees from Howard University and the University of Chicago Divinity School and a doctorate from United Theological Seminary: *incendiary*

(10), *controversial* (9), *racist* (9), *inflammatory* (4), *radical* (3), *provocative* (2), *explosive* (2), *anti-American* (2), *bombastic* (2), *paranoid* (2), *learned* (2). In part, white America, statelier in its religious practice, was unused to the more flamboyant African American style of preaching. In part as well, Reverend Wright could ham it up a bit on camera. At times, in fact, he even managed to turn the tables on his interviewers, interrogating them instead.

Mostly, however, what the media reflected was offense at the content of Wright's message. There was a perplexed offense at this kind of intrusion of religion into politics, a religious intrusion that castigated America. From the perspective of liberal, white opinion in America, Bush's invocation of religious language might have been in bad taste, but there nevertheless was widespread agreement even among liberals that, as John McCain put it, "America is the greatest force for good in the world."

Americans are prone to a kind of nation worship that might be considered idolatrous by all the so-called religions of the book: Judaism, Christianity and Islam. By the same token, Wright's prophetic critique of America was from the perspective of nation worship itself idolatrous. Accordingly, in the manner Foucault calls *governmentality*, Wright was ideologically disciplined and with Wright, incidentally, Barack Obama too. Thus, on 29 April 2008, Obama publicly repudiated his pastor.

Conclusion

The relation between religion and state reflects the state of religion at the current time. In America, the state of religion is complex, as is the relation between religion and the state. As is well known, in comparison with Western Europe, Australia and Japan, the United States is religiously exceptional. It is religiously exceptional in being still largely religious and being religious in complex ways. The majority of Americans say religion is important in their lives, and a large percentage at least report attending religious services regularly.

For all its religiosity, religion in the United States has not been immune to privatization. Yet, although the New Age and kindred movements have certainly made inroads within the United States as in Europe, religion in the United States has tended to be privatized in a more straightforwardly religious and less commodified way. A very great percentage of America's religious holds very theologically conservative views. Over 40 percent reject the concept of evolution in favor of a literal reading of the creation story in Genesis. The focus of such conservative religion is, as Luckmann suggests, the salvation in the next life of the individual soul. Although there is now evidence of profound change among the youngest cohort of Evangelicals (Sullivan, 2010), issues of social justice have not been on the Evangelical agenda.

The privatization of religion in America shows up clearly in public sphere debates. There, as in other industrialized countries, the norm is for discussion to be entirely secular. What is striking about such privatization, however, is an effect that has been little noted aside from Luckmann's discussion. Luckmann specifically suggests that one consequence of religious privatization will be a corresponding privatization of morality.

Up until now, Luckmann's prediction has received little attention and accordingly little empirical validation. In two of the cases examined here, however – the public sphere debate about Iraq and the commentary on the torture of prisoners at Abu Ghraib – a privatization of morality is clearly to be observed. If any state actions at all have a moral bearing, the list should certainly include unprovoked attack on another sovereign state and the torture or inhumane treatment of prisoners. In terms of JWT alone, the first is a flagrant violation of *Jus ad Bellum* criteria and the latter of criteria for *Jus in Bellum*. Yet in the entire secularized portion of discussion about these issues in the American public sphere, moral – or even legal – deliberation was sparse. And when there was moral commentary in the secularized portion of the debate, it was frequently muted or disguised as prudential commentary. If it matters that states direct themselves in moral ways, then such privatization of morality ought to be of significant concern.

The privatization of morality in secularized discussion of state behavior shows up more clearly when contrasted with the comparative density of moral commentary emanating from the religious sector. What also shows up thereby are the limits of religion's privatization. Put somewhat paradoxically, we might conclude that while society privatizes religion, not all religion is privatized. Indeed, even outside the examples examined here, America in particular is known for the intrusion of religion into public sphere debate. Usually, that intrusion is associated with right-wing religious sentiment, resisting, among other things, gay marriage, abortion and the teaching of evolution in public schools. Here as well in the example of Bush's war rhetoric, we could observe in America the remaining power of at least a dilute civil religion that takes something beyond a privatized commodified form.

It was, however, in the religious resistance to the American state's treatment of prisoners and its attack on Iraq that we saw something else. We saw in the first place continuing in the modern era a strong moral sensibility that is not privatized. More, insofar as that sensibility happens to have been a religious one, we saw, secondly, evidence that at least in America, there is an important strand of religion that has escaped privatization and commodification.

We could see as much in the controversy over Reverend Wright and again, something more. The liberation theology represented by Reverend Wright was again, neither privatized nor commodified. It was instead a strong, counterhegemonic commentary on the state. The "more" we saw in this case was that the exclusion from the public sphere of such commentary is not something necessarily impersonal and inexorable. On the contrary, it was effected by human agents, anxious to avoid any hint of national self-condemnation. The significance of such fact is that what human agency endeavors to exclude can also by human agency be reincluded. The future trajectory of religion thus remains indeterminate.

References

Bellah, Robert. 1967. "Civil Religion in America." *Daedalus* 96.1: 1–21.

Bellah, Robert, Richard Madsen, William M. Sullivan, Ann Swidler and Steven M. Tipton. 1985. *Habits of the Heart: Individualism and Commitment in American Life*. Berkeley, CA: University of California Press.

Berger, Peter. 1967. *The Sacred Canopy*. Garden City, NY: Doubleday.

Burchell, Graham, Colin Gordon and Peter Miller. 1991. *The Foucault Effect: Studies in Governmentality*. Chicago: University of Chicago Press.

Etzioni, Amitai. 2004. *The Communitarian Reader: Beyond the Essentials (Rights and Responses)*. New York: Rowman & Littlefield.

Gilgoff, Dan. 2009. "Poll: Most Evangelicals and Catholics Condone Torture in Some Instances." *US News and World Report*, 30 April 2009. Online at: http://www.usnews.com/blogs/god-and-country/2009/04/30/poll-most-evangelicals-and-catholics-condone-torture-in-some-instances.html (accessed 22 June 2011).

Hagemann, Julia, Alexander Nikolaev and Douglas Porpora. 2007. "Some Did Dare Call It Torture." Paper presented at the "Media, War and Conflict" conference in Milwaukee, WI, April 2007.

Hollis, Martin and Steven Smith. 1990. *Explaining and Understanding International Relations*. Oxford: Oxford University Press.

Jenkins, Alexander, Alexander Nikolaev and Douglas Porpora. 2008. "The USENET Debate on Iraq." Paper presented to the 2008 annual meeting of CITASA (American Sociological Association), Boston, and at meetings of the Eastern Sociological Society, Baltimore, MD.

Kagan, Donald, Gary Schmitt and Thomas Donnelly. 2000. *Rebuilding America's Defenses: Strategies, Forces, and Resources for a New Century*. New York: The Project for a New American Century.

Kerry, John F. 2002. "We Still Have a Choice on Iraq." *New York Times*, 6 September 2002, 23.

Lukes, Steven. 2004. *Power: A Radical View*. New York: Palgrave Macmillan.

Luckmann, Thomas. 1967. *The Invisible Religion*. New York: Macmillan.

_____. 1996. "The Privatization of Religion and Morality." In Paul Heelas, Scott Lash and Paul M. Morris (eds), *Detraditionalization: Critical Reflections on Authority and Identity*, 72–85. Oxford: Wiley-Blackwell.

_____. 1997. "The Moral Order of Modern Societies, Moral Communication and Indirect Moralizing." Paper delivered at Collegium Budapest, Institute for Advanced Study, Budapest, Hungary.

McGuire, Meredith B. 2008. *Lived Religion: Faith and Practice in Everyday Life*. New York: Oxford.

National Religious Campaign Against Torture. 2006. "Torture is a Moral Issue." Online at: http://www.educationforjustice.org/bin/view.fpl/1404/article/4993.html (accessed 10 April 2006 – registration required).

Neuendorf, Kimberly A. 2002. *The Content Analysis Guidebook*. Thousand Oaks, CA: SAGE.

Neuhaus, Richard. 1986. *The Naked Public Square: Religion and Democracy in America*. Grand Rapids, MI: Eerdmans.

Nikolaev, Alexander and Douglas Porpora. 2007. "Talking War: How Elite U.S. Newspaper Editorials and Opinion Pieces Debated the Attack on Iraq." *Sociological Focus* 40.1: 6–25.

Parsons, Talcott. 1977. *The Evolution of Societies*. Englewood Cliffs, NJ: Prentice-Hall.

Porpora, Douglas and Alexander Nikolaev. 2008. "Moral Muting in US Newspaper Op-eds Debating the Attack on Iraq." *Discourse and Communication* 2.2: 165–84.

Rabbis for Human Rights – North America. 2006. "A Jewish Statement Against Torture and Other Cruel, Inhuman and Degrading Treatment of Detainees Under United States Control." Online at: http://www.rhr-na.org/resources/human-rights-topics/torture-and-indefinite-detention/95-jewish-statement-against-torture-and-other-cruel-inhuman-and-degrading-treatment-of-detainees-under-united-states-control.html (accessed 10 April 2006).

Rice, Condolezza. 2000. "Campaign 2000: Promoting the National Interest." *Foreign Affairs* 79: 45–62.

Robinson, Eugene. 2005. "Denial, Now and 30 Years Ago." *Washington Post*, 3 June, A23.

Smith, Christian. 2003. *The Secular Revolution: Power, Interests and Conflict in the Secularlization of American Public Life*. Chicago: University of Chicago Press.

Sullivan, Amy. 2010. "Young Evangelicals: Expanding Their Mission." *Time*, 1 June. Online at: http://www.time.com/time/nation/article/0,8599,1992463,00.html (accessed 22 June 2011).

Swatos, William H. Jr and Kevin J. Christiano. 1999. "Secularization Theory: The Course of a Concept." *Sociology of Religion* 60.3: 209–28.

Thucydides. 2009. *The Peloponnesian War*. New York: Oxford.

US Conference of Catholic Bishops. 2004. "Letter to Congress on Human Rights and Torture: 2004." Online at: http://www.usccb.org/issues-and-action/human-life-and-dignity/war/torture/letter-congress-human-rights-and-torture-2004.cfm (accessed 22 August 2011).

Van Dijk, Teun A. 1985. *Macrostructures*. Hillsdale, NJ: Lawrence Erlbaum.

———. 2000. *Ideology: A Multidisciplinary Approach*. Los Angeles, CA: SAGE.

Walzer, Michael. 2000. *Just and Unjust Wars: A Moral Argument with Historical Illustrations*. New York: Basic Books.

Weber, Max. 1946. "Science as a vocation." In C. Wright Mills and Hans H. Gerth (eds), *From Max Weber*, 129–56. New York: Oxford University Press.

Zizek, Slavoj. 2009. *The Fragile Absolute: Or, Why is the Christian Legacy Worth Fighting For?* London: Verso.

Chapter 7

CHURCH, STATE AND SOCIETY IN POST-COMMUNIST EUROPE

Siniša Zrinščak

University of Zagreb

Introduction

The collapse of communism is most usually symbolically equated with the fall of the Berlin Wall in 1989 (about twenty years ago), although in some countries it is reckoned a bit later.[1] But the term "post-communist Europe" is not an adequate one for variety of reasons. Two of these reasons are worth mentioning in connection with the content of this chapter. First, the term simply acknowledges that some countries have a communist past, but does not say anything about the main features their new social orders have developed during years of post-communist transformation. Second, there are numerous post-communist countries,[2] countries which range from the center of the continent through the southeast to Eastern Europe, or from the Czech Republic and Slovenia through Macedonia and Albania to Ukraine and Moldova. These are countries with different histories,

---

1 This chapter was written on the basis of work done in the research project Religion and Values Central and Eastern Research Network (REVACERN) from 2007 to 2009, funded by the European Union and coordinated by the University of Szeged, Hungary. For more details about the project, see http://www.revacern.eu/. Previous versions of this chapter were presented at the first International Sociological Association Forum on Sociology: "Sociological Research and Public Debate" (Barcelona, 2008), at the conference "Religion and the State: Regional and Global Perspective" (Sydney, 2009), and in Zrinščak (2009a and 2009b).

2 The number of post-communist countries in Europe is higher than the number of Western European countries: there are 22 post-communist countries which are members of the Council of Europe, the largest pan-European organization. For details see: http://www.coe.int/aboutCoe/index.asp?page=47pays1europe&l=en (last accessed 5 October 2011).

social and cultural specificities and social development possibilities with, in a word, *profound* social differences despite 45 (or, in the case of the majority of ex-Soviet Union states, 70) years of common past. Therefore, the term "post-communist Europe" used in this chapter is simply a technical one. In addition, the chapter covers only part of post-communist Europe: countries that joined the European Union in 2004 (Czech Republic, Hungary, Poland, Slovakia and Slovenia) or in 2007 (Bulgaria and Romania) and one country which is set to become the twenty eight member state of the European Union in July 2013 (Croatia).

Finally and most crucially, the main argument of this chapter is that issues and dilemmas concerning church-state relations are basically the same in "new" European Union member states and in "old" European Union member states. Post-communist states – at least those analyzed in this chapter – after years of transformation to pluralist democracy and market economy and particularly transformation connected with European Union membership do not represent any special case in terms of church-state relations, a view that might differ significantly from Western European analysis. Besides, there are considerable differences among the countries analyzed; post-communist countries should not be seen as a homogenized case regarding their church-state relations. Still, there are many issues present both in Western and Eastern Europe concerning these relations, which are of sociological interest and should be analyzed via a comparative perspective of church-state relations in Europe in general.

Therefore, this chapter paper will:

- give an overview of church-state relations in Eastern and Western Europe;
- give a sociological religious portrait of particular countries concerning social expectations concerning church-state relations; and
- analyze main issues and dilemmas in church-state relations, point out possible explanations and suggest directions for future research.

Comparative Framework: Church and State in Western Europe

This chapter concerns issues and dilemmas which are basically the same in "old" and "new" European Union member states. This argument is present in the available literature and is widely shared by different authors, although mainly those writing from legal points of view. Interestingly, church-state relations are principally a domain for lawyers rather than sociologists,[3] but what is of more

---

3 Although there are some notable exceptions (Beckford and Richardson, 2007; Richardson, 2004, 2006, 2009; Shterin and Richardson, 2000, 2002; Berger, Davie and Fokas, 2008; Doe, 2004, etc.) a similar observation has recently been made by

interest is that there is not much cooperation between these two scientific perspectives. More specifically, sociological literature speaks about church and state but primarily approaches them from different angles, researching the position of minority religions or religious education issues. These are certainly very promising approaches, but other aspects of church-state relations present in the literature written by other experts should be brought into the general discussion.

Church-state relations in Western Europe, i.e. "old" European Union members with much longer democratic histories, can serve as a comparative framework for studying church-state relations in post-communist Europe. Authors basically agree that three different models are distinguished (Ferrari, 2003a, 2003b, 2003c; Torfs, 2007; Robbers, 2005). The first type can be found in countries with state or national church, such as England, Denmark, Finland, Greece, etc. France is well known as an unique country based on a strict separation model, although similar models (at least concerning legal separation rather than a general social attitude toward religion) can be found in the Netherlands and in Ireland. The majority of European countries fall into the third category, usually called the cooperative model, which is characterized by constitutional separation of church and state coupled with mutual cooperation based on agreements between state and different (usually historically dominant) religions that have important and officially recognized/supported social tasks and significance. In the case of the Catholic Church, these agreements (concordat in some cases) have been negotiated and signed between the Holy See and the respective countries.

Models speak little about the details and actual positions of different religions in any particular country. Deeper and more specific analysis can reveal details about the social position of minority religions, the concrete exercise of religious rights and religious freedom, norms guaranteed by constitutions or international agreements (e.g. Richardson, 2004). In addition, two questions of particular interest arise. First, are there any commonalities in terms of church-state relations which can be found among different European countries. More precisely, can we speak at least partly about an emerging European model of church-state relations, particularly keeping in mind the Europeanization process, or deepening of European Union integration? Second, and in connection with the first question, in which directions are church-state relations developing?

M. Koenig (2009: 298): "Church-state relations [is] a topic that had for a very long time been left to historians and legal scholars." Similarly: "There has been very little sociological commentary on the various definitions and conceptions of religion found in law. This is despite the obvious sociological importance a legal definition of religion has" (Sandberg, 2008: 157).

Although legal authors agree that there is no single European model of church-state relations, some of them nevertheless argue over evidence of a distinctive European dimension. Torf (2007) distinguishes between level A, the very basic level present in all European countries visible in the attribution of religious freedom to all religious groups and level B, which concerns the typical European leveling of support to some religious groups which consequently receive a kind of privileged treatment. Robbers (2005), particularly examining European Union laws, acknowledges the European Union's neutrality in relation to religious and philosophical issues but also its basic respect of religious needs and churches' right to self-determination. Still, history and traditions are very present and influence the persistence of different models despite countervailing tendencies. As has been pointed out by Madeley (2003: 2, 9), the "hand of history" is extremely visible because religions deeply influenced the creation of modern European nations and states. All this suggests a possible answer to the second question. There is a trend toward disestablishment. One commonly cited example is the Swedish Church, which changed its status in 2000 and has since then no longer been the state but the "folk" church (Gustafsson, 2003; Edgardh and Pettersson, 2010). Though it is not possible to argue about disestablishment on the basis of this single example, additional support can be found (in terms of recognition and support by the state) in debates about similar possible moves in several other countries. In these countries, changes from confessional to nonconfessional school education and more equal rights for minority religions have also been obtained. Disestablishment is in fact another reason for Ferrari (2008) to argue about the emergence of the common European trend.

At the same time, contrary tendencies are also noted. Some European countries have become very restrictive toward a wide range of minority religions (Richardson and Introvigne, 2001) and debates about the positions of Islam and its public role have become very intense (Casanova, 2007, 2008). There are arguments about antidisestablishmentarianism (Madeley, 2003: 17), the surge of religious persecution (Robbins, 2003) and the rise of government regulation over religion (Fox, 2009, 2010). Even though they seem oppositional, all these briefly presented viewpoints are of interest and should not be analyzed separately. Contradictory tendencies all constitute social reality. Sociological research should rely on all of them. Moreover, viewpoints on religion and state differ according to theoretical and ideological standpoints and it is common to find in the literature the same reality completely differently analyzed by different authors. Even the different official treatment of the issue of religious rights (and consequently that of church-state relations) by international organizations is noted. As argued by Richardson and Garay (2004), the European Court of Human Rights demonstrates its authority concerning religious rights to the majority of post-communist countries (like Bulgaria, Romania, Russia and other post-Soviet states), even while it retains its traditional deference to original member states of the European Union.

Church and State in Post-communism

Church-state relations faced different challenges and passed through different phases after the fall of communism. The first years of the post-communist period brought a general embracing of religious freedom which was extended equally to traditional and minority religions and created a space for new religions to enter previously closed and hostile religious societies. However, traditional churches and conservative parties found it unjustified to grant the same privileges to traditional churches (which had suffered during the years of communism) and newly arrived religions, some of which (it has been argued by those who opposed equal treatment of different religions) possessed "suspicious" features. Yet this kind of social reaction was very different in Russia and some other post-Soviet states, which have on record very inimical and completely antidemocratic treatment of minority and nontraditional religions (Barker, 1997; Shterin and Richardson, 1998, 2000) than in the majority of other post-communist countries. These countries actually have become more or less similar to the majority of Western European countries in their differential treatment of different religions whilst coping more or less successfully with demands for religious freedom. The tension between a differential treatment and striving toward religious freedom for all different religions is in a fact a major similarity between Western and Eastern European countries. Still, many authors point to the fact that although these latter countries do not follow the restrictive "Russian pattern" of dealing with nontraditional religions, they nevertheless have (serious) problems dealing with religious pluralism (e.g. Črnič, 2007; Sarkissian, 2009; Borowik, 2006; Tomka and Yurash, 2006; Révay and Tomka, 2006, 2007; Kuburić and Moe, 2006).

Taking into account all available research on a number of post-communist states, I am extending the argument about the common European trend according to literature present in Western Europe to Central Eastern Europe and exemplified in essential principles: "substantial respect of individual religious freedom, guarantee of the autonomy and, in particular, the self-administration of the religious denominations, and selective collaboration of the states with the churches" (Ferrari, 2003a: 171–8; 2003c: 421; 2008: 110). The argument is based and should be underlined on the notion of separation of church and state, which is the constitutional norm prevailing in post-communist countries. It basically means a distinction between the areas which belong to the state and those which belong to the church, thus denoting a mutual respect of their mutual autonomy. As outlined by Ferrari, the separation does not mean that the state does not have the right to help religious communities by its own resources in various forms of cooperation between states and different religious communities. Still, and crucially, the cooperation is selective in both Western and Central Eastern European countries and concerns mainly traditional religious communities, eliding the rights and social possibilities of different, usually minority, religions. The selectivity has stricter or looser ways of manifesting in different countries. The crucial questions concern the meaning of a constitutional or legal provision of the "separation" and of the "equality" of all religions before law and how different religions (different sizes, different histories, different attitudes toward societies) should be treated following these legal requirements. One of the underlying theories in most sociological papers, usually not explicitly stated, is the "human rights approach" which indicates that, if there are stipulations of "separation" and "equality" and if basic international and European documents guarantee equality based on beliefs, then selectivity (or selective cooperation between state and some religions) is not justified. The reality does not support this approach; as in Western Europe, post-communist Europe balances between religious freedom and a two (or three) tier system which ascribes different rights and different privileges to different religious communities. A summary of different aspects of church-state relations in post-communist countries is presented in Table 7.1.

Socioreligious Profile of Post-communist Europe

Historical legacy, both in terms of the communist past and of longer overall social development, is the factor influencing development of church-state relations in post-communism. However, these relations are shaped inside very concrete historical circumstances and consequently inside very concrete socioreligious landscapes. In researching the socioreligious background of church-state relations, there are several facts already pointed out in sociological research that have to be put together in order to understand the rather complex image of religious changes in post-communism. First, the trend of revitalization was widely acknowledged and discussed. Measured by different indicators, the revitalization of religion was a part of overall social changes in all countries, although to different extents and in different timeframes. However, a distinction should be made between the revitalization visible in the public appearance and role of religion (mainly regarding traditional churches, but after some time also newly arrived religions) and the revitalization visible in the rise of individual religiosity according to different indicators (like belonging, church participation, belief in God and particularly behavioral consequences of religious believing).

Table 7.1. Church-state relations in eight post-communist countries

	Bulgaria	Croatia	Czech Republic	Hungary	Poland	Romania	Slovakia	Slovenia
Basic religious freedom	Yes + possible limits	Yes	Yes	Yes	Yes + possible limits	Yes	Yes + possible limits	Yes
Separation	Yes + Eastern orthodox Christianity as traditional religion	Yes	Yes	Yes	Yes	Not clear	Yes + reference to St Cyril and Methodius spiritual heritage	Yes + reference to St Cyril and Methodius spiritual heritage
Concordat	No	Yes	Pending	Yes	Yes	No	Yes	Yes
Special rights	Yes, although the degree is not the same in all countries (for details see the next row), while other religious communities (particularly those that are not traditional) may be registered but do not enjoy special rights, or can act as other nongovernmental organizations							
Agreement/ privileges	Yes; Orthodox Church + registered denominations	Yes; Catholic Church + communities with agreements with the state	Yes; 26 registered churches and religious societies	Yes; Catholic Church and different rights of larger religions, although lower than in other countries	Yes; Catholic Church + 14 communities with special rights	Yes; Orthodox Church + 15 registered communities	Yes; Catholic Church + 14 registered communities	Yes; Catholic Church + traditional churches with agreement, although small privileges
Restriction (based on Fox, 2008a)	High	Low	Low	Low	Moderate	High	Low / moderate	Low
State involvement	High	Moderate	Low	Low	Moderate	High	Moderate	Moderate

Sources: Own analysis based on: Črnič (2007); Devetak, Kalčina and Polzer (2004); Ferrari and Durham (2003); Fox (2008a); Robbers (2005); and Schanda (2003, 2009). Because some of the sources are not so accurate there might be some recent changes in respect to data presented (particularly those connected with numbers of registered communities), but the overall picture seems to be rather stable and indeed reflects the overall situation in the longer period, i.e. the end of 1990s and 2000s.

The newly acquired public role of religion has not always developed in parallel with the rising of individual religiosity. Second, and in connection with the previous statement, revitalization is not the sole factor able to explain religious changes in post-communism. There are other important factors (ethnic, cultural, political) that have influenced religious changes, and even a lot of secularizing tendencies (both those inherited from the secular past and those connected with the "Westernization" of post-communist countries). Thus, another increasingly posed question is whether the revitalization was just a feature of the dissolution of communism and the rise of new democratic and market-oriented societies, which today (slowly but in some countries very visibly) gives way to "natural," "European" secularization and moreover, European secularism. Third, all these issues have to be put in a specific national context, as among post-communist countries there have been those with high religiosity (like Romania and Poland) and those with low religiosity (like the Czech Republic and former East Germany). Fourth, the specificity of the national context has been further underlined by the strong links between religious and ethnic belonging throughout Eastern Europe, the most prominent examples being in cases of war and of dissolution of former federal states, as in the former Yugoslavia during the 1990s.

This chapter will contextualize and briefly discuss levels of as well as trends in religiosity in the countries analyzed. Data presented comes from the Aufbruch research project carried out in 1997 and 2007.[4] This international project's aim was to examine the position of religions and churches in transitional countries during communism and after the fall of the Berlin Wall. It was a cross-sectional and longitudinal study comprised of quantitative and qualitative methods. Questionnaire surveys, the quantitative part of the project, were designed to investigate value systems and religious orientation in these countries. In both years a questionnaire survey was conducted, but some new questions were added in 2007. A representative sampling was made in each of the countries. In 1997 ten ex-communist countries were involved – Lithuania, Poland, Ukraine, Czech Republic, Slovakia, Hungary, Romania, Slovenia, Croatia and East Germany – and in 2007 the survey was extended to Moldavia, Belarus, Serbia and Bulgaria.

Belonging to religious community[5] was a majority orientation in a majority of countries in 2007, except in the Czech Republic where less than 20 percent

---

4 For more information about the research and about results see Tomka and Zulehner (2008). I personally was able to access the data through my participation in the REVACERN research project (see note 1), and would like to thank Professor A. Máté Tóth for this opportunity.

5 It should be noted that the wording of this question could generate misunderstandings. For example, "belonging to religious community" and "belonging to church" have different meanings in the Croatian language; questions about belonging to community can result in lower percentages than those about actually belonging to different confessional groups. See also Ančić (2011: 6) and Tomka (2006).

of respondents expressed belonging and in Hungary, where belonging was at the level of about 50 percent. Two Orthodox countries, Bulgaria and Romania, have exceptionally high belonging, followed by Poland, Croatia and Slovakia. Comparison to 1997 reveals contradictory tendencies: a small rise in Slovakia, a stable situation in Romania and a fall of around 7.0–8.5 percent in Croatia, Czech Republic, Hungary and Poland.

Religious self-identification represents a partly different picture from the one based on confessional belonging. It is expected in sociological research to have a difference between confessional and religious identification and to have a lower level of religious identification than of confessional identification. However, comparing the 2007 versions of Figures 7.1 and 7.2 shows very different situations. In Croatia and Hungary, there is no difference between confessional and religious identification (of course, in line with the fact that we counted in the category of religious people those who identified themselves

Figure 7.1. Belonging to a religious community: "yes" responses (%)

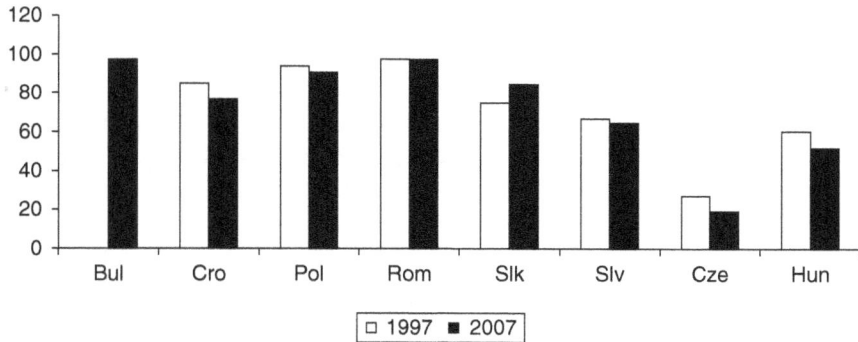

Figure 7.2. Religious self-identification – those who declared themselves very religious and to some extent religious (%)

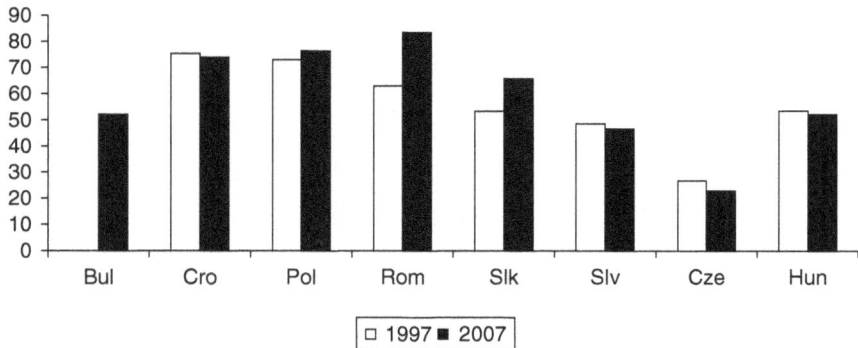

as very religious and also those who identified themselves as to some extent religious). In other countries, the difference is quite significant, the highest difference (almost double) being in Slovakia. It is rather unusual in sociological research to find a higher religious identification in comparison to confessional identification, as we did in the Czech Republic (though the difference was not so significant). It is interesting to note that the same tendency was already noted for Russia, which was partly explained by the role of public religion in a specific post-communist context, not performed exclusively by specific religious communities. A considerable part of population wants to be religious and supports its public appearance but does not trust and belong to any religious community (Agadjanin, 2001). If this tendency were to continue in the future, it would need to be further analyzed in the context of different meanings of "believing" and "belonging" in different European countries (Davie, 2000). The comparison between 1997 and 2007 also shows another important tendency: a stable situation or even rise of religious identification particularly marked in Slovakia and Romania.

As expected, participation at services is lower than other dimensions of religiosity in the majority of countries. The exception is Poland with a very high participation rate, followed by Romania, Slovakia and Croatia. Of particular interest is Bulgaria, with a much lower participation rate in comparison to other religiosity indicators (particularly "belonging to the religious community"). Romania also has a lower participation rate in contrast to the very high religiosity indicators in the country, which can be an indication of the "Orthodox specificities" of these two countries. In sum, religiosity is markedly present in countries analyzed, though there are significant differences among them. In terms of religious changes in the period 1997–2007, they can be confirmed, although an overall stability has still been more present than

Figure 7.3. Participation at services – at least once a month or more often (%)

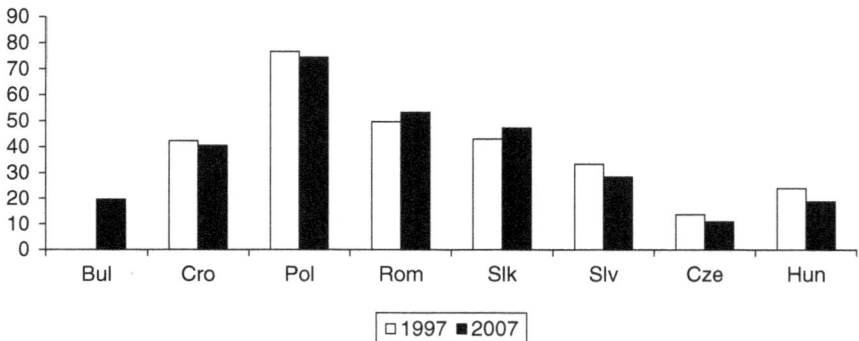

any clear revitalization or secularization tendencies.[6] Grouping of countries is extremely difficult as there are different values of different indicators, but based on the similar analysis of the same pool of data there are some consistent groupings (Ančić, 2011). Concerning religious belonging, one group forms Romania, Slovakia, Poland, Bulgaria and Croatia with the highest level, Slovenia and Hungary form the middle group, and the third and lowest level is occupied by the Czech Republic. Concerning religious self-identification, Romania, Poland and Croatia form the group with the highest religiosity, the Czech Republic is again the country with the lowest religiosity and this time we can put Bulgaria, Slovakia, Hungary and Slovenia in the middle group.

Church-State Relations: Social Expectations

Studies about church-state relations do not usually talk about people's social expectations. They take legal points of view focusing on constitutional or other legal provisions, rights and obligations or sociological points of view focusing on the position and rights of all religions. But as history is considerably present in contemporary church-state relations in Europe and as religions still have considerable social significance and perform important social tasks, it is of interest to take into consideration what the public thinks about and expects from churches, particularly traditional ones.[7] Thus, it is necessary to complement the socioreligious images of countries with public social expectations which in fact considerably shape the social role of religions and which consequently illuminate relevant issues for church-state relations.

According to the data presented in Table 7.2, respondents in a majority of countries are satisfied with the level of publicity of big Christian churches, as they opted for the answer "quite appropriate" publicity. However, there are considerable differences between countries. In some countries, there is a substantial number of people who think that churches acquired too much publicity. Croatian, Polish and Slovenian respondents tend to think that churches gain too much publicity, as to a lesser extent do the Slovakian public, while in Bulgaria and Romania one third of people (or more) think quite the opposite. Although in Croatia, Poland and Slovenia there are similar proportions of those who think that churches acquired too much publicity, the proportion was higher in 2007 than in 1997 in Croatia and Slovenia and much lower in 2007 than

---

6 Stability is for example the main conclusion about concluded reason for religious changes in Croatia, drawn from the European Value Survey data 1999 and 2008 analysis (Črpić and Zrinščak, 2010).

7 It should be noted that the analysis here is restricted by the type of data available from the Aufbruch research project.

Table 7.2. "Do you think that, during the last decade, the big Christian churches acquired too much or not enough publicity?" (%)

Country	Too much		Quite appropriate		Not enough	
	1997	2007	1997	2007	1997	2007
Bulgaria		7.4		50.3		42.3
Croatia	38.1	44.1	45.1	41.4	16.7	14.5
Poland	67.6	45.8	26.9	45.9	5.5	8.3
Romania	28.0	16.2	40.3	50.6	31.7	33.3
Slovakia	32.4	32.7	53.7	57.8	13.9	9.4
Slovenia	37.6	43.1	48.6	46.5	13.8	10.4
Czech R.	14.5	19.8	65.3	62.5	20.1	17.7
Hungary	23.2	19.5	56.3	61.8	20.5	18.6

in 1997 in Poland. Starting from an assumption that the 1990s were years of acquiring this publicity in comparison to the communist years, the situation in Croatia and Slovenia requires deeper analysis. The general opinion about public presence of churches in countries seems also to not be in line with the general level of religiosity or with secularization or revitalization tendencies in respective countries.

A similar picture transpires from the answers (not presented here in detail) to the question of whether the public is satisfied with the general development of big Christian churches in the last ten years. A substantial majority in almost all countries opted for the middle position – neither unsatisfied nor satisfied – followed by those who opted for the satisfied position. The middle position got a bit less support in 2007 than in 1997.

Tables 7.3 and 7.4 show interesting views on the role of churches in contemporary societies. First, it is discernable that generally, the social role of churches is not seen to be in contradiction to the development of democracy, although there are some divisions in this view. Disagreement is particularly high in Slovenia and the Czech Republic and agreement exceptionally high in Romania, followed by Poland and Bulgaria. Further, agreement is much higher in 2007 than in 1997 in Romania and Poland. This is of particular interest, as religion (and particularly the Catholic Church) was a crucial factor in the democratization of previous communist states (Casanova, 2001). It is clear that support is higher in all countries concerning economic development and the possible ethical role of religion than it is concerning the case of democratic development, even though there is still a high level of rejection in Slovenia and the Czech Republic. This level of support obviously reflects transitional economic problems (like the rise of unemployment and poverty) and widespread opinions that the economic development during

Table 7.3. "For strengthening democracy is it important to ensure that churches would have a role to play?" (%)

Country	Disagree		Neither agree, nor disagree		Agree	
	1997	2007	1997	2007	1997	2007
Bulgaria		18.4		34.5		47.1
Croatia	34.0	38.1	32.6	26.1	33.4	35.8
Poland	34.7	27.3	31.6	22.7	33.7	50.1
Romania	19.3	9.8	29.3	17.8	51.4	72.4
Slovakia	27.0	33.3	34.7	31.3	38.3	35.4
Slovenia	27.0	58.7	27.2	24.3	27.9	17.0
Czech Republic	40.7	52.7	31.4	26.2	27.9	21.1
Hungary	30.3	35.0	27.8	27.6	41.8	37.4

Table 7.4. "For the economic development of our country, is it important to follow the moral principles of religion?" (%)

Country	Disagree		Neither agree, nor disagree		Agree	
	1997	2007	1997	2007	1997	2007
Bulgaria		15.8		30.1		54.1
Croatia	35.1	28.1	32.1	27.6	32.9	44.4
Poland	26.0	18.3	28.4	20.6	45.7	61.1
Romania	20.6	4.7	26.7	17.4	52.7	78.0
Slovakia	34.0	28.3	34.0	30.9	32.1	40.7
Slovenia	50.6	47.7	26.8	29.5	22.6	22.7
Czech Republic	45.8	42.7	29.4	30.6	24.8	26.7
Hungary	34.1	29.3	28.2	25.8	37.6	45.0

1990s was not in accordance with ethical principles and thus only widened social inequalities. Opinions welcoming the role of churches in disputed aspects of social development are also visible from other survey questions and can partly explain the relatively high social support of the social role of churches in some countries.

The 2007 questionnaire (in contrast to the 1997 questionnaire) included many new questions about the social role of churches, including the three presented in Table 7.5. General support for at least the first two categories ("Europe needs Christianity to preserve social spirit needs" and "Christianity strengthens freedom in Europe") is considerable, with the notable exceptions of Slovenia and the Czech Republic. In Croatia, Slovakia and Hungary less than half of the population show their support, while in other countries

Table 7.5. Attitudes to the general role of churches in Europe – those who agree (%) (2007)

Country	Europe needs Christianity to preserve social spirit needs	Christianity strengthens freedom in Europe	God should have been mentioned in the European Constitution
Bulgaria	63.6	64.2	46.0
Croatia	43.0	49.5	33.1
Poland	59.3	66.5	53.2
Romania	75.2	80.0	66.2
Slovakia	46.4	48.9	38.2
Slovenia	19.5	24.1	15.8
Czech Republic	24.6	30.9	9.3
Hungary	48.7	49.4	26.5

popular support is quite high. However, divisions clearly exist regarding mentioning God in the European Constitution: high support (more than 50 percent) is visible only in Romania and Poland, with a little less than 50 percent in Bulgaria. It is obvious that the support expressed for the general role of churches in Europe is not extended to the political realm (the issue of God in the European Constitution).

This last hypothesis is further justified by a series of questions (not shown here in the tables) which measured attitudes toward particular social and religious roles of churches, such as to educate and raise people in faith, to support and foster relations between people, to alleviate social needs, to teach people to be more attentive to each other, to participate in public life, to strengthen the national spirit, to support morality, to reconcile people with each other, to take an official position on important social issues and to teach people to help the needy. These statements can be classified as religious (e.g. to educate people in faith), moral-social (e.g. to foster relations or to teach people to be more attentive), and as more social-political (to alleviate social needs or to take an official position). The answers show that, in these first two general issues, support of church involvement is particularly high in almost all countries, ranging usually from 60–90 percent. In the last group of (sociopolitical) issues, support is a bit lower, but in the majority of countries it is still above 50 percent. In line with that, the official participation of churches in public life is supported, though not unanimously. Concerning all of the above classified issues, two countries stand out as exceptions: Slovenia and Romania. In Slovenia support is the lowest, while in Romania it is the highest.

Figure 7.4. "Is it appropriate when the big Christian churches deal with…?" – "yes" responses (%)

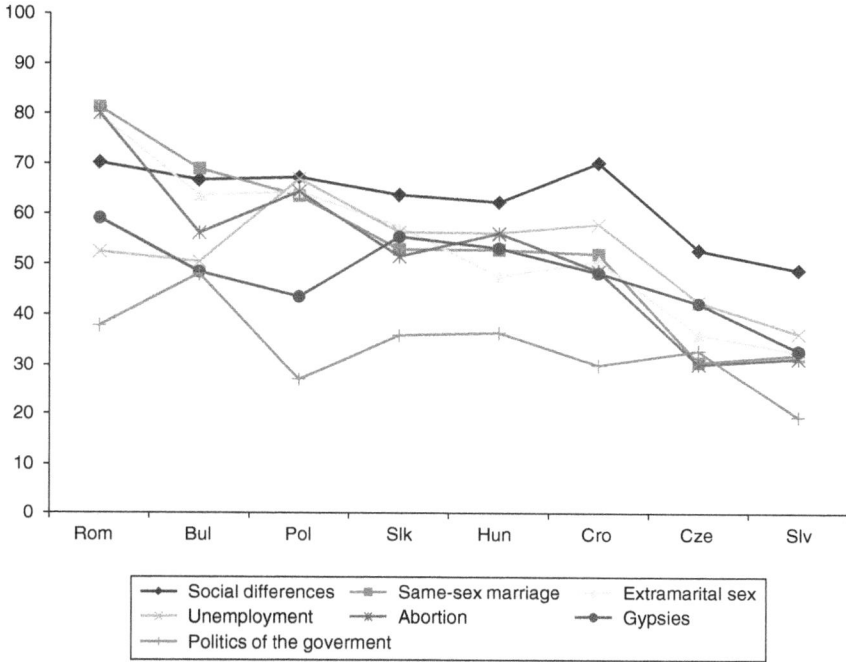

Social differences	Same-sex marriage	Extramarital sex
Unemployment	Abortion	Gypsies
Politics of the goverment		

Figure 7.5. "Is it appropriate when the big Christian churches deal with…?" – "yes" responses for all countries (%) (except Bulgaria in 1997)

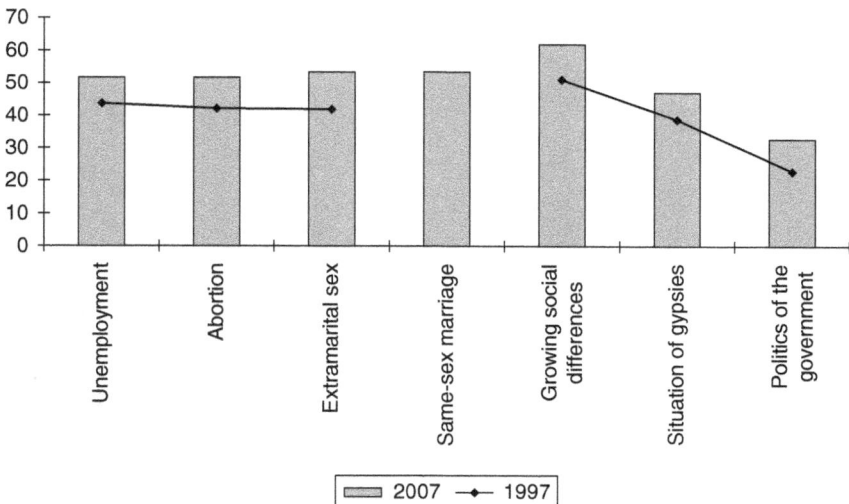

2007   1997

Acceptance of the voice of big Christian churches depends on the issue at stake, but ranges from general acceptance (about 50 percent or more) in most cases to general nonacceptance in the case of the politics of the government (Figures 7.4 and 7.5). Of particular interest is that the level of acceptance is much the same in, for example, the cases of unemployment and abortion, which are very different issues. Moral statements about issues of sexuality usually provoke opposing attitudes and heated social debates. The highest acceptance rate concerns growing social differences, showing that this is the most pressing social issue in all post-communist societies. Although the picture is not unambiguous, there is a general acceptance of churches' authority, but not at the levels of politics.

The crucial insight into the role of churches in post-communist societies comes from the questions (Figure 7.6) about church institutions like kindergartens, schools, retirement homes, hospitals, unions and media: do we have too little of them or too many? Do we want to have them or not? Most importantly, who should finance them? These questions also illustrate respondents' views on the ability of state and different private institutions (profit or nonprofit) in satisfying their social needs.

These results show that there is, in general, very high acceptance of different church institutions, particularly kindergartens, retirement homes and hospitals and less acceptance in the case of schools. Obviously, there is much space for church-owned institutions in connection with unfavorable social situations

Figure 7.6. "Would you say that the churches and religious communities still have too little, or already have too many, of the following institutions?" – "already too many" responses (%) (2007)

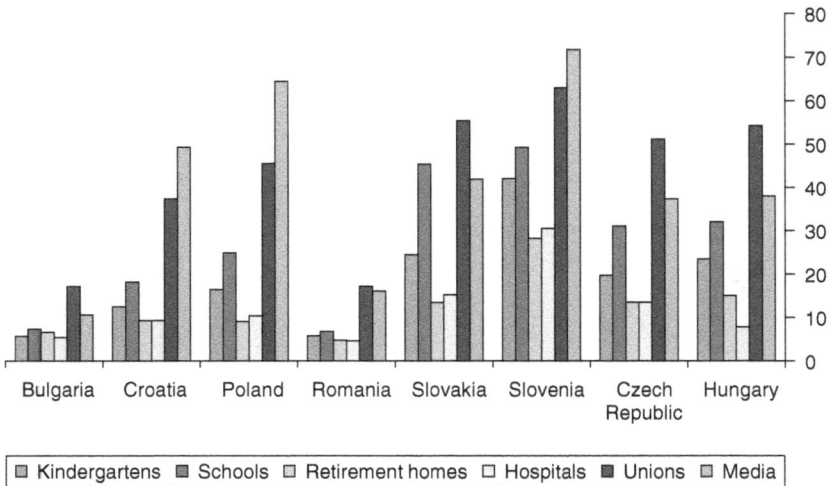

and particularly with the lack of social services governments have been able to provide. The least acceptance is for unions and media, although in that last case acceptance differs much between countries, ranging from 89.4 percent in Bulgaria to only 28.2 percent in Slovenia. Slovenia is the country with the lowest acceptance regarding all issues. Also concerning all these issues, the Czech Republic is not similar to Slovenia (as it is in the other previously analyzed questions) but to countries with generally higher acceptance rates.

Data from Table 7.6 indicates different views about donations to churches, which is demonstrated by the majority of answers being affirmative in Croatia, Poland, Romania and Slovakia, whilst not in other countries. However, donations to churches also depend on the specific system of financing of churches in respective countries, which is not further elaborated on. Age differences are visible in a sense that in all countries, the elderly support the church through donations more than their younger counterparts. Concerning the religious self-estimation, more religious obviously support the most, while in general in more religious countries (Croatia, Poland and Romania) even those who are partly religious or to some extent nonreligious support considerably. That points to the importance of the general religious climate in a given society, or to the general role of a (dominant) church that obviously has a considerable social role beyond a purely religious one. Concerning the gender differences, women in general support more, although there are differences that can be explained by the particular situations of different countries.

Readiness to pay regular contributions to churches is not supported by a majority, except in Romania. Even in the more religious Poland and Croatia, readiness is expressed by less than 50 percent of respondents. Obviously, there are many reasons for this, and the economic situation is the most important one: even before the 2009–10 economic crisis, the post-communist countries were still catching up very slowly to Western Europe's economic level, meaning that a considerable proportion of their populations suffer rather poor living conditions. There are age differences, but they are not as consistent as they were in the question about donations to religious communities (Table 7.6). The individual level of religiosity has a considerable impact and in terms of gender, women are more ready to give money than men. Interestingly, readiness to pay was higher in 1997, particularly in Croatia, Poland and Slovenia.

Although it is not easy to draw any conclusion as different issues provoke different viewpoints, some patterns of responses are still detectable among countries. Romania, Poland and (to a lesser extent) Bulgaria are countries in which approval of the public and social role of churches is the highest. It can be even said that Romania is a unique case, with particularly high approval of religious influence in all social issues. Slovenia and the Czech Republic are at the other end of the spectrum, though we can observe significant approval

Table 7.6. Donations to religious communities or paid contributions to the church (%) (2007)

2007	Apart from occasional donations, have you or someone from your family during the last year given a donation to a religious community or paid a contribution to the church? ("yes" answers in %)							
	Bulgaria	Croatia	Poland	Romania	Slovakia	Slovenia	Czech R.	Hungary
Age								
18–29	13.3	58.9	57.7	68.0	53.2	39.5	11.2	28.2
30–39	16.8	61.6	61.4	76.1	61.8	44.8	20.5	30.1
40–49	17.1	68.4	63.8	80.5	56.0	39.8	26.2	38.4
50–59	22.1	60.7	69.7	76.5	66.5	49.4	23.3	40.6
60+	21.6	73.3	75.2	81.6	71.7	61.7	32.9	55.4
Religious self-perception								
Very religious	43.8	84.5	77.4	87.5	86.7	89.0	78.5	76.9
To some extent religious	24.9	69.2	67.8	77.6	71.9	69.1	61.2	53.8
Neither religious nor nonreligious	8.7	48.7	48.9	60.8	38.9	36.0	26.0	18.4
To some extent nonreligious	6.8	41.9	43.1	45.9	32.0	25.2	13.9	5.0
Absolutely nonreligious	9.3	10.4	20.0	71.4	13.7	6.5	3.3	8.6
Sex								
Male	16.0	62.3	64.3	75.2	57.3	41.1	18.3	37.6
Female	20.5	68.8	66.9	77.3	65.3	54.5	27.3	41.8

Table 7.7. Readiness to pay regular contribution to the church / religious community of church taxes (%) (2007)

2007	If it would be necessary for supporting your religious community, would you be ready to pay a regular contribution of church taxes to the church/religious community? ("yes" answers in %)								
	Bulgaria	Croatia	Poland	Romania	Slovakia	Slovenia	Czech R.	Hungary
Age								
18–29	27.6	42.5	40.1	84.0	39.5	19.5	14.9	33.3
30–39	45.5	42.6	38.4	89.8	51.5	20.1	12.3	36.0
40–49	35.8	43.2	46.0	89.4	49.0	23.1	23.0	47.5
50–59	35.3	50.8	41.3	89.6	57.0	32.5	18.2	49.4
60+	30.9	41.2	53.7	91.8	61.8	43.3	31.7	57.7
Religious self-perception								
Very religious	58.3	66.8	58.6	94.2	86.1	78.7	77.4	78.6
To some extent religious	46.6	41.1	45.6	91.0	58.7	44.7	49.3	65.4
Neither religious nor nonreligious	21.8	22.5	24.0	79.2	27.3	15.9	18.7	24.5
To some extent nonreligious	14.3	21.4	16.7	54.5	17.4	3.7	5.6	20.0
Absolutely nonreligious	16.7	3.4	23.1	42.9	2.2	0	4.5	8.5
Sex								
Male	33.2	39.6	40.8	88.3	43.6	24.1	17.6	39.8
Female	35.2	46.8	46.9	89.0	58.3	33.5	22.8	50.8

of church ownership of social institutions in the Czech Republic. Croatia, Slovakia, Hungary and (again to a lesser extent) Bulgaria occupy the middle of the spectrum. This grouping is similar to the previous analysis (same pool of data), which also detected three groups of countries (Ančić, 2011). The highest social expectations from religion are to be found in Romania and Poland. The second group consists of Hungary, Bulgaria, Slovakia and Croatia, while the lowest approval is noted in the Czech Republic and Slovenia. However, the factorial analysis extracted two factors, the first one being the sociocultural role of religion and the second one being the sociopolitical role of religion (Ančić, 2011).[8] Respondents from Romania and Poland are more in favor of a sociocultural role of religion, respondents in Bulgaria and Croatia are against it and Slovaks and Hungarians are in between.[9] Concerning the sociopolitical role, it is widely accepted in Romania, less accepted in Bulgaria and least accepted in Slovakia, Croatia, Poland and Hungary.

Religion, Church-State and Public Social Expectations: Concluding Notes

The main aim of this chapter was to give an overview of the development of church-state relations in Western and Central Eastern Europe and to demonstrate that there is no unique post-communist case. Post-communist countries differ greatly from each other (concerning both legal arrangements and sociological profiles). The above analysis shows that there are, in fact, not many differences between Western and Central Eastern (post-communist) countries as they face a very similar problem: how to balance historically shaped church-state relations that favored traditional churches with the rising of religious (and in general, sociocultural) pluralism.[10] As in Western Europe, there are different ways of dealing with pluralism and of rearranging church-state relations after the collapse of communism (Table 7.1).

The principal concern of this chapter is whether there has been a connection between the religious profile of countries and their church-state relations and

---

8 Sociocultural factors consist of items such as: "religion can give spiritual comfort, reconcile people, support morality, support relations between people," etc., while the sociopolitical factor refers to participation in public life, holding of official positions on important social issues and strengthening of the national spirit (Ančić, 2011).

9 It is very important to recognize that these factors do not operate in Slovenia and the Czech Republic, probably due to a very low acceptance of analyzed items in these two countries.

10 Though this chapter analyzes mainly Central Eastern European countries, this claim is based on the available literature about Western Europe, partly presented in the subchapter "Comparative Framework: Church and State in Western Europe."

indeed, between church-state relations and public expectations about the social role of religions. The main argument is that public social expectation is the relevant factor for studying church-state relations and that this factor has been neglected so far in sociological studies. The analysis confirmed these assumptions to a great extent. It is observable that there is no clear link between a simple account of religiosity and church-state relations. However, if Table 7.1 is to be read in light of responses *about* religiosity, then even though the simple link is missing, one can conclude that there has been slightly stronger restriction and state involvement in countries with higher religiosity (with the notable exception of Bulgaria, although despite a lower level of religiosity there is a high confessional belonging in Bulgaria). Social expectations make the picture a bit more consistent as in general, higher religiosity also means higher social expectations and higher social involvement of traditional churches. Two things are important here. The first is that in the majority of countries the public (according to survey results) welcomes the social role of religion (particularly that of big Christian churches) and moreover, that this role embraces the strengthening of democracy across different governmental issues and the church ownership of different social institutions.[11] Simply, the significance of the social role of big churches is evident and is the factor that greatly influences church-state relations. Second, there are notable differences among post-communist countries. The Slovenian and Czech respondents are much more against the social role of religion (particularly of traditional religions), and these are at the same time countries in which differences between religions with privileges and religions without privileges are not so large. In terms of church-state relations, Hungary is similar to these two countries and is always somewhere in the middle in terms of social expectations. Slovakia and Croatia are countries with high or moderate religiosity, moderate social expectations and (consequently) countries that approve the significant role of traditional religions and allow these religions moderate social involvement. Poland is also a country with moderate state involvement, but with a more significant role for traditional churches. Bulgaria and Romania have many similarities in terms of higher state involvement, higher social expectations and somewhat higher restrictions toward nontraditional religions, although Bulgaria is a country where religiosity is high on the basis of confessional belonging and lower on the basis of religious self-identification. As underlined several times in the chapter, Romania is a country with exceptionally high religiosity considering all indicators. Bulgaria and Romania are also Orthodox countries in which state involvement in religious matters is historically

---

11 The role of churches in the welfare field has been an important aspect of the development of modern European societies, and despite the secularization process, remains of continuing importance (Van Kersbergen and Kremer, 2008; Opielka, 2008; Van Kersbergen and Manow, 2009). This analysis is yet to be done for Central Eastern European countries.

higher than in Catholic or Protestant countries. That points to other social and cultural factors that are relevant for the creating and sustaining of church-state relations, which are not elaborated in this chapter.

As the intention of the chapter was also to introduce post-communist church-state relations to the general discussion about church and state, this last section will briefly discuss the findings in the context of possible future research. Namely, there are at least two visible contradictions in church-state relations in many European countries, post-communist countries included. They are normatively and at least ideologically devoted to concepts of "separation," "neutrality" and "equality," but at the same time continue with the different regulation of different religions. Secondly, there are marked differences between countries that at the ideological or normative levels supposedly follow the same or very similar principles. Historical influence, as already explained, is one of main reasons for this phenomenon (Madeley, 2003; Ferrari, 2008; Casanova, 2008). Still, the question remains as to why the histories continue to be so powerful with respect to rapid social changes in contemporary societies. Gunn (2006) underlined that it is not only history per se but *perceived national identity* or *founding myth* that country has about itself.

> Thus, I hypothesize, the differences among these countries cannot be explained simply by their histories and different legal systems and cultures, but also by understanding the "founding myths" and the "perceived identities" that are widely (and naively) shared by the populations... Those who are responsible for regulating religion...will often see "neutrality," "equality" and "nondiscrimination" not through some relatively "objective" lens, but through the rose-colored glasses of the founding myths and perceived identities. (Gunn, 2006: 37)

That fact is also underlined by other authors, like Casanova (2007, 2008) who points to how collective European identity has been questioned and shaken by the role of Islam and other immigrant religions which increasingly influence contemporary Europe. Similarly, Hervieu-Léger (2006) emphasizes the importance of historical and religious context for current European public debates on social and ethical issues, claiming that although religious institutions lose power, symbolic structures they shape have a remarkable capacity to influence the local culture. This indicates a need to complement studies of church-state relations with more general studies about the challenges of identity construction in contemporary social processes and the contemporary social significance of religion beyond the secularization trend and debates.

This is an approach that is very relevant for both Western and Eastern Europe. However, in an account of religious development in Central and Eastern Europe (CEE), Borowik (2007) listed five reasons for distinguishing CEE from the rest of Europe when discussing the role of religion: (1) Christianity arrived later here than in the West; (2) this is the area of parallel existence of Latin and Orthodox Christianity; (3) religion was consolidated at the same time as and was an important factor in nation and state-building processes; (4) CEE felt the influence of strong antireligious and antidemocratic communism; and (5) religion is a part of the total social transformation after the collapse of communism. It is not certain to what degree these reasons distinguish Eastern Europe from the West, but reasons 3, 4 and 5 explain the importance of religion to the post-communist region for state- and nation-building (Zrinščak, 2002, 2006; Marinović, Jerolimov and Zrinščak, 2006). That means that for historical reasons, religion is in Central Eastern Europe far more involved in contemporary social processes in comparison to Western Europe, although recent developments in different Western European countries might suggest that differences between Western and Eastern Europe are not so profound.

Another important issue that has to be further researched is the connection between church-state relations – or, more clearly, church-state separation – and democratic development. This question has dominated sociological research in post-communism, as the issue of minority religion has been studied from the point of view of both separation provisions and human rights and religious freedom provisions. Without going into detail, it can be said that the connection exists but is not particularly strong. Fox (2008b) found that state religious exclusivity is connected to poor human rights records, but that this relationship is weaker for Western democracies and that the reason might be a high respect for human rights in liberal Western Europe irrespective of church-state relations. Similarly, Stepan (2001: 222) argues that the construction and reconstruction of tolerance, not the conceptual separation of church and state, influences democratic development and religious freedom in Europe. Furthermore, the degree of separation of state and churches at least in Europe does not have any significant influence on religious vitality (Pollack and Pickel, 2009). However, people expect much from churches and although there are normative expectations that churches should respect functional differentiation in modern societies (Pollack and Pickel, 2009), the situation has been (as explained in this chapter) extremely complicated. Simply, three concepts are crucial and should be further researched in relation to each other: "church-state," "public social expectations" and "religion and identity formation."

References

Agadjanin, Alexander. 2001. "Public Religion and the Quest for National Ideology. Russia's Media Discourse." *Journal for the Scientific Study of Religion* 40.3: 351–65.

Ančić, B. 2011. "What Do We Want from Religion? Religiosity and Social Expectations in Central and Eastern Europe." Forthcoming in András Máté-Tóth and Cosima

Rughiniş (eds), *Space and Borders. Current Research on Religion in Central and Eastern Europe*. Berlin: Walter de Gruyter.

Barker, Eileen V. 1997. "But Who's Going to Win? National and Minority Religions in Post Communist Society." In Eileen V. Barker and G. Babiński (eds), *New Religious Phenomena in Central and Eastern Europe*, 25–62. Kraków: Nomos.

Beckford, James A. and James T. Richardson. 2007. "Regulating Religion." In James A. Beckford and N. J. Demerath (eds), *The SAGE Handbook of the Sociology of Religion*, 396–418. London: SAGE.

Berger, Peter, Grace Davie and Effie Fokas. 2008. *Religious America, Secular Europe?: A Theme and Variations*. Aldershot: Ashgate.

Borowik, Irena (ed.) 2006. *Religions, Churches, and Religiosity in Post-Communist Europe*. Kraków: Nomos.

———. 2007. "The Religious Landscape of Central and Eastern Europe after Communism." In James A. Beckford and N. J. Demerath (eds), *The SAGE Handbook of the Sociology of Religion*, 654–69. London: SAGE.

Casanova, José. 2001. "Civil Society and Religion: Retrospective Relations on Catholicism and Prospective Reflections to Islam." *Social Research* 68.4: 1041–80.

———. 2007. "Immigration and the New Religious Pluralism: A EU/US Comparison." In Thomas Banchoff (ed.), *Democracy and the New Religious Pluralism*, 59–84. Oxford: Oxford University Press.

———. 2008. "The Problem of Religion and the Anxieties of European Secular Democracy." In Gabriel Motzkin and Yochi Fisher (eds), *Religion and Democracy in Contemporary Europe*, 63–74. London: Alliance Publishing Trust.

Črpić, Gordan and Siniša Zrinščak. 2010. "Dynamism in Stability: Religiosity in Croatia in 1999 and 2008." *Društvena istraživanja* 105–6.1–2: 3–37. In Croatian.

Devetak, Silvo, Liana Kalčina and Miroslav F. Polzer. 2004. *Legal Position of Churches and Religious Communities in South-Eastern Europe*. Ljubljana, Maribor and Vienna: ISCOMET.

Doe, Norman. 2004. "A Sociology of Law and Religion – Towards a New Discipline: Legal Responses to Religious Pluralism in Europe." *Law and Justice* 152: 68–92.

Edgardh, Ninna and Per Pettersson. 2010. "The Church of Sweden: A Church for All, Especially the Most Vulnerable." In Anders Bäckstrom and Grace Davie with Ninna Edgardh and Per Pettersson (eds), *Welfare and Religion in 21st Century Europe: Volume 1. Configuring the Connections*, 39–56. Farnham: Ashgate.

Ferrari, Silvio. 2003a. "The Legal Dimension." In Brigitte Maréchel, Stefano Allievi, Felice Dassetto and Jørgen Nielsen (eds), *Muslims in the Enlarged Europe. Religion and Society*, 219–51. Leiden: Brill.

———. 2003b. "The European Pattern of Church and State Relations." *Comparative Law* 20: 1–24.

———. 2003c. "Conclusion. Church and State in Post-Communist Europe." In Silvio Ferrari and W. Cole Durham Jr (eds), *Law and Religion in Post-Communist Europe*, 411–19. Leuven: Peeters.

———. 2008. "State Regulation of Religion in the European Democracies: The Decline of the Old Pattern." In Gabriel Motzkin and Yochi Fisher (eds), *Religion and Democracy in Contemporary Europe*, 103–12. London: Alliance Publishing Trust.

———. and Cole W. Durham Jr (eds) 2003. *Law and Religion in Post-Communist Europe*. Leuven: Peeters.

Fox, Jonathan. 2008a. *A World Survey of Religion and the State*. Cambridge: Cambridge University Press.

_____. 2008b. "State Religious Exclusivity and Human Rights." *Political Studies* 56.4: 928–48.

_____. 2009. "Quantifying Religion and State: Round Two of the Religion and State Project." *Politics and Religion* 2: 444–52.

_____. 2010. "The future of civilization and state religion policy." *Futures* 42.6: 522–31.

Gunn, Thomas Jeremy. 2006. "Managing Religion through Founding Myths and Perceived Identities." In Pauline Coté and Thomas Jeremy Gunn (eds), *La nouvelle question religieuse. Régulation ou ingérence de l'État? / The New Religious Question. State Regulations or State Interference?*, 33–48. Brussells, Bern, Berlin, Frankfurt am Main, New York, Oxford, Vienna: P.I.E. – Peter Lang.

Gustafsson, Goran. 2003. "Church-State Separation Swedish Style." In John T. S. Madeley and Zsolt Eneyedi (eds), *Church and State in Contemporary Europe: The Chimera of Neutrality*, 51–72. London and Portland, OR: Frank Cass.

Hervieu-Léger, Danièle. 2006. "The Role of Religion in Establishing Social Cohesion." In Krzysztof Michalski (ed.), *Religion in the New Europe*, 45–63. Budapest: Central University Press.

Kersbergen, Kees van and Monique Kremer. 2008. "Conservatism and the Welfare State: Intervening to Preserve." In Wim van Oorschot, Michael Opielka and Birgit Pfau-Effinger (eds), *Culture and Welfare State: Values and Social Policy in Comparative Perspective*, 71–88. Cheltenham: Edward Elgar.

Kersbergen, Kees van and Philip Manow (eds). 2009. *Religion, Class Coalitions, and Welfare States*. Cambridge: Cambridge University Press.

Koenig, Matthias. 2009. "How Nation-States Respond to Religious Diversity." In Paul A. Bramadat and Matthias Koenig (eds), *International Migration and the Governance of Religious Diversity*, 293–322. Montreal, Kingston, UK and Ithaca, NY: School of Policy Studies, Queen's University.

Kuburić, Zorica and Christian Moe. 2006. *Religion and Pluralism in Education: Comparative Approaches in the Western Balkans*. Novi Sad: CEIR in cooperation with the Kotor Network.

Madeley, John T. S. 2003. "European Liberal Democracies and the Principle of State Religious Neutrality." In John T. S. Madeley and Zsolt Eneyedi (eds), *Church and State in Contemporary Europe: The Chimera of Neutrality*, 1–22. London, Portland, OR: Frank Cass.

Marinović Jerolimov, Dinka and Siniša Zrinščak. 2006. "Religion Within and Beyond Borders: The Case of Croatia." *Social Compass* 53.2: 279–90.

Opielka, Michael. 2008. "Christian foundations of the welfare state: Strong cultural values in comparative perspective." In Wim van Oorschot, Michael Opielka and Birgit Pfau-Effinger (eds), *Culture and Welfare State: Values and Social Policy in Comparative Perspective*, 89–114. Northampton: Edward Elgar.

Polack, Detlef. and Gert Pickel. 2009. "Church-State Relations and the Vitality of Religion in European Comparison." In Gert Pickel and Olaf Müller (eds), *Church and Religion in Contemporary Europe: Results from Empirical and Comparative Research*, 145–66. Wiesbaden: VS Verlag für Sozialwissenschaften.

Révay, Edit and Miklos Tomka. 2006. *Eastern European Religion*. Budapest: Piliscsaba.

_____. 2007. *Churches and Religious Life in Post-Communist Societies*. Budapest: Piliscsaba.

Richardson, James T. 2004. *Regulating Religion: Case Studies from Around the Globe*. New York: Kluwer.

_____. 2006. "The Sociology of Religious Freedom: A Structural and Socio-Legal Analysis." *Sociology of Religion* 67.3: 271–94.

_____. 2009. "Religion and Law: An Interactionist perspective." In Peter Clarke (ed.), *The Oxford Handbook of the Sociology of Religion*, 418–31. Oxford: Oxford University Press.

Richardson, James T. and Massimo Introvigne. 2001. "'Brainwashing' Theories in European Parliamentary and Administrative Reports on 'Cults' and 'Sects.'" *Journal for the Scientific Study of Religion* 40.2: 143–68.

Richardson, James T. and Alain Garay. 2004. "The European Court of Human Rights and Former Communist States." In Dinka Marinović Jerolimov, Siniša Zrinščak and Irena Borowik (eds), *Religion and Patterns of Social Transformation*, 223–34. Zagreb: Institute for Social Research.

Robbins, Thomas. 2003. "Notes on Contemporary Peril to Religious Freedom." In James A. Beckford and James T. Richardson (eds), *Challenging Religion. Essays in Honour of Eileen Barker*, 64–73. London and New York: Routledge.

Robbers, Gerhard. 2005. "State and Church in the European Union." In Gerhard Robbers (ed.), *State and Church in the European Union*, 577–88. Baden-Baden: Nomos Verlagsgesellschaft.

_____. (ed.) 2005. *State and Church in the European Union*. Baden-Baden: Nomos Verlagsgesellschaft.

Sandberg, Russell. 2008. "Religion and the Individual: A Socio-legal Perspective." In Abby Day (ed.), *Religion and the Individual. Belief, Practice, Identity*, 157–68. Farnham: Ashgate.

Sarkissian, Ani. 2009. "Religious Reestablishment in Post-Communist Polities." *Journal of Church and State* 51.3: 472–501.

Schanda, Balázs. 2003. "Religion and State in the Candidate Countries to the European Union – Issues concerning Religion and State in Hungary." *Sociology of Religion* 64.3: 333–48.

_____. 2009. "Legal Status of Religious Communities in Central-Eastern Europe." REVACERN working paper (not publicly available).

Shterin, Marat and James T. Richardson. 1998. "Local Laws Restricting Religion in Russia: Precursors of Russia's New National Law." *Journal of Church and State* 40: 319–42.

_____. 2000. "Effects of the Western Anti-Cult Movement in Development of Laws Concerning Religion in Post-Communist Russia." *Journal of Church and State* 42: 247–71.

_____. 2002. "The Yakunin v. Dworkin Case: Analysis of a Major Legal Case Involving Minority Religions in Russia." *Religion in Eastern Europe* 22: 1–38.

Stepan, Alfred. 2001. *Arguing Comparative Politics*. Oxford: Oxford University Press.

Tomka, Miklos. 2006. "Is Conventional Sociology of Religion Able to Deal with Differences Between Eastern and Western Development?" *Social Compass* 53.2: 251–65.

Tomka, Miklos and Andrij Yurash. 2006. *Challenges of Religious Plurality for Eastern and Central Europe*. Lviv: T. Soroka.

Tomka, Miklos and Paul Zulehner. 2008. *Religionen und Kirchen in Ost(Mittel)Europa. Entwicklungen siet der Wende. Aufbruch 2007*. Wien-Budapest: Loisir

Torfs, Rik. 2007. "Religion and State Relationship in Europe." *Religious Studies Review* 4.1: 31–41.

Zrinščak, Siniša. 2002. "Rôles, attentes et conflits: La religion et les Eglises dans les sociétés en transition." *Social Compass* 49.4: 509–21.

_____. 2006. "Anonymous Believers as a Sociological Challenge: Religions and Religious Changes in Post-Yugoslav States." In Irena Borowik (ed.), *Religions, Churches and Religiosity in Post-Communist Europe*, 68-80. Krakow: Nomos.

_____. 2009a. *Legal Patterns and Social Reality of the Status of Religious Communities*. REVACERN working paper (not publicly available).

_____. 2009b. *Social Expectations Concerning the Church-State Relations*. REVACERN working paper (not publicly available).

Part II

FROM PIETISM TO CONSUMERISM

Chapter 8

CHINESE RELIGION, MARKET SOCIETY AND THE STATE

Jack Barbalet

Hong Kong Baptist University

Introduction

The familiar discussion of the nexus between religion and economy has emblematic representation in Max Weber's classic account of the elective affinity between Calvinism and the spirit of modern capitalism (Weber, 1991). Weber's demonstration of the supportive role of religious belief for capitalistic development is reversed, however, in his treatment of the history of China in which it is argued that Confucianism and Daoism had a compelling restraining impact on economic rationalization (Weber, 1964). This reversal has an additional dimension, insofar as an unintended consequence of the development of an expanding market economy and concomitant industrialization in China since the Deng Xiaoping reforms in 1978 has been to provide a space for religious expression unprecedented since the advent of the communist regime in 1949, and possibly even before this time given the predominantly negative policies toward religion by the state during the republican period from 1912. Indeed, since the onset of the reform period in the 1980s there has been not only more evidence of religious commitment and activity in both rural and urban areas but also changes in the nature of individual religions and in the numbers of religious adherents.

The most striking religious changes in the People's Republic of China (PRC) over the last 25 or so years have been twofold. The first consists of the reforms in both Buddhism and Daoism, especially in outreach and growth in the numbers of temples, priests and adherents or participants, which have largely been state sponsored or supported. The second is that the Christian presence in China and its diversity has significantly expanded.

However, apart from the permissive and regulatory role of the state in each of these developments, these trends do not point in the same direction. A good deal has been written about the growth of Christianity in China, but it is possibly the least understood of these changes. Much of the Christian expansion is in the PRC's rural sector (Huang and Yang, 2005) and while the Protestantism that is currently growing in major cities may be seen by some of its adherents as supportive, even expressive of a free market economy, a more comprehensive profile of Chinese Christianity suggests a tendency to social and economic conservatism.

It will be shown in the discussion below that a revival of Buddhism and Daoism, which on the surface appears even less remotely connected with the promotion of market economy in the PRC than Christianity, is an important mechanism in the provision of investment required for economic development in China. This is because the growth of Buddhism and Daoism both attract and are fueled by overseas Chinese contributors to the mainland economy. The capacity of the overseas Chinese to invest in the PRC derives from their success in business, commerce and finance in East and Southeast Asia. This development raises doubts concerning Weber's account of the negative impact of Confucian and Daoist orientations for capitalistic activity. This is because the overseas Chinese population that has been economically successful is generally endowed with the traditional Confucian and Daoist outlook Weber saw as responsible for inhibiting the development of capitalistic orientations and practices. Both of these aspects of the relationship between Chinese capitalism and Chinese religion shall be discussed in what follows. While these issues arise through the historical recentness of China's embrace of a market economy, it should not be assumed that its principles are entirely foreign to China, a matter raised in the following section.

Laissez-Faire and Daoism: Wu Wei

Joseph Needham, the distinguished author of the multivolumed *Science and Civilization in China* (1954–2004), famously demonstrated that practically every significant invention in human history originated in China: not only gunpowder and printing but also alcohol, ball bearings, the magnetic compass, paper, toilet paper, the stirrup, the toothbrush and so on. Not only physical but also social technologies can be sourced to Chinese origins. While no Needham-like figure has yet written *Social Science and Civilization in China*, it can be shown that the concept of a laissez-faire instrument of Chinese political economy, for instance, was not only clearly articulated 100 years before Christ but also that the Chinese doctrine of laissez-faire was self-consciously borrowed by the eighteenth-century French economist, François Quesnay, in development of his physiocratic theory (Gerlach, 2005; Hudson, 1961: 322–6; Reichwein, 1968: 99–110). Anticipating Adam Smith by 1,850 years, the great Han Dynasty historian Sima Qian wrote:

There must be farmers to produce food, men to extract the wealth of mountains and marshes, artisans to produce these things and merchants to circulate them. There is no need to wait for government orders: each man will play his part, doing his best to get what he desires... When all work willingly at their trades, just as water flows ceaselessly downhill day and night, things will appear unsought and people will produce them without being asked. For clearly this accords with the Way and is in keeping with nature. (Chien, 1979: 411)

It is evident within this passage that the conceptual root of the economic notion of laissez-faire reported here, directed against feudal practices of interference, is Daoist.

The water metaphor contained in the passage above is characteristic of the principal Daoist texts dating from the third century BC, namely the *Daode jing* (sometimes referred to as the *Laozi* after its putative author) and the *Zhuangzi*. But more important in demonstrating the Daoist nature of Sima Qian's discussion is the way in which the passage above expresses the key Daoist principle of *wu wei*. *Wu wei* can be translated as "doing less" or "noncoercive action." The passage above from Sima Qian paraphrases sections of the *Daode jing* in showing that the performance of trade and the division of labor occur in the absence of government engagement which itself indicates that "this accords with the Way [or Dao]" and in doing so is consonant with nature:

It is simply in doing things non-coercively (*wuwei*) that everything is governed properly...do things non-coercively (*wuwei*) and the common people will develop along their own lines. (Ames and Hall, 2003: 82, 166)

The point of these passages from the *Laozi* – and also those from Sima Qian – is that a state that practices *wu wei* does less, yet everything is accomplished in accordance with the needs of the state.

It is not necessary, of course, to go back to the Han Dynasty to locate evidence of pre-1978 Chinese inclinations to laissez-faire or market capitalism. Well before China embraced a market economy in the 1980s, southern Chinese migrants in East and Southeast Asia from the mid-nineteenth century and throughout the twentieth century were successfully engaged in capitalist activities. It will be shown below that the capitalism of the overseas Chinese, ironically, has been an instrumental factor in the more recent development of a capital market in the PRC, with the help of the Chinese state. It will also be shown that Daoism continues to play a role in Chinese capitalist success, as it did in the formulation of laissez-faire doctrine during the Han Dynasty. It might be mentioned parenthetically that in the PRC today, there is continuing application of Daoist principles to analysis of economic development. Since 2000 there have appeared in Chinese social science and Party journals a number of articles in which Daoist concepts, especially *wu wei* and related notions, are applied to understanding the development and operation of China's market economy (see Barbalet, 2011). Given the continuing importance of Daoism to Chinese self-understanding of markets and to an account of the Chinese economy, it is necessary to mention a number of issues relating to the distinctive features of Chinese religion.

Chinese Religion

It is often noted in indicating the complexity of Chinese traditions that Daoism, for instance, is both a religion and philosophy. We shall return to this distinction below. Before doing so, however, it is important to understand that the concepts of both religion and philosophy were until recently unknown to Chinese language and culture. The current Chinese term for religion, *jiao*, is an abbreviation of a word imported at the beginning of the twentieth century from Japanese and sinicized as *zong jiao*. An earlier Chinese term, *san jiao*, used from the ninth century to refer to Buddhism, Daoism and Confucianism collectively, means not "three religions" but "three teachings" (Sun, 2005: 232–3; see also Ashiwa and Wank, 2009: 9). The Chinese term for philosophy, *zhexue*, is also a Japanese invention created at the end of the nineteenth century by combining the Chinese characters for wisdom (*zhe*) and study (*xue*). Before this innovation there was instead only study of the canon or great books (*jing xue*) and the traditions of the masters (*zi xue*) (Yijie, 2007: 33–4). Daoism, then, offers a way of seeing the world as a means of being in it – it is one teaching (*yi jiao*) and the texts of Daoism, for instance the *Laozi* and *Zhuangzi* and their purported authors, can be objects of study (*jing xue*). Daoism as a "religion" and "philosophy" in this sense, then, refers only to the fact that it is a pedagogic practice and that the practice is associated with books that can be the objects of contemplation, reflection and commentary.

At the present time in the PRC, Daoism may increasingly appear to be like a religion in the Western sense because it is increasingly transformed by regulation, training, professionalization and outreach that derive from modern political requirements and cultural transformations (Yang, 2005; Dean, 2009). The philological asides of the previous paragraph help make sense of the commonplace observation that the notion of "Chinese religion" presents certain problems of specification and classification because an understanding of religion in the Western sense – of focus on a deity, a sacred-profane dichotomy, transcendence and so on – is not readily located in the Chinese cases. The asides also lead us to other aspects of Chinese tradition in addition to the modernizing forces to which Daoism and Buddhism are today subjected, which are themselves suggestive of certain limits on how far these "teachings" can go in becoming religions in the Western sense. For the sake of making the argument it is necessary, though, in spite of what has been written above, to refer to Chinese "religion" in order to more clearly indicate the nature and context of these cultural practices and patterns of thought.

In an important sense, Chinese religion and European religion can be regarded as practically opposites. Chinese religion has always been polytheistic and nonexclusive, whereas European religion is monotheistic and exclusive. In China, priests and what would pass in the Western sense as clergy have traditionally been small in number and poorly organized (Yang, 1961: 307–27). Unlike Western religion, Chinese religion has historically failed to provide social services or education (Yang, 1961: 335–9), although this is subject to modest change today (Yang and Wei, 2005: 69–70; Lang, Chan and Ragvald, 2005: 163). Chinese religious nonexclusivity and therefore the absence of exclusive patronage has contributed to the organizational weakness of Chinese religion, whereas Western religious exclusivity has led to a disciplined clergy and well-organized laity. Marcel Granet summarizes the Chinese case:

> The Chinese are not divided up into followers of one or another of the three faiths; in circumstances fixed by tradition they appeal at the same time to Buddhist or Taoist priests, even to [Confucian] literati or officials. Not only do they never submit to a dogmatic parti pris, but when they have recourse to specialists, they do not show towards them the veneration of the sort due to members of a clergy. (Granet, 1975: 144)

A final striking difference to be mentioned here between Chinese religion and European religion is their relationship with the political state. The Chinese state – imperial and republican as well as communist – has always constituted a powerful force over and against organized (perhaps it is more accurate to say in light of the above remarks, disorganized) religion, and the Chinese tradition is one of political dominance over and control of religion (Yang, 1961: 180–217). While there have been periods of state patronage, the typical orientation of the state towards religion since the early Ming Dynasty in the fourteenth century has been a mix of regulation and prohibition (Brook, 2009). The early history of Christianity, on the other hand, prior to the Reformation, was of a continentally organized church empire against small and divided secular governments. Against this background, the politically instrumental utility of national Protestant churches to European states provided reform churches with a power which they may still call upon and exercise in defense of their own independence.

The image of the weakness of Chinese religion created in the preceding paragraph relates to its organizational capacities, but a further characteristic of Chinese religion that requires special consideration is its enduring cultural presence and force. Before pursuing this theme, however, it is necessary to say something about Confucianism, which has so far been ignored. Western commentators have frequently regarded Confucianism as a religion even though the absence of religious consciousness with regard to it on the part of adherents suggests that the appellation is misplaced. Indeed, the failed attempt to establish a Confucian religion during the republican period for largely political reasons (Yang, 1961: 355–8; Sun, 2005: 234–6) suggests the artificiality and misleading nature of the idea that Confucianism is a religion in any meaningful sense. This is not to say that there are not elements of Confucianism that arguably possess religious qualities, such as self-cultivation productive of social order or harmony expressed in a clear ethical code through a positive orientation to ritual practices (see Yang, 1961: 244–77). Perhaps more important than the observer ascribed as opposed to adherent experienced religious characteristics of Confucianism is its long-standing and complex relationship, since the ninth century, of opposition and creative engagement with both Buddhism and Daoism, that has seen each contest, adapt to and mimic aspects of the others over a long period of Chinese history.

The last point above can be taken to imply that Confucianism, Buddhism and Daoism have changed through their mutual interactions. Of course, such interactions are not the only sources of change, but they do suggest that not one of these three traditions can be regarded as entirely unitary entities when considered over historical time. The point has been made that Confucianism, for instance, is "not one philosophy, but many" and that while "Neo-Confucianism, a movement dating from the late T'ang…is not only significantly different from what went before, (it is) very far from a unified philosophy itself" (Nivison, 1959: 4). Daoism even more than Confucianism can be seen as a single label that covers a number of quite different movements and purposes. In a seminal paper that has become the source of much controversy, Herrlee Creel has shown that Daoism is in effect three, not one set of principles and practices (Creel, 1977).

Creel distinguishes "contemplative" and "purposive" Daoism associated respectively with the *Zhuangzi* and the *Daode jing*, one cultivating an understanding of the Dao or Way to achieve inner strength and the other to achieve a means of power and kingly council (Creel, 1977: 4–6). At an historically later period, a set of practices and doctrines were consolidated into a movement that went on to manifest variant and divergent forms, but with the continuing purpose of attaining immortality for its practitioners, which amalgamated elements of folk immortality cults, Buddhist organizational forms and the Daoist name (Creel, 1977: 7–8). Creel names this third type of Daoism not "religious" Daoism but Hsien Daoism – *hsien* being an immortal – because the "immortality in question was a perpetuation of the physical body" (Creel, 1977: 7). The means used to achieve everlasting life or at least extraordinary longevity included drugs and alchemic practices, breath control and gymnastics, dietary management and macrobiotics, moral (Confucian) virtue, sexual techniques, magical rites and charms and talismans – all of which are opposed or ridiculed in the *Zhuangzi* and the *Daode jing* (Creel, 1977: 8–9). The important point, which it is not Creel's purpose to make, is that irrespective of their logical and historical relationship the anarchistic contemplative Daoism which promotes inner self-cultivation, the instrumentally purposive Daoism which navigates social and political power and the curative and restorative Hsien Daoism which extends and improves life and living have all been contemporaneously available for nearly two thousand years within the Chinese cultural framework of doctrinal and practical nonexclusivity.

The characteristic organizational weakness of Chinese religion, for want of a better term, belies its enduring cultural presence and power. The real strength of Chinese religion arguably derives from what C. K. Yang, following Durkheim, calls its "diffused" form (Yang, 1961: 296–300). A religion is diffused when its outlook and concepts are insinuated in and dispersed through secular social institutions and in that sense are a part of those institutions. Yang reserves this concept for his discussion of folk religions and especially ancestor worship, neither of which have the benefit of organized sanction or rationale. But Confucianism, Buddhism and Daoism (in each of its three forms) have a continuing diffused, that is noninstitutional representation in many aspects of Chinese life and culture. In the domain of self-cultivation, for instance, Confucian and Daoist concepts are essential for understanding Chinese practices; in business, military strategy and environmental policy purposive Daoist concepts predominate; in medical and health matters and in the rhythm of mundane life, Hsien Daoist rituals prevail; and so on. These and related traditions are diffused through Chinese culture and many of their key concepts are given representation in the Chinese language itself. The significance of the cognitive framework of Chinese religions will be taken up below.

State Management of Religion and the Market Economy in China Since 1978

Twenty-first century China can justifiably be seen as a site of religious effervescence. In addition to the appreciable rise in Christianity there have also emerged new religious movements, the best known being Falun Gong (Ownby, 2004). Alongside these changes and arguably more important for an understanding of current political and economic developments in the PRC is a revival of Buddhism and Daoism, a significant aspect of which includes the rebuilding of damaged or destroyed temples. The activity of temple rebuilding is state sponsored, privately funded and quite central to the ongoing expansion of economic development.

As a large proportion of temples in China were traditionally communal property, it was not unusual even in imperial times for them to be put to nonreligious use as the need arose, a process hastened with the formation of the republic in 1912 and secular modernization that continued after 1949 with the establishment of the PRC (see Yang, 1961: 326, 368). It has been estimated that by the end of the republican period half of China's local temples had been destroyed, and that during the period of the Cultural Revolution (1966–76) tens of thousands of the remaining Buddhist, Daoist and other temples were destroyed as part of active antireligious campaigns (Goossaert, 2003). In contrast to the events of the 1960s and 1970s in the PRC, there has emerged from the early 1980s a new tolerance toward religion. The third constitution of the PRC promulgated in 1978 introduced limited guarantees of religious freedom. Such freedoms have been extended in Article 36 of the subsequent 1982 constitution, which remains current. Article 36 indicates a move from state prohibition to state regulation of religion; it declares that while religions are not to "engage in activities that disrupt public order, impair the health of citizens or interfere with the educational system of the state" the state shall "protect normal religious activities." What these normal activities might be are not specified except in the negative case as indicated. This qualified relaxation of overall hostility towards religion from the late 1970s has accelerated to a positive acceptance of aspects of religion in particular religions so that by the mid-1990s there have been permitted, even encouraged, large-scale and vigorous efforts at restoration and refurbishment of temples and other religious buildings destroyed during the Cultural Revolution. By 1996, for instance, 1,722 Daoist temples had been restored and opened (Dean, 2009: 193).

The new qualified acceptance of religion in the PRC is an aspect of a broader liberalization that has accompanied China's incorporation into the international capitalist economy and its entry on to the world political stage.

While state suppression of religious movements such as Falun Gong (Tong, 2009) and the smaller Dongfang Shandian (Eastern Lightning) continues in the PRC (Dunn, 2009), the constitutional guarantees of freedom of religious belief and practice are given meaningful expression for Buddhist, Daoist, Catholic, Protestant and Islamic organizations that are affiliated with the state-controlled umbrella bodies (see Yang, 2007: 636–8). A link between China's religious liberalization, especially the rebuilding of Buddhist and Daoist temples, and the development – indeed exuberant blossoming – of a market economy in the PRC is to be found in a further and connected dimension of government reorientation since the mid-1980s, namely a reversal in attitude to the Chinese Diaspora. Temple rebuilding attracts overseas Chinese investment. There is a new motto for capital acquisition given voice by local government in the PRC: "Build the religious stage to sing the economic opera" (Yang, 2006: 109).

The changing official attitude in the PRC to the overseas Chinese is central for an understanding of both the revival of religion and the development of a capital market. From Liberation (1949) up until the immediate post–Cultural Revolution period, the Chinese political leadership entertained a thorough and intense suspicion of the overseas Chinese. As the PRC has joined the globalized international market, the economic skills of the overseas Chinese and their capacity to provide investment capital that had earlier led to their stigmatization as "Capitalist Roaders" have been evaluated positively by official forces in the PRC since the 1980s. Those skills and that capacity are now seriously sought by the Chinese market economy. Indeed, since the 1980s there has been much official encouragement of overseas Chinese to invest in the PRC. One means of attracting overseas Chinese investment has been through the temple door. After opening its borders as a consequence of the Deng Xiaoping reforms, the PRC has facilitated visits by significant numbers of overseas Chinese persons who since liberalization have returned to family home sites in the PRC for religious and mortuary rituals (Fan, 2003; Lai, 2003). The program of temple rebuilding mentioned above has coincidentally and conjointly been encouraged enormously through donations made by overseas Chinese individuals and families (Yang and Wei, 2005: 71–2, 86; Lang, Chan and Ragvald, 2005: 157–9). In this way, the erstwhile "Capitalist Roaders" are led to occupy an important place in the course of Chinese economic development (Maddison, 2007: 172–3; Redding, 1993: 231ff.). Indeed, up to the mid-1990s overseas Chinese investors from Hong Kong, Taiwan and Singapore contributed 75 percent of foreign capital to China, and if other overseas Chinese are included the figure goes up to 85 percent, amounting to approximately US$200 billion (Hamilton, 2006; Redding, 1995; Sen, 2001: 3).

Capitalism, China and Max Weber

It is not simply the magnitude of growth and strength of China's market economy that is so impressive, but also that it erupted against all expectations. It could be argued, of course, that in effectively abandoning socialism, embracing the market and joining capitalist globalization, China's economic growth was inevitable. The limitations of this argument can partly be seen in India's failure to enjoy Chinese levels of economic expansion. It is important to notice, as mentioned above, that during the nineteenth and twentieth century mercantile and financial dynasties were formed within overseas Chinese communities, demonstrating the way in which market opportunities could be realized by persons who adhered to Chinese religions. Nevertheless, in an argument that continues to hold the attention of many sociologists, Max Weber insisted that traditional Chinese religions and the familial commitments associated with them are antithetical to the development of capitalism (Weber, 1964). However, in the face of recent Chinese economic success in both overseas Chinese populations and in the post-1978 PRC, the task must be to explain afresh how Chinese religion and associated family structure might be related to capitalist development.

Weber's characterization of Chinese religion in *The Religion of China* is to demonstrate the cultural basis of a failure in Imperial China to develop rational or modern industrial capitalism. Weber holds that traditional Chinese values in the form of Confucianism promoted an orientation of talent to state service, to scholarly pursuits that tended to preserve tradition and at the same time to dissuade thinkers from innovation. Confucianism, according to Weber, generates a rationalism that leads persons to adjust to the world rather than encouraging them to change it (Weber, 1964: 248). Daoism, Weber says, promotes an orientation to simplicity in life and harmony with nature. Both of these philosophies or religions are held to discourage capitalistic accumulation and profit seeking. While this broad characterization of Chinese traditional values is more or less descriptively accurate for the period covered by Weber's study, it is quite a different matter to claim that these values were causally implicated in the failure to develop industrial capitalism in Imperial China. Indeed, it is likely that the key inhibiting constraints on Chinese economic development were not cultural. John Hall, for instance, has shown that at crucial times in its long history the imperial Chinese state chose to limit capitalism even as it developed for political reasons (Hall, 1986: 33–57). In more directly addressing Weber's concern regarding the absence in China of the development of industrial capitalism, Mark Elvin (1973: 286–315, 1983) argues that a failure to continue an historically established pattern of innovation necessary for industrialization, which occurred around 1820 through an insufficiency of demand – what he calls a "high-level equilibrium trap" – inhibited capitalist industrialization in China.

Evidence of both political and economic structural limitations challenge the adequacy of Weber's argument that "rational entrepreneurial capitalism...has been handicapped [in China]...by the lack of a particular mentality" (Weber, 1964: 104). It is not, however, the purpose here to claim that consideration of Confucianism and Daoism is irrelevant to an understanding of economic processes and especially entrepreneurial activity in Chinese cultural areas. But it is important to recognize, contrary to Weber's approach, that the social consequences of culture, and values in particular, are not internal to the culture or values themselves but are contextually effective. Therefore, the relationship between any given value set and economic outcomes for those holding them may vary with changing opportunities and constraints. While Weber attributes Chinese petty bourgeois hoarding to Confucian notions of thrift, for instance, there is no way of knowing whether his theory-laden proposition implies a spurious relationship without first paying attention to the constraints on opportunities for consumption or investment, which Weber fails to do (Weber, 1964: 245).

Weber's inclination to treat institutions in terms of what he sees as the values inherent in them has led to serious misunderstanding concerning the function of key institutions, including the family. In the *Protestant Ethic*, for instance, Weber writes that Protestant vocation or calling generates emotional detachment and depersonalizes family relations, thus early modern European entrepreneurs are presented as individuals free of family ties and traditional obligations. This perspective on the family is more forcefully stated in his later studies, especially in *The Religion of China* (Weber, 1964: 237, 240–1, 244), where it is argued that family and community are sources of traditional constraint that inhibit the capitalist ethos of profit making for its own sake as a result of religious values. This argument is seriously mistaken, however, both for Western capitalism and Chinese capitalism. Before considering Chinese religion and capitalism, it is necessary to say something about the family in capitalist development. This is because the motor of economic growth is familial capitalism rather than socially isolated individuals imbued with self-possessed acquisitiveness in both Europe and in the Chinese diaspora from the nineteenth century.

Family as a Resource for Capitalist Development

The unit of enterprise and the major proximate sources of commercial and business attainment in early modern Europe was not the individual entrepreneur free of family responsibility and commitment, but rather individuals who were economically enriched by kinship networks and marital alliances who thereby had immediate access to reputation, credit and uniquely reliable associates (Grassby, 2000). The pattern of European familial capitalism persisted into the nineteenth century (Farrell, 1993; Scranton, 1983) and continued even to the twentieth century, even though by this time national markets for long-term investment were functioning (Postan, 1935: 5–6) thus rendering family credit less important. Writing in the early 1970s, Maurice Zeitlin indicated that in spite of the widespread belief concerning managerial control, the majority of firms in the United States, for instance, continued at that time to be subject to family control and that a large number of the financial institutions that controlled firms which were not directly owned by families were themselves family owned and controlled (Zeitlin, 1974). A more recent study suggests that the incidence of family ownership in the United States may be as high as 80 percent and possibly rising (La Porta, Lopez-de-Silanes and Shleifer 1999; see also Church, 1993).

This brief excursion into Western familial capitalism has the purpose of suggesting that examination of the role of the Chinese family in capitalist enterprise, which a number of studies of both overseas and mainland Chinese business have focused upon (Redding, 1993; Whyte, 1996), is not to highlight an exceptional Chinese contribution to a course of capitalist development but to indicate a neglected but significant aspect of the sociology of capitalism in general. The resources appropriate to capitalistic market production and exchange include financial credit, business information and know-how, reputation for reliability, able associates, trustworthy and low-cost workers and translocal networks. Strong kinship and marital alliances supply these resources in abundance.

Indeed, the significance of the family for economic activity is demonstrated in consideration of employment costs. Economic theories understand labor costs in terms of supply and demand for skills and effort capacities. Quality labor, though, is not simply at the top end of these latter factors but imbued with what John Stuart Mill calls "moral qualities" (Mill, 1940: 110–11). Quality labor, then, can be trusted to work at a high level of efficiency with relatively little supervision whatever its skill or effort capacity. The preparedness of employers to pay above the market rate for workers with these moral qualities is addressed by efficiency wage theory. Family labor, though, simply reverses efficiency wage theory because quality labor is not only efficiently selected through family relations but in family enterprises is frequently paid well below market rates without risking labor turnover, sabotage or shirking. The role of wives working for low or no wages in family firms as business managers or accountants is well known in the West and has recently been demonstrated for family enterprises in the PRC's private sector (Goodman, 2004, 2007; Tsai, 2007: 112–14). This is not to say that inefficiency and nepotism cannot occur in family firms (see Redding, 1993: 133–4), but that familial capitalism is not *necessarily* nonrational, as Weber maintains. Indeed, the application of transaction cost analysis and agency contract theory to family enterprises identifies the aspects of and conditions under which familial capitalism may operate at high levels of market rationality (Pollak, 1985; Steier, 2003).

Chinese families, because they are constituted by transgenerational and lateral networks, are particularly adept at providing the resources for or means of capitalistic agency (Goody, 1996: 151–61; Whyte, 1996: 9–13). Differences between Chinese and Western families in business derive from cultural differences – much is made, for instance, of the Confucian basis of Chinese family structure and practices – but there are also highly salient contingent differences. Gordon Redding, for instance, notes:

> The environments in which [overseas Chinese business families] are accustomed to operate have not been notable for their hospitality to business enterprises or to Chinese entrepreneurs. Such entrepreneurs have developed a well-justified wariness in the face of officialdom and a well-honed set of defensive weapons to ensure their survival in an uncertain world. (Redding, 1993: 4)

These learned characteristics are particularly useful when operating within the orbit of the capricious administration of the PRC. While familial capitalism is not necessarily the only factor in the development of post-1978 Chinese market capitalism, it is an important one (Whyte, 1996: 9).

Action: Opportunity Structures and Resources

As indicated above, Chinese families are an efficient basis of the provision of *means* for engaging in capitalist activity by reducing the transaction costs of credit and finance and by lowering the agency costs of management, administration and labor. It will be shown here that Chinese religion is particularly important in effectively increasing the *opportunities* for applying those means in money making. But this requires a very different approach than Weber's to both religion and action.

The close fit between Weber's sociology of religion and his theory of action is readily located in *The Protestant Ethic*, for instance: Weber approaches religion by identifying the values implicit in religious doctrine as a primary source in the social actor's construction of meaning which in turn is generative of individual motivation or the orientation of action. But the understanding of action in terms of values as the basis of motive raises a number of problems, not the least of which are that effective values are more likely to be the outcomes of actions rather than their antecedents and motives are largely inaccessible and frequently innumerable for any given action (Barbalet, 2009). Much more important for understanding action are two factors which Weber tends to neglect. While he notes in the *General Economic History* that "rational capitalism...is organized with a view to market opportunities" (Weber, 1981: 334), Weber tends to have very little to say about structures of opportunities for action (Barbalet, 2008: 218–19, 221) and he also tends to ignore the means required for the achievement of opportunities (Barbalet, 2008: 123–5). If we think of capitalism in terms of opportunities for money making through market exchanges and the particular resources required to take advantage of or to mobilize for those opportunities, then a general form of motivation can be simply assumed and individual motives cease to be of theoretical interest in understanding economic action. If we think of action in terms of opportunities and resources or means then the family, for instance, can be seen as one source of the means required for market exchanges as indicated above and perception of opportunities can be treated as part of a cultural-cognitive apparatus within which religion may play a role.

The apprehension of novel opportunities for profit making – through the discovery of a market niche, for instance, or a new way of deploying existing resources – is widely recognized as fundamental for market success under capitalist conditions. The concept of opportunity structure therefore addresses the question of the potential for new profit generation and the expansion of the market and economic activity. The significance of opportunity structures is understood in practice by all economic actors. However, theoretical discussion of opportunity has been marred by naturalistic and individualistic assumptions. For instance, in his important statement of the theory of the entrepreneur, Joseph Schumpeter regards opportunities or what he calls "possibilities" as something that are "offered by the surrounding world" and are simply "always present" (Schumpeter, 2008: 79, 88). Schumpeter's supposition that there is no need for a mechanism to generate or realize manifest opportunities from latent "possibilities" is a reflection of his conceptualization of entrepreneurship in terms of individual will and motivation (Schumpeter, 2008: 93–4). While more recent studies have focused on the entrepreneur's characteristically astute grasp of opportunities, their theoretical framework continues to assume that individual mental processes of cognition are sufficient bases of explanation (Mitchell et al., 2002; Shane, 2004). The approach proposed here, on the other hand, places the perception of opportunities not in individual cognitive psychological processes but in cultural apparatuses, including religious frameworks.

While opportunities may be latent in existing arrangements, as Schumpeter holds, opportunities are necessarily prospective – not material – realities and become manifest only when they are taken. Opportunity structures therefore only exist as hypotheses or as constructed or discovered possibilities dependent on a particular conjectural perception. Like all perception, the involvement of anticipation and therefore emotion and imagination are central to the formation of opportunity structures, including those for profit making. Religion may play a role here if religion is part of a cultural apparatus that contributes to the notional location or formation of opportunities for profit making. Whether Protestantism, for instance, can be part of such a cultural apparatus must be a matter for empirical investigation. Because religious dissenters, as critics of an established order, may possess novel cognitive orientations or capacities, it is possible that if they are business orientated they could perceive opportunities for profit making that may not otherwise be visible. The difference between this argument and Weber's is large. It is not that Protestantism leads to a capitalistic ethic but that should Protestants be capitalistically involved, then their religion, not as a set of values but as a culturally provided cognitive framework, may generate a perception of opportunity for profit through affective and imaginative appraisal of future prospects irrespective of whatever motive may direct them to profit making.

Weber implicitly and unintentionally raises the question of opportunity in a way compatible with the manner it is set out here. Toward the end of *The Religion of China* he says enigmatically in the context of his preceding remarks that "The Chinese in all probability would be quite capable, probably more capable than the Japanese, of assimilating capitalism which has technically and economically been fully developed in the modern cultural area" (Weber, 1964: 248). How they might achieve this Weber does not say, apart from a suggestion that cultural osmosis may be the mechanism – he refers to Canton (now Guangzhou) as one place it has happened because of the large numbers of foreigners there (Weber, 1964: 242). It must be noted, though, that in a slightly later work Weber claims that the Japanese are more likely than the Chinese to "take over capitalism as an artefact from the outside" (Weber, 1960: 275). Given Weber's insistence on the incongruity of the values of Chinese religion and capitalism – in which the motive for profit making as an end in itself in market exchanges cannot be deduced from the values of Chinese religious ethics – it is ironic that the cognitive structure of Chinese religions can function as instruments in expanding the horizon of capitalistic opportunities, as indicated below.

Chinese Religion and Expanding Opportunity Structures

It was mentioned above that Chinese religions cohabit within a polytheistic culture of nonexclusivity. It is feasible to suppose that this nonexclusivity has played a role in the advancement of China's post-1978 market economy insofar as the mindset of religious nonexclusivity is part of a cultural apparatus which, in the context of market exchanges, encourages the perception and apprehension of opportunities which may otherwise not be apparent. Because of the lateral elective cognitive mobility available within the Chinese religious universe, which is an aspect of religious nonexclusivity, there is an increased likelihood of a sharpened awareness of an expanding range of possible opportunities in any given situation. But within the lattice of Chinese religious nonexclusivity, the different religions do not equally play a role in encouraging an expanding appreciation of market opportunities. Therefore, it is necessary to give consideration to the different capacities of Buddhism, Confucianism and Daoism to contribute to the likely apprehension of market opportunities.

Chinese Buddhism comprises a number of different "schools" but is unified in being "this worldly" (*Mahayana*) rather than "other-worldly" (*Theravada*) in its concerns (Liu, 2008: 218–9). Chinese Buddhist acceptance of performance of mundane activities in achieving nonattachment or nonselfhood (the absence of enduring identity) in renunciation of the world and profit seeking within it contributes to a cognitive apparatus that limits rather than expands the optional set within an opportunity structure. The general and therefore potentially transferable ethical prescriptions of Buddhism similarly offer no encouragement that it might cognitively support an expansive opportunity structure. Buddhist ethics assume the impossibility through moral regulation of improvement of a social order comprising persons with human desires and interests. The affective or emotional direction of Buddhism, therefore, is disengagement from and aversion to this-worldly economic action.

Confucianism, in emphasizing a "middle way" (*zhong yong*) approach to life and conduct, encourages neutrality, stability and avoiding extreme positions. This has the effect of confining the appreciation of opportunities to a limited range of prospects and stabilizing rather than radically expanding the optional set within an opportunity structure. Because Confucianism is restricted to precedent and has a this-worldly orientation – it both faces the past and is realist – it tends to be restrictive of imagination. At the same time, however, the Confucian understanding of fate does include a significant agentic element: persons establish their own fate by planning ahead, applying their best abilities and taking responsibility for their own actions. According to Confucian teaching, the controlling capacity of fate is not at the level of the selection and execution of a course of action but in whether such actions might succeed or fail (Yang, 1961: 229, 272–3). Thus fate, rather than another human agent, is responsible for the success or failure of a given person's action. On balance, then, and especially relative to Buddhism, Confucianism tends to cognitively expand rather than contract the optional set of any given opportunity structure.

The presentation of Daoism in Weber's *Religion of China* emphasizes what he sees as three essential qualities: its mysticism (Weber, 1964: 180–8), its focus on macrobiotics and immortality (Weber, 1964: 191, 204) and its traditionalism – "more traditionalist than orthodox Confucianism" – predicated on the use of magical techniques (Weber, 1964: 205). In his account, Weber confuses and conflates what were earlier in this chapter distinguished as contemplative, purposive and Hsien Daoisms, rendering his globalizing assessment unsustainable. Weber's claim that the *Laozi* or *Daode jing* contains an exposition of "contemplative mysticism" (Weber, 1964: 186) reflects what has been described as an antagonistic Confucian interpretation (Hansen, 1992: 7) widely accepted by the Christian missionaries who wrote many of the sources Weber drew upon. Indeed, one scholarly assessment is that the leading Daoist ideas are "more intellectual than mystical" (Granet, quoted in Creel, 1970: 15), although there is no consensus about this in the literature. While some scholars insist on the mystical nature of *Daode jing* (Schwartz, 1985) others see it as an antimystical and naturalistic or protoscientific work (Needham, 1956; Moeller, 2006; see also Lau, 1963: xxxviii–xli). The principle text of Daoism, *Daode jing*, while appearing to some as a set of mystical poems is at the same time readily seen as a handbook of statecraft, with a purpose of political counsel and kingly advice anticipating Machiavelli's *The Prince*. Indeed, the politically instrumental orientation of the text is demonstrated throughout a third-century commentary by Wang Bi (1999), a work which continues to inform the Chinese understanding of the *Daode jing*. Neither is it possible to show that *Daode jing* or *Zhuangzi* advocate magical means or are necessarily traditionalist. Traditional thought and practice, rather, are vulnerable to a key deconstructive tendency within purposive Daoism (Needham, 1956: 33–164). These are the inherent attributes of Daoism that positively encourage nonexclusivity and an experimental expansion of the optional set within any given opportunity structure. These latter are achieved through development and promotion of the concept and practice of what might be described as "paradoxical integration."

Paradoxical integration entails that opposite elements of a thing are interdependent and mutually supportive, best represented in the relationship between *yin* and *yang*. The opposition between elements of a paradoxical integration is not contradictory in the Western sense that one element eliminates the other, but rather is held to give rise to generative relationships of a number of types between opposites. *Daode jing* is a veritable handbook of paradoxical integration, with more than forty percent of the text occupied with examples and expositions of paradoxical integration. Thus, according to the *Daode jing*, opposites are held to be mutually productive of each other, for instance, that in order to achieve a purpose its opposite must be attempted, that a thing seems to be quite other than it is, and so on (Ames and Hall, 2003: 80, 133, 140–41). The Daoist notions of strength in weakness and advantage in threat or danger generate perceptions of opportunities in market engagements which might otherwise not materialize.

Daoism has been relatively neglected in considerations of Chinese religion, probably because it is institutionally weaker than Buddhism. The diffuse nature of Chinese religion, however, means that its importance and influence cannot be measured by the number of its supporters but by the pervasiveness of its concepts. The conventional approach of associating overseas Chinese business success with Confucian principles, for example, is based on the assumption that Chinese family dynamics are Confucian (Haley, Haley and Tan, 2004; Haley, Tan and Haley, 1998; Redding, 1993; Whyte, 1996). There is more than an element of truth in this supposition, even though it neglects the importance of Daoist ideas concerning family and marital relations. These ideas round out and strengthen Confucian precepts associated with the durability of Chinese families, especially in terms of Daoist encouragement of discovering "the natural" course in relationships and in emphasizing the importance of the feminine and therefore encouraging a certain type of regard for women.

Conclusion

Chinese religion and China's market economy can be seen as mutually supportive in a number of ways. First, the revival of Buddhism and Daoism in post-1978 China has been a conduit for investment in the market economy of the PRC from the Chinese diaspora. Second, the success of overseas Chinese since the nineteenth century in capitalist ventures in East and Southeast Asia suggests a positive relationship between market rationality on the one hand and Chinese religion and family on the other that raises questions concerning the received Weberian perspective. Third, an approach to religion as part of a cultural apparatus instrumental in the apprehension of opportunity structures for capitalistic activity is outlined in the chapter, which indicates the significance of Chinese religious nonexclusivity in general and Daoism in particular for successful market engagements through opportunity perceptiveness.

Throughout the chapter, the significance of the relationship between the political state and religion has been indicated. The long historical relationship in China between the state and religion has been characterized as one of state regulation of religion moderated by brief interspersed episodes of patronage or prohibition. Regulatory relations have frequently included co-option of religious forces for state purposes. This is demonstrated in the present post-1978 period by the state sponsored but privately funded program of temple restoration that is a conduit for capital investment in the PRC by overseas Chinese.

In contrasting Chinese and Western religion it was shown above that a Chinese term for religion, *zong jiao*, was invented in the nineteenth century because none had previously existed. Religion in the modern Western sense of a belief system supported by doctrine, organization and leadership has simply been absent in Chinese society. Chinese traditions of temples, ritual practices and ceremonial practitioners relate to local communities and the rhythms of their needs in multifunctional spaces in which liturgy has little salience and performative elements prevail. In this context the introduction of a concept of "religion" as a system of belief carried by a congregation organized by a professional clergy challenges traditional community rituals and practices by separating out "superstition" and also "culture" from "religion" to the detriment of the traditional forms (Ashiwa and Wank, 2009: 9–12; Dean, 2009: 188–91). Thus, the nineteenth-century invention of Chinese religion, which Weber draw upon and contributed to, in this sense was a further instrument of state regulation in the service of modernization.

An aspect of Chinese religion, to use the term on notice, which has remained more or less outside the reach of state regulation and control, is referred to above as its "diffused" aspects. This includes the conceptual and dispositional elements of a cultural legacy that exist in language and idiom. This aspect of Chinese religion is signal in the acumen of Chinese business in generating an expansive opportunity structure necessary for market engagement, as indicated in discussion above.

References

Ames, Roger T. and David L. Hall. 2003. *Daodejing: A Philosophical Translation*. New York: Ballantine Books.

Ashiwa, Yoshika and David L. Wank. 2009. "Making Religion, Making the State in Modern China." In Yoshiko Ashiwa and David L. Wank (eds), *Making Religion, Making the State: The Politics of Religion in Modern China*, 1–21. Stanford, CA: Stanford University Press.

Barbalet, Jack. 2008. *Weber, Passion and Profits: "The Protestant Ethic and the Spirit of Capitalism" in Context*. Cambridge: Cambridge University Press.

———. 2009. "Action Theoretic Foundations of Economic Sociology." *Wirtschaftssoziologie. Kölner Zeitschrift für Soziologie und Sozialpsychologie*, Sonderheft 49: 143–57.

———. 2011. "Market Relations as *Wuwei*: Traditional Concepts in Analysis of China's Post-1978 Economy." *Asian Studies Review* 35.3: 335–54.

Brook, Timothy. 2009. "The Politics of Religion: Late-Imperial Origins of the Regulatory State." In Yoshiko Ashiwa and David L. Wank (eds), *Making Religion, Making the State: The Politics of Religion in Modern China*, 22–42. Stanford, CA: Stanford University Press.

Chien, Szuma. 1979. *Selections from Records of the Historian* (trans. Yang Hsien-yi and Gladys Yang). Peking: Foreign Languages Press.

Church, Roy. 1993. "The Family Firm in Industrial Capitalism: International Perspectives on Hypothesis and History." *Business History* 35.4: 17–43.

Creel, Herrlee G. 1977. "What is Taoism?" In Herrlee G. Creel, *What is Taoism? And Other Studies in Chinese Cultural History*, 1–24. Chicago: University of Chicago Press.

Dean, Kenneth. 2009. "Further Partings of the Way: The Chinese State and Daoist Ritual Traditions in Contemporary China." In Yoshiko Ashiwa and David L. Wank (eds), *Making Religion, Making the State: The Politics of Religion in Modern China*, 179–210. Stanford, CA: Stanford University Press.

Dunn, Emily C. 2009. "'Cult,' Church and the CCP: Introducing Eastern Lighting." *Modern China* 35.1: 96–119.

Elvin, Mark. 1973. *The Patterns of the Chinese Past*. Stanford, CA: Stanford University Press.

_____. 1983. "Why China Failed to Create an Endogenous Industrial Capitalism." *Theory and Society* 13.3: 379–91.

Fan, Lizhu. 2003. "Popular Religion in Contemporary China." *Social Compass* 50.4: 449–57.

Farrell, Betty G. 1993. *Elite Families: Class and Power in Nineteenth-Century Boston*. Albany, NY: SUNY Press.

Gerlach, Christian. 2005. "Wu-Wei in Europe. A Study of Eurasian Economic Thought." Working Paper No. 12/05. London: Department of Economic History, London School of Economics.

Goodman, David S. 2004. "Why Women Count: Chinese Women and the Leadership of Reform." In Anne Elizabeth Mclaren (ed.), *Chinese Women: Living and Working*, 19–41. London: Edward Elgar.

_____. 2007. "Narratives of Change: Culture and Local Economic Development." In Anne McLaren (ed.), *The Chinese Economy in the 21st Century: Enterprise and Business Behaviour*, 175–201. London: RoutledgeCurzon.

Goody, Jack. 1996. *The East in the West*. Cambridge: Cambridge University Press.

Goossaert, Vincent. 2003. "Le Destin de la Religion Chinoise au 20ème Siècle." *Social Compass* 50.4: 429–40.

Granet, Marcel. 1975. *The Religion of the Chinese People*. Oxford: Basil Blackwell.

Grassby, Richard. 2000. *Kinship and Capitalism: Marriage, Family and Business in the English-Speaking World, 1580–1740*. Cambridge: Cambridge University Press.

Haley, George T., Usha C. V. Haley and Chin Tiong Tan. 2004. *The Chinese Tao of Business: The Logic of Successful Business Strategy*. New York: Wiley.

_____. 1998. *New Asian Emperors: The Overseas Chinese*. Oxford: Butterworth Heinemann.

Hall, John A. 1986. *Powers and Liberties*. London: Penguin.

Hamilton, Gary G. 2006. *Commerce and Capitalism in Chinese Societies*. London: Routledge.

Hansen, Chad. 2000. *A Daoist Theory of Chinese Thought: A Philosophical Interpretation*. New York: Oxford University Press.

Huang, Jianbo and Fenggang Yang. 2005. "The Cross Faces the Loudspeakers: A Village Church Perseveres under State Power." In Fenggang Yang and Joseph B. Tamney (eds), *State, Market, and Religions in Chinese Societies*, 41–62. Leiden: Brill.

Hudson, Geoffrey Francis. 1961. *Europe and China: A Survey of their Relations from the Earliest Times to 1800*. Boston, MA: Beacon Press.

Lai, Chi-Tim. 2003. "Daoism in China Today: 1980-2002." *China Quarterly* 174: 413–27.

Lang, Graeme, Chan, Selina and Ragvald, Lars. 2005. "Temples and the Religious Economy." In Fenggang Yang and Joseph B. Tamney (eds), *State, Market, and Religions in Chinese Societies*, 149–80. Leiden: Brill.

La Porta, Rafael, Florencio Lopez-de-Silanes and Andrei Shleifer. 1999. "Corporate Ownership around the World." *Journal of Finance* 54.2: 471–517.

Lau, D. C. 1963. "Introduction." In *Lao Tzu, Tao Te Ching* (trans. D. C. Lau), vii–xlv. London: Penguin Books.

Liu, JeeLoo. 2008. *An Introduction to Chinese Philosophy: From Ancient Philosophy to Chinese Buddhism*. Oxford: Blackwell.

Maddison, Angus. 2007. *Contours of the World Economy*. Oxford: Oxford University Press.

Mill, John Stuart. 1940. *Principles of Political Economy* (ed. J. W. Ashley). London: Longmans.

Mitchell, Ronald K., Lowell Busenitz, Theresa Lant, Patricia P. McDougall, Eric A. Morse and J. Brock Smith. 2002. "Toward a Theory of Entrepreneurial Cognition." *Entrepreneurship Theory and Practice* 27.2: 93–104.

Moeller, Hans-Georg. 2006. *The Philosophy of the Daodejing*. New York: Columbia University Press.

Needham, Joseph. 1956. *Science and Civilization in China: Volume 2, History of Scientific Thought*. Cambridge: Cambridge University Press.

Nivison, David S. 1959. "Introduction." In David S. Nivison and Arthur F. Wright (eds), *Confucianism in Action*, 3–24. Stanford, CA: Stanford University Press.

Ownby, David. 2004. "The Falun Gong: A New Religious Movement in Post-Mao China." In James R. Lewis and Jesper Aagaard Petersen (eds), *Controversial New Religions*, 195–214. New York: Oxford University Press.

Pollak, Robert A. 1985. "A Transaction Cost Approach to Families and Households." *Journal of Economic Literature* 23.2: 581–608.

Postan, M. M. 1935. "Recent Trends in the Accumulation of Capital." *Economic History Review* 6.1: 1–12.

Redding, S. Gordon. 1993. *The Spirit of Chinese Capitalism*. Berlin: Walter de Gruyer.

———. 1995. "Overseas Chinese Networks: Understanding the Enigma." *Long Range Planning* 28.1: 6–19.

Reichwein, Adolf. 1968. *China and Europe: Intellectual and Artistic Contacts in the Eighteenth Century*. New York: Barnes and Noble.

Schumpeter, Joseph. A. 2008. *The Theory of Economic Development: An Inquiry into Profits, Capital, Credit, Interest, and the Business Cycle*. New Brunswick, NJ: Transaction Publishers.

Schwartz, Benjamin I. 1985. *The World of Thought in Ancient China*. Cambridge, MA: Harvard University Press.

Scranton, Philip. 1983. *Proprietary Capitalism: The Textile Manufacture at Philadelphia 1800–1895*. Cambridge: Cambridge University Press.

Sen, Gautam. 2001. *Post-Reform China and the International Economy: Economic Change and Liberalisation under Sovereign Control*. London: The Global Site.

Shane, Scott Andrew. 2004. *A General Theory of Entrepreneurship: The Individual-Opportunity Nexus*. London: Edward Elgar.

Steier, Lloyd. 2003. "Variants of Agency Contracts in Family-financed Ventures as a Continuum of Familial and Market Rationalities." *Journal of Business Venturing* 18.5: 597–618.

Sun, Anna Xiao Dong. 2005. "The Fate of Confucianism as Religion in Socialist China: Controversies and Paradoxes." In Fenggang Yang and Joseph B. Tamney (eds), *State, Market, and Religions in Chinese Societies*, 229–53. Leiden: Brill.

Tong, James W. 2009. *Revenge of the Forbidden City: The Suppression of the Falungong in China, 1999–2005*. New York: Oxford University Press.

Tsai, Kellee S. 2007. *Capitalism without Democracy: The Private Sector in Contemporary China*. Ithaca, NY: Cornell University Press.

Wang, Bi. 1999. *The Classic of the Way and Virtue: A New Translation of the Tao-te ching as Interpreted by Wang Bi* (trans. Richard John Lynn). New York: Columbia University Press.

Weber, Max. 1960. *The Religion of India: The Sociology of Hinduism and Buddhism* (trans. and ed. by Hans H. Gerth and Don Martindale). New York: The Free Press.

––––––––. 1964. *The Religion of China: Confucianism and Taoism* (trans. and ed. Hans H. Gerth, with an introduction by C. K. Yang). New York: The Free Press.

––––––––. 1981. *General Economic History* (trans. by Frank Knight). New Brunswick, NJ: Transaction Books.

––––––––. 1991. *The Protestant Ethic and the Spirit of Capitalism* (trans. Talcott Parsons). London: HarperCollins.

Whyte, Martin King. 1996. "The Chinese Family and Economic Development: Obstacle or Engine?" *Economic Development and Cultural Change* 45.1: 1–30.

Yang, Ching Kun. 1961. *Religion in Chinese Society: A Study of Contemporary Social Functions of Religion and Some of their Historical Factors*. Berkeley, CA: University of California Press.

Yang, Der-Ruey. 2005. "The Changing Economy of Temple Daoism in Shanghai." In Fenggang Yang and Joseph B. Tamney (eds), *State, Market, and Religions in Chinese Societies*, 113–48. Leiden: Brill.

Yang, Fenggang. 2006. "The Red, Black and Gray Markets of Religion in China." *Sociological Quarterly* 47: 93–122.

––––––––. 2007. "Oligopoly Dynamics: Official Religions in China." In James A. Beckford and N. J. Demerath (eds), *The SAGE Handbook of the Sociology of Religion*, 635–53. London: SAGE.

Yang, Fenggang and Dedong Wei. 2005. "The Bailin Buddhist Temple: Thriving under Communism." In Fenggang Yang and Joseph B. Tamney (eds), *State, Market, and Religions in Chinese Societies*, 63–86. Leiden: Brill.

Yijie, Tang. 2007. "Constructing Chinese Philosophy in Sino-European Cultural Exchange." In Karyn I. Lai (ed.), *New Interdisciplinary Perspectives in Chinese Philosophy*, 33–42. Oxford: Blackwell.

Zeitlin, Maurice. 1974. "Corporate Ownership and Control: The Large Corporation and the Capitalist Class." *American Journal of Sociology* 79.5: 1073–1119.

Chapter 9

HINDU NORMALIZATION, NATIONALISM AND CONSUMER MOBILIZATION

Arathi Sriprakash and Adam Possamai

University of Western Sydney

This book has sought to map some of the relationships between religion, the state and advanced capitalism in different political and social arenas across the globe. In India, accelerated and uneven modernization following the nation's economic liberalization in the early 1990s provides an interesting context to examine these relationships, specifically given the significant rise of Hindu nationalism in this period. Hindutva (loosely "Hindu-ness"), an ideology advocated by Hindu nationalist movements, exerts significant influence in parliamentary politics and arguably more insidiously, in social life in contemporary India. Although it has been argued that modernization and associated secular practices have repressed religion from public life, since the 1980s we have seen a deprivatization process of religion in many places in the world (Casanova, 2006). This chapter follows on this perspective and discusses the ways religious expression may adapt to and diffuse through public spaces and practices of modernity with regards to the political projects of Hindutva and consumer mobilization more specifically.

We consider the ways Hindu assertion diffuses through the consumption of information, images, sounds and goods. The saturation of popular media and consumer practices with Hindu cultural markers has in many ways constructed forms of "Hinduness" as "Indianess," particularly among the urban middle classes. Through the construction of a Hindu normalcy, the operation of power with nonhegemonic and non-Hindu groups is made less visible and thus unchallenged. In the second half of the chapter we take up this concern in the context of development activities in India, particularly fundraising efforts that have involved Indian diasporic networks. We explore how Hindu nationalism has emerged in some philanthropic efforts with disturbing consequences. We also consider the ways philanthropies appeal to the diasporic "donor-consumer" by constructing a homogenous, culturally unified Indian nation, making religion (and Hindu dominance) less explicit. Through this imagination of India and its "development," the relations of power, particularly around religion, caste and class, once again risk being unchallenged.

Religion in Consumer Society

Consumption has always been part of social practice. Consumption for leisure and lifestyle has opened out as a social practice beyond the dominant classes since hyperindustrialization has taken place in many societies. In present times of mass consumption, consumer society presents itself as all-inclusive with access for groups across social and economic hierarchies. Indeed, for Bauman (1998), a "normal life" in a consumer society is the life of consumerism, which involves making choices among all the displayed opportunities. A "happy life" is then defined as taking as many of these opportunities as possible. The poor in consumer society are not necessarily those who do not have shelter but are those ones who have no access to a normal or "happy" life. This is to be a consumer *manqué*, as Bauman (1998: 38) explains:

> In a society of consumers, it is above all the inadequacy of the person as a consumer that leads to social degradation and "internal exile." It is this inadequacy, this inability to acquit oneself of the consumer's duties, that turns into bitterness at being left behind, disinherited or degraded, shut off or excluded from the social feast to which others gained entry. Overcoming that consumer inadequacy is likely to be seen as the only remedy – the sole exit from a humiliating plight.

Consumer culture is the outcome of the massive expansion of the production of capitalist commodity. The outburst of the capitalist system has created a vast reservoir of consumer goods and sites for purchase and consumption to be "enjoyed" by the various classes of our society. This has lead to growing dependence on mass leisure and consumption activities. Some view this as leading to more egalitarianism and individual freedom (e.g. Certeau, 1988) and others see it as an increase in the ideological and seductive manipulation of the masses by the dominant class (e.g. the Frankfurt School and the American New Left). This manipulation would distract the masses from considering an alternative to our society, which could improve our social relations.

Religion takes an interesting role in contemporary consumer societies. Religious groups produce commodities, or put positive values in some commodities, that can be bought by the religious consumer. Some groups are more involved in consumer activity than others and practices can vary from Hare Krishna devotees selling books or food at a university campus to Christian shops selling books and other artifacts to the Church of Scientology charging fees for each level of spiritual development or to New Age shops offering goods that can help the spiritual actor on his or her quest. It cannot be claimed that religion has always been protected from consumer culture until now – one might be familiar with the narrative of Jesus protesting against the merchants in the temple. However, what is of contemporary relevance is the way in which religion has been seemingly immersed into consumer cultures; a cause for some to celebrate and others to resist. It would now appear that for a group to spread its beliefs and values, the group has to speak a language that the majority of people can understand: that of consumption. For example, some Christian evangelical groups are producing cultural artifacts (e.g. movies, computer games, pop music...) to promote their faith in consumer society and are also preventing contraliteralist Christian artifacts (e.g. stories promoting evolutionism) from entering the same social and cultural space (Possamai, 2005).

Postwar consumer culture has dominated Western lifestyles with mass-produced commodities. This culture, instead of building a sense of belonging for groups – e.g. class, subcultures, political parties – appears to create a fragmented society in which religion is only one part. Indeed, in this consuming world, the individual becomes his or her own authority; the late modern person in the West no longer tolerates being told what to believe and what to do. Consumer choice is not limited to shopping but is extended to education, health, politics and religion. People are now "free to choose" and the market culture might be turning us into consumers rather than citizens (Lyon, 2002: 12). The consumer is faced with a proliferation of "spiritual/ religious/philosophical knowledges," which they research and experience. However, as Davie (2000: 172) underlines, when it comes to consumption and monastic discipline for example, people choose what they like from the rigors of the order (e.g. listening to Gregorian chants) but rarely embrace the whole ascetic discipline.

In a recent book by Carrette and King (2005), the coagulation between religion and consumption is characterized in a very negative light, as exemplified by this quote:

Today in most British cities you will find old church buildings that have been sold off to become business offices, supermarkets, public houses, nightclubs and private apartments. However, it is not primarily the sale of buildings that we are concerned with here, but rather of the "cultural capital" of the religious for the purposes of consumption and corporate gain. From the branding of perfumes using ancient Asian concepts and the idea of the spiritual ("Samsara" perfume, "Zen" deodorant, "Spiritual" body-spray) to clothe the product in an aura of mystical authenticity, to the promotion of management courses offering "spiritual techniques" for the enhancement of one's work productivity and corporate business-efficiency, the sanitised religiosity of "the spiritual" sells. (Carette and King, 2005: 16)

In this perspective, "spirituality is turned into a product or a kind of brand name for the meaning of life" (Carette and King, 2005: 53). Moving beyond this characterization, are we interested in the relationship between religion, consumerism and the state? Is the state simply a structure that overtly regulates religious citizens to be consumers, or could there be other, perhaps less visible social relations at work?

Analyses of religion, consumerism and the state in Western societies have shown how religion has been dedifferentiated in the public sphere through market forces that are increasingly unregulated by the state. Religion has been deprivatized (Casanova, 2006) and has appeared as a social force on the same footing as other social forces (e.g. political parties, unions etc.). Following this line of thinking, Beaumont (2008a, 2008b) recently studied the deprivatization of religion as an outcome of the development of neoliberalism in a Western context. With the rolling back of the neoliberal state from its welfare activities in several domains in public life, faith-based organizations have increased their penetration in the public sphere. We see, for example, the prevalence of faith-based organizations running facilities and programs targeting urban poverty. This has reached a turning point in which we find politicians, social activists and commentators claiming that some religious organizations are better equipped for such actions than the current welfare state. With the advent of neoliberalism, faith-based organizations changed from simply offering charity work to being strong actors in the provision of welfare and social services. We have thus seen the potential deprivatization of faith-based organization in the public sphere. It becomes clear in this case that the advent of the neoliberal state has had the unintended consequence of partly bringing religion back into the public sphere.

But how do we understand the interaction between religion and market forces that are buoying consumer societies beyond the Eurocentric perspective, which has had a long history of demarcating the church-state relation? Gopalakrishnan (2006) has provided an interesting argument in his work on Hindutva and neoliberalism in contemporary India. He analyzes the political project of Hindutva, an expression of "Hindu-ness" that has been a considerable force in India's social history since the nineteenth century. As an assertion of cultural nationalism, Hindutva configures the "origins" of India as a Hindu civilization. Gopalakrishnan sets out to understand the resonances and tensions between Indian neoliberalism and Hindutva as political projects that have had a near simultaneous rise in influence in India since the late 1980s. He argues that Hindutva and neoliberalism share "similar visions of the relationship between the state, society and the individual" (2805), despite tendencies to view religious-oriented projects and market-oriented values as incompatible.

Gopalakrishnan begins by examining the ways in which both Hindutva and neoliberal discourses reduce social processes to individual choices and decisions. For the former, society is shaped by the choices of Hindu morality, values, character; discourses which individualize actions and thereby elide social power relations (such as caste, class or gender). This, as Gopalakrishnan argues, resonates with neoliberal technologies (for instance, of "consumer choice" gestured to above) that presume social behavior as "voluntary transactions between rational, utility-maximizing individuals" (2805). The construction of social processes as individual, autonomous human action means that problems or divisions in society are also seen to be addressed by attending to the self. For example, a Hindutva narrative suggests "harmony" in society is achieved through "harmony" in the human body. For neoliberalism, marketized forms of civil action enable people to help society by helping themselves (i.e. self-esteem movements for social good, or appeals to help the national economy through consumer activity).

Key to the interests of our chapter is Gopalakrishnan's discussion of how Indian neoliberalism and Hindutva both take up in their political projects the rhetoric of transformation and a "new society." This was nowhere more apparent than in the Hindu-right Bharatiya Janata Party (BJP)'s glossy, forward-looking election slogan of "India Shining" in 2004. Driving the rhetoric of social transformation are the core principles of each project – Hindu rule and *dharma* in Hindutva and the market in neoliberal discourse. As an example, Gopalakrishnan quotes the BJP's 1998 election manifesto, which states the party's vision of "the world's oldest cradle of civilisation transform itself yet again into a benign global power, contributing her material, intellectual, cultural and spiritual energies…to save the world from the gathering civilisational crisis" (2805). Working in parallel to this is the transformational agenda of Indian neoliberalism. Neoliberal discourses invoke the utopian market, underscoring "notions of a new, 'developed' and wealthy society" (2805) with modern, urban consumer tastes and practices.

Gopalakrishnan's analysis provides a way of thinking about how religious expression (and in this case religious-political projects) can adapt to market technologies in India. We began this section by describing the ways in which pervasive consumer cultures normalize consumer identity. As religious expression finds ways of adapting to market technologies, we might expect to see the normalization of *religious*-consumer identities. In the next part of this chapter we explore how social forces around Hindu-nationalism have been mobilized through consumer activity in India. Our main point of interest is to consider the ways in which consumption of "Hinduism" has constructed a Hindu-normative India despite the country's religious and social diversity – arguably to the disadvantage of already marginalized groups.

Consumer Mobilization and Hindu Normalization

The religious, linguistic and cultural heterogeneity of the modern Indian nation is well known. It has been argued that earlier communities in India had, as Kaviraj (1992: 26) noted, "fuzzy boundaries." This was partly because religion, caste and endogamous groups were based on social principals not primarily tied to territory, but also partly because "traditional communities, unlike modern ones, are not enumerated." It has been argued the notion of "Hindu community," "Hindu-ness" and a "Hindu way of life" were reified under colonial rule. Basu (2008) suggests the discursive construction and enumeration of a unitary "Hindu people" in the colonial state involved the consolidation of a single Hindu identity that made eight centuries of Islamic culture invisible. Richard King (1999) argued in his paper "Orientalism and the Modern Myth of 'Hinduism'" that "Hinduism" as a single world religion is itself a nineteenth-century construction and that the present-day usage of "Hinduism" has emerged from colonial representations of the general features of Indian society rather than of a single religion. Further, there have been various attempts by Hindu leaders themselves to eradicate "folk" remnants of Hinduism such as ritualistic healing and communication with the dead (Sinha, 2005). The construction and "normalization" of Hinduism and Hindu-ness in India has a longer history than the contemporary contexts we examine below.

The notion of a singular, unifying "Hinduism" is widely mobilized by Hindu nationalist movements. In the postcolonial democratic state, Hindu nationalism and associated Hindutva ideologies were institutionalized through the formation of political organizations such as the Rashtriya Swayamsevak Sangh (RSS) and the Bharatiya Janata Party (BJP). Rao (2004) examines how these political parties have circumvented constitutional commitments to secularism, which promotes the separation of politics and religion. When accused of spreading communal bigotry, such parties argue that "Hinduism/ Hindutva is not a religion but 'a way of life'" and in doing so advance a Hindu majoritarian reading of secularism (Rao, 2004: 394). The BJP has forged a powerful role in national politics in India, seeking to protect Hindu interests in a religiously diverse landscape. The party was elected to power in 1998 and served until 2004. It currently holds power in five states. The political-economic conjuncture in which the strengthening of Hindu nationalism occurred was marked by significant market reforms and expansion of media and communications.

The opening up of India's economy in 1991 saw the increased participation of the country in global markets, the expansion of electronic media, the growth of the middle classes, and associated consumer-oriented practices. In the popular imagination, India had arrived on the world stage. This saw the emergence of what Hansen (1999) called a "double discourse" in the Hindu nationalist movement: national pride in the country's upward trajectory was coupled with self-depreciation of India's capitulation to external interests, goods and values. Bose (2009) notes that this double discourse "catered to a growing middle class which was anxious to integrate into the global economy without losing their cultural integrity" (Bose, 2009: 25). The maintenance of this integrity occurred through the relocation and reconstitution of Hindu discourses, images and practices into modern ideals of consumption. In neoliberal India, pietism and consumerism were not always constructed in opposition to each other.

Indeed, there has been significant research and commentary on the ways in which consumer goods and mass media have transmitted, constituted and reinforced both Hindu religiosity and Hindu nationalist ideology in India (cf. Johnson, 2000; Page and Crawley, 2001; Rajagopal, 2001). Murty (2009) provides a detailed analysis of the ways in which Hindutva ideologies found expression in Indian popular cinema from 1990–2003, a time when Hindu nationalism gained particular momentum in the political arena. Arvind Rajagopal's (2000) book *Politics After Television: Hindu Nationalism and the Reshaping of the Public in India* explored the expanding consumption of television image and narrative and its production of a Hindu national imagination. State-broadcast television enabled far-reaching communication across a society "beset by deep economic and cultural cleavages" (Rajagopal, 2000: 119). But for the Indian state, the new visibility of audience ratings, popularity and profits also meant "the gap between state pronouncements and public sentiments acquired unprecedented salience" (ibid.: 119). Rajagopal focused his analysis on the immensely popular television series broadcast of the Hindu epic *Ramayan*. The highly rated mass adulation of the series was used by the Hindu nationalist BJP to stir public interest in the Ayodhya dispute. Hindu nationalists asserted the Babri Mosque was constructed on the site of a former Hindu temple and the birthplace of the Hindu god Ram (the lead character of the televised epic *Ramayan*). There were violent outcomes of this campaign, and in 1992 Hindu nationalists were involved in the demolition of the mosque. (See Rao 2004 for an incisive analysis of the legal battles arising from this incident, which brought the tensions between constitutional commitments to secularism and federalism in Indian politics into focus.)

Indeed, television, the internet and new media have played a significant part in creating networks through which religious and nationalist interests travel, especially for diasporic communities. Khilnani (2003) captured the confluence of piety and consumerism, describing the "novel" Hinduism found on urban Indian streets: "where holographic gods dangle on well-used key chains and cassettes of devotional ragas are played in traffic jams" (Khilnani, 2003: 186). In Indian business management, Birtchnell (2009) reports that "modern and liberal Indian business leaders are committed to integrating a set of beliefs into their working lives" (268), those beliefs being as Birtchnell argues a "Hindu ethic" that has been refashioned in India as "cultural capital." Rajagopal (2001) examined the "brand logics" in India's expanding market through which a Hindu cultural identity was constructed through consumer products and services. The adoption of Hindu symbols and practices by businesses does not merely signify a marketing strategy to reach new consumers, but also, given the rhetoric of "consumer choice," that "the economic and cultural spheres are apparently working through a model of consent, creating an apparently expanding middle class, and at the same time, a wider acceptance of Hindu dominance" (Rajagopal, 2001: 773).

Rajagopal's point is that Hinduva "travelled on the back of expanding markets... inserting itself into spaces party politics had not developed systematically, thus bringing itself closer to people, and advancing its cause" (780). The consumer has been mobilized in the branding of Hindu India.

Examining the normalization of Hinduism particularly by urban, middle- and elite-class Indians, Anustup Basu (2008) provides a particularly insightful analysis of how the expansion of the Indian electronic media space has enabled new forms of Hindu power. Through the concept of "informatic modernization," Basu explores the ways contemporary Hindu assertion "does not pertain to orders, spaces, genres and enclosures of modern knowledge, but to a diffuse but kinetic ecology of sights and sounds" (Basu, 2008: 244). Basu draws examples from Indian cinema in which the assemblage of Hindu signs, language, imagery and sounds takes an "informatic" form whereby "disparate elements can be orchestrated together without completing a story as such" (ibid.: 246). He reflects on the ways in which similar processes of assemblage produce a "metropolitan Hinduness", which is "not just marked by representational clamour of subjects and identities, but is an innocuous yet omnipresent suffusion of metropolitan life and language" (ibid.: 249). Through this assemblage, signifiers of the Hindu are abstracted, historical identities are fractured or made irrelevant and hierarchies are recalibrated to be based on aesthetic qualities, lifestyles, merit, etc. Religious identities are reinscribed by consumer identities. However, by normalizing the metropolitan consumer subject through this mode of apparent religious and social inclusion, the social practices through which the religious "other" and the Hindu "self" are constituted are made invisible. As Basu argues "it is thus always possible for the Hindu to either hate the Muslim community or express despair over its practiced 'medievalisms' and at the same time to have 'Muslim' friends" (ibid.: 249–50).

Of course, the older and more explicit forms of Hindu assertion continue to shape social and political life in India. What we see in the examples above are the ways in which Hindu power as majoritarian normalcy is distributed by networks of information and products enabled particularly in the so called "new" consumer India. As Basu concludes his analysis, "it becomes, quite insidiously, a matter of absolute normalcy to become Hindu in the global metropolis" (ibid.: 250).

Indian Diasporic Networks and Consumer Citizenship

We turn now to consider the implications of such Hindu normalization for India's "development" activities, particularly concerning the influence of Indian diasporic communities. As Indian consumers have been mobilized within the nation-state to create a modern "Hindu" India, arguably so too have the diaspora beyond national borders. Though a heterogeneous group, the Indian diaspora are often characterized as successful, entrepreneurial professionals and there have been significant moves to encourage diasporic capital and influence back to India as part of the country's "development." It is estimated there are 25–40 million Indian émigrés worldwide, with reports that India has the largest volume of diasporic remittances in the world (Bose, 2008). Indian links with diasporic networks have been encouraged through, for example, dual citizenship arrangements, state-sponsored conventions, conferences for nonresidential Indians (NRIs) and community movements and associations. While NRIs have been extended citizenship rights, there are questions around the denial of similar rights for Kashmiris, Gujarati Muslims and other marginalized groups: "NRIs were to be 'welcomed home' even as other communities were driven out" (Gopalakrishnan, 2006: 2809).

Bose (2008: 127) has explored how diasporic communities have a hand in reshaping "the material aesthetic and ideological landscapes of their homelands" through remittances, investments, property ownership and cultural influences. Within India, idealized diasporic "tastes" and "interests" have had significant influence over the nature of urban development projects (such as Westernized malls and NRI housing developments), higher education programs (course content oriented towards the globally mobile consumer), cinematic and media representations (of the chic, tech-savvy, English speaking Indian) and transnational business relationships. Sumit Sarkar (2008: 430) reminds us that these products of economic liberalization in India have been accompanied by "an increasingly aggressive emphasis on 'Hindu' cultural-religious identity." Hindu assertion (whether explicit or implicit) in these realms has led Gopalakrishnan (2006) to argue that diasporic influence has redrawn India's social boundaries around a supposedly unitary community – a product of what he sees as the alliance between neoliberalism and Hindutva.

In his research on diasporas and development, Bose (2008) has traced the flow of capital into India through diasporic networks. He discusses how a number of initiatives by both Hindu-right and center-left Indian governments over the last two decades have strengthened relationships between India and its diasporic communities. The potential "good" of such relationships might be seen in terms of "development assistance, economic aid, increased trade, greater cultural connections and understanding and so on" (124). However, Bose also raises caution about the potentially detrimental and deleterious effects of diasporic assistance. He examines the unintended outcomes of diasporic development activity, for example the mass displacement of people as a result of the Narmada Valley Development Dam Project that had attracted significant diasporic financial support.

Bose also discusses the entanglement of diasporic communities in more explicit ideological projects to "reshape, resurrect, defend or even enlarge homelands" (Bose, 2008: 126). There has been some critique of diasporic support for Hindu nationalist projects in the name of Indian "development." Commentators have claimed that "Hindu fundamentalism has reemerged in India with a new virulence, partly funded by the overseas Indian diaspora" (Vicziany, 2004: 113). Bose describes the active international fundraising efforts by the Vishwa Hindu Parishad (VHP, or World Hindu Council). The VHP is one of the many entities of the *sangh parivar*, the name given to the "family" of Hindu nationalist organizations which have networks that extend beyond India. Bose reports on the extent of influence of the VHP and its disturbing consequences with regards to the 2002 communal violence in the state of Gujarat:

Perhaps most alarming has been the vocal support and justification offered by some within diasporic Hindu communities in North America and Western Europe following the pogroms against Muslims...VHP functionaries abroad were particularly active in their defence of the shocking events and sought to minimise the evidence that state authorities were complicit in the murders and brutalisation of the Muslim community in Gujurat. (127)

We see here how the transnational travels of Hindutva ideology have positioned Hindu nationalism as "both the globalizing face of Indian politics, and the bearer of a violent and brutal form of religious chauvinism" (Rajagopal, 2001: 775).

Another controversy that raised concerns over the nature of diasporic mobilization for Indian development activity involved the United States-based India Development and Relief Fund (IDRF). Vicziany (2004) presents a very critical case against the IDRF. She argues the IDRF presented itself as a nonprofit nongovernmental organization which sought to contribute to community housing, education and sanitation, as well as disaster relief. However, Vicziany reports that the IDRF has been part of the Hindu nationalist *sangh parivar.* The organization has received a substantial amount of money through diasporic fundraising efforts: "In 2000 alone, over US$3.8 million was collected by the IDRF in America" (109). International money, it is argued, was used to fund sectarian programs and to benefit Hindu communities over other groups during disaster relief. Bose (2008) reports how critics of the IDRF launched a public campaign to highlight the problematic connections between diasporic fundraising for development and the growth of Hindu nationalist ideas in India.

As Vicziany (2004) is careful to note, it is uncertain how far diasporic funding to Hindu nationalist "development" organizations was driven by sympathy for religious nationalist projects or how far donors were "tricked" into their support. What is significant is the mechanisms of this potential "trickery." Such development organizations are potentially able to take on discourses of democracy, which can conceal sectarian motives or the privileging of certain groups. As Kaviraj (1995: 312) observes, "since Hinduism is the religion of the majority, this makes it easy for its advocates to speak the language of democracy." As the consumption of goods and images in modern India is seen to "normalize" markers of Hindu society, do philanthropic and development organizations address their diasporic donor-consumers through Hindu majoritarianism? How far does the normalization of Hindu-India configure Indian "development" in terms of Hindu interests?

There is an emerging literature that explores neoliberal consumer-citizenship and the ways in which philanthropic activities (of nonprofit organizations and otherwise) extend their "products" to reach consumer-citizens. Banet-Weiser and Lapsanksy (2008: 1255) note in their work on brand culture and consumer citizenship that "the logics of neo-liberalism have permeated spheres that have traditionally been understood as separate from the everyday workings of capitalism, such as social activism." We see this in the rise of "fair trade" goods and seemingly class-based practices of "ethical" consumerism. Jeremy Youde (2009: 203) writes that such "political consumerism functions as a form of social movement activity. Political consumerism focuses on a sense of social and political global responsibility exercised by consumers."

   This sense of social responsibility extends beyond the consumption of material goods, as we see in the construction of the philanthropic donor as a "donor-consumer." Raddon (2008: 42) for example examines the production of the normative neoliberal "caring" citizen who, "emulating the wealthy, gives time or money to help the less fortunate." New modes of philanthropy through consumer-citizenship or the contributions of the donor-consumer are seen as public acts, and Raddon argues that philanthropic organizations are increasingly modeled on business principles:

> The normative value of paying taxes, social movement activism, artistic and cultural creation, and the everyday work of caring for people within households and neighbourhoods diminishes in comparison to donating and fundraising. (42)

Slocum (2004) too suggests that citizens in neoliberal societies are now addressed as consumers. The consumer in politics can be seen either as a dupe who follows the hegemony of his or her country or as a political force when refusing to consume certain commodities (e.g. green consumerism and Stop the Sweatshops Campaign). In this sense, these citizens would be active in the consumption of commodities and values following the ethos of a new social movement. Kozinets and Handleman (2004) follow this line of thinking in their analysis of consumer movements. These movements want to challenge hegemonic consumption by organizing themselves around goals that resist particular industrial or marketing practices.

   What identities are constituted and reinforced through Indian diasporic fundraising that flows into India? Such "buying into" philanthropic practices have effects that are transnational: how, through this distance, is India and development imagined? After the controversy about diasporic fundraising for Hindutva-affiliated "development" programs, there have been efforts to highlight the need for ethical practices of nonresident Indian (NRI) investment and support in development activity. Bose (2008: 127) reports how the Association for India's Development (AID), a United States-based nongovernmental organization which runs development initiatives in India, has suggested that its members ask themselves "what kinds of developments in India are Indians in the US (and other countries) making possible?"

Kumarini Silva's (2010) recent research with AID members explores the construction of the diasporic philanthropic subject and the imagination of the Indian "homeland." Silva argues that AID tries to "connect the NRI to India through the pathos of nationalism and civic duty" (52). Through interviews with AID members in the United States, Silva shows how the language and practice of the Indian diaspora in "giving back" is steeped in neoliberal assumptions which allow the organization

> to construct their diasporic and expatriate selves as a monolith and India as a homogenous nation. Within this simplistic binary, where heterogeneity within both community and country are obfuscated, the activist relationship is constructed through an affective relationship between US –based economic success, vis-à-vis the non-resident-Indian (NRI), and diasporic nostalgia and longing for a "homeland." (48)

The construction of a homogenous Indian nation enables AID to "promote itself as a movement committed to an India that is united through culture rather than religion" (53). This was a way for the organization to distance itself from religious affiliation and potential communalism, and was also a useful marketing strategy to extend its reach to a wider set of donor-consumers. In terms of reaching and mobilizing diverse diasporic communities, narratives of unity are certainly powerful: "since this imagined community is constructed transnationally, rather than locally, it flourishes as a collective cause" (51).

In its newsletters, the AID organization produces narratives of what Silva calls a "domesticated utopia," asking diasporic Indians to identify with "the simple forest-dwelling Indian," the "children weaving carpets" and the "Indian organic farmer." Silva argues that this vision "preserves existing structural inequalities and differences in ethnicity, religion, class and caste. It does so by postulating an underlying liberal, universal 'Indian' subjectivity that orders and manages these differences as if they were of no consequence to development" (51). This "Indian" subjectivity, like our earlier discussion of Hindu normalization, assembles India in ways that make invisible the practices and distribution of power that marginalizes minority communities. As Silva suggests, India is constructed by AID as "one nation far away from a geography that is riddled by separatist politics" (51).

Philanthropic discourses that play down religion by emphasizing a common "Indian culture" may well make Hinduism and forms of Hindu assertion less explicit in NRI activity. However, Lal (2003) has argued that there is an "anxiety of influence" especially among the middle-class, "modern" Hindu Indian diasporic community about the invisibility of Hinduism as a "world religion" despite successful "Indianization" in international business,

media and technology. As an example of this anxiety, he describes how
diasporic Indians are questioning the relatively weak position of India in
United States foreign policy, especially compared to that of China and
particularly when the democratic politics of India would suggest it to be a
more suitable partner. According to Lal, further dimension of this anxiety
stems from the significant global focus on Islam in comparison to a rare
interest in Hinduism: "to be Hindu is to be nearly condemned to oblivion"
(30). At the same time as a resurgence of militant Hinduism is happening in
India, Lal suggests that many NRIs perceive that Hinduism should be more
visible outside of India. His descriptions of religious marginalization attempt
to explain how Hindutva as a form of Hindu assertion is able to gain traction
among Hindu diasporic communities. The efforts of such movements to
homogenize a "Hindu" identity is an exercise in "transforming it into a world
religion, and placing it within categories of knowledge that would make it
into a proper religion" (35).

   We have seen in this section how consumerism and religion are interpenetrated
in such a way as promoting the development of a religious view that is closely
linked to nationalist and developmental projects. It should be noted, as a last point
for this section, that the confluence of religion and consumerism does not indicate
an "anything goes" characterization of religious consumption. For example, Lal
(2003) makes reference to the "American Hindus Against Defamation" who have
been campaigning against the inappropriate "commercialization" of Hinduism.
One example is the campaign against the toilet seat manufacturer Sittin' Pretty,
which placed pictures of Shiva and other Hindu deities on toilet seat covers.
The merging of religion with nationalism does not always lead to positive
consumption (i.e. the promotion of certain types of consuming practices) but
also to a type of negative consumption (i.e. the prevention of certain types of
consuming practices).

Theoretical Discussion

To understand this intersection of religion, consumption and neoliberal state
strategies, we need to revise current theories on consumerism. Featherstone
(1991) identified three theories of consumer culture. The first analyzes
consumerism as a stage of capitalist development in which the consumer is
faced with hegemonic force from a technocratic society (e.g. the Frankfurt
School and the American New Left). The second is a more sociological
concern about how people delineate their class and status and how they
create distinction via their consuming habits. The consumer is located in
a specific social class that inscribes his or her presence in a social field by
creating a social distinction from other social classes (e.g. Bourdieu). The third

is concerned with the creativity of consumer practices and how this leads to an aesthetics and emotional pleasure of consumption. The consumers are seen as quasi-heroic people who can create their identities by playing with the system and constructing their own identity for themselves in selecting what is available in the consuming system (e.g. Certeau).

Adapting these theories to the field of religion, we would find that the first theory would see religion used as a commodity for a source of profit and/ or as a way to maintain status quo in a technocratic society. If religion for Marx was an opium during modernity, consumerism in this perspective has become the opium par excellence in which religion is now but a part. With the second perspective, we would have specific strata of a society consuming religion for specific purposes and in distinction from other strata. We would see here, for example, some middle-class Christian evangelical groups consuming according to their faith while distinguishing themselves from other groups such as atheists (e.g. refusal to consume stories supporting evolutionism). The third perspective would see the religious person consuming in an apparently free-floating fashion. An example of this would be the New Ager who is interested in commodities from various religions, as consumption in this case is not strictly limited to one religion only (Possamai, 2005).

With reference to the political projects of Hindutva and consumer mobilization, we find limitations with these three theories. The first theory would see this phenomenon as providing profit for the upper classes and/or technocrats and as maintaining the status quo of the neoliberal state. While Hindu assertion has been expressed at the national level in party politics, it is in fact aiming at changing the status quo through, paradoxically, neoliberal means. For this nationalistic movement, religion is used to carry its ideals rather than just act as a source of profit or control. With regards to the second theory, it could be argued that the majority of these religious consumers are from a middle-class background; however, the Hindu nationalist movement is not bound by class only. For the last theory, we clearly have a case here of people consuming with a specific social and cultural outcome in mind, and this goes beyond the consumption of the self only. To move forward in the understanding of this case study, we need to work on a hybrid theory between the first and second perspectives.

Bourdieu's research was centered on class. In his analysis of consuming practices in France, he developed his theory of capital to understand how classes operate and create distinctions between themselves. For example, a working-class person has a different cultural capital than someone from a higher class and might consume a beer at a pub rather than a vintage wine in an upmarket cafe. However, if we were to adapt Bourdieu's use of class to that of a movement – in this case a religious and nationalist movement – we could argue that this case study offers a window into the consumption of a movement that aims to promote a religion with a specific nationalist agenda as a form of distinction from other religions (e.g. Islam in India) or other political forces rather than other classes.

When Bourdieu argues that the taste and distaste of a class is an act of distinction, in this case the positive and negative consumption of a group or movement is also an act of distinction that goes beyond or across class analysis. His adapted theory helps us to understand Hindu nationalism as not only a movement with a specific goal, but also as a movement that creates distinction with other religious and nationalist groups. However, this movement is not just a pro- or contra-consumer movement, it is a transformative social movement that attempts to change India according to its nationalist and religious views. It is also a transnational movement as it gains traction with its diasporic communities. People are mobilized into the movement through practices of consumption. And here we find the connection with the first theory in this approach that explains the consumer as a normalized self compelled to consume. But in this case, it is not consumption that is for the benefit of capitalism but rather for the benefit of a movement. Consumption is not reinforcing the status quo of a neoliberal society, but rather using the tools offered by a neoliberal society to change the status quo. What we have here is a transformative and transnational movement that mobilizes consumers for a specific combined nationalist and religious agenda. The normalization of a Hindu India may enable Hindu nationalist agendas to operate in the background of consumer practices while an imagined "unified" India is foregrounded.

Conclusion

Processes of desecularization are usually understood to occur through religious groups politically reentering the public sphere (Kepel, 1994; Lawrence, 1998), the cultural transactions between religious and spiritual groups and individuals via consumer culture and popular culture (Bauman, 1998; Possamai, 2005) or the growth of a type of religious social capital generated by the transnational networks of new immigrant and ethnic communities (Possamai and Possamai-Inesedy, 2007). Through the exploration of the specific case study of Hindu nationalism, we have been able to explore a specific non-Western desecularized path. Here, the confluence between nationalistic and religious agendas has been carried through consumer cultures of a transformative and transnational social movement. Adapting Bourdieu's theory of class, it can be argued that this movement creates a type of social distinction when it comes to its consuming practices with regards to religion and nationalism. However, connecting this case to the theories from the Frankfurt school, this movement also aims at normalizing its consumers not because of a technocratic or capitalist agenda, but because of a specific nationalist and religious agenda.

References

Banet-Weiser, Sarah and Charlotte Lapsansky. 2008. "RED is the New Black: Brand Culture, Consumer Citizenship and Political Possibility." *International Journal of Communication* 2: 1248–68.

Basu, Anustup. 2008. "Hindutva and Informatic Modernization." *Boundary* 35.3: 239–50.

Bauman, Zygmunt. 1998. "Postmodern Religion." In Paul Heelas (ed.), *Religion, Modernity and Postmodernity*, 55–78. Oxford: Blackwell.

Beaumont, Justin. 2008a. "Faith Action on Urban Social Issues." *Urban Studies* 45.10: 2019–34.

———. 2008b. "Faith-Based Organisations and Urban Social Justice in the Netherlands." *Tijdschrift voor Economische en Sociale Geografie* 99.4: 382–92.

Birtchnell, Thomas. 2009. "From 'Hindolence' to 'Spirinomics': Discourse, Practice and the Myth of Indian Enterprise." *South Asia: Journal of South Asian Studies* 43.2: 248–68.

Bose, Anuja. 2009. "Hindutva and the Politicization of Religious Identity in India." *Journal of Peace, Conflict and Development* 13. Online at: http://www.peacestudiesjournal.org.uk/dl/Issue 13 Article 8 formatted.pdf (accessed 22 June 2011).

Bose, Pablo. 2008. "Home and Away, Diasporas, Developments and Displacements in a Globalizing World." *Journal of Intercultural Studies* 29.1: 111–31.

Carette, Jeremy and Richard King. 2005. *Selling Spirituality: The Silent Takeover of Religion.* London and New York: Routledge.

Casanova, José. 2006. "Rethinking Secularization: A Global Comparative Perspective." *Hedgehog Review* 8.1–2: 7–22.

Certeau, Michel de. 1988. *The Practice of Everyday Life.* Berkeley and Los Angeles: University of California Press.

Davie, Grace. 2000. *Religion in Modern Europe: A Memory Mutates.* Oxford: Oxford University Press.

Featherstone, Mike. 1991. *Consumer Culture & Postmodernism.* London: SAGE.

Gopalakrishnan, Shankar. 2006. "Defining, Constructing and Policing a 'New India.' Relationship between Neoliberalism and Hindutva." *Economic and Political Weekly*, 30 June 2006: 2803–13.

Hansen, Thomas. 1999. *The Saffron Wave: Democracy and Hindu Nationalism in Modern India.* Princeton, NJ: Princeton University Press.

Johnson, Kirk. 2000. *Television and Social Change in Rural India.* New Delhi: SAGE.

Kaviraj, Sudipta. 1992. "The Imaginary Institution of India." In Partha Chatterjee and Gyanendra Pandey (eds), *Subaltern Studies. Volume VII*, 1–40. New Delhi: Oxford University Press.

———. 1995. Religion, Politics and Modernity. In Upendra Baxi and Bhiku Parekh (eds), *Crisis and Change in Contemporary India*, 295–316. New Delhi: SAGE.

Kepel, Gilles. 1994. *The Revenge Of God. The Resurgence of Islam, Christianity and Judaism in the Modern World.* University Park: Pennsylvania State University Press.

Khilnani, Sunil. 2003. *The Idea of India.* Penguin Books: London.

King, Richard. 1999. "Orientalism and the modern myth of 'Hinduism.'" *Numen* 46.2: 146–85.

Kozinets, Robert and Jay Handleman. 2004. "Adversaries of Consumption: Consumer Movements, Activism, and Ideology." *Journal of Consumer Research* 31: 691–704.

Lyon, David. 2000. *Jesus in Disneyland: Religion in Postmodern Times.* Cambridge: Polity Press.

Lal, Vinay. 2003. "India in the World: Hinduism, the Diaspora, and the Anxiety of Influence." *Australian Religion Studies Review* 16.2: 19–37.

Lawrence, Bruce. 1998. "From fundamentalism to fundamentalisms: A religious ideology in multiple forms." In Paul Heelas (ed.), *Religion, Modernity and Postmodernity*, 88–101. Oxford: Blackwell.

Murty, Madhavi. 2009. "Representing Hindutva: Nation and Masculinity in Indian Popular Cinema, 1990 to 2003." *Popular Communication* 7.4: 267–81.

Page, David and William Crawley. 2001. *Satellites over South Asia*. New Delhi: SAGE.

Possamai, Adam. 2005. *Religion and Popular Culture: A Hyper-Real Testament*. Brussels, Bern, Berlin, Frankfurt, New York, Oxford, Vienna: European Interuniversity Press.

Possamai, Adam and Alphia Possamai-Inesedy. 2008. "The Baha'i Faith and Caodaism: Migration, Change and De-secularisation(s) in Australia." *Journal of Sociology* 43.3: 301–17.

Raddon, Mary-Beth. 2008. "Neoliberal Legacies: Planned giving and the new philanthropy." *Studies in Political Economy* 81: 27–38.

Rajagopal, Arvind. 2000. *Politics After Television*. Cambridge: Cambridge University Press.

_____. 2001. "Thinking through Emerging Markets: Brand Logics and Cultural Forms of Political Society in India." *Economic and Political Weekly*, 3 March 2001: 773–82.

Rao, Badrinath. 2004. "Religion, Law, and Minorities in India. Problems with Judicial Regulation." In James T. Richardson (ed.), *Regulating Religion: Case Studies from Around the Globe*, 381–413. New York: Kluwer.

Sarkar, Sumit. 2008. "Nationalism and poverty: Discourses of development and culture in 20th century India." *Third World Quarterly* 29.3: 429–45.

Silva, Kumarini. 2010. "Global nationalisms, pastoral identities: Association for India's Development (AID) negotiates transnational activism." *South Asian Popular Culture* 8.1: 47–55.

Sinha, Vineeta. 2005. "Persistence of 'Folk Hinduism' in Malaysia and Singapore." *Australian Religion Studies Review* 18.2: 211–34.

Slocum, Rachel. 2004. "Consumer citizens and the Cities for Climate Protection campaign." *Environment and Planning* 36: 763–82.

Vicziany, Marika. 2004. "Globalization and Hindutva: India's Experience with Global Economic and Political Integration." In Gloria Davies and Chris Nyland (eds), *Globalization in the Asian Region*, 92–118. Cheltenham: Edward Elgar Publishers.

Youde, Jeremy. 2009. "Ethical Consumerism or Reified Neoliberalism? Product (RED) and Private Funding for Public Goods." *New Political Science* 31.2: 201–20.

Chapter 10

CLASH OF SECULARITY AND RELIGIOSITY: THE STAGING OF SECULARISM AND ISLAM THROUGH THE ICONS OF ATATÜRK AND THE VEIL IN TURKEY

Meyda Yeğenoğlu

Bilgi University, Istanbul

1920s Republic

When the military interrupted parliamentary democratic politics in Turkey in 1980, the Turkish population did not know or predict that this was indeed the harbinger of far-reaching transformation in the position Islam has been used to occupying in the social and public life of Turkey. José Casanova's (1994) thesis about the significant "deprivatization" of religion applies well to the noteworthy presence that Islamic religiosity has achieved in Turkey's social, cultural, political and economic life in the last two decades or so. The term "deprivatization" signifies the emergence of new historical developments that entail the reversal of a certain secular trend, involving the entrance of religion into the public sphere and the arena of political contestation. Religion is called upon not simply to defend the territory that has been allocated to it,

> but also to participate in the very struggles to define and set the modern boundaries between the private and public spheres, between system and life-world, between legality and morality, between individual and society, between family, civil society and state, between nations, states, civilizations and the world system. (Casanova, 1994: 6)

Following Casanova's thinking, it is possible to talk about a process of "deprivatization" of Islam in Turkey since the 1980s. Since then, not only has Turkey's political life become fairly volatile and unpredictable, but the social and cultural life has been characterized by the confrontation or clash of secular and Islamic ways of living, styles of dressing and manners, targeting the constitution of bodies and subjectivities.

Cohabitation of the social, cultural and political space by secularists and Islamists in Turkey since the establishment of the republic in the 1920s has not been easy. Secularism became the official state ideology of the republic founded by Mustafa Kemal Atatürk. In an attempt to establish a new sense of nationhood and a new social order, the Kemalist project took secularism, progress and Western modernity as the founding principles of its ideology. The sociopolitical repudiation of the Islamic Ottoman past was pursued in a top-down manner, institutionalizing secularism as the defining characteristic in Turkey's constitutional make-up.[1] The establishment of the republic in the early twentieth century was secured through authoritarian measures rather than a democratic or popular consensual process. Since the authoritarian nationalism of Kemalist secularism tried to achieve social unity by eradicating the public visibility of religious, ethnic and other sorts of differences, public claims for recognition of differences have become the core of the politics of resistance. As Asad (2006) suggests in his discussion of French secularism (which constituted the role model for secularism in Turkey), the call for *unity* and *integration* is an integral aspect of centralized state control. For Asad, "the preoccupation with unity has been a central feature of authoritarian discourse and the requirement of loyalty to symbols of the nation is central to that political tradition... Those who are to be unified or integrated are required to submit to a particular normative order" (496). This normative order in Turkey has been secular modernization.

In creating a new united secular socious, the utmost importance was placed upon appearances in the public realm. The newly established republic began wiping out the visibility (if not the existence) of all religious signs and practices from the public domain. This aim of secularization of the public and political domain was accompanied by a strong emphasis on transposing religion to a matter of private and individual faith. In addition to the banning of many visible markers of Islam (through initiatives such as the introduction of the Western calendar, replacement of the Arabic script with the Latin

---

1 A wide range of social scientists have studied the process of secular modernization in Turkey as well the "return" of Islam to the sociopolitical scene. See Berkes (1999), Çağaptay (2006), Çolak (2003), Çolak and Aydın (2004), Gülalp (2003) and Çınar (2008).

alphabet, closure of *medreses, tekkes* and Sufi orders, closure of Shari'a courts, implementation of Swiss Civil Code and promotion of certain types of music rather than others on state radio channels), a special significance has also been given to the way Turkish people look in their manners, dress and lifestyles. The Kemalist project did not limit its formation of a new society to the radical reorganization of the public realm. The private sphere was also subjected to a thorough intervention. Even matters that have to do with forms of socializing have become targets of reformation for the new secular elites. Consequently, issues that were deemed to be key to a modern/Western social life have been subjected to a scrupulous reformulation, revision and resignification so as to cut their umbilical ties with Islam and to lodge secularization in people's life-worlds. This desire, and its accompanying processes that aimed to establish a new republic out of what was regarded to be a religious and backward society by the secularist elite, implied the constitution of a *new subject population.*[2] This resulted in the formation of a Western-looking new republican elite group, who view those who do not conform to the new social and cultural decorum and punctilios as backward, traditional and Islamic. The public sphere has thus been thoroughly reshaped as a nonreligious sphere. Hence, what characterizes Kemalist secularism is not simply the separation of the domains of the private and public and the mapping of this separation onto the religious and secular, but the "protection" of the public from the intrusion of the religious and thereby the privileging and sacralizing of the public domain's secular nature.

With the institutionalization of the Kemalist ideology of the republic, the secular has become the defining ingredient of the hegemonic social imaginary of Turkey. In making the secular the new foundation, ethos, ideology and defining principle of the republic, extra weight was placed on appearances and visible signs as markers of the new regime. As a consequence, apparently trivial issues such as men's hats and women's veiling were highlighted as issues of social remedy or as part of the program of Westernization. Modernization was identified with Westernization and the ideology of Westernization gained

---

2 I am using the term "subject population" in the Foucauldian sense to refer to technologies of power that mark, stamp, invest, inscribe and act upon bodies. I want to allude to the productive principle of power that constitutes the subject and subject population in their materiality. The subjection of the bodies and souls of people to power should not be seen as a simple process of subordination or as a repression. Rather, subjection needs to be seen as a process, which secures, maintains and puts in place a subject. Therefore, it needs to be understood as a process of *subjectification*: at the same time a creative and coercive process. Thus, I want to allude to the *productive, creative yet coercive* processes by which secular modernization in Turkey has created new subjects in its materiality. I discuss the interrelation between the constitution of bodies, subjectivities and veiling/ unveiling in my *Colonial Fantasies* (1998).

additional symbolic value. Men's traditional headgear (the *fez*) was replaced with the European hat. Although women's veiling was not outlawed, women were strongly discouraged from wearing veils, as the Islamic attire was mapped onto backwardness. There was an excessive emphasis placed on women being educators of future generations. Their lives, manners and appearances became a major social target of Atatürk's, what Gellner (1981) calls "didactic secularist" reforms. This didactic reorganization of the society brought, as one scholar puts it, "Islamic authority under the full and absolute control of the secular state... The institutionalization of secularism involved bringing all religious activity under the direct control and monopoly of the secular state" (Çınar, 2005: 16). This adamant control of Islam not only secured the formation, survival and weight of the secular state and of the secular elites, but it also managed to allocate Islam a specific slot in the socious, a particular place that was and is meticulously controlled, regulated and supervised. In an attempt to contain the unregulated dissemination of Islam in the public realm, certain practical measures were taken. The new penal code's banning of the use of religion for political purposes, the removal from the constitution of the article that defined the Turkish state as "Islamic," the closure of self-governing religious centers and the granting of the authority to regulate and supervise mosques and all sorts of religious activities to the newly established Directorate of Religious Affairs (Çınar, 2005: 17) were some of the means by which the republic constituted a secular public sphere in the early twentieth century. It was through this *exclusive inclusion* of Islam that the Kemalist ideology managed to launch a secularist ethos in Turkey. This official secular nationalist ideology, which the Turkish state chose for itself as the governing narrative for its self-staging and presentation, represented a radical rupture from the Ottoman Empire. The institution of this new sociopolitical order ascribed to the state a controlling hand on religion and preeminence and authority over religious institutions. It would thus not be unwarranted to claim that this official order remained substantially unchallenged until the 1980s. It is with "return of the religious" that the hegemony of the secularist nationalist ideology of Kemalism began to be unsettled and destabilized.

1990s Islamic Challenge

The Kemalist sacralized protection of the public sphere from the intrusion of religious signs and the system of control and subordination it managed to institute since the establishment of the republic in 1923 have begun to be challenged in the name of freedom of religious expression. In opposition to the authoritarian and centralized secularism of the state, the military, the courts and the educational institutions, a religio-political discourse is questioning the hegemonic distinction between the public and private. Hence, there is a quizzical political atmosphere emerging about the state's unrestricted hold and authority over the definition and shaping of public identity. Thus, the polarization between Islamists and secularists and the growing schism between discourses of Islamism and secularism are some of the critical issues that have come to shape public life in Turkey since the 1980s. This period has witnessed a rapid increase in the visibility of objects, discourses and issues that are marked as Islamic. Although Islam's presence in various forms has been maintained during the whole twentieth century, surviving in informal social gatherings, literature, poetry and music, Islamic formations had to maintain a low profile and avoid public visibility (Çınar, 2005: 18). In comparison to this low profile, it is now possible to talk about Islam's "comeback" into the public domain.

It was after the 1980 military coup that Islamic groups and practices started gaining public presence. When the parliamentary regime resumed in 1983 in Turkey, the military regime's backing of Islamist groups against the left had paved the way for the flourishing of Islamist groups. Islam's first major challenge to the hegemony of secularism was publicly visible through the use of the headscarf among female university students in the 1980s. The Refah Party's prominent attention to the headscarf issue as a political matter enabled the party (established after the parliamentary regime was restored in 1983) to achieve a more overtly Islamic character. The enormous electoral success of the Refah Party in the 1994 local elections can be regarded as a turning point in the history of Turkey insofar as the unchallenged continuance of Kemalist secular ideology is concerned. Following the local elections, the Refah Party became the top party in general elections in 1995. Its leader Necmettin Erbakan became the prime minister in the coalition government in 1996. However, with the infamous postmodern coup of 28 February 1997, when the National Security Council gave a declaration to the government asking it to take strict measures against the threat of rising Islamism in the country, the coalition government was dismantled. After the cessation of the Refah Party, the Fazilet Party was established in 1998. As far as code of belief, cadre and directorial structures are concerned, the Fazilet Party was a carryover of the Refah Party that lasted until 2001. With the split of the Fazilet Party in 2001, the AK Party was founded. Generally speaking, the AK Party is less confrontational with the secular military, more moderate in its Islamic line, follows economic liberal policies, and is militantly pro-European. Regarding the characterizing features of the AK Party, it can be portrayed as having a liberal conservative ideology and social value system, taking its essential charge from Islam and Islamism. The AK Party has been in government since 2002, displaying major electoral victories both in 2002 and 2005. (For a detailed exposition of current sociopolitical developments, see Çınar, 2005.)

The period after the 1994 municipal elections when the Islamic Welfare Party won the major cities needs special attention. It was in this period that the Kemalist elite and the military managed to lay the discursive and organizational ground of an *irrational fear and phobia of Islam*. This psychic condition appealed to the populace and achieved quite substantial popular support. Due to increasing concern about Islamists becoming a vital force in the social, cultural and political life of Turkey (expressed in a way that is akin to Europe's current Orientalist and Islamophobic fantasy about the "threat of Islamization"), the Welfare Party's victory in local elections was experienced almost like a sharp and sudden pain by the secular establishment. The psychic condition and the neurotic response[3] that followed the 1994 local elections have since set the tone of the relation between these two groups, becoming even more highlighted and intense. This was a special historical moment in Turkey's social and political life, when the secularist elite of the republic had experienced major shock, utter dismay and consternation to such an extent that it might be legitimate to describe the psychic condition as total discomposure. The victory of Islamic parties in municipal elections both in Istanbul and in many other major cities resulted in alarm, extreme agitation, frenzy and panic. This condition has resulted in a lack of any rational social negotiation between the contending groups and thus needs to been seen as indicative of unconscious forces that participate in the structuring of the political domain.

---

3 In the 1994 local elections, the Welfare party's achievement of a major victory in many cities, especially in Istanbul, was certainly key in the creation of this secularist hysteria. Also, the fact that not only the district municipalities were obtained but also the municipality of greater Istanbul was of central importance in the formation of an anxiety-ridden and greatly irrational fear and phobia. This phobic sociopsychic condition was formed by the dissemination of rumors that have contributed to the formation of a new imaginary cultivating the idea that the secular lifestyles of middle-class people, especially women, are under tremendous threat. As it was believed that Islamic groups' major obsession was with the control of women, most concerns have revolved around the issue of gender. Navaro-Yashin (2002) cites several of the rumors that were put into circulation immediately after the municipal elections. Most rumors had to do with public appearances, lifestyles and women. Some of these were as follows: women would no longer be able to have a public life without wearing proper Islamic clothes as it was believed that Islamists were there to impose Islamic ways. Nor would they allow women to work or vote. (A female friend of mine, on hearing the election results, got physically ill: her blood pressure went up too high. I met her with a blood clot in her eye the next day caused by crying through the whole night, as she truly believed that she would be forced to be veiled.) Another rumor of concern for the secular middle class was that they would no longer be able to consume alcohol in restaurants and bars. Many jokes, stories and rumors have been instrumental in the creation of secularist apprehension about the future that is waiting for Turkey. These rumors added to the formation of an imaginary that was very similar to the Orientalist fantasy "The Muslims are Coming."

For this reason, to be able to offer an analysis of the ways in which Islamists and secularists have positioned themselves against one another over the last 20 years in Turkey, one has to attend to the unconscious processes that structure the domain of the political and the role of these processes in the constitution of the Islamic/secularist schism.[4] I will examine below the dynamics that lie behind this nonrational dimension. In discussing this, I will examine how certain objects are articulated and utilized in the public domain. Standouts among the large number of objects used both by Islamists and secularists are the headscarf used by Islamist women and icons of Atatürk used in various forms by secularists. These objects have become significant in the staging of *secularity* and *religiosity*, not only because they have been deployed in a wide range of contexts and with great frequency, but also because they have been instilled with strong symbolic value.

Objects and Their Social Life

Certain objects and their transformation into fetish objects played a vital role in the creation of a bifurcation between Islamist and secularist groups. Fear and paranoia about an Islamic threat has led to the fetishization as well as the commoditization of certain objects and symbols among secularist groups. Consequently, we have started witnessing widespread usage of icons of Atatürk (in homes, offices, cars, on dresses and even on bodies), resulting in an excessive cultural emphasis on his symbolic image.[5] This new embracing of the Atatürk figure by secularists also includes regular visits to his mausoleum (akin to visits to a shrine or some other place of worship) whenever a contentious social or political issue emerges. On the other hand, Islamists utilize women's headscarves in an almost fetishistic manner to symbolize their public visibility and presence in social and political life.

By examining the increased vitality these objects have gained, one can reach a good understanding of how certain objects move in and out of mere commodity status and attain a social and symbolic life. These objects certainly did exist before the hype, emotion and paranoia about the Islamic "threat" achieved such a heightened condition. However, objects never exist in a pure state. They receive a new life as a result of their commoditization, and commoditization is about acquiring a new value. If we follow the

---

4 Navaro-Yashin (2002: 5) also alludes to this unconscious and nonrational dimension of the political.

5 In her ethnographic work, Esra Özyürek (2005) offers a detailed description of the ways in which pictures of Atatürk proliferate in homes and businesses as a potent symbol of the secular Turkish state.

Saussurean principle of language and difference, objects do not have any absolute meaning and value. The meaning of an object is always determined in a social relation; therefore, its symbolic value is set reciprocally. Moreover, the meaning of an object is determined in relation to other objects and it never exists independently of the desire that infuses it with value. The desire that infuses and marks certain objects with particular values and meanings is certainly not a product of an individual undertaking, but is always conditioned and structured by a particular social imaginary.

To be able to understand how certain cultural meanings are mobilized in Islamist and secularist politics in Turkey, we need an analysis of the "life history of objects" and the "cultural biography" (Appadurai, 1986) of the things used in the clash between secularism and religion. By examining how certain objects are positioned and articulated, we can reveal the kind of imaginary these groups create, both of themselves and of each other, while staging their relation to religion and to secularism.

There is an interesting contrast between the ways in which wars of symbolism or wars of objects have been managed by Islamists and secularists. Among Islamists, the women's headscarf was attributed a high symbolic value and hence a market has developed for it.[6] However, interestingly, in an attempt to counter the symbolism of Islamists, the secularists did not necessarily wage their politics of identity through women's cloths. Instead, the excessive use of Atatürk icons has become the means through which the secularist groups signify publicly their politics of protection of the secular foundations of the republic. Consequently, the headscarf and icons of Atatürk have achieved new symbolic values and meanings in relation to each other.

Symbolism of Cloth

The *raison d'être* behind the symbolic importance of the headscarf can be understood when one takes into consideration the way Islam has been lodged in the secular republican heritage of Turkey. It is perhaps the didactic secularism outlined by Gellner that can explain why an apparently simple issue of clothing – the banning of university students' wearing of headscarves which occurred in the early 1980s and still continues – has turned into a matter of major social clash and confrontation between secularism and Islamism in the current Turkish political conjuncture. Secularism was not only established in an authoritarian manner in Turkey, but it has become

---

6 Navaro-Yashin (2002) offers a detailed exposition of the development and proliferation of a new market for manufacturing of the veil and the portrait of Atatürk. See especially chapter 3.

the hegemonic nationalist mode in which the Turkish state has managed to constitute its public self-image. Through didactic secularism, the state has been able to dominate the public, cultural and psychological life of people in Turkey. Any challenge to secularism since its inception has been perceived as a fundamental challenge to Turkey's very being. Hence, secularism was able to maintain its legitimacy without allowing counternarratives to flourish. But the political conjuncture in Turkey since the 1980s has revealed a precarious side to the overtly unchallenged legitimacy of this secular hegemony. Examining the dialectic between Islamists and secularists and the way in which secularity in Turkey tries to maintain its hegemony in the face of the challenge posed by Islamists can give us hints about the fantasies and therefore about the unconscious processes involved in this political battle.

In an attempt to dislodge the secularist erasure of the traces and presence of Islam from the public domain, Islamists placed great emphasis on the headscarf worn by women. The headscarf functioned as a very convenient visible symbol, not only of the presence of people with Islamic faith, but also of the presence of a *way of living* that is guided by the principles of Islam. The headscarf came to signify that Islam is present and alive not only as an individual faith, but as a collective social and cultural set of principles guiding people, manners and styles of living. But most important of all, it signified that the sacralized and defended space of the public was now becoming vulnerable to the intrusion of religious signs. Muslim women entering the public space with their Islamic headscarves implied the destabilization of the principles of centralist Kemalist secularism and the Kemal attempt to redefine the parameters of the public domain. Hence, the increasing number of female university students wearing headscarves came to signify *publicly* that Islam is present in people's life-world.

Although the headscarf appears to be an item of individual preference, it has also become translated into the lexicon of a major political battle. It not only came to symbolize Islam's *public presence*, but was also transformed into a key term in the vocabulary of a grand political discourse that based itself on democratic and basic human rights, freedom of religious expression and individual liberties. We will be far from comprehending the transformative journey of the symbolism of the headscarf from being a private and individual question of piety into being a question of Islam's public presence and freedom of expression and rights if we simply think that people in Turkey have become more religious and have started challenging the foundations of the secularist republic. This sort of explanation would simply mimic the paranoiac secularist politics that is alive in Turkey today. This paranoiac politics insists that the headscarf is a sign of a hidden agenda of Islamist political actors, whose ultimate aim is to replace the secular republican regime with an Islamist one.

However, the public emphasis on the question of the headscarf – starting in the 1980s and intensifying through the 1990s and 2000s, especially among urban, modernized and educated groups of Islamist activist women – is far from indicating the Islamization of Turkish society. If we remain within statistical logic and point to the total number of women in Turkey who wear the Islamic headscarf, we will not be able to understand the changing nature of Turkish people's relation to religion. It is important that our analysis attends to the changing nature of the *religiosity* in Turkey's social and cultural life. I deploy Olivier Roy's (2006) term "religiosity" rather than religion to refer to the manner in which people live their relationship to religion (3). Roy suggests that, as a result of the processes of globalization, the return to religiosity is everywhere in the world. The "return" of Islam in Turkish social and political life is also conditioned and influenced by global processes. Unfortunately, examination of Islamism as social movement and of the global sociopolitical dynamics behind its becoming a worldwide phenomenon is outside the scope of this essay.

The *changing nature of religiosity* in Turkey would make sense by understanding its mirror opposite: the *changing nature of secularity*. In other words, understanding either the changing nature of religiosity or of secularity in Turkey can only be possible by considering their interaction with each other. Hence, I use the term secularity to allude to the manner in which people's relation to the secular republican social and political order is lived, experienced and imagined. Thus I will suggest that it is not secularism per se, but *secularity* that has changed in response to or in its interaction with the increasing visibility of Islam and things associated with Islam in the Turkish people's lives. It is the nature of the interaction between the religious and the secular that has changed and gained a new life of its own. However, to be able to understand the metamorphoses or transmutations of secularity and religiosity in Turkey since the 1980s, we will need to develop a theoretical framework that attends to the processes that differentiate and mark certain practices, signs, languages, symbols and discourses as belonging to the realm of either the religious or secular. The current scholarship exemplified in the works of Talal Asad (2003), Gil Anidjar (2008 and 2003), Tomoko Masuzawa (2005) and Hent de Vries (2007 and 2006) offer new conceptual and theoretical lenses through which we might understand not simply what religion is about but, at the same time, the nature of the processes by which the field of religion is constituted in genealogical terms. If we follow the spirit of this current scholarship, it is no longer possible simply to delimit a space called the religious and examine the "what is" of religion. Asad's (2003) framework discourages us from regarding the secular as a space which was gradually emancipated from religion. As he suggests, "it is this assumption that allows us to think of religion as 'infecting' the secular domain or as replicating within it the structure of theological concepts" (191). The distinction between the secular and religious is problematized by another scholar as follows: "one can argue that within the semantic of the modern religio-secular paradigm, processes of 'religionization' – i.e. the signification of certain spaces, practices, narratives and languages as religious (as opposed to things marked as secular) – and 'secularization' are constitutive of each other" (Dressler, 2008: 281).

Rather than seeing the secular and the religious as two distinct experiential realities, I suggest that we understand them in their interaction and hence in their reciprocal shaping and constitution of one another. Dressler's terms *religionization* and *secularization* correspond somewhat to my suggestion regarding the new forms of *religiosity* and *secularity* in Turkey. With these terms, I want to be able to capture the ways in which people's imaginary and real relationship to those things called religious and secular are structured and shaped. Rather than attempting to decipher what secularism and Islamism *are* in Turkey, examining the processes, symbols, narratives and practices that contribute to the marking of certain things as religious and others as secular will enable us to comprehend the dynamic, processual and relational nature of the secular and of the religious.

Sacralized Public Space

Marking the headscarf as a site of rural traditionalism and lower-class ignorance, the republican secularist fashioning of the public sphere in the formative years of the republic in the 1920s instituted women's unveiling as a key signifier, not only of the emancipation of women from religion and ignorance, but of the modernization of the country. From the 1980s onward, the activism of students insisting on attending universities wearing their headscarves constituted a major challenge to the authority of the Kemalist secularist sacralization of public spaces. As education was regarded as one of the key institutions in the path of modernizing Turkey, female university students' claim to be able to attend educational institutions without giving up signs of religiosity was met with great unease. To make sense of this unease, we can perhaps accept Talal Asad's (2003) suggestion that secularism is not simply about separating the fields of religion and politics, but also about the suppression and control of religion by the secular. For Asad, secularism is first and foremost about instituting a division or opposition between the secular and religious and thus entails the production of the religious by the secular so as to constitute the latter as the norm and accord to itself a privileged position. What maintains secularism's authority is precisely this power to institute the opposition between itself and the religious. Thus what constitutes a major challenge to secularism is not simply the making visible of religiosity. Rather, it is the conflation of the neat binary between the secular and the religious that makes maintenance of the opposition no longer possible that constitutes such a troubling destabilization to the privilege and authority of the secularist surveillance of the public.

The official response to the increasing visibility of the Islamic headscarf on university campuses and hence the conflation of the opposition between the secular and the religious came with the decree of the National Security Council in 1997. It demanded tighter measures against the threat of Islamization. A ban on the headscarf was one of those measures.

A more striking and perhaps definitive example of the mixing or confusion of the binaries between private and public, religious and secular is the 1999 Merve Kavakçı case. What we witness in the Kavakçı case is a furious reaction to any sign of the entrance or intrusion (to use the parlance of secularist discourse) of the headscarf into the sacred institutions of the state. Merve Kavakçı, a 30-year-old woman educated as an engineer in the United States, was elected as an MP for the Islamist Virtue Party in 1999 and insisted that she attend the oath ceremony in the parliament in her headscarf. Merve Kavakçı's insistence was retorted in a physically powerful manner when she entered the parliament to take her seat. The members of the parliament started banging on their desks and chanting the slogan "Turkey is and will remain secular" (which became a famous song of praise among the secularists), thus forcing Kavakçı to leave without being sworn in (see Göçek, 1999).

Prime Minister Bülent Ecevit's speech in criticism of Merve Kavakçı's insistence on wearing her headscarf is symptomatic of the desire to keep the private and the public distinct and to keep the state as the guardian of the public:

> In Turkey, nobody interferes in the clothing and the headscarf of women in private life. However, this is not a domain of private life. Those who serve here, have to suit the tradition and the rules of the state. This is not the place to challenge the state. (Quoted in Dressler, 2008b: 15)

Similarly, Süleyman Demirel, the then-president of the republic was another figure who criticized Kavakçı on the grounds that she was creating trouble and accused her of being an *agent provocateur* controlled by foreign powers. Moreover, he saw Kavakçı's headscarf as symbolizing the movement which aimed to transform Turkey into an Iran, Afghanistan or Algeria. "The chief prosecutor used Kavakçı's action to start a lawsuit against her party for inciting her to take a stand against the secular principles of the state, and to eliminate, once and for all, all party members who were like vampires constantly sucking on the blood of the nations" (Demirel cited in Göçek, 1999: 523).

Popular opposition to Kavakçı was no less hysterical. Her neighbors decorated their windows with posters of Atatürk so as to send the message that the threat to the secular order established by Atatürk, presumed to be posed by Kavakçı's wish to be present in the space of the parliament with her headscarf on, would not go unanswered. The widespread media campaign against Kavakçı portrayed her as a decoy of an Islamist party whose hidden aim was to institute an Islamic state in Turkey. This negative campaign launched by the popular secularist media interrogated Kavakçı's moral character and her private life was put under scrutiny. Consequently, it was discovered that she had earlier received American citizenship. Her Turkish citizenship was taken away on the grounds that she attained American citizenship without following the appropriate bureaucratic procedures in notifying the Turkish state about her desire to retain dual citizenship. With the removal of her Turkish citizenship, Kavakçı's MP position was annulled. (For a detailed explication of the case of Merve Kavakçı, see Göçek, 1999.)

Both the political plight of Merve Kavakçı, and female students' insistence on wearing their headscarves to university, need to be seen as the destabilization of the very opposition between the private and public that the secularist narrative had established. They should function as an important reminder that despite the prevailing secularist argument's relegation of religion to the private domain, religion has never ceased to appear in public space. The very act of separating religion from other domains – in particular from the domains of politics and culture – and the production of religion by the very forces of secularist narrative do not imply that religion's mode of presence is simply enclosed by secularism, especially in the context of the geopolitics of today's globalized world.

Icons of Atatürk

In opposition to the symbolism of the headscarf, the secularist groups have used icons of Atatürk in an excessive manner to make their politics visible in the public domain. Atatürk posters have always been present in Turkish people's official and social lives since the establishment of the republic, though not so much in their private lives. But interestingly, not only has the sheer quantity of icons of Atatürk that people are using in their private lives increased, but the form of these icons has drastically changed. In contrast to the traditional colossal statues and posters of Atatürk, imagery of Atatürk transformed into smaller, private and individual items. To give a context for the importance of the icon of Atatürk, I must mention that it was widely used during the establishment of the republic to cement the disparate groups of the nation and build the fantasy and cult of the origination of the new nation. Atatürk posters have been persistently used in state offices, but in the 1990s the imagery of Atatürk began to take the form of *individualized objects*. People started wearing Atatürk pins, displaying him on car stickers and, later and most strikingly, wearing his signature or portrait as tattoos on their bodies.

Obsession with the imagery of Atatürk arrived at a pinnacle with the Islamic Welfare Party's victory in the general elections. The army's intervention into politics in 1997 was effected by the banning of its leader from politics and the deliverance of a powerful warning against the "threat of Islamism." It came to be named a postmodern coup, as its intervention into parliamentary democracy was exercised not in the usual military manner and has not resulted in the dissolution of the parliament, but was accomplished through a new mode that can be called a "simulated coup." With this coup, the hype about using Atatürk images in a personalized, privatized manner in people's offices, homes and on their bodies intensified. We can interpret the privatized and individualized usage of Atatürk icons as an effort by secularist groups to symbolize that the *people* and not simply the state were now functioning as the guardians of the secular regime.[7]

---

7 This emphasis on "people" in the secularist narratives is highly problematical. The secularist narratives' reference to "people" and attribution to them of a certain kind of spontaneity in the guardianship and support of the secular regime is very dubious and far from being accurate. One example that might help us to question people's spontaneous support of the secular regime is that of the seventy-fifth Republic Day celebrations. Özyürek (2005) offers us a very illuminating example by unraveling how the seventy-fifth anniversary celebration ceremony was also a highly organized and planned event designed to convey an anti-Islamist message. During the authoritarian single-party regime, the centralized Turkish state had centrally planned and organized an orderly and choreographed demonstration to celebrate the tenth anniversary of the republic. However, with the 1994 local electoral victory of the Islamist party, Islamist mayors of cities turned out not to be too eager about providing passionate celebrations of the Republic Day. The military's strong warning against the government on 28 February 1987 was instrumental in setting the tone of a certain narrative and psychosocial atmosphere which can be translated as "It is the people with their free will who are now willing to act as the guardians of the secularist ideology and secular regime." The desire to orchestrate the seventh-fifth anniversary by allocating millions of dollars for the celebrations and to delegate the History Foundation, chaired by well-known city planner İlhan Tekeli, as the organizing agent of the celebrations, demonstrates strikingly that those celebrations were far from being spontaneous and were far from being an expression of the "free will" of the people. It was İlhan Tekeli who came up with the idea of participatory "festival-like celebrations" as opposed to the hierarchical organizations of the state. Tekeli mentioned to Özyürek (2006) in an interview that one of the most important motives for the seventy-fifth anniversary celebrations was to make an

However, having Atatürk's signature and portrait inscribed as a tattoo on one's body is also instructive about an interesting desire, and we can perhaps make sense of this desire when we situate it in the context of the waging of a war of symbols. The headscarf, no doubt, is a bodily item. The woman who wears a headscarf, in a way, transforms her body into a ground of a political battle.[8] If we follow the Foucauldian principle of inscription of bodies and the power of objects and discourses to produce particular types of bodies by inscribing them in particular ways, then this desire to carry Atatürk icons on one's own body, especially in response to the use of headscarf, can be seen as a struggle waged through bodies. The veiled woman's manner of being in public with or without a headscarf certainly entails different forms of embodiment. Thus secularists, in the battle with the increasing presence of religiosity in the public sphere, have developed a belated or responsive desire in an effort to find a matching item that has a comparable weight in terms of its bodily effects.

In addition to the frenzied interest in Atatürk iconography, a pattern of secularist demonstrations has developed. The excessive use of the Turkish flag came to identify a particular political message: the people's guardianship of the secular regime. The Turkish flag was also used to repeat the republic's anxiety around unity and integration and centralized state control. In addition to expressing their desire to have the principles of the republic inscribed on their bodies, guardians of the republic wanted to convey the message that they were capable of reinstituting and maintaining their hold on the united and integrated secular nation.

What was so unusual about these demonstrations was that the middle-class urban bourgeois women who earlier had barely had any explicit political commitment or taken part in street politics became the central actors of secular guardianship. They were also the key consumers of Atatürk icons. There are two dimensions of the explanation as to why urban middle-class women were so eager to embrace the role of "guardianship of secularism." With the

---

anti-Islamist statement. He underlined that "as enlightened Turks...we felt responsible for the republic and wanted to do something against the religious uprising" (138). Perhaps this ideology of "expression of people's free will and their guardianship of the secular regime" instituted during the seventy-fifth anniversary celebrations has since shaped the nature of the secularist form of political expression. Many of the protests against the Islamist government have been accompanied with excessive use of the Turkish flag and the slogan "Turkey is and will remain secular" and have all been infused by the aura: "It is now people who are expressing their free will."

8   For a detailed discussion of how the veil is turned into a ground of battle between Islamists and the Kemalist elite in the formative years of the republic, see my *Colonial Fantasies* (1998).

establishment of the new republican regime, secularism was promoted as an issue of lifestyle, in particular of middle-class lifestyle. Great emphasis was placed on secularist lifestyles and secularism was associated with Western habits of eating, socializing and dressing. In general, the kind of social and public life one pursued became an important signifier of one's allegiance to a secular and modern Western society. Islamic forms, cultural and social habits were associated with backwardness and traditionalism. Another explanatory dimension is that these groups were the key beneficiaries of the newly established republic, with its emphasis on education and its encouragement of women taking part in social-public life.

As the above examples illustrate, neither the headscarf nor Atatürk icons are motionless, inert and lifeless objects. Rather, following the understanding Appadurai develops in *The Social Life of Things* (1986) we can see them as *things in motion*. This would involve understanding the symbolism of these objects as a *processual* issue; such a focus on process enables us to engage with the question of objects used in the Turkish battle between secularism and Islamism as a question of signification, relationality and opposition and thereby to track their social and cultural movement, their paths, diversions, directions and mutations. This will enable us to explicate the cultural issues surrounding their classification and labeling as well as the political and ideological framework which envelopes their articulation. In other words, the articulation of these two objects into the discursive battle between a particular secularity and religiosity indicates that these are not lifeless, motionless or neutral items, but cultural and political devices that are open for articulation and rearticulation and can have a transformative capacity depending on the ways they are used. Here I am not simply making the straightforward and well-known point that to consume an object is inevitably to convey a message. Beyond this familiar point, following Appadurai's argument, I am suggesting that the consumption of the Islamic headscarf and the icon of Atatürk in opposition to each other politicize both the *reception* and the *consumption* of these objects. By consuming the headscarf and the icon of Atatürk, Islamists and secularists are making symbolic statements and sending particular messages. However, perhaps as importantly as sending particular messages, they are also receiving messages (Appadurai, 1986: 31). In other words, *by consuming certain objects that are marked in particular ways, secularist and Islamist groups in Turkey are receiving messages about the value of their Islamism and secularism and their relation to religiosity and secularity.* The distribution of knowledge about these objects, and the schedule of values that mark certain objects as religious or secular, are of key consequence to the vitality gained by the objects in the staging of religiosity and/or secularity.

Paranoid Nationalism: By Way of Conclusion

Secularism can be regarded as a public discourse that is fighting for a kind of legitimacy that is not identical to the legitimacy it was striving for in the 1920s, which was established in a didactic manner. It would thus be misleading to simply suggest that Islamism is becoming more widespread or intense in the social, political and cultural life of Turkey. The visibility Islamic ways have gained is not simply a matter of *degree* but of *type*, in the sense that the nature of religiosity in Turkey has also changed since the 1920s. This change contributed to the fantasies, fears and imagery about Islam. It is important to note that secularity and Islamic public presence have gained new twenty-first century faces through their relationality. To understand how the relation between the two has progressed, we can perhaps talk about the *staging of religiosity* and *staging of secularity*. My reason for deploying the term *staging* should not imply that my argument presumes a "real" or "authentic" Islam or secularism behind their staging. Rather, I want to emphasize the *performativity* that is associated with both. To understand the characteristics of this performativity, it is important that we attend to the nature of the relation both groups establish with the objects they manipulate (headscarf and Atatürk's icons) as their quintessential signifiers.

As mentioned above, it is possible to talk about the flourishing of a particular secular psychic condition in Turkey since the 1990s. The more serene and confident secular posture of the early republican elite displaced itself into a kind of frantic and irrational fear and phobia of things deemed Islamic or religious in the 1990s. The rational and self-possessed assuredness of the 1920s secular elite no longer surrounds the elite's relation to secularism today. Rather, there is every sign of an insecure attachment that I would like to identify with a term I borrow from Ghassan Hage (2003): *paranoid nationalism*.

Particularly after the electoral victory of the Islamic Refah Party in local elections in 1994, secularists developed a condition of panic, alarm and anxiety at the idea of a "religious invasion" of the domains of the political and public. Increased consternation about the threat of Islamization is what characterizes the self-presentation of mainstream and popular media and secular elite groups. This paranoid condition, to follow Hage's understanding, brought with it intense "worrying" as a result of feeling threatened. Such a defensive attitude flourishes because of an insecure attachment to a nation that is incapable of properly nourishing its citizens. Worrying thus results in the exertion of "a form of symbolic violence over the field of national belonging," obliterating other possibilities and modes of belonging. The paranoid nationalist imaginary forecloses the possibility of a relation with the other.

One instance where one can discern this paranoid imaginary in Turkey is the systematic and persistent questioning of the "motives" of Islamists. The Islamic movement and people are attributed "hidden motives" behind their apparent political behavior, particularly via the use of the Islamic notion of *"takiyye."* According to this concept, which can be translated as "dissimulation," a Muslim is justified in hiding his or her real motives if the circumstances are unfavorable to the exercise of his or her faith. The concept of *takiyye* is often used by the secularists indiscriminately without analysis of any specific behavior as an umbrella term for Islamic politics in general. The whole of Islamic political behavior is thus reduced to so many ways of covering a larger secret political plan to establish an Islamic hegemony and finally an Islamic regime of Shari'a. As Asad (2003) notes, the attempts by Muslim movements to reform the social body through parliamentary intervention will be opposed as "antidemocratic," as was the case in Turkey in 1997 and in Algeria in 1992. Primarily, the intolerant attitude towards the deprivatization of religion by secularists was "because of the motives imputed to their opponents rather than to anything the latter have actually done. The motives signal the potential entry of religion into space already occupied by the secular. It is the nationalist-secularists themselves, one might say, who stoutly reject the secularization of religious concepts and practices here" (199–200).

As outlined above, in defending the secular heritage and principles of Turkey, new patterns of expression have emerged. Secular sentiments, symbols and ceremonial and ritualistic practices are being deployed such as attending Atatürk's mausoleum, excessive use of the Turkish flag and images of Atatürk and the use of the slogan "Turkey is secular and will remain secular" on almost every occasion. Such expressions can be seen as a process of *sacralization and transcendentalization of the principles of secularism.* This sacralized defense of the principles of secularism in turn feeds the paranoid nationalist response. The insistence on the categorical separation of the religious and the political leaves no room for a different and more responsible articulation of religion with the secular.

However, the split and opposition between the secularists and Islamists in today's Turkey is only an apparent one. This is the other reason why I will prefer to use the term "staging," as this term will help me in suggesting that the *contemporary form of Islamic religiosity and the new faces of secularity are constitutive of each other.* A closer analysis of the discourse of secularists reveals that it is very much imbued with a religious language and way of doing things. The Turkish secularists suffer from inadequate secularization and the current staging of secularism evidences the sacralization of secularism. For this reason, ironically, secularist discourse is imbued with the language of religion in its fight with religion. On the other hand, Islamist politics inherited the authoritarian management of culture from the elitist secularist system that denied it legitimate existence. The discourse and the symbolic world embodied by the historically hegemonic secularist elite was authoritarian and the secularist infusion of the discourse of Islamism must be acknowledged as an intermingling with authoritarianism. Thus, it is important that we remain critical of any suggestion of categorical and clear-cut distinctions and differences between religiosity and secularity in the Turkish case.

References

Anidjar, Gil. 2008. *Semites: Race, Religion, Literature*. Stanford, CA: Stanford University Press.

_____. 2003. *The Jew, the Arab: A History of the Enemy*. Stanford, CA: Stanford University Press.

Appadurai, Arjun. 1986. "Introduction: Commodities and the Politics of Value." In Arjun Appadurai (ed.), *The Social Life of Things: Commodities in Cultural Perspective*, 3–63. Cambridge: Cambridge University Press.

Asad, Talal. 2006. "Trying to Understand French Secularism." In Hent de Vries (ed.), *Political Theologies in a Post-Secular World*. New York: Fordham University Press.

_____. 2003. *Formations of the Secular: Christianity, Islam, Modernity*. Stanford, CA: Stanford Univesity Press.

Berkes, Niyazi. 1999. *The Development of Secularism in Turkey*. New York and London: Routledge.

Casanova, José. 1994. *Public Religions in the Modern World*. Chicago and London: University Chicago Press.

Çağaptay, Soner. 2006. *Islam, Secularism and Nationalism in Modern Turkey: Who is a Turk?* New York and London: Routledge

Çınar, Alev. 2005. *Modernity, Islam, and Secularism in Turkey: Bodies, Places and Time*. Minneapolis: University of Minnesota Press.

Çolak, Yılmaz and Aydın Ertan. 2000. "Dilemmas of Turkish Democracy: The Conflict Between Kemaalist Laicism and Islamism in the 1990s" In David W. Odell-Scott (ed.), *Democracy and Religion: Free Exercise and Diverse Visions*, 3rd volume of the Kent State University Symposium on Democracy, 202–20. Kent, OH: Kent State University Press.

_____. 2003. "Nationalism and the State in Turkey: Drawing Boundaries of 'Turkish Culture' in the 1930s." *Studies in Ethnicity and Nationalism* 3.1: 1–19.

De Vries, Hent (ed.) 2006. *Political Theologies: Public Religions in a Postsecular World*. New York: Fordham University Press.

_____. (ed.) 2007. *Religion: Beyond a Concept: The Future of the Religious Past*. New York: Fordham University Press.

Dressler, Markus. 2008a. "Religio-Secular Metamorphoses: The Re-Making of Turkish Alevism." *Journal of American Academy of Religion* 76.2: 280–311.

_____. 2008b. "Debating Secularism in Turkey: Public/Private Distinction, the Alevi Question, and the Headscarf." Paper presented at the "Religion, Secularism, and Democracy" conference, Istanbul, 7–9 July 2008.

Gellner, Ernest. 1981. *Muslim Society*. Cambridge, MA: Cambridge University Press.

Göçek, Müge. 1999. "To Veil or Not to Veil: The Contested Location of Gender in Contemporary Turkey." *Interventions* 1.4: 521–35.

Gülalp, Haldun. 2003. "Whatever Happened to Secularization? The Multiple Islams in Turkey." *South Atlantic Quarterly* 102.2–3: 381–95.

Hage, Ghassan. 2003. *Against Paranoid Nationalism: Searching for Hope in a Shrinking Society.* London: Merlin Press.

Masuzawa, Tomoko. 2005. *The Invention of World Religions: Or, How European Universalism Was Preserved in the Language of Pluralism.* Chicago: Chicago University Press.

Navaro-Yashin, Yael. 2002. *Faces of the State: Secularism and Public Life in Turkey.* Princeton, NJ: University of Princeton Press.

Özyürek, Esra. 2006. *Nostalgia for the Modern: State Secularism and Everyday Politics in Turkey.* Durham, NC: Duke University Press.

Roy, Olivier. 2006. "Islam in Europe: Clash of Religions or Religiosities?" In Krzysztof Michalski (ed.), *Condition of European Solidarity, vol. II: Religion in the New Europe*, 1–10. Budapest: Central European University Press.

Yeğenoğlu, Meyda. 1998. *Colonial Fantasies: Towards a Feminist Reading of Orientalism.* Cambridge: Cambridge University Press.

Chapter 11

GRAMSCI, JEDIISM, THE STANDARDIZATION OF POPULAR RELIGION AND THE STATE[1]

Adam Possamai

University of Western Sydney

Gramsci viewed popular religion as having the possibility of being a progressive movement against the bourgeois hegemony produced and reproduced in symbiosis with official religion and the state. In this pre–mass consumption society, there was the germ of a revolt in popular religion that could help the revolutionary push needed and guided by earlier Marxists. The goal of this chapter is to argue that with the entry of popular religion into the consumer societies of the Western world, popular religion has not moved further in terms of its opposition against the state. A case study of hyperreal religions and more specifically of Jediism will form the thread of the chapter. Following Simmel and Beck, I will argue that popular religion, like money, now individualizes and standardizes and by this process loses its oppositional strength.

Introduction

In pre-consumer and pre-cyber culture, Gramsci argued that popular religion could help with counterhegemonic forces and that this could offer an opposition to the state. Could this still be the case today? Jediism is a spirituality that has been inspired by the *Star Wars* franchise. It is a subset of popular religion that has emerged in consumer and cyber culture and will be used as a case study for the purpose of this chapter.

---

1 Many thanks to Elena Knox, who provided some research assistance for this chapter.

Jediism has infiltrated a few censuses around the world and is actively present on the internet. On "The Jediism Way,"[2] an internet site dedicated to presenting Jediism as a religion, we can find a specific view of the *Star Wars* mythos that does not direct its focus exclusively on the myth and fiction as created by the movie director George Lucas but upon "real life" examples of Jediism:

> Jediism is not the same as that which is portrayed within the Star Wars Saga by George Lucas and Lucasfilm LTD. George Lucas' Jedi are fictional characters that exist within a literary and cinematic universe. The Jedi discussed within this website refer to factual people within this world that live or lived their lives according to Jediism, of which we recognize and work together as a community to both cultivate and celebrate... The history of the path of Jediism traverses thought which is well over 5,000 years old. It shares many themes embraced in Hinduism, Confucianism, Buddhism, Gnosticism, Stoicism, Catholicism, Taoism, Shinto, Modern Mysticism, the Way of the Shaolin Monks, the Knight's Code of Chivalry and the Samurai warriors. We recognize that many times the answer to mankind's problems comes from within the purified hearts of genuine seekers of truth. Theology, philosophy and religious doctrine can facilitate this process, but we believe that it would be a futile exercise for any belief system to claim to hold all the answers to all the serious questions posed to seekers of truth in the 21st century. Jediism may help facilitate this process, yet we also acknowledge that it is up to the true believer who applies the universal truths inherent with Jediism to find the answers they seek.

In the bulk of its online representations, Jediknightism, or Jediism, is presented as an old religion remythologized to a contemporary public. Old techniques of development of the self such as meditation, yoga and shamanism are used towards this Jedi path. The stories of *Star Wars* are in fact presented as a support for a mix-and-match of various religions and philosophies from the past and present.

One of the messages from the same "Jedi Knight Movement" discussion list quoted above states about "Jediknightism":

> Life on planet earth has become much more complex – the churches, although meaning well, many times fall short of the mark of addressing the complexities. The political arena many times disappoints us and falls short of inspiring either ourselves or others to action.

---

2 See www.jediism.org.

We can read from this statement that people who embrace this religion are critical of mainstream religions and of political movements. Left without these grand narratives they embrace another type of narrative:

> Storytelling is an age-old tradition that has followed mankind for millennia – and has been used effectively for transferring ideals, from philosophers to prophets. It is an ideal medium to both entertain and enlighten simultaneously, which is why it is so powerful and its effects so profound when used expertly.[3]

The spiritual actors from this religion consume popular culture and add it to a kind of religious bricolage. This spirituality is part of what I have called hyperreal religion/spirituality (Possamai, 2007), which is a simulacrum[4] of a religion partly created out of popular culture that provides inspiration for believers and consumers. At one end of the spectrum, we can find individuals rejecting institutionalized religions and practicing Jediism (appropriated from the *Star Wars* movies) and Matrixism (from the *Matrix* trilogy) and neopagan groups using stories from the *Lord of the Rings* and *Harry Potter*. At the other end of the spectrum, practitioners still involved in mainstream religions such as Christianity reveal themselves as being influenced or inspired by, for example, the *Da Vinci Code*. These contemporary expressions of religion are likely to be consumed and individualized, and thus have more relevance to the self than to a community and/or congregation.

As already argued elsewhere (Possamai, 2008), the syncretic aspects of hyperreal religion as differentiated from official codified religion bear some striking resemblances to popular religion. Although hyperreal religion has some clear popular elements and is not led by an elite group, its members are quite literate and computer savvy and certainly not part of a subordinate group, contrary to the classical understanding of popular religion. It is because of this new practice of using commodified popular culture for religious purposes that hyperreal religion is a new subset of popular religion. This will be developed further below.

Star Wars' first three movies (episodes 4, 5 and 6) involve a Jedi Knight on his path to developing himself. This has led many consumers of these movies to be inspired by a spirituality informed by the franchise. In this case, believers and consumers reinvent old religions such as shamanism, Buddhism, Taoism and even Catholicism to validate the Jedi religion, and apply them in an

---

3 See http://groups.yahoo.com/groups/Jedi_Knight_Movement/ (accessed 25 October 2002 – registration required).
4 As inspired by the work of Jean Baudrillard (1983).

individualized way to a new spirituality of the self. However, another crucial aspect of these movies appears to be of less importance to the development of this spirituality in cyberspace. The Jedi knight in the movies, Luke Skywalker, fights against an oppressive regime led by an emperor and his right-hand man, Darth Vader. A rebellion (which could have been called a revolution) from a subordinate group succeeds at the end of the first trilogy, pointing out that the religion portrayed in the movies has a strong revolutionary nature. However, most devotees of this work of popular culture are predominantly concerned with a spirituality of the self.

In chat rooms and forums dedicated to Jediism, few discussions are posted about political issues. Examining three sites (The Jediism Way, http://www. thejediismway.org; Temple of the Jedi Force, http://www.templeofthejediforce. org, and Temple of the Jedi Order, http://www.templeofthejediorder.org), one can observe that the bulk of the discussion is about individual spiritual training rather than collective political development. When politics is mentioned, it is mainly in the context of current affairs or in the citing of various ideologies without evidence of a specific goal or organizing principle. From my observation in September–October 2009 of the discussion in these three sites, it appears that, while not apolitical, Jediism is more interested in the peacekeeping, protective and defensive ideologies derived from the *Star Wars* series than in the incitement of governmental overthrow also present in the movies.

One interaction is worth mentioning here. At the beginning of 2009, a "newbie" to Jediism posted a message to argue that in the hands of a Jedist, politics could be a very positive thing. He states:

> Communism, in my opinion, is essentially the best avenue of approach. The basic underlying tenet of Communism is basically to free those whom are being oppressed or exploited… Every Jedi should feel compelled to relieve the suffering of the opposed [sic] and to combat the spread of Capitalism, as a means to exploit and oppress those like the third world, and even those at home.[5]

Two hours later, a senior member of this Jedi group replied to this message by stating that the implementation of communism had failed and that "Stalin was an ass and Mao an idiot." There followed from this remark a heated exchange of messages between the newbie and the senior member which led to some name calling, even when a third party tried to intervene to calm the

---

5 http://www.thejediismway.org/index.php/topic,55.0.html (accessed 2 July 2009 – website since discontinued).

situation down. The whole exchange of messages lasted a bit more than a day, and no one has since posted anything on that specific discussion board. This exchange could be interpreted in two ways. The first interpretation would be that there has been some discussion against capitalism in Jediism and that there might be the germination of some counterhegemonic forces slowly emerging. The other is simply that this political spark quickly ran out of heat and became insignificant among all the messages in the forum. How to reflect on this incident? Would Jediism and other popular religions on the internet provide the type of counterhegemonic forces that Gramsci was looking for? Or would these forces only present an illusion that would never lead to social change, or even to opposition against the status quo?

This chapter attempts to explain this case study by first exploring popular religion and its revolutionary strength according to Gramsci. It then addresses the position of spiritualities on the internet and their possible counterhegemonic strength through a "participatory culture." The chapter finally makes reference to the work of Simmel and Beck in order to understand how consumer culture has affected popular religion and how the standardization of popular religion might have affected the revolutionary power of popular religion.

Revolutionary Aspects of Popular Religion?

In its worst possible interpretation, popular religion can make reference to the "vulgar," the "superstitious," the "hopelessly irrational," the "socially retrograde" and the "idiotic" (Berlinerblau, 2001). Popular religion reflects the lived and unstructured religion of subordinated groups and is a term that has developed mainly in contrast to institutionalized, established and/or official religion which has a rationalized, codified and written down theology. Popular religion refers to the religion of the people when they subvert the codified official religion of the elite group by, for example, changing the official liturgy of the established religion to their own liking, bringing eclectic elements into a syncretic set of beliefs from other religions that are not officially recognized or simply following a previous religion in opposition to a new official one (these examples are context-dependent).

To move forward in our sociological discussion, Berlinerblau (2001: 13) extrapolated two broad understandings of popular religion from Weber:

1. "Popular Religion" is that religion, whatever its contents, practiced by groups among the masses characterized by nonprivileged social and economic status
2. "Popular religion" is constituted by specific types of practices and beliefs (i.e. magic, an antirational orientation, a close bond with nature,

a "this-worldly" religious attitude, heightened concern with salvation and savior-figures) held by a particular group

In Parker's (1998: 205) view, "unlike the [official] religion of reason characteristic of the intellectual elites and clergy, popular religion is a religion of rites and myths, of dreams and emotions, of body and the quest for this-worldly well-being." Although popular religion comprises a multitude of unorganized elements, often in contradiction, some theorists define popular religion specifically in terms of class divide;[6] the upper class belonging to official religion and the lower to popular religion. These theorists, following the legacy of Gramsci, sometimes see popular religion as a form of contestation against dominant culture, thinking that this type of religion has the possibility of being a progressive movement.

Gramsci viewed the state as two distinct but interwoven fields: political society (the field of force and domination) and civil society (the field of hegemony). This creates what he called the "integral state," which is a sociopolitical order with hegemonic equilibrium as a key characteristic and is constituted by a "combination of force and consent which are balanced in varying proportions, without force prevailing too greatly over consent" (Gramsci, quoted by Fontana, 2002: 159). While "force and domination" implies the use of coercion or armed force over other groups, hegemony makes reference to the intellectual and moral leadership of one group over others to such a point as the latter become "allies" and "associates" of the former.

The church, this official religion, was part of what Althusser would later call an ideological state apparatus. To maintain hegemony, the church managed over the years to keep popular religion in check:

> The strength of religions, and of the Catholic church in particular, has lain, and still lies, in the fact that they feel very strongly the need for the doctrinal unity of the whole mass of the faithful and strive to ensure that the higher intellectual stratum does not get separated from the lower. The Roman church has always been the most vigorous in the struggle to prevent the "official" formation of two religions, one for the "intellectuals" and the other for the "simple souls." (Gramsci, 1991: 328)

Gramsci sees the subaltern culture as different and in opposition to the church's official values; however, this opposition is not always conscious or explicit (Nesti, 1975). Popular culture comprises a multitude of unorganized

---

6 Others, like researchers in Latin America (e.g. Blancarte, 2000) would present this more
  in relation to ethnicity.

elements often in contradiction. Gramsci argues that some of the elements have a potential to lead to novelty and to a contestation against the state. These elements could be framed to build a collective consciousness within the popular mass and lead to an organized opposition against hegemonic power.

Gramsci does not make reference to popular religion as a whole when it comes to reaching this revolutionary strength. As he clearly points out, some elements of this subaltern culture cannot be of help as they are remnants of past historical periods and not in line with, for instance, the development of the Italy of his time as an industrial society. Indeed, he states that there is a need to combat "the residues of the pre-capitalist world that still exist among the popular masses, especially in the field of religion" (Gramsci, 1991: 392). These popular religious movements, for Gramsci, can be both progressive and regressive and only their progressive attributes have the potential to be counterhegemonic. Gramsci is here explaining how some progressive movements have already attempted revolt but have been at a later stage absorbed by the church, counteracting their revolutionary power.

> Many heretical movements were manifestations of popular forces aiming to reform the Church and bring it closer to the people by exalting them. The reaction of the Church was often very violent: it has created the Society of Jesus; it has clothed itself in the protective armour of the Council of Trent; although it has organised a marvellous mechanism of "democratic" selection of its intellectuals,[7] they have been selected as single individuals and not as the representative expression of popular groups. (Gramsci, 1991: 397)

Gramsci (1991: 331–2) also makes reference to other examples such as the creation of strong popular mass movements centered on strong personalities such as St Dominic and St Francis. Instead of allowing such division, the church again managed to absorb these personages by creating new religious

---

7 Gramsci, in his prison notebooks, believed that intellectuals are bound to their class of origin. Intellectuals cannot form a single group, but are divided into subgroups that emerge from and serve specific classes. The bourgeoisie produces its intellectuals, as does the proletariat. Intellectuals, for Gramsci, thus work for the interest of their own class and are called within this perspective "organic intellectuals." He thus viewed the role of working class intellectuals as having a key role within the Marxist revolutionary movement. And it would be the role of these organic intellectuals to frame the consciousness of the people who are involved in popular religion to help towards a revolt against the bourgeois state.

orders, and thus counteract counterhegemonic processes. For Gramsci, The Society of Jesus was the last of the great religious orders as its origins were reactionary.

Engels already studied heretical movements in the twelfth century, and it is no surprise that Gramsci was interested in them as well (Nesti, 1975: 351). Engels discovered two types of heretics; those who were revolting against the land extension of the aristocrats, and those who wanted to revolutionize the entire system, demanding political and cultural autonomy to create a more egalitarian society in light of Christianity's perceived origins. Indeed, Engels (1959: 170) analyzed the origins of Christianity and discovered that there were strong similarities between the working-class movement in modernity and the first Christians. Both preached forthcoming salvation from bondage and misery, but while Christianity placed this salvation in a life beyond death in heaven, socialism situated it in this world. However, early Christianity later became a dogmatically fixed universal religion through the Nicene Council (325 AD), which changed the early positive nature of this religion into one that has been negatively analyzed by the above authors.

Gramsci's notions of state and hegemony would need to be adapted to the global context, as radical sociocultural changes have occurred since the time of his writings. Robinson (2005) can here be of help, as he has reworked Gramsci's notion of the state to a contemporary setting. Robinson is inspired by Gramsci's understanding of a hegemony which is not operated by states (that would be a statist view of hegemony) but rather by social groups and classes operating through states and other institutions. As dominant social groups and classes have become transnational, their hegemonic power can no longer been seen as being located within a specific state any longer. To adapt Gramsci to today's world, Robinson makes reference to the transnational state (TNS).

The TCC [Transnational Capitalist Class] has been attempting to position itself as a new ruling class group worldwide and to bring some coherence and stability to its rule through an emergent TNS apparatus. What would a potentially hegemonic bloc – henceforth referred to as a globalist bloc – under the leadership of the TCC look like? It would clearly consist of various economic and political forces whose politics and policies are conditioned by the new global structure of accumulation. At the center of the globalist bloc would be the TCC, comprised of the owners and managers of the transnational corporations and private financial institutions and other capitalists around the world who manage transnational capital. The bloc would also include the cadre, bureaucratic managers and technicians who administer the agencies of the TNS, such as the IMF, the World Bank, and the WTO, other transnational forums, and the states of the North and the South. (Robinson, 2005: 565)

Although we could still expect today's popular religions to be antagonistic toward specific states, we could also envision them working at the global level, counterhegemonic not to one state only but to this transnational state in general.

Popular Religion: From Gramsci to Today

Enzo Pace (1979) notes that, for Italian scholars, popular religion is a class phenomenon. It is followed especially by the subaltern classes and most predominantly, but not exclusively, by the agricultural classes. Davidson (1991) reminds us that peasantry formed the majority of the population in Gramsci's time. We can thus expect Gramsci to have been inspired by the same understanding of popular religion. However, popular religion is not always the religion of the underprivileged.

Making such a distinction solely between the learned and the illiterate is not always fruitful. Over the last centuries many of the elite who have wanted to gain knowledge from "popular religion" have studied it and have codified some aspects of it. One might remember that during the Middle Ages and the Renaissance, popular magic moved from the inarticulate classes to the intellectual ones. For example, Jean Pic de la Mirandole, Paracelsus and John Dee were learned men who delved into popular religion and its magic to codify and rationalize it. This magic, also called esotericism, changed through the modern and late modern periods to influence New Age spiritualities. Through the ages, this "magic" has been commodified and gentrified (Possamai, 2005).

Another case in point is the birth of neopaganism in the late 1940s, during which Gerald Gardner (1884–1964) published an ethnography of contemporary witches. For Gardner, witches had ancient knowledge and powers handed down through generations and he claimed to have been initiated into their nature religion. The alleged ancient nature religion (previously seen as a folk and popular religion) that Gardner codified in his writing led to the birth of current neopagan movement. By this example, it could be argued that contemporary neopaganism is a reinterpretation of the popular religion of certain folk people. However, many neopagans live in cities, are literate and tend to come from middle-class backgrounds.

Popular religion in the Western world has been gentrified. It is no longer the prerogative of the peasants and/or lower classes, but it is now accessible, if not carried, by the middle classes as well.[8]

One way to define popular religion is to use a social constructionist approach (see Beckford, 2003) – basically arguing that understandings of popular religion are in tension with official religion (Berlinerblau, 2001; Possamai, 2008). Popular religion exists because official religion desires to distance itself from more populist types of magical practices. However, popular religion has become so complex in recent years in the Western world that the dichotomy between these two religious subfields is not as clear-cut as it used to be. Over the years, we have seen more elitist forms of religiosity (e.g. Troeltsh's (1950) mysticism and Campbell's (1978) secret religion of the educated class) merging with forms of popular religion and vice versa. I have detailed this bridge between these two religious fields within consumer culture elsewhere with the help of Jameson's theory on the cultural logic of late capitalism (Possamai, 2007, 2008) and especially of his work on high and popular culture. Enzo Pace (1987), by using Niklas Luhmann's theory on Complex Society, also reached the same conclusion that mysticism (in Troeltsh's sense) is becoming a form of religious neopopulism. As popular religion becomes a more complex synthesis, it might be better to understand it as religion that takes "account of subjective needs, of emotional communication, of face to face rapport, as opposed to all the cold forms of functioning of the traditional religious institution" (Pace, 1987: 12–13).

To return to Jediism and hyperreal religions, it can easily be argued that they fulfill their members' subjective needs. They are all able to express themselves on the internet and construct for themselves by themselves their view of Jediism. Emotional communication happens via chat rooms in which people are able to express themselves freely, especially behind pseudonymic masks. In these forums and chat rooms, people do not have to show their faces and can even pretend they are a different gender and age. Some might even have more than one cyber name. These hyperreal religions might have been able to develop due to the fact that people can play with their identities and not suffer from the stigma attached to following a "nerdy" or "wacky" religion. Further, people participating in these cyber activities can do it without any fear of offline discrimination or harassment, as they do not ever have to meet in geographical space.

However, it would be hard to argue that Jediism has liturgies in the classic sense (Houk, 1996), although it is as decentralized and syncretic as popular

---

8 This is not limited to Western countries. Howell (2006) writes from Indonesia that many Muslim and non-Muslim middle-class people have developed an interest in new Western spiritualities.

religion can be. Nevertheless, it can easily be argued that it has instead e-text liturgies. Often, in these chat rooms, text tends to be reproduced as if it were part of an oral conversation. Further, this e-oral liturgy is kept online, allowing other people to share and intervene. This creates a new type of face-to-face rapport between actors in popular religions that deal in online oral or e-text liturgies.

Syncretic aspects of hyperreal religion bear some striking resemblances to similar aspects of popular religion. However, the extent of this syncretism in contemporary Western societies has broadened significantly since the time of pre–mass consumption. It mixes even more heteroclite elements from religions, philosophies and now from global contemporary popular culture. It is because of this new practice of using commodified popular culture for religious purposes that hyperreal religion is a new subset of popular religion.

A Counterhegemonic Process?

Within the literature on media, Jenkins (2003) studied the participatory phenomenon of the *Star Wars* culture. Although he did not address Jediism, strong similarities can be drawn from his research with that on hyperreal religion. Jenkins discovered that *Star Wars* fans on the internet emulate or parody some of the *Star Wars* stories and create their own work (e.g. homemade movies, pictures and stories). For example, an internet database for fan film production has close to three hundred amateur-produced *Star Wars* films. These works are no longer photocopied and/or recorded from tape to tape, sent via (snail)mail and thus only accessible to a few dozen people, but are put on the internet to be reached by the world. Alternative media production has become more visible in mainstream culture. These artists/fans create their own stories, which could be interpreted by some as questioning the hegemonic representation of their culture. To reflect this process as amplified by online circulation, Jenkins (2003: 286) uses the term "participatory culture":

> Patterns of media consumption have been profoundly altered by a succession of new media technologies which enable average citizens to participate in the archiving, annotation, appropriation, transformation, and recirculation of media content. Participatory culture refers to the new style of consumerism that emerges in this environment.

It can be argued that participatory culture also encompasses hyperreal religionists. They now have the ability to discuss their spiritual works on the internet and share them with others, something that would have been difficult to accomplish to such an extent with the use of a photocopier (or even a publishing company!). The internet offers people a vehicle for sharing with the world their construction of themselves (e.g. through photographs, video and biography). Some include their views on spirituality; these can attract other people toward idiosyncratic spiritualities in a way that was not possible pre-internet. People from all over the world can join in the discussion at any time and take part in e-activities. Through this they might contribute to their own, or someone else's, spiritual construction, usually by virtue of a pseudonym and/or feeling more free to speak in the online world than in the offline one.

As Jenkins remarks about *Star Wars*' participatory culture, the web has allowed a return to a type of folk-understanding of creativity that was present before the Industrial Revolution. Before this revolution, folktales, legends, myths and ballads were built up over time as people transformed them into more personally meaningful texts. But with the Industrial Revolution, culture became privatized and copyrighted, over time allowing corporations to control "their" intellectual property and thus impose upon the general population the status of consumers rather than cultural participants. Jenkins describes this phenomenon during this industrial time:

> The mass production of culture has largely displaced the old folk culture, but we have lost the possibility for cultural myths to accrue new meanings and associations over time, resulting in single authorized versions (or at best, corporately controlled efforts to rewrite and "update" the myths of our popular heroes). Our emotional and social investments in culture have not shifted, but new structures of ownership diminish our ability to participate in the creation and interpretation of that culture.

Star Wars fans are now able to take part in the formation and discussion of the *Star Wars* culture via the internet, evoking participatory folk culture before the Industrial Revolution. Including for the purpose of this chapter folk theology as part of folk culture, similarities can easily be drawn between hyperreal religion and folk theology, which is generally characterized by decentralization, oral liturgies, dynamic and syncretic belief systems and consensus-based leadership (Houk, 1996). Because of the popular ability to participate in the creation and interpretation of new spirituality on cyberspace by and for the self, one could infer potential leverage against various ideological state apparatus. Spirituality accruing new meanings on the internet could be a counteraction against a church's effort to control the "official" text/liturgy. But is it really?

Standardization

Would this counterhegemonic possibility exist within current Western popular religions? Does the internet allow for such a process? To address this question, we need to focus on the key aspect of contemporary popular religions (and even contemporary spirituality at large): individualization. Beck's work is enlightening.

Beck (2002) makes reference to a triple individualization process in late modernity. The first process is the "disembedding" process, that is the individual's liberation from any prescribed social forms and commitment. He or she is no longer bound to follow any dominant traditional institutions (e.g. class, family, church). Through the elevation of the educational system, increases in disposable income, changes within the family and new labor conditions, the individual has gained a new freedom in late modern society. For example, in the sphere of religion, people can explore different religions, pick and mix various parts electively and construct a personal spirituality. As an illustration, in Australia it is now less important for Irish migrants to be Irish Catholics like our forbears. We can still remain Catholic, but we can also explore and choose *à la carte* other religious elements to create a personal identity and spirituality; or move away from Catholicism and still consume *à la carte*, such as studying astrology, being interested in Tibetan Buddhism, rereading the Bible and rewatching the *Star Wars* saga. Beck sees in this behavior a liberating dimension from traditional structures. However, liberation has consequences.

The second process, a direct consequence of the first, is "the loss of traditional security with respect to practical knowledge, faith and guiding norms." Beck sees this as the "disenchantment" dimension. The individual in late modern society is increasingly uprooted as he or she is deprived of the cultural signifiers of traditional culture. As Varga (2007: 146) argues, "the individual is – to paraphrase Sartre – 'thrown into choice,' and collective memory is becoming ever more fragmented."

Indeed, with the advent of globalization, uncertainty through job insecurity has resulted from the delocalization of industry from the West to the "rest." Generations X and Y do not know if they will live in the same place for the rest of their lives and they cannot be certain they will last with a partner until their deathbeds. If there is a constant in the lives of these people who have lost the traditional cultural security of their ancestors, it is that they have to live with uncertainty (Possamai, 2009).

Beck's two types of processes are not new in social theory, however his third is of great importance to the argument of this chapter. Beck's third process of individualization, "reembedding," is a new type of social commitment.

Through reembedding the individual is, paradoxically, more dependent on social institutions than ever before. To be able to make a choice, a structure needs to be put in place that allows such a thing, and this structure depends upon institutions. Thus to be a liberated individual, one is dependent upon, for example, education, consumption, welfare state regulation and support. As Beck (1992: 131) observes, "individualization becomes the most advanced form of societalization dependent on the market, law, education and so on." The individual is free from traditional commitments such as class and family, but these constraints are exchanged with a dependency upon external control such as the labor market and consumption to a level never encountered before. This paradoxical dependency leads to a process of standardization in which choice might not appear to be so liberating. The market, money, law, mobility, education and so on are institutions that have created a new type of dependency:

> Individualization means market dependency in all dimensions of living… The individual is indeed removed from traditional commitments and support relationships, but exchanges them for the constraints of existence in the labor market and as a consumer, with the standardizations and controls they contain. The place of *traditional* ties and social forms (social class, nuclear family) is taken by *secondary* agencies and institutions, which stamp the biography of the individual and make that person dependent upon fashion, social policy, economic cycles and markets, contrary to the image of individual control which establishes itself in consciousness. (Beck, 1992: 131–2)

One may also remember Simmel, who claims in his *Philosophy of Money* that money exercises its function as a standard value. Turner (1986: 97) explains that money, for Simmel, "creates greater interpersonal freedom through impersonal exchange relations, but at the same time makes human life more subject to bureaucratic, quantitative regulation." In this sense, money, like individuation, liberates people from any prescribed social forms and commitment but creates as well a quantitative regimentation of individuals: a standardizing process.

To illustrate this standardizing process in terms of religion, let's move to Beckford (2003), who makes reference to a type of standardized individuality. People might decide to go on a spiritual path towards a new self-identity such as being "born again," "saved," "enlightened," "clear" or, may I add, a "Jedi Knight." It is believed that working towards this new self-identity will be an investment that will have some practical effects in the everyday life of the individual.

> In other words, involvement in these individualized forms of religion is not so much a flight or escape from the pressure to make lifestyle choices as an expression of the same kind of "standardized individuality." An

analogy with restaurants will make this point clearer. A wide range of cuisines is on offer in late-modern societies, thereby increasing the choices facing customers. But many restaurants belong to transnational corporations; and their menus reflect hybridized and standardized notions of taste. In short, the appearance of diversity and choice masks underlying pressures towards standardization. Individual customers are certainly free to exercise their choice but they can only choose from items on the menu. (Beckford, 2003: 213)

This, I have argued (Possamai, 2005), has created a religious stasis that is linked to the stasis of culture in general. Culture within late modernity cannot create anything new (Jameson, 1991); apparent novelties in culture are simply strategies – e.g. "pastiche," "retro," "appropriation," "simulation," "intertextuality" and "resurrectionism" – of the culture industry to make quick profit. As Hassan (1999: 308) claims, "the stasis of culture within late capitalism has thus produced a culture which is bounded and predetermined by the immediate needs of the culture industries." By continuously rearranging, repackaging, reviving and reinventing culture, the culture industry produces an *effect* of "difference", "innovation" and "creativity." However, the appearance of actual innovation is really illusory and created by technological advances. For example, the superheroes from recent movies such as *X-Men, Spiderman, Daredevil, The Hulk, The League of Extraordinary Gentlemen* and *Hell Boy* look less tacky due to the use of computer-generated images. However, even if they are more attractive to the young generation than the old Superman movies and Batman television series, the content – even if it is more mature – is nothing new.

My point about the stasis of religion does not question the religious vitality of our time period, even if it can be argued that this vitality can be standardized. The widespread creative use of technology to express and support a religion allows individualized religions to flourish, as is the case for hyperreal religions. Personal religious involvement in spirituality is strong; however, it could be argued that there is a hybridized and standardized notion of religious/spiritual taste in this period of late capitalism. This might be seen as a paradox. If we come back to Hassan's (1999) discussion of cultural stasis, we find that no new cultural forms can develop "naturally" as they once did because they are part of the logic of purely capitalist production and consumption. Religion today might be argued to be part of this logic of purely capitalist consumption. Due to the hyperconsumption of religion (Possamai, 2007) by the social actors that we have studied, no new religious form has the time to develop "naturally" because of the standard way it is individualized almost as soon as it is produced.

Gramsci referred to the way the church managed to absorb counterhegemonic religious movements into its order to counteract their oppositional stance. In the case of popular religion in contemporary Western societies, consumer culture counteracts this oppositional stance at a global level. If the church was a strong ally to the state in Gramsci's Italy in controlling popular religion, then with regard to the transnational state of today it appears that consumer culture might have replaced the church as the controlling agent of popular religion, and might be regarded as the ideological (transnational) state apparatus *par excellence.*

Through this standardization of religion/spirituality specifically and culture in general, it becomes hard to believe that a counterhegemonic germ could be found in twenty-first century popular religions. Even if they have some elements of counterhegemonic force against the transnational state (e.g. reappropriating copyrighted elements of popular culture for spiritual work; contestation against religious institutions), these facets are weak compared to the essential development of the level of class/group consciousness detailed by Gramsci. Perhaps we have not moved in any different direction since Gramsci's time. Although we are faced with a transnational state rather than a nationally bounded state and although popular religion in the Western world is now more articulated due to its gentrification process, the combined processes of the standardization and stasis of religion/culture would prevent any counterhegemonic spark from growing into the full-blown force urged by Gramsci. Perhaps the key to understanding this process is to cite a popular French proverb *"plus ça change, plus c'est la même chose"* (the more things change, the more they stay the same), meaning that turbulent social and cultural changes do not affect reality on any deeper level than to cement the status quo.

Conclusion

Looking at Weber, Turner (2009) found that global commercialism has inverted the traditional relationship between the virtuosi (the carriers of official religions) and the mass (the consumers of popular religions). As the educated and elite carriers of religion are now challenged by a global spiritual marketplace, we might expect from the mass that has gone through a process of individualization that elements of contemporary popular religion could lead to the progressive advancement that Gramsci saw in the popular religions of the Italian peasantry.

With the internet and its participatory culture, there are strong indications that popular religion online could have a counterhegemonic strength and thus achieve the potential that Gramsci alluded to. However, according to

Beck, the individualization process is standardized today, dependent on larger social institutions and structures such as the labor market and consumption in a way that has never been stronger. Popular religion does not escape this phenomenon and thus cannot escape its standardizing process. According to this view, there would be no possibility of any counterhegemony towards the transnational state, as all possibilities are bounded within a worldwide religious marketplace.

References

Baudrillard, Jean. 1983. *Simulacra and Simulation*. New York: Semiotext(e).

Beck, Ulrich. 1992. "Individualization, Institutionalization and Standardization: Life Situations and Biographical Patterns." In Ulrich Beck, *Risk Society: Towards a New Modernity*, 127–38. London: SAGE.

Beckford, James A. 2003. *Social Theory and Religion*, Cambridge: Cambridge University Press.

Berlinerblau, Jacques. 2001. "Max Weber's Useful Ambiguities and the Problem of Defining 'Popular Religion.'" *Journal of the American Academy of Religion* 69.3: 605–26.

Blancarte, Roberto. 2000. "Popular Religion, Catholicism and Socioreligious Dissent in Latin America. Facing the Modernity Paradigm." *International Sociology* 15.4: 591–603.

Campbell, Colin. 1978. "The Secret Religion of the Educated Classes." *Sociological Analysis* 39.2: 146–56.

Davidson, Alistair. 1991. "Antonio Gramsci." In Peter Beilharz (ed.), *Social Theory: A Guide to Central Thinkers*, 127–32. Crows Nest, NSW: Allen & Unwin.

Engels, Frederick. 1959. *Basic Writing on Politics and Philosophy*. Garden City, NY: Anchor Pub. Co.

Fontana, Benedetto. 2002. "Gramsci on Politics and State." *Journal of Classical Sociology* 2.2: 157–78.

Gramsci, Antonio. 1991. *Selections from Prison Notebooks*. London: Lawrence & Wishart.

Hassan, Riaz. 1999. "Globalization: Information Technology and Culture within the Space Economy of Late Capitalism." *Information, Communication & Society* 2.3: 300–17.

Howell, Julia. 2006. "The New Spiritualities, East and West: Colonial Legacies and the Global Spiritual Marketplace in Southeast Asia." *Australian Religion Studies Review* 19.1: 9–33.

Jameson, Fredric. 1991. *Postmodernism or, The Cultural Logic of Late Capitalism*. Durham, NC: Duke University Press.

Jenkins, Henry. 2003. "Quentin Tarantino's Star Wars?: Digital Cinema, Media Convergence, and Participatory Culture." In David Thorburn and Henry Jenkins (eds), *Rethinking Media Change: The Aesthetics of Transition*, 281–313. Cambridge, MA: MIT Press.

Houk, James. 1996. "Anthropological Theory and the Breakdown of Eclectic Folk Religions." *Journal for the Scientific Study of Religions* 35.4: 442–7.

Nesti, Arnaldo. 1975. "Gramsci et la religion populaire." *Social Compass* 12.3–4: 343–54.

————. 1979. "The Debate on Popular Religion in Italy." *Sociological Analysis* 71–75.

————. 1987. "New Paradigms or Popular Religion." *Archives des Sciences Sociales des Religions* 64.1: 7–14.

Parker, C. 1998. "Modern Popular Religion. A Complex Object of Study for Sociology." *International Sociology* 13.2: 195–212.

Possamai, Adam. 2005. *In Search of New Age Spiritualities*. Farnham: Ashgate.

———. 2007. *Religion and Popular Culture: A Hyper-Real Testament*. Bruxelles, Bern, Berlin, Frankfurt am Main, New York, Oxford, Vienna: European Interuniversity Press.

———. 2008. "Popular Religion." In P. Clarke and P. Beyer (eds), *The World's Religions: Continuities and Transformations*, 479–92. London and New York: Routledge.

———. 2009. *Sociology of Religion for Generations X and Y*, London: Equinox.

Robinson, W. 2005. "Gramsci and Globalisation: From Nation-State to Transnational Hegemony." *Critical Review of International Social and Political Philosophy* 8.4: 559–74.

Troeltsch, Ernst. 1950. *The Social Teaching of the Christian Churches*. 2 vols. London: George Allen & Unwin.

Simmel, George. 1990. *The Philosophy of Money*. London: Routledge.

Turner, Bryan S. 1986. "Simmel, rationalisation and the sociology of money." *The Sociological Review* 34.1: 93–114.

———. 2009. "Max Weber on Islam and Confucianism. The Kantian Theory of Secularization." In Peter Clarke (ed.), *The Oxford Handbook of The Sociology of Religion*, 79–97. Oxford: Oxford University Press.

Varga, Ivan. 2007. "Georg Simmel: Religion and Spirituality." In Kieran Flanagan and Peter Jupp (eds), *A Sociology of Spirituality*, 145–60. Farnham: Ashgate.

Part III

CONCLUDING COMMENTS

Chapter 12

CONCERNING THE CURRENT RECOMPOSITIONS OF RELIGION AND OF POLITICS

Patrick Michel

Centre National de la Recherche Scientifique
and
École des Hautes Études en Sciences Sociales, Paris

Although it seems impossible to provide a definition of "religion" that would likely be consensual,[1] religion yet appears to be an essential analytical key to account for the transformations of the contemporary world. Hence the new visibility religion has acquired in the public and scientific debate in the last few years: the debate has shifted from discussions specific to the sociologists of religion to an appropriation of religion by different disciplinary and theoretical approaches. This has led to interpretations through the religious lens of, among other things, ethnic conflicts, terrorism, the political evolution of the Middle East, the management of immigration, and even the "civil unrest" in the suburbs of France.[2]

This new visibility of religion does nothing to prevent it from representing a continuing enigma: is religion still disappearing? Or is it endlessly reemerging? Besides, when religion is foregrounded nowadays, it is often something else that is at stake: the relation to the other (and thus to pluralism) or rather, identity and consequently the relevance of the criteria that will allow us to define identity. A precondition of this milieu is the inability to find a register of discourse that is better adapted to what tries to be formulated. Herein religion

---

1 See "La religion, objet sociologique pertinent?" (Michel, 2003: 159–70).
2 The 2005 "civil unrest" of October and November was a series of riots involving mainly the burning of cars and public buildings at night in the periphery of big cities in France. President Jacques Chirac announced a national state of emergency on 8 November. These events led the political authorities to (re)open the file of national identity.

would be the vehicle through which could be articulated, in the words of Michel de Certeau, "both the necessity and impossibility of taking hold again of the whole" (2003: 142).

The task set out here against a background of ever-increasing tension between believers and institutions and a wider problem of religious apportionment and flow, is to articulate, from a resolutely theoretical perspective, a few remarks around three closely interwoven themes: the relation between religion, utopia and democracy; the need for a political approach to the religious; and the role of religion in the global world.

Religion, Utopia, Democratization

According to Lucien Febvre, the first duty of an historian is to date with precision. And trying to do this, with regard to the relation between politics and religion, compels us to go back to the founding moment in our period, i.e. 1989, which was considered by Eric Hobsbawm (1996) – as we all well remember – as marking the end of the "short twentieth century."

Different actors belonging to different scenes have pointed at Pope John Paul II as the one who "defeated communism."[3] But although religion played a part in the long process of the exit from communism in the Soviet bloc, the responsibility rests first with the Soviet system's initiation of religion as the instrument that questioned the system's own legitimacy. By putting forward the theory that the exhaustion of religion is a strong indicator of the advancement of the project of building an "harmonious society" and thus constituting religion as the only register that it would refuse to ideologically integrate, the Soviet-type system built religion into the only space that would become irreducibly alien to it. Religion became an "elsewhere" that developed into (provided that there were actors who could operationalize

---

3 See the subtitle of Bernard Lecomte's book, *La Vérité l'emportera toujours sur le mensonge* (1991). Lecomte quotes Pope John Paul II, who claimed during the general audience he granted 21 February 1990 that "it was God who defeated in the East" (15). Observing in the speech he made on his arrival in Prague on 21 April 1990 that "the claim of building a world without God and even against God has proved to be an illusion," the pope subsequently opened up in *Centesimus annus* (III, 24) about his vision of the deep reasons behind the upheavals that took place in Europe in 1989: "The true cause of the new developments was the spiritual void brought about by atheism, which deprived the younger generations of a sense of direction and in many cases led them, in the irrepressible search for personal identity and for the meaning of life, to rediscover the religious roots of their national cultures, and to rediscover the person of Christ himself as the existentially adequate response to the desire in every human heart for goodness, truth and life." See "La religion, objet sociologique pertinent?" (Michel, 2003: 159–70).

its potentiality (which has not been the case everywhere)) a triple liberating process: at the individual level, at the level of the fabric of community, and at the level of the reiteration of a nation through the assertion of its indelibly inscribed religious belief.

But the responsibility of the Soviet system does not end there. The existence of this system (and of the mechanism of legitimization through which it was built up, whatever may have been its forced concessions to reality) led to an ideologization of democracy, constituted into a space that embodied Good against the "Empire of Evil." This sudden emergence of ethical categories was the result of a particular political enchantment by which communism aimed to constitute a utopia as the ultimate reservoir of legitimacy for the Soviet system.

The collapse of communism brought to light a process that had started long before, a process in which communism itself takes part. Although 1989 assuredly marked the beginning of a new era, this era should not be assessed according to the criteria of the breakup. Rather, it should be assessed according to a continuity that is not closed by this event, but vindicated and prolonged. From this perspective the problem of the very definition of politics emerges in a new light.

The main issue of the era begun by the collapse of communism could well stem from the difficulty for all contemporary societies in abandoning some of these "enchanted" political categories. In its long-term history, communism has represented an attempt to curb disenchantment simply by sacralizing politics (which in the ultimate analysis amounted to disposing of politics). Communism, although it did not reenchant the world, contributed to stop the process of disenchantment.

The fact that the communist undertaking did not last long (it was confronted by the obvious erosion of its credibility very early on, and thus forced to make many settlements with a reality that it could not control or recapitulate) does not change the fact that the kernel of a mechanism of legitimization organized around the reference to utopia was to remain intact during the whole period. Communism's very existence was at stake. The end of communism is without a doubt the (definitive?) disqualification of utopia as the bedrock of the mechanism for the legitimization of politics. This is despite attempts here and there (for example via the political instrumentalization of religion in the aftermath of the 9/11 crisis) to give the utopian notion back some plausibility. Hence the demand and the urgency to redefine our conceptual tools.

The positioning of communism within the political field was formed temporally and spatially around a utopia, not only in the communist countries, but also in noncommunist countries. The existence of an "actual" communism materialized by the Soviet Union and its empire served as an organizing principle in contemporary space, a locator of bearings. A frontier physically separated the free world from what was beyond the Iron Curtain. It also organized a relation to time, since it ascribed a logic to it: the fight against the enemy – and a horizon: the perspective of defeating the enemy. The meaning of the collapse of communism is thus not exhausted with the acknowledgement of the end of a system (ideological, political economic, military, etc.). As one of the two opposite poles that structured the contemporary space, communism gave form to and organized this global space. Its disappearance thus affects the whole space. Communism was totalizing everything, including the opposition it aroused. Its collapse detotalizes everything, that is to say that it pluralizes everything. It is in accordance with this view that the idea has been put forward that all contemporary societies are post-communist societies, in the sense that they all had to manage the effects of the disappearance of communism.

The year 1989 is analyzed here not as a fundamental break but as a decisive step in a process that had started long before and which continues today. This "disenchantment of the world" nowadays affects the political arena, after having concerned only the religious arena for a long time. After an absolute religion founded the political order and after communism's attempt to reenchant the world strove to make credible a political absolute, we are now confronted with a situation in which the absolute, whatever its nature, would globally be unbelievable. This opens onto a world of pluralism and relativism characterized by new modalities of articulation of a believing that is somewhat untied from its relation to any content of belief. It is a matter of urgency that we scrutinize our current theoretical categories and elaborate a sociology of movement, i.e. a sociology of the itineraries of meaning which would ultimately allow us to decipher trends in the evolution of the contemporary world, the redistributions these trends induce and the recompositions of the believing that they require.[4]

A Political Approach to Religion

Here is a twofold acknowledgement from which stems a central hypothesis. First, we are in fact utterly unable to define the whole extent of the effects of a trend towards the individuation of relation to meaning, this trend being broad and universal (not limited to the so-called "Western" societies, but affecting all contemporary societies according to specific modalities). The religious appears here as the vehicular or the revelatory element of this individuation of believing and also as a potential resource by which groups might curb,

---

4 See Michel (1994).

contest or even refuse individuation and the strong tendencies it may seem to reiterate. The religious field promotes its own existence here by supplying the requisite indexes to ensure its translation, ontological tools by which we might "get to grips" with these trends.

Secondly, and from the same perspective, we should acknowledge the limits with which "traditionally" developed analyses concerning the religious must contend. The contemporary processes of decomposition-recomposition experienced by our societies emphasize the obsolescence of a conceptual apparatus, a notion articulated for the most part within theories of secularization and – accordingly rather than contrarily – within the "religious creations" of modernity (whether it be a "hyper-" or a "post-" modernity).

Hence the necessity of rethinking the relationship of our societies with believing, by thinking anew through the believing, and of drawing out a renewed and effective intellectual toolbox from this reflection.[5]

The need for such a renewal is evidenced by the existing confusion. Religion is de facto often analytically constituted as an object exterior to social evolutions, its relation to which can be consequently studied. There would thus be, for instance, a "religious dimension of globalization."[6] Globalization would bring about adaptations, adjustments and/or transformations affecting religion. In fact, such an approach, which perpetuates the idea that there is a religious field characterized by an (at least relative) autonomy, stems from a double premise. First, the premise that assumes it would be possible to equate the mutations of the contemporary believing to what can be perceived in the sole register of the religious. Secondly, the premise that a conception of this religious, forged in and through the reference to an organizing stability, would remain usable enough to identify and validate any evolutions induced by contemporary global movement.

These presuppositions are at work in the way certain types of questions are formulated and handled mediatically, politically and also scientifically. Is religion favorable to some form of economy or other? Is religion (or some denomination or other, most notably Islam) compatible or not with democracy? Or again, more trivially, is there a "renewal" or a "return of religion" or even a "revenge from God"? Is secularism threatened?

Finally, it is important to come back to Michel de Certeau's statement that when politics gives ground, the religious comes back. But if it comes back,

---

5 This is contrary to the approach of Danièle Hervieu-Léger, who declared that she didn't "accept the way the sociology of religion was eclipsed into a vast socio-anthropology of the believing, which would comprehensively grasp its issues and its functioning" (1987: 28).

6 See for example the special report on "Effervescences religieuses dans le monde" in *Esprit* (March–April, 2007).

it is most certainly not in its own guise. Such visibility would first fulfill the function of stressing a deficit of politics that is so cruel that it would not have the political words to tell itself. Hence politics' recourse to the religious as a register of articulation. Against a background of the exhaustion of the believable, the generalized wavering of reference points and markers and the urgency and simultaneous impossibility of building a renewed relation to totality, the credibility of politics is now being questioned even more than the credibility of religion.

A traditional mode of analysis of the relation between politics and religion consists of taking a look at the political positioning of the great religious institutions and denominations in order to figure out the strategies implemented and redeployed in the contemporary world. This mode of analysis is admittedly not devoid of interest. Nevertheless, as it privileges institutions, it perpetuates a reading that does not account for much larger processes and whose contemporary reliance on religion (moreover, often in the mode of its extrainstitutional resurfacing) produces what can only be symptoms or revealers.

Consequently, it is an approach through the "believing" that must be substituted, a view to which Georges Balandier ascribed in *Le dédale* (1994: 175, my translation) when he emphasized how much

> the space of the believing is the site where a working reconfiguration is now taking place... Some memory is being recomposed there, some continuity is being restored, some meaning is being looked for, as well as the revealing/revelatory signs of burgeoning affinities with a world that is continually transforming itself.

The believing is the mechanism, necessarily dynamic and therefore evolutionary, through which some meaning is looked for and allocated. This mechanism has the distinctive feature that all its configurations have simultaneous elements of anticipation and lateness with regard to time. Delay arises because the believing, as an undertaking to allocate meaning, tends to curb movement by endeavoring to translate movement into already felt categories of meaning. Anticipation exists because the believing, as an undertaking to allocate meaning, tends to orient movement, inscribe it in these felt categories in order to modify them or inscribe it into new categories which it contributes toward inventing. The believing consists of all the constant reshuffle carried out for the purposes of managing this contradictory simultaneity between anticipation and delay. It is therefore the privileged space of an adjustment, the place where a coincidence is felt (and where it is to be felt).

This believing is particularly solicited – and disrupted – in situations characterized on the one hand by acceleration of movement and on the other by the urgent need to define a new relationship with movement.[7] By movement, I mean simultaneously the transformations that take place on a scene/stage, the state of consciousness of these transformations and the procedure that leads, on the basis of this state of consciousness, to the articulation of a relationship with the transformations. The speeding up of this movement is combined with the lack of plausible bearings that traditionally allowed us if not to frame then at least to pretend that framing was possible. In other words, we have exited a time when it was possible to substantiate the existence of stabilities organizing reality and entered an era in which reference to these stabilities no longer appears to be globally or wholly convincing or credible.

Religion and the "Global" World

The speeding-up of contemporary movement, quite widely confused with that felt due to a "globalization" with which all societies are confronted, induces multiple and profound transformations, one of the major dimensions of which affects "individuals." This issue of individuation in the new context of globalization seems to constitute the privileged juncture at which the ongoing evolutions can be questioned: does the emergence of the "modern individual" constitute the unavoidable arrival point of all evolutions? To what extent is this individual, in the words of Amartya Sen (2000, 2005), the "only invention of Europe" as the spreading of this model consequently partakes in a form of violence imposed by the West on other "civilizations"? (We are obviously overlooking the issue, recurrent in the discourse of some social actors on the international stage, of knowing if this "individual" does not represent a "dead end.")

The effects of globalization have been described many times: free flow in a space thought to be unified, simultaneity in a supposedly worldwide time. The individual is precisely supposed to be the basic entity of this scene. There is a redistribution of the roles given to the different authorities that concurs with the making of the individual. In the context of this redistribution, which is largely conditioned and shaped by the economy, religion fulfills new functions. Whereas within modernity religion constituted one of the vehicles of individualization as well as the barrier that had to be broken down in order to reach it, a certain form of religion has set itself the role on the globalized stage

---

7 As I set out to show in my analysis of the public's reactions at the Museum of Religion in Glasgow (1999).

of producing an individual who is "compatible" with the rules in force in the market world. These rules apply entirely in this case insofar as they constantly trace and retrace the profile of a producing and consuming individual who is as adapted as possible to the market logics.

The modern process of individualization occurred in a context of confrontation between institutional religion and the state, a process stemming partly from the action of the latter through various bodies, most particularly through education. As for contemporary individuation, it is a form of contestation of the primacy of the state and it testifies to the existence of a process of privatization in which the functions that were granted to the state in modernity are now dependent on private initiative. The way the new Evangelical community institutions endeavor to manufacture a globalized individual according to entirely integrated market principles appears to be particularly significant in this milieu.

The "constant and generalized progression" of conservative Protestant Christianity, in the words of David Martin (2001: 81–2), compels us to revisit the idea of a continuous and irreversible secularization of societies that are upset by the logics of a plural modernity. The progression compels us so much that it could have been used to support the reverse theory of a desecularization or even of a "return of God" or the "reenchantment of the world" (to take up the titles of the books published by Harvey Cox and Peter Berger,[8] who used to be the great theoreticians of secularization and are now confessing that they were radically mistaken about the interpretation of a world that becomes, according to them, "more furiously religious than ever" (Berger, 2001:15)). It is in this vein that neo-Pentecostalism has been presented as the religion of the future.

In the North American conservative conception of society and of the world, of which neo-Pentecostalism is a major vehicle of diffusion, the frontiers between politics, religion, economy and ideology tend to fade, if not disappear. The collapse of communism has admittedly deprived this denomination of the enemy that was giving it a certain meaning. But, when interpreted as a sign of divine blessing, this very collapse outlines the horizon of a planet with American colors, a project which is informed by a "theology of prosperity and wealth" serving the "mission" America would have to see through. According to this view, the relationship with Islam is essential, since Islam (which is necessarily radical) appears to be the other religion which would be constantly gaining ground. It also appears to be the religion of the Other, which would substantiate the existence of a "clash of civilization" in which, like in the Cold War, the United States would embody Good.

---

8 Peter L. Berger (ed.), *Le Réenchantement du monde* (2001); Harvey Cox (trans. Michel Valois), *Le Retour de Dieu: Voyage en pays pentecôtiste* (1995).

The parallel with radical Islam is also likely to make sense in the register of contemporary identities and of the generalized wavering that identities are experiencing because of recompositions induced by economic and cultural globalization. Just as radical Islam would be the pure product of the confrontation with a Western modernity that is simultaneously desired and rejected – a privileged space of the articulation of fantasies and frustrations – the progress of conservative Evangelism would constitute, as such, an interpretative grid of modalities of management of the reconstruction of identitary mechanisms. This would allow the adherent to "come to grips" with movement. And, ultimately – to come full circle – the increase in the power of fundamentalism would seem to evidence the big comeback of religion on the domestic, transnational and internal scenes.

The individual whose primacy is displayed on the globalized stage is not the one stemming from the modern process of the emergence of the autonomous subject, from the emancipation from the community logics and the forced affiliations that kept her/him in check. However, contemporary individuation takes advantage of modern individuation in terms of legitimization. But contemporary individuation aims to produce more than an autonomous individual; it aims to produce an individual who adheres to renewed forms of communities in close line with the demands of the world market. In the constant interaction affecting contemporary societies – production of the global from the local and recomposition of the local by the global – the making of the individual can only be understood as the making of the compatible individual. And if religion has a central place in this procedure, it is because it is one of the most effective registers in which to recompose a totality in line with the ideological demands that shape and affect a specific moment in the history of a contemporary society.

Several questions emerge. The first concerns the reasons for the particular aptitude that is recognized and/or allotted to religion and which religion can take advantage of in order to pretend to display itself as such in the public space (in recomposition). The second question ponders whether, when religion is at stake, it is not in a generic way. (The religious experience relevant to the management of and making of a compatible individual is not the traditional one organized by the fiction of autonomous fields but, to take up the category of Zygmunt Bauman (2006), a "fluid" religion that rejects the institutional model handed down by a monopoly and which is almost perfectly illustrated by neo-Pentecostalism.) The third question interrogates the idea that what is fundamentally at stake is not religion or the making of the individual, but religion's capacity to spread a model and to make people believe in the emergence through religion of an individual. The subsidiary issue here is the nature of the institution; it is clear that in the context thus described, autonomous individual actors are in possession of an operationality that cannot be compared with the one that "historical" (in particular, Catholic) churches could boast of. The nature of the institution/operation presents a fourth problem: does the making of a compatible individual amount to a pure manipulation which, under the guise of religion, pursues the purpose of setting up and spreading a model and eliciting submission to the modalities of the functioning of said model?

In any case, religion does not have a meaning of its own. It is, above all other definitions, a repertoire that provides opposing parties with the necessary resources to articulate (or rearticulate) a relation to the self, to the other, to the world. This repertoire is neutral insofar as the content it offers is so flexible that it can be used to serve contradictory as well as accepted strategies.

What is highlighted here is the lost relevance of the criteria traditionally used to justify the stability of the identitary mechanism. But it is not an absolute loss; the criteria are somewhat recycled by the very circulation caused by the loss of relative relevance. In other words, a movement of oscillation constitutes a strong indicator of identity deregulation, denoting a space in which a redefinition is at work. Oscillation thus becomes the major characteristic of a social landscape in which identities are simultaneously felt as being organizing centralities and being inescapably relativized in a situation of constant circulation between different supplies and articulations of content (which of course does not imply that an adherence to one supply or another cannot take place at a given time and for a given period).

The oscillation does not constitute the space of a potential reconstruction but one that is mapped out by various propositions of reconstructions to which the individual is asked to adhere. Two of these can be distinguished: the identity that stems from a sense of belonging (organized by the reference to "ethnicity" or to the "nation") and the identity that stems from an adherence (shaped by religion). The major difference between the two is the claimed absence of reference to a hierarchy in the case of ethnic identity and the insistence on submission to a hierarchy in the case of an identity reformulated through religion (a submission that is likely to be exported to other registers, and in particular to the political register).

Indeed, privatized religion mobilized for the management of the consequences of globalization on societies deterritorializes itself at the same time as ethnicity (or the national factor) is being activated. Yet this activation, which also stems from the global, takes place due to the reiteration of the origin in the context of reasserting the relevance of territory as regards identitary demands. This paradoxical evolution of the relation to territoriality – erasing or exceeding vs. reaffirmation – forces us to rethink the issue of belonging through the lens of a structuring tension in which the choice of criterion becomes central. In other words, depending on whether someone defines himself or herself by his/

her ethnicity or by his/her religion, the issues of the relation to the territory, to politics and to legitimacy will be articulated according to different terms. The problem is that quite often both criteria are used simultaneously, producing many contradictions. Privatized religion disqualifies ethnicity on grounds of paganism.[9] Ethnicity successively turns out to be able to reappropriate practices by raising them to the rank of religious practices and thus mobilizing the religious register in the context not only of identitary assertion but also of the directly political demand to share or exercise power.

The current world is characterized by an intense fluidity between religion, economy and politics. The feeling of acceleration experienced in contemporary societies because of globalization – which proceeds through a reindifferentiation – problematizes the idea of the existence of distinct fields and therefore the resulting analysis that draws attention to the mechanisms of exchange between said fields. From this perspective, religion was grasped in its relation to the economy and/or politics in the knowledge that it was not exhausted by the interactions thus described and ultimately had retained a supposedly specific nature. What was necessary was for academics to attempt to check the fact that what was happening in any of the fields turned out to be likely to be transferred into another.

The first function of a religious actor is to sell religion and to conquer market shares against the strong competition created by the increased pluralization of the religious supply. Therefore there is not (or not anymore) any reason to raise the question, induced by the privatization of religion, of whether business is at the service of religion or whether religion is a business. This is because religion and business both partake of the same global logic, as they are registers within a common matrix whose object is to produce a stand on contemporary societies. The problem here is no longer that of the relation between fields thought to be different. It is the problem of the modalities of circulation in a global space whose actors are able to simultaneously slip into all multiple roles.

The remarks that have been articulated here draw the outline of a program that aims at seizing the recompositions of the believing in order to constitute them into so many indicators and modes of management of the transformations taking place nowadays. These transformations include a triple redistribution of the relation to time, the relation to space and the relation to authority; a triple crisis affecting identity, mediation and centrality; and a triple disadjustment of political deficit, the explosion and inadequacy of the supply of meaning, and the strong decrease and withdrawal of credibility.

---

9 For instance, in Latin America, Indian peoples' demands for recognition can be expressed through the rediscovery of traditional religions. Denouncing paganism thus constitutes a resource used to fight against these demands.

References

Balandier, Georges. 1994. *Le Dédale – Pour en fi nir avec le XXème siècle*. Paris: Fayard.

Bauman, Zygmunt. 2006. *La Vie liquide*. Paris: Le Rouergue/Chambon.

Berger, Peter. L. (ed.) 2001. *Le Réenchantement du monde*. Paris: Bayard.

Bernstein, Carl and Marco Politi. 1996. *His Holiness (John Paul II and the Hidden History of Our Time)*. Paris: Plon.

Certeau, Michel de. 1973. *L'Absent de l'histoire*. Paris: Mame.

Cox, Harvey. 1995. *Le Retour de Dieu: Voyage en pays pentecôtiste* (trans. Michel Valois). Paris: Desclée de Brouwer.

Hervieu-Léger, Danièle. 1987. "Faut il définir la religion? Questions préalables à la construction d'une sociologie de la modernité religieuse." *Archives de Sciences Sociales des Religions* 63.1: 11–30.

Hobsbawm, Eric. 1996. *The Age of Extremes: A History of the World. 1914–1991*. New York: Vintage Books.

Lecomte, Bernard. 1991. *La Vérité l'emportera toujours sur le mensonge*. Paris: JC Lattès.

Martin, David. 2001. "La poussée évangéliste et ses effets politiques." In Peter L. Berger (ed.), *Le Réenchantement du monde*, 81–2. Paris: Bayard.

Michel, Patrick. 1994. *Politique et religion – La grande mutation*. Paris: Albin-Michel.

_____. 1999. *La religion au muse: Croire dans l'Europe contemporaine*. Paris: L'Harmattan.

_____. 2003. "La religion, objet sociologique pertinent?" *Revue du Mauss* 22: 159–70. Paris: La Découverte.

Petit, Jean-François. (ed.) 1990. *La Documentation catholique*. Paris: Bayard.

Schlegel, Jean-Louis. 2007. "Effervescences religieuses dans le monde." *Esprit*, March–April 2007.

Sen, Amartya. 2000. *Un nouveau modèle économique: Développement, justice, liberté*. Paris: Odile Jacob.

_____. 2005. *La Démocratie des autres: Pourquoi la liberté n'est pas une invention de l'Occident*. Paris: Payot.

Chapter 13

PUBLIC RELIGIONS AND THE STATE: A COMPARATIVE PERSPECTIVE

Jack Barbalet, Adam Possamai and Bryan S. Turner

The preceding chapters highlight a number of aspects of religion which depart from, fundamentally modify and recontextualize the received wisdom about religion, especially as it has been understood through the prism of classical sociology. Each of the distinct sources of the classical perspective outlines an understanding of religion that – while contrasting with other understandings – has been taken with the others to represent the various facets of religion in the modern world. And yet none of these facets of religion is today found in forms projected by the sociological luminaries.

Émile Durkheim famously characterized religion in terms of a distinction he believed inherent in all religions, namely that between the sacred and the profane. The sacred, Durkheim held, was a symbolic form of the enduring and defining values of the society itself in which the religion in question resides. But the coherence of a more or less societally wide normative consensus that Durkheim assumes in making this claim is in fact not to be found in modern societies. This is largely because the populations of modern societies are not unitary in terms of their origins and historical memory, either through geographic mobility that accompanies modern occupational careers or through international migration, which has been a major demographic factor throughout the twentieth century and promises to continue in the present. Associated with these trends, the idea of the sacred – which requires a traditional understanding of received meaning supported by ritual practices – has given way if not to a scientific to at least a mundane utilitarian and therefore market set of values. These values coexist with quite a different idea of spirituality that does not compliment so much as displace the idea of the sacred which Durkheim found in the religions of settled and unified societies.

Against what is often thought of as Durkheim's view of religion's conservative function, Max Weber saw the revolutionary possibility of rationalizing religion – finding its apotheosis in ascetic Protestantism – which transforms the world. But rather than generating the cognitive and emotional tensions Weber described that would lead to major historical changes, religion today more typically serves an opposite function of smoothing existential disjuncture and disharmonies by offering various types of comfort in the world. If ascetic Puritanism is implicated in the development of capitalism, as Weber argues, the success of capitalism and the ever-expanding markets it encourages have caught religion in their own nets. Religious beliefs, practices and adherence are today arguably packaged and provided as consumer goods available in religious markets that trade in branded identities and lifestyles. This is a palliative of well-being and more palpably, a provider of materially social and economic welfare.

Karl Marx's famous view of religion as both the "sigh of the oppressed creature" and the "opiate of the masses" (Marx and Engels, 1972: 38) is possibly closer to the reality of religion today than either Durkheim's or Weber's vision, but the grandiose form of its expression is too bold and unitary to capture the diversity of the forms of religion, the uses to which religions are put by adherents and the ways in which the meaning and practices of religions are renegotiated and transformed by those who adopt or consume them. However, even more telling of the limitations of Marx's vision is his expectation that religion would simply decline through the progressive development of economic institutions. It is of particular interest that one of Marx's intellectual sources, Adam Smith, in an important but neglected discussion of religious institutions as (potential) recipients of state revenue, outlines a clear materialist sociology of religion which projects a continuing future for religious organizations necessarily subject to changing form and purpose (Smith, 1979: 788–816).

The departures from the classical sociological vision of religion, provided by the preceding chapters of this book, can be understood in terms of a number of changes that might be summarized by the term "globalization." The view that globalization, as late modernist phenomena involving the extension of international markets and the mores of rational organizational form, could reasonably be expected to convey associated norms of modernity including secularization is not challenged here. But secularization in this context cannot mean the absence of a religious presence but rather transformations in its role or function and location in social, economic and cultural processes. A changing vision in understanding the nature of religion implies changes in the way the concept of secularization is understood. Whereas historically earlier representations of secularization meant a decline in the significance of religious institutions and symbols, it can now be shown that in fact these latter gain a certain credence, even nourishment from global tendencies which at the same time changes their efficacy and usefulness for adherents. Having said this, it must be added that globalization does not promote an undifferentiated religious transformation.

It is important to appreciate that distinct aspects of globalization are associated with different types of religious changes and that these are achieved through a range of dissimilar mechanisms. In the broadest terms, it can be noted that some religious developments arise in opposition to globalization and are reactive defenses against what are taken to be despoliation of existing religious and cultural values. Militant Islam is an obvious example of this type of relationship between globalization and religious revival. Another possibility is that religious reinvigoration and modification is not primarily sponsored by globalization as a negative reaction, but arises as a consequence of distributional struggles subsequent to certain structural consequences of globalization. Aspects of Hindu revivalism and the political mobilization of religion in India may be described in these terms. A further relationship between global currents and revivalism is entailed in new opportunities for religious expression provided by aspects of globalization. The expansion of existing religions and the development of new religious movements in China is arguably an instance of this last variant of encouragement of religion by globalization. Aspects of these and similar developments are discussed in a number of the chapters above.

Against this background of the significance of globalization for religion in the modern period, there are two interrelated changes in particular that are characteristic of religion. Firstly, as religion has been constructed through globalization as a unified and recognizable institution, it is also increasingly managed by the state as a set of services that can contribute to welfare provisions in society. Religions appear to thrive in secular societies that provide little coordinated welfare for their citizens. This might explain at least in part the success of religious organizations in the United States and the current religious developments in China where the state-managed professionalization of traditional religions has encouraged an outreach and welfare function they previously did not possess. This management of religion typically involves an upgrading of religion to make it technically efficient and rational, as the discussion of Singapore in the chapter on religion in authoritarian states indicates.

Secondly, globalized religions are constantly and inevitably drawn into the global circuits of capital insofar as they are themselves converted into lifestyles and institutions offering services that cater to the needs of those participating in their activities. These participants may still be described as their congregations, but might more realistically be called their clients.

While much of popular religion is shaped by secular consumerism, there are also powerful forms of opposition to capitalism that draw upon a more traditional language of religious protest, most prominently of course the growth of "political Islam" as noted above. Our conclusion therefore supports a particular interpretation of secularization, namely that it involves a merger between religion and consumerism and the erosion of the sacred by science, urbanization, industrialization and political instrumentalism.

In a differentiated global religious market, the various segments of the religious market compete with each other and tend to overlap. The new spirituality, for instance, which may be seen as an alternative to organized religion, is genuinely a consumerist religion; fundamentalism, on the other hand, appears to challenge Western consumer values. But in doing so it is in fact operating on the principle of individual or market choice – "buying" in a religious market – a lifestyle based on special diets, alternative education, health regimes and mentalities. The global religious market is highly fragmented into fundamentalist groups, charismatic movements, Pentecostalism, traditional religions, spirituality and so forth, but these are all to varying degrees influenced by a consumerist ethos in which a choice between alternative offerings is made by an individual in satisfaction of a "preference." The consumer markets or audiences for religious services are also fragmented by class, gender, education, region and so forth. The triumph of popular democratizing global culture is now having a deep impact on traditional hierarchical, patriarchal religions of the past. Perhaps the most important development in modern religion is the changing status of women in religious communities. A principal organizational development of the late twentieth century has been the ordination of women in a variety of Protestant churches and within non-Orthodox branches of Judaism. Indeed, it is possible that women will become increasingly important in religious leadership (Tong and Turner, 2008). Gender is a crucial feature of the new consumerist religiosity where women increasingly dominate the new spiritualities. Women will be and to some extent already are the "taste leaders" in the emergent global spiritual marketplace.

While globalization theory has concentrated attention on modern fundamentalism (as a critique of traditional and popular religiosity) and on religious radicalism (as a critique of American foreign policy), perhaps the real effect of globalization is the triumph of heterodox, commercial, hybrid popular religion over orthodox, authoritative professional versions of the spiritual life. Their ideological effects cannot be controlled by religious authorities and they have a greater impact than official messages. In Weber's terms, it is the triumph of mass over virtuoso religiosity. David Martin (2002) provides a brilliant account of the various ways in which Pentecostalism has prepared the lower middle classes for participation in the emerging consumer economy of

Latin America. In a similar fashion, reformist Islam in Southeast Asia provides newly urbanized people, especially women, with values and practices that are relevant to life in complex, multicultural urban spaces where international corporations have provided employment for young women willing or able to leave their villages for work in the megacities.

Contemporary manifestations of religion are basically compatible with the lifestyles of a commercial world in which the driving force of the economy is domestic consumption. Megachurches have embraced the sales strategies of late capitalism to get their message out to the public. On these grounds, we would argue that modern religions are compromised because the tension between the world and the religion is lost. We may define these developments as a form of social secularization. Following Casanova (1994), who distinguished three dimensions of secularization – the differentiation of secular spheres from religions norms and institutions, a decline of religious belief and practices, and the marginalization of religion to a privatized sphere – we can argue that with social differentiation, the market no longer plays to the tune of religion. Furthermore, these secular developments are global rather than local. The result is a sociological paradox or set of paradoxes. Religion has erupted into the public domain, being associated with a number of radical or revolutionary movements from Iran to Brazil and from Poland to Columbia, but at the same time religion is subject to subtle changes that have brought about secularization through commodification. More precisely, as a number of the chapters above have demonstrated, the secularization of religion has occurred through a double movement: democratization and commercialization. The sense of mystery and awe surrounding the ineffable character of the sacred has been eroded by the ethos of liberal democracies in which egalitarian, immediate and intimate relations are valued over hierarchical, distant and formal relationships. Religion is further corroded by the loss of any significant contrast between the sacred and the world. Religion has specialized in providing personal services and therefore has to compete with various secular agencies also offering welfare, healing, comfort and meaning. In this competition, religious groups have by and large taken over the methods and values of a range of institutions operating within what we can for want of a more sophisticated term call "the leisure industries."

Given the developments mentioned in the preceding paragraph, it can be seen that the state can intervene in the management of religion in civil society under two very distinct circumstances. In the first, fears about security from the presence of radical religion force the state to develop strategies to bring such groups under adequate surveillance and control. These strategies may include more systematic control of migration and the repatriation of troublesome minorities. In the second, there may be anxieties about the quality of religious services and a fear that cults may adversely influence youth. However, across a broad spectrum of politics – from the most repressive authoritarian states to liberal democratic regimes – states are drawn into the management of religion. The root cause of both sets of circumstances is in general terms globalization. Global labor markets produce religious diversity through migration and global religious competition produces innovation, including the employment of commercial strategies to promote religious growth. These trends point to a general erosion of the liberal tradition in which religion could be regarded as a matter of private conscience outside the orbit of state affairs.

References

Casanova, José. 1994. *Public Religions in the Modern World*. Chicago: University of Chicago Press.
Martin, David. 2002. *Pentecostalism: The World Their Parish*. Oxford: Blackwell.
Marx, Karl and Fredrick Engels. 1972. *On Religion*. Moscow: Progress Publishers.
Smith, Adam. 1979. *An Inquiry into the Nature and Causes of the Wealth of Nations, Volume II*. Oxford: Oxford University Press.
Tong, Joy Kooi-Chin and Bryan S. Turner. 2008. "Women, piety and practice: A study of women and religious practice in Malaya." *Contemporary Islam* 2: 41–59.